BURKE
& HARE

BURKE, THE MURDERER!

Drawn from life in the Lock-up House on the day before his execution by his own consent.

BURKE
& HARE

OWEN DUDLEY EDWARDS

"I regret that we have not sent the best of our citizens to your
country."
— Eamon de Valera, Taoiseach, Republic of Ireland,
to Robert MacIntyre, Chairman, Scottish National Party

THE MERCAT PRESS
EDINBURGH

First published 1980 by Polygon Books
Second edition 1993 by Mercat Press
53 South Bridge, Edinburgh EH1 1YS

© Owen Dudley Edwards 1980, 1993

ISBN 1873644 256

Printed in Great Britain by
The Cromwell Press, Melksham

For
BRUCE,
MARGARET,
ROBERT
and
E.U.S.P.B.

Photograph/Owen Dudley Edwards with the skeleton of William Burke.

Biographical Note

Owen Dudley Edwards was initially led to his subjects by something he holds in common with them; he too is an Irish Catholic now making a contribution to higher learning in Edinburgh. Born in Dublin of a distinguished literary family, Owen Dudley Edwards has earned a growing reputation as scholar, author and journalist.

He is at present Reader in History at Edinburgh University. He is a regular contributor and reviewer for radio and television, the *Irish Times* and *The Scotsman*. His previous works include *Celtic Nationalism*; *Mind of an Acitivist: James Connolly*; *1916 The Easter Rising* and *P.G. Wodehouse: a Critical and Historical Study*. More recently he has written *The Quest for Sherlock Holmes: a Biographical Study of Arthur Conan Doyle*; *Macaulay*; *Eamon de Valera*, and has edited *The Fireworks of Oscar Wilde*; *A Claim of Right for Scotland*; and (as general editor) The Oxford Sherlock Holmes (9 vols.).

Contents

Acknowledgements

I happily reaffirm the many thanks I distributed in the first edition of this book (1980). Alas, many of the recipients are now beyond renewed thanks. I list all persons once more leaving the specificities of their services to the earlier edition, partly because of pressure of space here dictated by the need to say something of changes in my knowledge since first publication, partly because of changes to the people and institutions since then which would make the expression of thanks outmoded or the updating of it anachronistic. But time can make no difference to my gratitude to: Bruce Young, Robert Sutherland, Margaret Roxton, Professor Neil MacCormick, the late Very Rev. Anthony Ross, O.P., Professor Thomas Devine, Professor Bruce Lenman, the late Professor Robert Dudley Edwards and the late Síle Ni Shúilleabháin (my parents), Ray Footman, Patrick Rayner, the late Professor Dennis Roberts, William Brown, the late Ian Rae, Julian Russell, Alan Bell, Rev. Conrad Pepler, O.P., Dom Mark Dilworth, O.S.B., the late Right Rev. David McRoberts, Nicolas Barker, Professor George Shepperson, Rhodri Jeffreys-Jones, Tom Nairn, Robert McIntyre, A. G. Donaldson, Griselda Donaldson, Edward Spiers, George Johnstone, Professor Robert Morris, Professor Rosalind Mitchison, William Ferguson, John Arnott, Allen Wright, Roger Savage, Sir John (Lord) Cameron, Lionel Daiches, Q.C., David Campbell, Charles Wilde, Paul Harris, Ailfrid Mac Lochlainn, the late Professor David Greene, Ben Shepherd, Magnus Magnusson, Professor G. J. Romanes, I. B. Macleod, A. A. Shivas, J. S. K. Stevenson, C. N. Stoddart, Professor Christopher Smout, Professor V. G. Kiernan, James Hutcheson, William Kilpatrick Campbell, Louis Appleby, Graham Sutton, Rory Knight Bruce, David Johnston, Timothy Willis, Adam Griffin, Neville Moir, Jamie Donald, Alasdair G. Mathers, Judith Baldwin Mathers, Professor Roy Foster, Bonnie, Leila, Sara and Michael Dudley Edwards. It is with pleasure I now add the names of Tom Johnstone, Seán Costello, Allan Boyd and D. Ainslie Thin.

Introduction

C'est ici, qu'en désaccord avec la plupart des biographes, je laisserai MM. Burke et Hare au milieu de leur auréole de gloire.
— Marcel Schwob, *Vies Imaginaires*

William Burke and William Hare were Ulster Catholics of the agricultural labourer class who came to Scotland around 1818 to work as navvies on the Union Canal. Burke had had previous experience in the Donegal militia. They followed a variety of occupations after the canal had been cut. They met in 1827, when Hare and his recently married wife were running a lodging-house and Burke and his Scottish mistress, Helen MacDougal, came in as lodgers. They became aware of a famine in subjects for the fiercely competing Edinburgh anatomists and ultimately murdered sixteen persons (fifteen in joint operations) for payment by the famous extramural teacher of anatomy Dr Robert Knox. Their initial involvement seems to have been accidental, and it seems clear that despite folklore neither of them engaged in the business of grave-robbing. Ultimately they separated, Burke and Helen going to their own lodgings, but the murder partnership continued. It finally came to grief when they murdered an old Gaelic-speaking Irishwoman whose original name seems to have been Mary Docherty. Information was given against them by lodgers of Burke's who were also relatives of Helen MacDougal by the name of Gray. Burke and Helen were arrested, the body was recovered — the only one to reach the police — and the Hares were also taken into custody. The Lord Advocate, Sir William Rae, despaired of a firm case in that Burke and Hare had perfected a method of murder by suffocation which left no clear signs of violent inducement of death upon the corpse. He therefore persuaded the Hares to turn King's Evidence, and Burke and Helen MacDougal were brought to trial on Christmas Eve, 1828. They obtained the services of the best counsel in Scotland, whose law, very exceptionally for those times, offered prisoners full legal representation and celebrated the tradition of readiness to accept paupers' briefs by even the foremost lawyers. Burke was convicted of the murder of Mary Docherty. The murder charge against Helen MacDougal was found not proven. Abortive proceedings were commenced against Hare by the family of one of his victims, but after much urging by Rae, the prosecution was quashed. Hare was smuggled over to England where, some weeks before, Helen MacDougal was also reported to have gone; Margaret Hare got back to her native Ulster. Nothing more is known about any of them. Burke made two confessions in jail, an official one on 3 January and another in the presence of officials to the Edinburgh *Evening Courant* on 21 January. Neither of these were published until, after Burke's execution, Hare was out of the country. Burke was hanged at Edinburgh on 28 January before a crowd estimated at 25,000 and then, according to law, his own body was dissected by Knox's rival, Professor Alexander Monro, who held the Chair of Anatomy at Edinburgh University. After riots among students and the crowd to gain admission to the lecture, Professor Robert Christison arranged for the viewing of the body by the curious, and on 29 and 30 January some 30,000 are credited with having passed by the body, as impressive a crowd as a lying-in-state could seek in those days. Burke's body remains on view today in the Anatomy Museum in Edinburgh University. Various distinguished persons of Edinburgh intellectual society obtained and treasured pieces of his skin. A century later William Roughead in his edition of the trial recorded his possession of "an authentic specimen of it, resembling in colour and texture a piece of an old leather strap".

I had intended to write a book on Burke and Hare which would use the facts established or asserted in connection with their case as revelatory of the nature of Irish immigration in Scotland, in the early nineteenth century, and of world migration in general during that era. I wanted to write something about Scottish history with an Irish flavour to be published by my friends and colleagues at Edinburgh University Student Publications Board and it struck me that two famous Irishmen who had made a contribution to the development of Edinburgh education were an appropriate subject for another who was trying to. Also, I was — and am — concerned about the generalisations of social scientists and I felt I might help to put the feet of students on more solid ground by looking at a case-study of two persons among the huge mass of the Irish diaspora of whom a good deal was known. Also, I believe that historians do not make enough use of the evidence of criminal trials for social history, partly because a boyhood dream of becoming a criminal lawyer led me to read widely in the field although I never went on to study law. There were more frivolous motives. As an admirer of Conor Cruise O'Brien, who is writing a biography of Edmund Burke, it entertained me to find another Burke. Most importantly, I have grown to love Scotland and Edinburgh University and I wanted to be able to write something about the past of both.

But when this study was under way, it became clear to me that another book on Burke and Hare was needed. My terms of reference had meant that I would treat Burke and Hare as being humans rather than monsters. It became evident that none of my predecessors had taken such a view, with the result that their accounts of the case had become violently distorted. Moreover, things began to assume a different complexion on analysis. It became clear, for instance, that Dr Robert Knox was not simply a youthful expert kept out of a chair by an ageing incompetent, Professor Alexander Monro *tertius*, who relied on the lecture-notes of his illustrious grandfather; Knox was but one of several ambitious doctors, some more brilliant and some younger than he, and their competition was as much a motive for his voraciousness for corpses as the need to show up the wretched professor. The long debate, dragged out for the last century and a half on stage and screen, as to Knox's guilt or innocence in receiving murdered subjects proved quite irrelevant: my colleague Christopher Fyfe by discussing Knox's other scholarly interests proved to me what the reality was in that question. The Lord Advocate's investigation proved to be much more of a cover-up to protect the Edinburgh intellectual establishment and the needs of a police state demonstrably to protect its informers, than the impartial search which it had been taken to be. Sir James Moncreiff and Henry Cockburn had gallantly thrown their services into the cause of Burke and Helen MacDougal, but they did so partly with a view to discredit a Tory administration they detested and against which they had had a long-standing and active enmity: it was, in fact, an intensely *political* trial. Helen MacDougal was not, as all writers had claimed, guilty but found not proven on technical grounds and a brilliant defence; she was almost certainly innocent, and the grounds for her acquittal were even stronger than those urged by her brilliant advocate Cockburn. The Lord Advocate, in his desire to set at rest the possibly revolutionary instincts of an outraged proletariate, went to the utmost lengths to give it at least two victims, despite the poverty of his case against Helen. But the incompetence and diverse interests of the Lord Advocate, and the indifference and inefficiency of his team, made for a poor case for the prosecution, while a judicial bench, largely as deeply committed to the government as the prosecutors, did what it could — sometimes very ineptly — to rescue the prosecution. Hare's immunity was very seriously called into question by more impartial judges, and he only escaped by governmental *legerdemain*. Mob fury was indeed, as the Lord Advocate had feared, part of the dangerous tradition which stemmed back to the eighteenth-century age of democratic revolution and in Edinburgh's case to the Porteous riots of 1736; it would go on to fuel the Reform Bill crisis and the cholera riots of the early 1830s. On the other hand, despite Burke's and Hare's Catholicism, anti-Catholic sentiment played no part in the affair or its repercussions and this, too, despite the vehemence of the Catholic emancipation crisis which even then was thrusting Daniel O'Connell through the doors of an enraged House of Commons. Finally, William Burke was almost certainly not guilty of anything more than mass murder; he fought to save his woman, succeeded, and died in communion with his church with a just expectation of salvation. His involvement with murder was not that of a homicidal mercenary; it was that of a desperately tortured man whose discovery and death were probably welcome to him.

The academic historiographical *cliché* 'X Revisited' is, in keeping with its kind, patronising, pretentious and smug, and suggests a historian all too sure of his welcome. But 'Burke and Hare Revisited' emits an agreeable chill. Who would revisit Burke and Hare? It seems a particularly foolhardy proceeding. I have no personal yen for it, and can speak with authority having had at least one vivid dream of an early visit when the book was finished. Hare I recall as curiously neutral, Margaret Hare tolerantly contemptuous, Nellie MacDougal shrinking and nervous. But most of my conversation lay with Burke. He was quite extraordinarily charming, pleasantly appreciative of my attempts to humanise his reputation, really enjoyable company of the seductive kind which prolongs pub sojourns, and when he explained that he would now have to murder me it was in the most courteous possible way. My last recollection was of his apologetically grasping my nose between finger and thumb: he couldn't help himself, he explained, it was by now quite independent of Knox or gain. I awoke with relief, though with no more resentment — possibly less — than one retains against a deeply-valued friend who was tedious but not obnoxious at a party. I may have tried to explain he was killing a golden-egg laying goose, since I am his only friend known to historiographical science: but he hardly needed telling that he was killing a goose. Anyhow, I am still fond of him, but I really do not want to revisit him.

But a word should be said on the story's fortunes since 1980. My suspicion that Hare's much-bruited fate as a blind beggar was merely Victorian Morality's efforts to take the gilt off the government-provided gingerbread, proved shrewd enough when I found reports of Hare's demise in Belfast, in Derry, in New York, and in Chicago. So he ended as at least four corpses and nine blind beggars, a suitable fate for the unrequited murder of fifteen victims. My subsequent work on Arthur Conan Doyle as biographer and as editor documented his initial interest in the protection of supergrass Hare as revealed in his juvenile 'My Friend the Murderer' and in the mature Sherlock Holmes story 'The Resident Patient' (*Memoirs*); much later he used Burke as an inspiration for the morally odious and intellectually impressive Holy Peters in 'The Disappearance of Lady Frances Carfax' in *His Last Bow* whose eponymous eve-of-Great-War 'Epilogue' stars two German spies Von Bork and Von Herling. Conan Doyle's first year as an Edinburgh medical student, 1876–77, was Sir Robert Christison's last as an Edinburgh professor, though as member of University Court, Rectorial candidate, and father of the University Secretary he dominated the academic horizon in all of ACD's student years.

In 1829 Christison had published his *A Treatise on Poisons, in relation to Medical Jurisprudence, Physiology, and Practice of Physic* and in the copy presented to the Royal Medical Society of Edinburgh he included a marginal note recording his interviews with Burke after sentence: it discussed Burke's consumption of opium when his murder career made him an insomniac. Characteristically Burke seems to have been very helpful, recording a regular use of a pint a time. One wonders if Christison found him some opium to ease the horrors of his last weeks. The Royal Medical Society was so kind as to make me a Life Member in recognition of my small assistance with their archives; in view of this book, I feel the least I can do is to make myself also their Death Member, when the time arrives.

Some factual points have proved to need correction, or amplification. My literary conscience and former student Kenneth D. Mackay pointed out that children in rural Scotland even in this century were given whisky for nourishment; hence there is every reason to believe the infant killed with its grandmother in the case of the 'broken' (or, as it proved, unbroken) back would have been unconscious at the time of death. Commentators from Professor Karl Miller in the *London Review of Books* to Tom Johnstone of the Mercat Press have questioned Helen MacDougal's innocence, Miller arguing that for her to have remained in ignorance for a twelve-month puts her in the Meadowbank class of imbecility. But the woman who returned to the West Port after her trial was quite exceptionally limited in intellect; she was very lucky not to be lynched there, she seems to have betrayed her identity in every place to which she subsequently went, and her disappearance from history after the brickbat-shower in Gateshead probably means that she was quickly lynched. She may well have been retarded; for Hare to have advocated her murder to Burke would have been a little cool, even for him, had she not been a natural victim, and this quality could have been achieved by her being a near-idiot even more readily than merely by her status as a Protestant and a Scot. Burke may have adopted her in the first place as one adopts a domestic pet, and his violence in driving her off may have been prompted by her want of rational discourse, much as inopportune canine affection is driven off. Granted that she had been shell-shocked when the police arrived, she still acted very stupidly.

On the other hand I am increasingly convinced that Margaret Hare was implicated from the first, and master-minded the brilliant contrivance by which the Crown's offer of immunity or at most three, murders was transformed into immunity for fifteen murders. She could be stupid, as she was over Daft Jamie, but that seems more the product of unthinking enthusiasm than obdurate stupidity. She had an instinct for self-extrication from unwelcome situations (including, it may be, her first marriage) where Hare did not. Burke, as an intelligent, literate, working-class murderer was frightening to Sir Walter Scott and others; Margaret Hare as a woman at war against society was a much more disturbing figure, all the more because of her effectiveness. If anything the language of contemporary cursemongers on Burke and Hare far outdoes itself when the women come under discussion, and almost certainly because of male chauvinist fears of female homicidal dominance. But Margaret alone seems a real threat: even on the most hostile interpretation there is little sign of trouble from Helen.

Hare mentally as well as physically seems weaker than Margaret, and his repulsiveness is a standard feature of most accounts of the trial. Yet the very first cases indicate some personable qualities: Abigail Simpson of Gilmerton, for instance, seems to have found him a gallant, and so, more substantially, had Margaret herself. But his gaiety was of short duration. It may have been that the murders really did affect him as they did Burke, but such as to deepen his outward and inward misanthropy rather than simply proving he had murdered Sleep among other victims. Or it may have been that

Hare's difficulty in maintaining his charm turned his conquests sour: even Margaret seems to have found Burke more agreeable. Some of the stage versions have made Hare rather than Burke the corrupted innocent; and of course at some time he was an innocent, however impossible it proved for me to find that time. So my book is really half-success and half-failure, as I see it: I believe I understand Burke, I do not understand Hare. If Hare's confession ever turned up, we would have some chance of getting to terms with him. It is not beyond the bounds of possibility that a copy of it still exists in the papers of some custodian of public virtue too innocent to destroy it. As for Margaret Hare and Helen MacDougal, I grant that my theses are conjectural. 'Not proven' is much too valuable a verdict to be abolished, especially for the historian.

One of the prophecies of the book was fulfilled: Conor Cruise O'Brien did indeed write a masterpiece on Edmund Burke, entitled *The Great Melody* (1992). In general it was enthusiastically received, but Professor Roy Porter complained its quotations from Burke were 'stifling'. In the letter which, like a sensible author, he wrote to the editor but did not send, Cruise O'Brien opined that Porter was confusing Edmund with William.

In my own *City of a Thousand Worlds — Edinburgh in Festival* (1991), pp. 236–38, I discussed the Burke and Hare story in street theatre and on stage since the book. There was yet another version in 1992, *The Return of Burke and Hare*, dramatically suggesting such an event for the provision of heart-transplants in our own time. It was done with some splendidly loony foot-stamping musical numbers, but the thesis is grim enough. Privatisation of public health and perpetuation of private wealth could combine to ensure what the crowds of 1829–31 feared, the murder of the poor for the cure of the rich. Should such practices be discovered, the immediate miscreants will no doubt receive every known form of vilification, and the ultimate beneficiaries will be even more immune than hitherto.

The final point, I suppose, is that our own exploitation of one another makes Burkes and Hares of us all. On this logic William Burke is surely our superior. He paid the price for doing so. Most of us have not. Nevertheless he continues to be execrated as the 'infamous' murderer, thus distinguishing him from the rest of us. Humanity continues above all to follow him in the practice with which his name is most conspicuously associated, that of burking the issue. And yet that is surely the thing he did not do. He did not deny that he was a murderer, or that murder was a bad thing, after he had been found guilty; he did everything he could to protect what he

maintained were innocent associates including Knox as well as Helen
MacDougal; he would not glorify his crimes. In that last respect he
offers a pleasing contrast to many subsequent assassins, whether from
Ulster Catholic antecedents or from anywhere else.

Owen Dudley Edwards

Department of History
University of Edinburgh
12 August 1993

Chronology

1791
Birth of Robert Knox

1792
Birth of William Burke (as Liam de Búrca)

early 1790's
Birth of William Hare

1800
Act of Union of Great Britain and Ireland

1808
Birth of William Fergusson

1809
Burke enlists in Donegal militia, serving in Mayo

1810–11
Burke several times in and out of Regimental Hospital, Ballina

1814
First abdication of Napoleon, to Elba

1815
Return of Napoleon, culminating in battle of Waterloo

1816
Burke leaves militia

1818
Burke and Hare, unknown to one another, reach Scotland

1818–22
Union Canal dug from Falkirk to Edinburgh

1827
November
Burke meets Hare

Christmastide
Death and Sale to Knox of old Donald

1828
early
Murder and sale to Knox of Joe the Miller, of the Englishman from Cheshire, and of the woman from Gilmerton

April

Murder of Mary Paterson, afterwards sold to Knox, preserved, and painted under his direction

April–October

Ten other persons murdered by Burke and Hare and sold to Knox

October

Murder of 'Daft' Jamie Wilson, who resists, the body sold to Knox

Hallowe'en

Murder of Mary Docherty

All Saints' Day

Arrest of Burke and Helen MacDougal

All Souls' Day

Docherty body obtained from Surgeon Square by police; the Hares arrested

3 November

Examination of prisoners, Burke stating body received from man he never saw before

10 November

Examination of Burke and MacDougal, each of whom incriminate nobody

1 December

The Hares turn Kings' Evidence

8 December

Indictment served on Burke and MacDougal

Christmas Eve/Christmas Morning

Trial of Burke and MacDougal ending in Burke guilty, MacDougal not proven

26 December

MacDougal released

1829

3 January

Burke's official confession

16 January

Petition for prosecution of Hare

19 January

Release of Margaret Hare

21 January

Edinburgh *Courant* records Burke confession

26 January

Hearing on Bill of Advocation, Suspension and Liberation for Hare

28 January

Burke hanged at 8.15 a.m. before 25,000

29 January
Burke's cadaver lectured on by Professor Alexander Monro *tertius*
with riot at Old College
30 January
Burke's lying in state attended by 30,000
2 February
Advising on Bill of Advocation; prosecution of Hare disallowed.
Grant of petition with proposed action against Hare for assythment;
Hare imprisoned
5 February
Warrant withdrawn; release of Hare to coach
6 February
Hare mobbed in Dumfries with protective imprisonment
7 February
Hare at Annan, crossing border to England; publication of Burke's
confessions
9 February
Hare beyond Carlisle (last recorded sighting)
12 February
Riot at (Robert) Knox's house in Edinburgh
3 March
Knox burnt in effigy at Portobello
1832
Anatomy Act passed
1835
Decline in Knox's pupils
1844
Departure of Knox to Glasgow and thence to London
1862
Death of Knox
1877
Death of Knox's pupil and lover of Mary Paterson, Professor Sir
William Fergusson, FRCS, FRS, Hon. LL.D.(Edin.), Sergeant-
surgeon to Queen Victoria

The Irishness of William Burke

I will sing no more songs: the pride of my country I sang
    Through forty long years of good rhyme, without any avail;
And no one cared even as much as the half of a hang
    For the song or the singer, so here is an end to the tale.

If a person should think I complain and have not got the cause,
    Let him bring his eyes here and take a good look at my hand,
Let him say if a goose-quill has calloused this poor pair of paws
    Or the spade that I grip on and dig with out there in the land!

I had hoped to live decent, when Ireland was quit of her care,
    As a bailiff or steward in a house of degree,
But my end of the tale is, old brogues and old britches to wear,
    So I'll sing no more songs for the men that care nothing for me.

                        Dáibhí O Bruadair
           (adapted into English by James Stephens)

THE Irishness of Burke and Hare was an important feature in their story, although the modern folklore — the same which credits them with being graverobbers who took a shortcut — is often surprised to recall the fact. The precise significance of this Irishness has inevitably been a matter of sharp disagreement. Contemporary comment was curiously detached on the point: where the Irish connection received comment, it was generally in a social and economic context. The Catholic emancipation crisis of the 1820s was on the eve of its resolution, ending all but the most minor of civil disabilities for Roman Catholics — and in any serious sense the continued exclusion of Catholics from the British throne, the English woolsack and the Irish viceroyalty were by now of little importance in sober reality — and both then and later the threat of new Catholic power under Daniel O'Connell's mass popular leadership induced elitist and popular anti-Catholic responses. But Burke and Hare were not made further stars in the litany intoned where the enemies of Rome gathered: the murders of West Port never challenged the primacy of the tortures of the Inquisition and the fires of Smithfield

in Protestant commination services. Indeed, if the outcry against Dr
Robert Knox has any lesson to teach here, it is that neither the
Edinburgh mob nor the Edinburgh polite world had any particular
desire to shuffle the horror away from Edinburgh to alien
scapegoats.

The growth of racial attitudes among the educated classes as the
nineteenth century advanced made for a new view of the question of
Irishness. Ironically, Knox's own work in later life played a
considerable part in this evolution of racism, and one of its effects
was to draw a distinction between what Dylan Thomas called "the
doctor and the devils". Knox's guilt or innocence fascinated William
Roughead, James Bridie, Thomas and other writers; in a sense the
artistic and scholarly treatment of the question in the early twentieth
century carried with it the unspoken segregation of human types
which would have appealed to Knox himself so deeply. The Irishness
of Burke and Hare, explicitly or implicitly, accounted for their
their murderous propensities; and it also accounted — James Bridie
in particular made much of this — for their failure to carry their
murderous enterprise through with the efficiency and vigilance it
required. This last may seem a trifle unfair: if both the efficiency and
the inefficiency of the murderers are to be ascribed to their Irishness,
has Irishness any meaning save as an abusive epithet? In fact, the
prejudice behind these views is common to general white
Anglo-Saxon Protestant attitudes in Britain and America in the first
half of the twentieth century, and was extended to non-white races,
and to some non-Protestant white ones. The lesser breed was seen as
diabolically cunning *and* incredibly stupid. British and American
popular fiction of the day, whether concerned with ravening Indians
or embattled fuzzy-wuzzies, reeks with the idea. Guilt feelings
clearly played some part in the nurturing of the attitude. Oscillation
between the two points of emphasis owed something to fear. Because
Burke and Hare really are frightening to contemplate, racist
commentators found it comforting to stress their stupidity, much as
Irish jokes and Irish bombings keep pace with one another's increase
today. The sudden arrival of an extremely bloody Anglo-Irish war,
followed by an equally bloody and — to the outsider — bewildering
Irish civil war, deepened a sense of murderousness as an Irish racial
trait and this, too, had its effect on the historiography of Burke and
Hare; writers such as Lord Birkenhead who bore some personal
responsibility for the escalation of the Irish crisis into violence found
it particularly desirable to inculcate a racialist view of Irish violence
in their literary audience. It had the added advantage of being an

artificial explanation which obviated any necessity for real explanations.

The Dictionary of National Biography, in a notice by George Clement Boase, tells us that Burke was born in Orrery, county Cork, in 1792. Boase as a biographer had at least the advantage of being unlikely to sympathise with English racial stereotyping about Celtic murderousness and fecklessness — his other work included some celebration of his own Cornish genealogical antecedents — but he was little more than a professional biographical hack. Were his contributions to the D.N.B. brought together, they would fill a volume of that work; and, as was true of several of its other contributors with similar legions of subjects, he tended to rely on recent authorities, older biographical dictionaries, and standard sources he had pillaged with success for other topics. These very qualities have ensured the permanence of his own version of Burke, at least in the writings of subsequent contributors to dictionaries of biography. The latter can be faulted for their slavishness, Boase for his lack of critical awareness. For, so far as can be gathered, his Orrery story depends on the account of Burke and Hare in Grant's Old and New Edinburgh, a vigorous, exotic and multi-volume ragbag published in 1882 by Cassell; and the narrative includes a characteristically vivid account of the executions of Burke and Hare in the Lawnmarket. Boase might have been justified in his respect for Grant's ascription of the birth of William Burke, had Grant not been so damningly definite about the death of William Hare.

Snobbery seems to have been at the root of the problem as it has been at the root of so much else that is erroneous in studies of Burke and Hare. The title "Earl of Cork and Orrery" would no doubt have been well known to Grant, and still more to the multi-biographer Boase. Many accounts of Burke and Hare reported Burke as stating he had been born "in Orrey", and there exists no such place. But their mistake lay in thinking in upper-class rather than in lower-class terms. English upper-class speech sometimes elides syllables of proper names; Irish — and indeed Scots — lower-class speech elides letters of such names, particularly when the speaker derives from the Anglo-Gaelic frontier. What Burke was in fact saying was "Ur'ey", a word in which only the keenest ear could detect a subscript "n". It was his assertion that he was born in the parish of Urney, co. Tyrone.

There seems no reason to doubt him.

The parish is about three miles south-west of the town of Strabane, and lies today almost on the Northern Ireland border with Donegal. It is just south, and Strabane is just north, of the junction of

the rivers Mourne and Finn, before they come together as the Foyle.
It had been the scene of significant Catholic-Presbyterian confronta-
tion over a century and a half before the birth of Burke. The
Presbyterian church is one of the oldest in western Ulster, going back
to the mid-seventeenth century. It was restored at the end of the
century, when the victories of William III's armies against those of
James II determined that Protestant ascendancy would remain.
Urney Presbyterians would have been among those who fled to
Londonderry in 1689 there to withstand one of the most frightful
sieges in the history of these islands, while James's French allies and
Irish Catholic subjects laid waste the surrounding countryside.

Ireland is commonly a land of long memories, all the longer for a
peasantry who recalled largely imaginary lost glories as an antidote
for present deprivation and poverty. But memory in Ireland is no
casually consumed opium; it is normally deployed with maximum
effectiveness by interested parties. Memory was written and
unwritten. Written memory, among other things, included the title-
deeds of those Protestants who now possessed the best land.
Unwritten memory included the much vaguer title-deeds of those
Catholics who claimed to have once possessed it.

Almost certainly, Burke's first language was Irish. The fact that
witnesses testified to Burke's fluency in speaking Irish in Edinburgh
in 1828, a fluency which apparently convinced a native Irish speaker
as to his Gaelic-speaking origins, seems a very clear pointer to this.
Once English had been acquired by a family as its habitual form of
private speech there were few incentives to speak more than a few
phrases of Irish. Daniel O'Connell would sum the matter up in the
words: "Irish never sold the cow". Of course it had done, and of
course O'Connell knew it had, but once Catholics had advanced
financially to the level of cow-dealing, English was what they
needed. English increasingly became the language of all Irish
commerce. Burke's readiness to resort to Irish looks like confidence
in inherited rather than acquired skills. His whole ploy with Docherty
was to demonstrate that he was of her people, not just that he could
speak to her. A common Irish origin when Ireland was divided so
rigidly by caste, creed and ethnic origin meant little; a common Irish
linguistic origin meant everything. So William Burke comes before
us as a product of Gaelic Ireland, in its decline and on its frontier, but
Gaelic nonetheless.

Burke, indeed, stood at the commencement of his life not only at
one frontier, but at several. One of the singular qualities exhibited by
Burke throughout his brief public life was his exceptional

ecumenism, and while this, like much else about him, is unusual, it cannot casually be classified as unique. For if there was any real impact in Ireland of the democratic and libertarian ideals of the American Revolution, it was among the Ulster Presbyterians. Religion in eighteenth-century Ireland was important not for belief but for status. Protestant Episcopalians had land, status and power; Presbyterians and other Protestant dissenters suffered many forms of discrimination; Catholics lay at the bottom of the social and economic pyramid. Much has been made of a few isolated Protestant espiscopalian statements in favour of Catholic emancipation, but it was the Presbyterians in the 1780s who really produced the most deeply-felt pleas for the Catholics. By the 1790s the thrust of the richer Catholics into commercial life and the new expectations of the Presbyterians resulted in a jostling between castes and the London government for the support of the former untouchables, but in certain Ulster Presbyterian circles the ideological commitment to the Catholic cause remained generous and strong. These coincided with rising sentiments of Presbyterian tenant-farmer hostility to espiscopalian landlordism, shading into agrarian skirmishes, and at the end of the decade, insurrection in eastern Ulster. In eastern Tyrone, especially in the better agricultural lands, Protestants outnumbered Catholics thickly enough, but in the extreme north-west whence William Burke came, observers such as Edward Wakefield noted that the Protestants were very thin on the ground indeed. Protestant episcopalian high society, such as was typified by the Marquess of Abercorn (whose opulent estate, Baronscourt, lay near the Burkes' hovel), expressed its exclusiveness at the expense of its Presbyterian fellow-Protestants even more pointedly than at that of the wretched Catholics. The latter had neither the income nor the legal position to offer competition. Wakefield early in the next century noted but one Catholic in the entire county with sufficient wealth to be permitted to serve on a Grand Jury.

One singular fact about the religious frontier in Tyrone is the presence of folklore concerning Catholic eccentrics who from time to time would visit Protestant churches as well as their own, as William Burke was to do in his maturer years. But the paucity of Protestants in the neighbourhood would throw Burke more firmly back on his Gaelic origins. In fact, it is most likely that in the initial instance he did not think of himself as William Burke at all, but as Liam de Búrca.

The only other member of Burke's family of whom we know anything by evidence other than his was his brother Constantine, and

during the great days of Burke and Hare he inhabited poor quarters
in the West Port. Constantine as a first name was found in Scotland
and Cornwall in the early nineteenth century. The Cornish-
Caledonian connection arises from an alleged Christian mission to
Scotland from St Constantine of Cornwall, as a result of which one
of the earlier Christian kings of Scotland is credited with the name.
What this means for us is that Constantine Burke received his
English name when he settled in Scotland, again a reminder of a
primarily Gaelic-speaking origin for the family. Had his
nomenclature become formally Anglicised in Ireland, it would have
been as Cornelius or possibly Conor. In casual English speech the
same abbreviation was employed as was used in Gaelic — Con — but
it is clear that Constantine obtained his original name in Gaelic and
not in English, or he would never have possessed it in so Scottish a
form. The Gaelic name is Conchubhar (pronounced Cruhoor or
Cruchoor, with the second "c" aspirate as in "Loch").

Gaelic Ireland was dying in Burke's youth, but it was powerful
enough to impress its imagery and escapism upon him. And he needed
it. His family belonged to the lowest order of the lowest caste in Irish
life — landless Catholic labourers.

The travellers Mr and Mrs S. C. Hall in their *Ireland. Its Scenery,
Character, &c.* (1843) quote the autobiographical statement of a "day
labourer, employed regularly, and receiving the usual rate of
remuneration — enough 'to starve upon'." The place was Sion Mills,
not far from Burke's birthplace, and the time the early nineteenth
century. There were seven children, and he often had to face them
with four potatoes, and bad ones, as the only food among them.
" 'God knows I used to think myself a selfish wretch for eating even
one, when the children's hungry eyes were on them; but I was hungry
too, and faint from work. My poor wife would go into Strabane, and
some there would do her a good turn of a hard summer, or in winter;
and she had a better command over the hunger than I had, for she
would purtend' " — so the Halls spelled his word — " 'sickness of
some sort or other after she'd throw the potatoes out on the table,
and go and lay on the straw that was our bed, and strive to sleep it
away. My eldest boy was more weakly than the others, and he had a
great relish for learning, and a gentleman took him, as a 'boy about
the place', to do a little of everything and learn when he could, which
he did, poor fellow; still there were eight of us on tenpence a day, and
the morsel of garden'."

William Burke was afterwards to claim a similar form of escape
for himself.

"It is slander," continue the Halls, "to characterise the Irish peasant as an idler; he is often idle, it is true, but only because, as often, his time is worth so little as to seem scarcely worthy of consideration. Not unfrequently, the waste of an hour involves the loss of but a single halfpenny; and it can seldom be said to cause the sacrifice of a solitary comfort or enjoyment — much less a luxury. A time is no doubt approaching, when hard labour will procure something more for the hard labourer than the mere means of preserving existence. . . ."

It was not. What was approaching was the great famine of 1845-50 and the decimation of the population whose rise had been pushing more and more of its poorest over the threshold of starvation. Was it for Burke alone that a future might seem to loom where hard labour would procure for the hard labourer the means of destroying existence that competed with his? There may have been something of the kind in the outbreaks of Irish agrarian warfare and vengeance, under the disguise of penalties for infringement of a code.

Yet the life of the Irish labourer in the 1790s was not one of unrelieved horror, and it was to the Gaelic heritage that he owed what surcease there was from the vicious spiral. Because Gaelic was to collapse so thoroughly in the early nineteenth century with the advance of state education and prospects for the newly enfranchised Catholics in migration to the industrialising North Atlantic world, we tend to lose sight of the fierceness with which it was often maintained amid remote rural poverty in the later eighteenth. Professor Thomas Flanagan remarks in his brilliant study *The Irish Novelists 1800-1850* "perhaps because external pressures upon it were so great, the Gaelic population held tenaciously to its language, customs and traditions". As he says, the Gaelic word lived "despised and hidden", but it lived. And within it lived the awareness of lost cultural richness, a vast wealth of folklore, a still thriving poetry, a vocabulary far richer and more varied than would ever be open to the Gaelic-speaking exiles forced into English. They seem to have been very conscious of what they were losing as they saw their world dying. Carleton's mother, asked to sing "The Red-Haired Man's Wife" in English, remarked that the English words and the Irish tune were like a man and his wife quarrelling — "the Irish melts into the tune but the English doesn't". The importance of the folklore and the poetry lies in the wealth of imagery, ornateness of reference and Homeric complexity of analogy with which they abounded.

Poets travelled and sang for reward and hospitality; song proliferated at the crossroads, in *ad hoc* gatherings in local cabins, and above all at wakes for the dead, and for the departing emigrants. Then the labourer, worn out with his toil of the day and his stammering subservience to his master in the alien tongue which meant so little to him, could luxuriate in the world that was his.

The poets themselves, from O Bruadair onward through the miserable years of eighteenth-century Ireland, were labourers; their physical frames wore out on poverty and degradation while their brains and tongues teemed with the triumphs of their ancestors and their art.

The folklorists were similarly in demand to produce long and complex renditions involving heroism, the supernatural, love, diplomacy and war, usually with careful allusions to the locality designed to lend a pleasing false authenticity whose mendacity and topicality would be well appreciated. These again would convey the nostalgia of past glory, and the charm of acquaintance with a world of normally invisible beings over whom the cruel contemporary world could have no sway. And they would remember also legends of the cunning tricksters who would turn words to such purpose that the law would become its own prisoner.

Professor John Kelleher and Mr Alf Mac Lochlainn have argued that the psychological impact of the loss of that Gaelic world must have been appalling for its exiles. A great vocabulary and a heritage of two thousand years was suddenly shrunk down into a few hundred pragmatic words. The spectacle of imaginative and far-ranging minds suddenly denied anything but the most banal forms of self-expression is one which clearly illuminates the movement into drunkenness, fighting, bitterness, brutality and crime. It was not that the old Gaelic world lacked violence: there was plenty of that. But if drink and fighting were resorted to very regularly in the dying Gaelic world, in the new land of the exiles drink and fighting seemed all that was left. True, there was also religion, the faith for which Gaelic Ireland had suffered so much, and which became the legal means of defining the extent of its degradation. But religion, in the early nineteenth century, would not be the organised force in the points of the emigrants' destiny which it would prove by mid-century and after. Priests were fewer, and some of the greatest focal points of Gaelic piety such as "stations" in the house and cults of local saints were as thoroughly lost to them. Small wonder, then, that Mrs Docherty should have suddenly seen her miserable world becoming miraculously enlarged and enriched ten times over when William Burke began to speak to her in Irish. What could have been more natural than that she would want to continue the conversation, perhaps with the addition of some of the old songs and stories? It was an attractive Death that spoke in Gaelic.

But the Gaelic itself came from a Death-encircled world. There were bitter land feuds which pressed much harder on the peasants and labourers who transgressed than on the mighty landlords. There were long sustained family feuds, about who had done what when, and whose father took a job or a holding whence another father had been fired or evicted, the story told and retold with circumstances of personal inadequacy reduced to invisibility while the treachery rose above that of Iscariot. There were grim, oath-bound organisations, Ribbonmen or their variants, where mysterious captains took terrible vengeance on defaulters or informers sometimes to the level of dwellings being fired and wives and children murdered along with the accused. There were endless faction disputes in which whole townlands aligned themselves, and the men broke heads while the children ambushed one another with stones. "These factions," observed Sir Walter Scott in 1825, "have been so long envenomed, and they have such narrow ground that they are like men fighting with daggers in a hogshead." With his customary economic insight on Irish questions, he had caught it as well as Yeats would later in the line "Great hatred, little room". The pressure of population to the square inch was bad and getting worse; the struggle for incredibly scarce resources and miserable privileges became more severe with each year. It is important to stress that this extended very heavily within the Catholic community. William Carleton in his story "The Party Fight and Funeral" tells of a bloody affray between Protestants and Catholics, but precedes it with excellent sociological relevance and apparent literary irrelevance with a long account of Catholics' faction-fighting among themselves, in which the main protagonist had risen to maturity before finally falling in the riot against the Protestants. The very work of the Gaelic bards and folklorists must have increased the propensity to violence. They sang of the great deeds of long-dead heroes, or of the lost battles of the previous century. The cults of highwaymen, better known as rapparees or tories, flourished long after their deaths as a glimmer of one means of preserving heroism and self-respect, and of course their character and deeds were glorified out of all resemblance to their rather squalid careers, Redmond Count O'Hanlon being the major legend in Burke's country. All that remained of heroic impulses and gentlemanly derring-do was the urge to distinguish oneself on local faction-fields. It was all that remained of the brave Cú Chulainn, the resourceful Fionn Mac Cumhaill, the proud O'Donnell, the mighty

O'Neill and the Brown Earl William Burke.

Death struck most frequently from malnutrition. However poor the corpse there would be a wake, if at all possible. A great wake did not necessarily mean a fine funeral. Carleton tells a cruel story of the wake of Larry McFarland, a fine occasion, despite the deceased and his wife having been labourers who died in total poverty with a son who would grow up to go to the scaffold; but of the funeral the narrator will say only "a poor berrin it was, a miserable sight, God knows — just a few of the nighbours; for those that used to take his thrate, and while he had a shilling in his pocket blarney him up, not one of the skulking thieves showed their faces at it — a good warning to foolish men that throw their money down the throats that haven't hearts asundher them". But the wake was vital — a folksong in English in the next century told of Finnegan who arose from his own coffin, after having been laid out and waked for dead, when a badly-aimed noggin of whiskey splashed on his features.

The origins of the wake are obscure, and one theory argues that the vigil was to ensure against the corpse's removal by evil-minded spirits; and as Carleton's characters would be quick to remark, by this epoch there were spirits enough and to spare at the wake the better to fight the other spirits off. Fear of theft of a body is very old. It surrounds the whole story of the Resurrection of Christ. It appears again and again in the *Iliad*. Strangely enough, Shane Leslie was told by the aged Rafferty that there was a genuine fear in those parts that bodies would be stolen by body-snatchers. He would have been speaking of the Carleton country, but Urney, close to urban centres such as Strabane and Derry, must have been ever more aware of any such propensity, since the means of reaching acquisitive members of the medical profession would have been much easier in that locality. The wake put paid to any chance of theft at that point, in that even with all the mourners fallen asleep the hue and cry after a lost body would have been too dangerous for body-snatchers to risk. But Rafferty tells of graves being watched for a week. It seems decidedly probable that William Burke had heard of the traffic in bodies before ever he left Ireland at all. It is far less likely that he ever took part in it. He certainly played no part in Scottish resurrectionism. But if he ever did have a hand in robbing a grave, it was in Ireland that he had it.

Quite apart from ressurectionism, the Tyrone border abounded in stories of games and antics to do with funerals, and here again Burke would have been early conditioned. Rafferty told a story of Carleton himself in this regard: "he met four men with a coffin, and they went into a publichouse, leaving the coffin out on the road, and Carleton went into it; and when they came out, they said 'the devil's in the coffin', and there wasn't a drop of Holy Water in the whole countryside they didn't pour over him and couldn't put him out". It is not a great step from jokes with coffins to jokes with bodies, especially if they have to be removed to perpetrate the jokes with coffins. Once again, it multiplies the appropriateness of Burke's Irish heritage.

The wake itself supplied merriment and games enough. "There were great games played at wakes in those times," asserted Rafferty, and spoke of "Clipping the Sheep, My Man Jack and Shuffle the Brogue". Clipping the Sheep, he remarked thoughtfully, was "powerful. It killed men betimes." And there would be dancing and singing, and the innumerable tributes to the dead, and poetry and recitations and narrations. So the system developed by Burke and Hare would seem to have been one of adaptation more than of originality. Their procedure was to invert the wake: party first, death second. If Burke had been acquainted with an unusually excitable performance of Clipping the Sheep, even that particular detail might prove to have been present at the original. Often enough the noise caused by the celebrations could be relied on to drown all other sounds. "At a wake," said Rafferty, "the people in the kitchen began singing against the people in the corpse-room. In the end there was contention which were the best singers." And contention, too, could lead to accidents, possibly even fatal ones.

From this world William Burke ultimately went forth with knowledge and possibly skills whose value only later became apparent to him. Like his fellow-emigrants, he went with the psychological burden of a lost Gaelic heritage and a shrunken range of reference. It would not be true to say that his ethnic origin gave him his homicidal propensities, but the socio-economic circumstances of his upbringing would have led him to hold life cheaper than, say, the British did. Or, at least, than the British did other than in their armed forces.

CHAPTER 2

Burke and the
Napoleonic Wars

"Waterloo? Of course I was at Waterloo. Wasn't I at Waterloo, Duke?"
"So your Majesty always says."
—Anecdote of George IV and the Duke of Wellington

WILLIAM Burke was probably not present at the battle of Waterloo, and it was a matter of extreme annoyance and exasperation to the Duke of Wellington that he was not. For William Burke as an individual he knew little ˉand cared less, although by one of these ironies which seem hell-made for the New Left Theatre, the Duke was in fact enjoying — or not enjoying — his sole real premiership at the time of Burke's trial and death. It was an arm of his government which brought Burke to the gallows and Hare to immunity. But the business was peripheral for the Duke: it was not Burke and Hare, but his other fellow-countryman, Daniel O'Connell, who most greatly exercised his mind. Burke and Hare he left to the Scotchmen. The closest he came to them was in sponsoring an Anatomy Bill through the House of Lords after it had passed the Commons; and he was forced to drop the Bill on 5 June 1829 after a hornets' nest had been conjured up with the aid of the Archbishop of Canterbury. A fresh Bill had to await London Burkers and a Whig government.

But in 1815 what William Burke represented was muscle and brawn and courage and discipline and the Duke could not get enough of it. "I have got an infamous army," he thundered to Lord Bathurst, fortunately unaware that he was thereby supplying Georgette Heyer with the title of a novel about him a hundred and twenty years thence, "very weak and ill equipped, and a very inexperienced Staff. In my opinion they are doing nothing in England. They have not raised a man; they have not called out the militia either in England or Ireland. . . ." The date of his despatch was 8 May 1815. And he was quite right. He never got the militia from either country, for a reason that seems virtually incredible to us today. The politicians had come to the conclusion that the militia could not be called out, although it was active, under arms and with a modicum of training, because in law the militia could only be called out for service overseas in the event of war. *And there was no war.* The battle of Waterloo is probably the most famous battle on the continent of Europe in which the British ever engaged: but they were not at war at the time. France was officially still under the restored Bourbons, and hence an ally. Napoleon's hundred days were, in law, a piece of local disorder in which British troops were being employed in what would nowadays be termed an international police action. So William Burke in the Donegal militia remained where he was, and the Duke roared for his arrival in vain.

So when the Duke needed William Burke to kill for him, he was not there, and when Burke finally did get himself into the killing business as a subject with the Duke once more in command, his services were not desired. It was an irony which went back far beyond the dawn of written history, and will doubtless go forward until the death of the last discharged soldier. Burke and countless others like him were trained for a profession which demanded quick responses, personal ingenuity, reliance on comrades and little squeamishness about the sanctity of human life, and when that profession had no further use for them, to what use were they to put the ethical and scientific education they had received? This is not to single out Wellington as one of the more inhumane war-lords of history; the evidence is that his instincts were more humane than most. But war is not humane, and the common soldier got little incentive to build up a sense of delicacy.

Wellington was not shouting for useless lumber on the eve of the most terrible engagement of his career. He and his brothers knew a great deal about the Irish militia; the Wellesleys produced Irish administrators as well as British generals, the Duke himself having been both. His term of office as Chief Secretary for Ireland lasted from April 1807 to April 1809, he was followed in it after an interval of but a few months by his brother, William Wellesley-Pole, who would last until 1812, and we may be reasonably certain that within those five years William Burke joined the Donegal militia which, like its fellows, lay under their command.

Burke's years in the militia meant a good deal to him. He was to speak of them afterwards with affection and ready resource, and it is probable that they were the best of his life. In this he was typical of many Irishmen before and after him. The Irish military tradition is a singular one. The volunteer element is particularly high; the

opposition to conscription is overwhelming. Motives for military
enlistment were socio-economic, not militaristic. But in the society
where a disadvantaged ethnic group is seeking to acquire equality of
status and power, by political blackmail as much as by anything else,
it naturally sought to avoid so unacceptable an admission as
mercenary motives. In fact mercenaries were exactly what the Irish
volunteers in the European, American and British armies were. A
remarkable anonymous eighteenth-century poem, *An Spailpín Fánach*
(the migrant labourer), tells of the author's intention to give up the
drudgery and the degradation of his wretched status for service in the
French army. Of course he, like most poets, insists on a lost grandeur
in his case, but it is his description of the economic conditions from
which he is fleeing that sounds the authentic note. His expression of
motives for his enlistment seem highly relevant to those of William
Burke half a century later: there was a frankness in the Gaelic
explanation which later English ones would lack.

When the British Government and the more reluctant Irish
administration dropped the barrier against recruitment of Catholics,
at first implicitly, and then openly, the labourers took the Saxon
shilling as readily as *"Spailpín Fánach"* had pledged himself to
" 'colours' na bhFranncach".

The origins of the militia are somewhat curious in themselves.
When Ireland had been denuded of troops during the American war
local volunteer regiments were raised by prominent Protestant
worthies. This was no idle action: John Paul Jones was raiding the
Irish and Scottish coasts and Benjamin Franklin in Passy had hired
some Irish smugglers to attack British shipping in the hope of
effecting exchanges of prisoners — the smugglers failed to pick up
prisoners but, like Jones, they raided to some advantage. There
remained the more ominous threat once the French had entered the
war in 1778 that a French armada might descend on Ireland,
something which the following year very nearly happened. But the
Irish Volunteers, as they were called, began to think of their own
grievances against the British government. Hitherto they had
accepted subordinate economic and constitutional status for the
Kingdom of Ireland and its Parliament in return for a free hand in the
repression of the Catholics, but now it began to seem that the fruits
of bigotry were hardly worth the costs. Ultimately the Volunteers
pressurised the British government to bring free trade and,
ultimately, constitutional independence (which in practice meant
that the British government had now to buy the Irish Parliament
instead of merely bullying it). And in the vortex of ideological

change induced by the revolutionary climate in the North Atlantic, elements in the Volunteer movement, notably the Presbyterians, actually began to concern themselves with the cause of the repressed Catholics. Ultimately the Volunteers won a considerable reputation for liberal influences. It was far from being wholly deserved. Certain elements in the movement, if not the greater part of it, remained wholly attached to the self-interest of their own socio-economic grouping, and Catholic advances in the initial instance owed more to the enlightened policies of Lord North than of his critics in the Volunteers. But in retrospect they looked good.

They also looked dangerous. After the steam had gone out of the movement an old proposal for setting up a militia was reintroduced. In part it came from some of the more conservative Volunteers, such as George Ogle, who urged the necessity of a force to maintain order in the absence of the army but who feared the momentum of independent military power in Volunteer hands. But he found support from such figures as Lord Hillsborough, who had been conspicuous for his hostility to the Americans and who wished to curb the power of those Protestant magnates who had looked so formidable in the Volunteer days. Both elements were at one in seeking a role for the militia to cut down agrarian rebels and Catholic sectarian attacks on the Protestants in the north-east — attacks which were in origin sometimes defences or reprisals against Protestant sectarian activists. The force ultimately was enacted into law in 1793. Local magnates undertook the work of building it up often in the spirit of the old Volunteers, but government control was maintained. A compulsory element entered into the recruitment, which duly elicited some ugly responses, but the militia fairly quickly became a fact of Irish life. The intermittent war with revolutionary France lent considerable force to the arguments for its acceptance.

The Donegal militia, which Burke was ultimately to join, had as its colonel Nathaniel Clements, styled Viscount Clements from 1795 to 1804, and then succeeding his father as the second Earl of Leitrim. Since Burke would know him only as Lord Leitrim, it is convenient for us to do the same. The *G. E. C. Complete Peerage* gives a fairly full account of the family, drawing on an American history, *Ancestors and Descendants of Robert Clements*, which was so rare that G. E. Cockayne had to obtain a copy from a private donor. But its rarity did not mean accuracy. It led G.E.C. to describe the militia as "the Donegal Regiment" stating it was disembodied and he retired in 1802. In fact, disembodiment proved only temporary and Leitrim remained the

colonel of the Donegal militia until in common with the rest of the
Irish militia it was disembodied in 1816. Otherwise G.E.C. is his
helpful and resourceful self. Leitrim was born in 1768, which puts
him at forty-odd when he obtained the services of William Burke. In
this he was decidedly senior to many other officers, some of whom
were little more than infants. In 1814 he received a request from a
father for a commission for his fourteen-year-old son, and officers of
even younger ages are found in actual service in other regiments.

Leitrim seems to have been a man of public spirit and courage. He
was a Whig in politics and sat in the Irish Parliament for ten years
until the Act of Union, after which he sat in the House of Commons
for Leitrim until he came into the peerage. He steadfastly supported
the Whig cause, despite resultant exclusion from the sweets of
office: his father, indeed, had obtained his peerage from Fox in 1783
but there were few families to take their loyalties so seriously. This
suggests a pattern of unusual political enlightenment at the head of
the Donegal militia. The extreme Whigs may have been conspicuous
in Ireland for their anti-Catholicism at the outbreak of the American
Revolution, but by the early nineteenth century the repressive nature
of the governments of Pitt and his Tory successors meant that Whig
principles could be assumed to imply somewhat liberal principles.
Leitrim's connections also indicated he would hold to something of
the traditions of the Irish Volunteers. His wife was the sister of Lady
Charlemont, whose husband's father had been known as the
"Volunteer Earl". And the Donegal militia differed from its fellows
in eschewing the ballot as a means of recruitment, thereby avoiding
the bad feeling and occasional flare-up which the element of
compulsion in that system induced. Leitrim raised his militia
throughout the county, of which he had become Governor in 1781,
by parochial assessment. His connections with the counties of
Donegal and Leitrim were extensive in the matter of land and
society, and he profited by the action of local magnates in collecting
money on an insurance system as a result of which the regiment
virtually paid for itself. His was largely a volunteer regiment.

Burke was almost certainly drawn into it partially as a result of
this public spirit. Directly his motives for leaving the status of a
labourer's son must have been akin to those of the *Spailpín Fánach*–

> Go deo deo arís ní raghad go Caiseal
> Ag díol nó ag reic mo shláinte,
> Ná ar mhargadh na saoire im shuidhe cois balla
> Im sgaoinse ar leath-taoibh sráide–

Bodairí na tíre ag tígheacht ar a gcapaill
Dá fhiafruighe an bhfuilim hirálta;
O! teanam chun siubhail, tá an cúrsa fada
Seo ar siubhal an Spailpín Fánach.

(I will go no more to Cashel town
Selling and wrecking my health and strength,
Nor at market-wall will I sit me down,
Thrown at the side of the high street's length.
While on horseback perched boorish farmers strong
Bawl at my head "Are ye hired today?"
Oh, the journey's mine though the course be long
And the wandering worker is on his way.)

But by the time he joined up Burke may have had one taste of status and economic betterment. It would seem that the same circumstance that liberated one of the children of the Halls' informant obtained in his case. He is reported to have become the servant of a Presbyterian minister. Some suspicion may attach to the story in that no such statement figures in any of Burke's narratives but despite the mythologising during the trial and afterwards there are points in favour of it. Protestant evangelical activities among the Catholics were to be a marked feature of Irish life in the early nineteenth century. Burke may in fact have been taken on as a prospective, or perhaps even an actual, if temporary, Presbyterian convert. It would account for his subsequent interest in evangelicalism and for his ecumenism in the militia itself. He ascribed the latter to the camaraderie of the militia but it could well have an antecedent point of departure.

If Burke had betrayed, or contemplated betraying, the church into which he had been born, for however brief a time, it would account for his silence on this passage in his life. It is clear that on the eve of his death he, for all of his ecumenism, very definitely wished to face his Maker in the affirmation of the faith of his fathers. It also seems likely that his Presbyterian employer would have been good for further opportunities. He may have been trained in a trade: if the Presbyterian minister's concern was to save a soul rather than to obtain a servant, it would account for the brevity of his service. What is also likely is that Burke's employer had drawn him over the border into Donegal, or else that he had associations with the county. This would explain why Burke, a Tyrone man, enlisted in Donegal, although extra-county enlistment had been illegal since 1797, and, given the scruple with which Lord Leitrim worked with all the individual parishes, an ecclesiastical link seems eminently possible.

Priests played some part in militia recruitment elsewhere in Ireland;
a Presbyterian minister seems an even more likely candidate for such
work. Finally Burke's success in obtaining the post of servant to an
officer again would be consistent with patronage from a person of
some consequence.

Burke says that he was in the militia for seven years, and there is no
reason to doubt him. His friend John Maclean said that he was
discharged "from the regiment after the battle of Waterloo".

One William Burke appears on the quarterly militia roll and
paylists of the Donegal militia for 1809 to 1815, remaining in service
throughout as a private in Captain Irwin's company. It is further
mentioned that he was in and out of the Regimental Hospital at
Ballina in 1810-11, and Ballina is the one place mentioned by Burke
in his own account, although the particulars given by him allude to
matrimony rather than to medical ailments. This would seem to be
conclusive, were it not for a curious circumstance. From 1812 the
records were maintained in much less detail; the paylist is for the
whole regiment. And from the beginning of 1812 there appear two
William Burkes, which in June 1814 become three. As Dr Roy
Foster, to whom I am deeply indebted for the research leading to
these facts, has remarked, William Burke seems to rival St Patrick in
the plurality of identity confronted by his historians. One of the
William Burkes — we cannot say which — left late in 1815, and it
could be that this is our one as it is consistent with the statement of
departure after Waterloo. But he could just as well be one of the two
still on the books in 1816. In any event the incursion of the second and
third William Burkes prevent us from being absolute in ruling out
European service outside of the militia or, indeed, service in
England. (The Donegal militia never left Ireland, nor did any Irish
militia units see service in Britain: George III emphatically objected
to Catholic troops being quartered on his Protestant realms. Two
regiments of the Irish militia were sent to Catholic Guernsey and
Jersey, neither of them being the Donegal.) The fact that all three
William Burkes concluded their service in Ireland makes it possible
for Burke to have been abroad, and yet to have settled initially in
Ireland after leaving the militia instead of commencing his British
career at that point. But the overwhelming balance lies with the
private in Irwin's company. One can only say that it is agreeable to
have found the first known source for Burke's life in Ireland,
exclusive of statements made when he rose to eminence in Scotland,
despite the fact that Ireland, having at last broken its silence, has been
somewhat over-generous in the breaking of it.

Whatever links Burke had formed in Donegal before his enlistment were to be speedily broken. The bogey of having armed the Catholics kept Government in a state of some anxiety about the militia during its lifetime. In fact the militia showed very little propensity to desert even during the year of greatest disaffection, 1798, and such of the men as fell into the hands of the French invaders were, for the most part, hostile to any thought of throwing their lot in with the insurgents and their European allies. The performance of the militia against the invaders had varied from the mad flight that became immortalised as "the races at Castlebar" to the intrepid defence of Collooney against veterans of Napoleon's Italian campaign; and in the bitter aftermath when the countryside was reduced to order after the defeat of the United Irishmen and the capture of the French, the militia earned an ugly reputation for ready recourse to gunfire against the faintest signs of civilian activity, as well as for plunder and loot on a fairly large scale. This was all ten years into the past in Burke's time but he would, no doubt, have been familiar with the militia tradition that life was cheap when pickings were considerable. But the allegations or fears of disaffection were ill-founded. Nevertheless the principle obtained from the first that the militia against the invaders had varied from the mad flight that became immortalised as "the races of Castlebar" to the intrepid defence of Collooney against veterans of Napoleon's Italian remained in the status of an occupying army in a country of uncertain loyalty which happened to be their own. County loyalty and identification were far stronger than national sentiment, and the Donegal, on its brief returns to its home base, was particularly conscious of alienation. County society took little pains to acknowledge their services, despite Leitrim's success in having rallied its financial support. A little before the time of Burke's enlistment one officer had bitterly complained during a home posting that "The Donegal regiment is as little thought of as when they were 200 miles from the county" and, given the remoteness of Donegal from the rest of Ireland, the distance was not extraordinary. Ballina, in county Mayo, would be comparatively local. By sea it is a very short distance from Donegal, though by land the vagaries of the Irish coastline add many Irish miles.

Burke had thus become an official nomad, and he would retain that nomadic status for the rest of his life. His primary loyalties then and later would be to comrades. The local inhabitants were to be exploited and entertained and, where necessary, assisted. They were to be liked and succoured; they were also, it might be, to be robbed and killed. The militia fought fires, helped with shipwrecks — both activities offering opportunities for public service and private plunder — and were even contemplated for navvy work. But self-enrichment rather than sympathy with disaffection was the real justification for anxiety about it.

Entertainment was important, and Maclean's insistence that Burke had been either a fifer or a drummer shows us a formalisation of his status as an entertainer. It accounts for the importance of music in Burke's subsequent career, as well as for his personal skill in flute-playing. It also accounts for Burke's stories of consorting with soldiers of several different religious faiths. The militia in general were primarily Protestant in officers, predominantly Catholic in the lower ranks. The Donegal would have had a higher proportion of Protestants, but Catholics were still heavily in the majority. But the regimental bands had a far higher proportion of outsiders. It was there that Englishmen and Scotsmen might be found, and even an occasional black. So, religiously, it would have been much more mixed than the mass of the private soldiers. And its work was attractive. Apart from ceremonial occasions and the provision of music for the troops, militia bands entertained the locals. The Donegals, under Lord Leitrim's direction, had been dressed with some cost and elegance. Conflict had existed in the regiment about the use of powder in the hair: an order of 1798 declared it to be "very prejudicial to the hair and apt to create vermin" and hence it was to be worn but twice a week, but by 1801 the lieutenant-colonel was strongly for it in that "it adds much to a soldier's appearance in point of dress, exclusive of the comfort of cleaning the hair". However much benefit Burke derived from this — and his head seems to have retained its hair until it fell into the hands of Professor Monro — he would have shared with the band the most exotic appearance of all the private soldiery. The band were invariably turned out in really striking uniforms, with appropriate effects on the local female population.

The two careers of Burke within the army, of manservant and of bandsman, suggest an immediate parallel with one of Charles Lever's most attractive characters. *Charles O'Malley* is set in the Napoleonic wars and while O'Malley and his servant Mickey Free saw Napoleonic warfare at first hand instead of, like the Donegal militia, waiting for an invasion that would never arrive, the self-images of Mickey and of Burke possess a decided similarity. That Mickey's songs are composed for British soldiers who are doing his assigned lackey-tasks in return for entertainment is noteworthy:

Bad luck to this marching,
Pipeclaying and starching;
How neat one must be to be killed by the French!
I'm sick of parading,
Through wet and cowld wading
Or standing all night to be shot in a trench.
To the tune of a fife,
They dispose of your life,
You surrender your soul to some illigant lilt,
Now I like Garryowen,
When I hear it at home,
But it's not half so sweet when you're going to be kilt.

Then though up late and early,
Our pay comes so rarely,
The devil a farthing we've ever to spare,
They say some disaster
Befell the paymaster;
On my conscience I think that the money's not there.
And, just think, what a blunder;
They won't let us plunder,
While the convents invite us to rob them, 'tis clear,
Though there isn't a village,
But cries, 'Come and pillage',
Yet we leave all the mutton behind for Mounseer. . . .

It will be obvious that the sentiments are conventional, if singularly felicitous, army grousing; the Donegals, of course, had little to complain of in the matter of pay, risked death only to the degree that locals might take out any grievances against society on the person of a solitary militia man — and there were occasional murders — while the plunder, though no doubt wholly insufficient, could still be obtained when the eye of Authority was diverted. But no song was ever the worse for a judicious mendacity. Nor is there any real likelihood that civilian life was to be preferred to military, by William Burke or any of his companions. We lack reactions to the final disembodiment, but during the abortive disembodiment of 1802 responses were very hostile. It was, said a militia officer apparently in the Donegals, "looked forward to with pleasure by some of our men, but far from agreeable, I believe, to the great bulk of them. . . . In fact, very few men, after having made a fair trial of the comforts of a soldier's life, can sit contentedly down to the labours and privations of 'life in a cabin'. Two hours on his feet at a time as a sentinel are very different from five or six at the bottom of a ditch or even behind a loom." The same witness, apparently, observed again, "Of the soldiers some were pleased at getting home but the greater

part regretted the loss of their regimental comforts. It was curious to
see them taking leave of their firelocks. One grenadier, I heard, as he
pitched his into the store, exclaim: 'There ye go darlin' an' be'jabers
I'd know the crack of ye in a thousand'.'' Burke himself would not
have found his youth and low stature a barrier to acceptance. Figures
for 1802 put one-sixth of the regiment as below 5 ft. 5 ins. (the
Armaghs of the same date had one-hundredth below 5 ft. 5 ins.) while
one-eighth were eighteen. Burke might have sung amusingly
grumbling songs but if his master (Captain Irwin? one wonders)
should have heard him, it would have simply resulted in a decision to
give him the prestigious status of bandsman. Indeed this seems the
most likely explanation for his obtaining it.

"Mr Whiskey had done a little mischief in our ranks," wrote
future Chief Secretary Castlereagh to his wife as the Londonderry
marched out of Limerick to face the French invasion at Bantry Bay in
1796, "but upon the whole for a first day's march (taking leave of
sweethearts and parting with the inhabitants who brought spirits in
quantities to them when they were chilled on the streets waiting for
stores which they never received) we did fairly well."

Mr Whiskey was ultimately to supply Burke and Hare with
motive for murder but he was also a major accomplice, and Burke
would have had the advantage of judging the potentialities of his
effects during army service. The knowledge of physical weakness
and inability for self-defence as a result of alcohol proved a useful
acquisition, and the militia would have supplied him with material
for observation. The mind does not necessarily connect an unfitness
for engaging in work with an unfitness for resistance to death, but in
a military situation the connection is an obvious one. The supply of
whiskey would in the west of Ireland have been very great indeed,
and what Burke and his fellow-soldiers obtained in large measure
from local admirers would have been poteen — the pale, potent
produce of illicit stills which abounded in the west in this period.

Burke made another set of acquaintances at this time, with
ominous significance for the future: the medical fraternity in the
Regimental Hospital at Ballina in 1810-11. The surgeons in the Irish
militia had been the cause of considerable scandal in their trafficking
in positions and influence. The appointment to a militia was felt to be
highly advantageous, and not considerably onerous. The threat of
war was not remote, but it was at least not as immediate as on the sea
or the continent, and the duties were not demanding. And the
perquisites were considerable. The ordinary militiaman was forced
largely to content himself with crude loot; the surgeon could obtain

much more refined and lucrative means of self-enrichment and self-advancement. Ultimately in 1804 the job-trafficking had been banned by the Viceroy, but of course the beneficiaries of it would still have been enjoying the rewards when Burke entered the hospital. It is quite likely that many surgeons further enriched themselves by the proscription of the traffic. It meant that their failure to pay their debts in finding regimental posts could not now be easily brought home to them. Nothing would be lost save honour. We can be very certain, also, that in an Irish army hospital the pretentions of the sawbones would be cut to pieces behind his back with much more precision than the cutting he himself undertook in his professional capacity. If scandal were to be imputed it would lose nothing in the retailing. Once again, this would be of future importance. The partnership of Burke and Hare always seemed to assume that surgeons would not ask questions; it assigned to them, in fact, the ethics and politics of a receiver of stolen goods. Nor do they seem to have given the surgeons credit for considerable intelligence. In this they were wrong, and the failure of Doctor Knox to denounce their proceedings arose not from his resemblance to the fashionable medical simoniacs of the Irish militia, but from a very different set of reasons which we will encounter later. The confidence of Burke and Hare in the low morals of the surgeons has been noted by earlier commentators, and may well be one of the wellsprings of the very widespread superstition that they started as resurrectionists. Previous acquaintance with medical men as receivers of stolen bodies would have accounted for the coolness with which Burke and Hare proceeded with them; no doubt they had heard some stories, but their confidence suggests a foundation in personal experience, in one case. Yet Burke denied to the end that he had ever been a resurrectionist; he seemed very sure Hare had not been; he could get into no additional trouble by confessing to such a thing; he was anxious to bring some measure of judicial punishment to bear on Hare and hence would hardly have suppressed any evidence that he could at least be sentenced for resurrectionism; and, above all, the version he gave after his conviction, and adhered to, as to the origin of the traffic in bodies militates wholly against a resurrectionist antecedent for either Burke or Hare. Now the point is cleared up. Burke assumed surgeons to be genteel criminals because he had known ones who were.

On the other hand it is unlikely that any of them were likely to have been mixed up in the body traffic. They could get all the bodies they wanted in a military hospital, and those of them who had research ambitions would have been unwise to become involved in resurrectionism while actually on military premises and under military surveillance. Financial speculation might be ignored, or even connived at. Graveyard-robbing was likely to unloose appalling recriminations from the local inhabitants; suspicion would automatically fall on the militia surgeons; and a threat of domestic disorder in a country which had witnessed invasion as recently as 1798, insurrection, as recently as 1803, and agrarian outrage, as recently as the day before yesterday, would bring down the wrath of the military authorities in a way that a modicum of pilfering would never do. Corruption was acceptable; pure scholarship was the danger. Once again, Burke's childhood background had abounded in stories of stolen corpses, and the hospital inmates might well have gossip about some surgeon who in student days had received stolen corpses, but we may safely doubt whether Burke had ever met a surgeon who was actively engaged in receiving stolen corpses, until he commenced his partnership with Hare.

Burke's associations with the band, whether as fifer or drummer, would have been all too likely to give him an even more unpleasant experience. The drum major was in charge of the execution of punishments, such punishment being inflicted by the drummers. The miscreant was punished with a cat-o'-nine-tails for which he then had to provide sixpence, and no cat-o'-nine-tails could be used on more than one person. In any event, it might well have exhausted its utility by such a time as it had discharged the sentences proscribed: contemporary punishments in the Irish militia include 200, 500 and 600 lashes for riotous conduct, 200, 500 and 800 lashes for drunkenness, 600, 800 and 900 lashes for desertion. A surgeon had to be present to feel the pulse of the victim from time to time and assert whether punishment could be continued without the risk of death. If Burke had been on the receiving end of more than one of these experiences, it would explain those visits to hospital, and it would also throw some further psychological light on his make-up. Yet his conduct is not that of a man soured by some hideous wound inflicted by Society; it would be consistent with what we know of Hare, but Hare was never cited as having a military background. On the other hand, the persistent story that he may have been a drummer suggests a very real possibility. Although he does not seem to have been a sadist, one frequent consequence of compulsorily or voluntarily administering corporal punishment, it is not much of a step from being trained to half-kill one's comrades to wholly kill one's more casual acquaintances. And Burke's methods of despatch were normally far more humane than those of the army. A sensitive man, indeed, forced to watch the growth of weals on the back, the empurpling of mounds of flesh, the opening of slits of blood, the enlarging of slits to streams and streams to rivers, the transformation of what once had been the strong and healthy torso of God's making into a hideous, raw, bleeding, pulpy mess — a sensitive man, forced to lay on the lash, look on that sight and hear those screams, might pray to have two moments to get his hand over the poor wretch's mouth and nostrils, stifle his breath and end his sufferings. Death would have seemed the ultimate kindness.

It will be questioned whether Burke was a sensitive man. He certainly was no more insensitive than the elite which had established such a system, arming the lower classes to do their killing for them, and holding them in subjection by such horrifying examples. An officer of the Irish militia remarked that a flogged man was "an unpleasant sight" but this aesthetic shortcoming was compensated for by the necessity "to discipline the ranks of the army" with their "many rascals who can be kept in order by corporal punishment only — who have no sense of shame so as to fear disgrace". It would not be fair to argue that the officer class revealed thereby that it regarded the ranks as less than human — no officer would ever have treated his horse in such a fashion. As Swift had pointed out, the lower Irish classes fell a long way below the equine creation in the estimation of the elite. But by now some level of enlightenment was emerging: members of the Protestant episcopalian, Presbyterian and Roman Catholic persuasions would all be open to such treatment if they responded to the call of their country or their own self-betterment and took places in the lower ranks of the militia. Only in the few militia forces directly associated with a tradition of sectarianism, such as the South Down, might a suspicion of religious discrimination emerge in the infliction of punishment on Roman Catholics, and even then the Protestants in the lower ranks would be much too numerous to escape being "made an example of". As for the attitude of non-military society, it is well evidenced by the way that the Dublin *Freeman's Journal*, an allegedly enlightened print, chose to allude to the matter. A militiaman sentenced to 250 lashes in 1793, at the very beginning of the corps's existence in Ireland, insisted that such a sentence was not justified in law: but his error, snickered the *Freeman*, "was ably illustrated upon his own parchment by half a dozen drummers". It is really rather surprising that a society with such public ethics should have thought anything unusual in the behaviour of Burke and Hare at all. It is hardly curious that the lower classes responded with black humour: Sam Weller's smile is very mirthless indeed when he tells Serjeant Buzfuz that "little to do and plenty to get" was what the soldier said when they ordered him 350 lashes.

The particular motive in enforcing so savage a standard of discipline in the Irish militia — even if the proceeding was not uncommon by the standards of the day — would have lain in the assumption that the militia's work lay in repressing internal disorder and that everything must be done to prevent any covert alliance between militiamen and potential rebels. Experience had shown that this eventuality was unlikely, but punishment was conceived not on the basis of actualities but of the remotest, most paranoid nightmares. The effect would be to leave a William Burke with the sense that all that mattered was not to be found out. A society as contemptuous of life and human dignity as that gave no standard of justice to be accepted. In all probability it held that the lower classes could only understand justice founded on ever-ready and brutal physical force. That Burke had emerged from a Gaelic world with its own abstract and complex sense of justice was beside the point. He had emerged from it; he had no choice but to accept the new forms. What happened was that he found the new much worse than the old, but if the new was unacceptable, the old was irrelevant. So he ultimately reverted to the law of the jungle, which at least had the merit of being older than either.

The repression of disorder was now the *raison d'être* of the militia's existence. For seven years at 1798 the possibility of a French invasion was very real. We now know that Napoleon was unenthusiastic about an Irish landing, and that the ridiculous estimates of Irish popular support given by Irish exiles to successive French revolutionary governments proved wholly baseless in practice, with consequent disillusion from the French authorities involved. But it was far from inevitable that Napoleon would continue to rule Ireland out; being Napoleon, it was far from inevitable that he would ever continue to rule anything out. Trafalgar, again it seems to us in retrospect, made an invasion impossible. But, again, that was not absolutely certain. The British, with their naval-centred historiographical eyes, see Trafalgar as the grand climax. But their ancestors confronted the succession of blow upon blow that followed it, as Napoleon wrote into history the names of Austerlitz, Jena, Eylau, Tilsit. The armies of empires and kings lay stretched supine before him, and the most vigorous of all his European opponents, the Czar Alexander, became instead his ally. It was idle to say that the danger of invasion was now over for Ireland. Was any danger at an end when you faced Napoleon? So, at least, felt the Irish agrarian outlaws signing their warning messages "Bonaparte", and so might have wondered the men, and even the officers, of the militia. There was a bad invasion-scare in 1811. Meanwhile the *esprit de corps*, if anything, increased. Lord Leitrim made quite a lot of it, and by the time Burke arrived he would have found an exceptionally united regiment. In one respect Leitrim's Whiggism must have increased it. It involved him with continued bickering against Tory opponents in Dublin Castle — including, of course, the brothers Wellesley, to wit the future Wellington and the present Wellesley-Pole. Their main hopes were now of using the militia as a training-ground whence volunteers could come for the European main line: Leitrim furiously responded that he would not have his regiment turned into a mere training-school whence others might reap the glory. The obvious answer would have been to have ordered the militia into the field, and Wellington, as we know, was cursing that this had not been done in time for Waterloo. But it is probable that Leitrim was unusually critical of the European war, among militia commanders. His family heritage connecting him with Fox and the Irish Volunteers would have committed him to peace abroad and self-reliance at home. Government ought not to be wasting men and treasure in propping up the wretched tyrants of Europe; but if Boney were to take himself or his agents of unrest to Ireland, the Donegals would give an account of themselves. Whatever else the Donegals may have learned from their Colonel, it was not admiration for the British Government. Meanwhile, their location in Mayo would have given them enough to do in watching for signs of local disaffection. The countryside had been the scene of the French invasion (and the infamous memory of the races of Castlebar put the Donegals on their mettle); moreover, co. Mayo, particularly that portion served by Ballina as a metropolis, is the most cruel, desolate and inhospitable of terrains in the whole of Ireland. Here have been found the most inhumane and rapacious of landlords; here, too, have emerged the most intransigent and influential of agrarian conspiracies, culminating after a century in the Land League of Mayo in 1879 which spread to the whole of Ireland and killed the landlord system. And it was here that Burke found the wife with whom he so temporarily settled near Ballina when the war was over — the war and the non-war that culminated in Waterloo.

Sir Henry McAnally, in his invaluable if cryptic account of the Irish militia, sums up by describing it as "a lump of Irish life being pressed into an English mould". As such it represented many things — the death of the Gaelic world, the reluctant admission that lower-class Catholics might be permitted to become cannon-fodder, the disappearance of socio-political independent power with its symbol of military display which the Protestant magnates had rekindled so noisily in the Irish Volunteers. It was also part of the integration of the Irish and British kingdoms under the Union of 1800. It was ironic that Burke should have served under a colonel who bridged the two eras so well — including the enlightenment of the future with the fiercely independent war-lord mentality of the past. But for all of Lord Leitrim's individuality, the Donegal militia was a first stage in not only migration, but emigration, even if Burke never left Ireland while in its ranks. It responded to new ways, demands, forms of expertise, necessities, opportunities and values, and it retained enough of the older ways to present Burke and his comrades with a taste of the soulless chill of a new vastness mingled with the intimacy of the old, personal cruelty. Even if its name did not become written in large letters in popular history, it did its work for what must be termed modernisation — for William Burke as for his fellows.

The Identity of William Hare

'Who or why, or which, or *what*,
Is the Akond of SWAT?

—Edward Lear

W E know neither when William Hare was born nor when he died. There is dispute about his place of birth and, unlike Burke's case, it is not a matter that can be established with relative certainty. We cannot be certain that the murders he committed with Burke were his only actions of that nature. The convenient death of his wife's previous husband cannot be dismissed without question. We can pin down the location and vocation of Burke for most of the years of his life, but all we have in Hare's case are ten years and, with the exception of the last two, the threads connecting any narrative of them are very ragged. Our principal source is his evidence and, unlike Burke's, it had every reason to be extremely selective. Burke might lie in his final written confessions to make a good story, or to bring rather more guilt home against Hare, or to protect Helen MacDougal, but he had few other reasons to lie and strong ones to tell the truth. Hare, on the contrary, would only save himself by taciturnity. Were he to make one false step, he was facing death. His adversaries watched him like hawks, and they included the foremost Scots lawyers of the day. Yet Hare, on the face of it a brutish, unlearned Irish labourer, outwitted them all both in facing cross-examination at Burke's trial and during the private prosecution of him by the relatives of Daft Jamie. As a result his autobiographical evidence is both sparse and suspect; as another result he remains the only mass murderer in modern history — members of the armed services apart — to have been in the hands of the authorities and yet to have gone free, without the slightest doubt in anyone's mind about his guilt. Comforting tradition insisted that Hare was thrown into a lime-kiln and finished his days as a blind beggar in London, an object of warning and reproach to the mid-Victorians — the critic Masson had nine different Hares pointed out to him. All we can say is that when last heard of, Hare was walking into England and had reached a point some miles south-east of Carlisle. And England holds her secret well.

Hare also seems, in any serious sense, beyond artistic enquiry. Burke as a proletarian Macbeth has poetry, dignity and courage, especially when all is lost—

> They have tied me to a stake; I cannot fly,
> But, bear-like, I must fight the course.

Or as a proletarian Richard III he could summon charm, laughter, humour and self-mockery to his aid, while being doomed to toss and turn in haunted sleep. But there is nothing of this in Hare.

His taciturnity in court is matched, according to Maclean, by dourness of manner and misanthropy of behaviour. He was an embittered and brutalised man, clever enough to contrive even his own escape, but with his strengths held to himself. He seems to have even less to do with coats of arms than Burke, yet he undoubtedly held true to the motto the Heralds assign to his family: *Fear Garbh a's maith* (A Rough Man is the best).

The closest he gets to literature — and it is not accidental — might be to the figure of one of the cut-purses or cut-throats surrounding François Villon in the Robert Louis Stevenson story "A Lodging for the Night", with Burke as a mute, inglorious Villon — and Stevenson knew his Burke and Hare. The analogy posits a world in which murder is a commonplace means of financial improvement. And murder seems a much more natural recourse in Hare, from what we know of his nature, than in Burke. Maclean is reported as describing him as "of a ferocious and tyrannical disposition, much inclined to quarrel, and very obstreperous when in liquor". (The contemporary journalistic stylisation of Maclean's language is as irritating a barrier as the vulgar rewrites in the press of today, but his meaning is clear enough.) "As an instance of this — in the end of last summer [1828 or possibly 1827] when M'Lean (the narrator), Hare, Burke and his wife [the allusion is evidently to Burke's mistress MacDougal and not to Mrs Hare], and others, were returning from the *shearing* at Carnwath . . . the whole party went into a public house west of Balerno, near Currie, to get some refreshment. The reckoning being clubbed, Hare took up the money from the table, and put it in his pocket; and for fear of any disturbance taking place in the house, Burke paid the amount out of his own pocket. On leaving the house, M'Lean observed to Hare it was a *scaly* trick to lift the money with an intention to affront them. On this

Hare knocked the feet from under M'Lean, and when prostrate on the ground, gave him a tremendous kick in the face with his foot. His shoes being pointed with iron, commonly called *caulkers*, wounded M'Lean severely laying open his upper lip." Maclean is described as being an old man, which makes a nasty story even nastier.

Hare seems a brutalised figure, and at times so much so as to raise questions about his sanity. Yet he had at least considerable cunning to defeat the lawyers. Burke's confessions in the condemned cell assign an element of leadership to him: that it was Hare who, with one of his lodgers dead by natural causes and no means of recovering rent due which would have been paid for by a military pension to have been collected the next day, bethought him of the doctors. This opens up the probability of the next allegation, that it was Hare who then had the first idea of murdering someone for the same purpose. Now, the latter may be true. Violence came naturally to Hare — it was not his fault that the old man Maclean had not been killed by the shock of that "tremendous kick" or that some vital organ had not been mortally injured, the throat, for example. But Burke, who genuinely resented getting his deserts while his betrayer and partner in crime went free, was evidently anxious to bring the point home. On the basis of what we now know, Burke had knowledge of the surgeons, had probably formed unfavourable views of their moral probity, and had the quickness of wit to have put forward such a solution as selling the body for dissection. It seems far less consistent with the duller Hare. And while Hare *might* have had some acquaintance with surgeons and the gossip surrounding resurrectionism, we know Burke *did* have personal experience of surgeons. Also, it would be like the agreeable Burke, anxious to please the man who was then his landlord, and ready with a contrivance which would remove a grievance from his morose companion and make for more pleasant company. Once again, whether Hare did or did not suggest the murder in the first instance — and on balance I think he was the one who did — the scientific care with which suffocation was selected as a method sounds like the received wisdom of the former patient at the Regimental Hospital in Ballina. He may even have encountered a case in hospital: patients could suffocate in bed of their phlegm or vomit. Hare, of course, might have heard of such a case also, but less would have been made of the absence of marks of death than would be true of death in a hospital. Hence the cry of the *Caledonian Mercury* after the trial, seeking to bring guilt home to Dr Knox and the medical fraternity, is an important question to which it assigned the wrong answer:

Now, we ask, WHO taught Burke, a common Irish labourer of the
very lowest class, to commit murder after a fashion, the science
displayed in which is a subject of wonder and dismay to many of the
most skilful anatomists in this city, with three of whom we have
conversed in regard to it, and found them overwhelmed with horror
and amazement? *Who*, we say, taught Burke? — for that he was *tutored*
as to the mode of committing the crime, no human being can entertain
a shadow of doubt. We will answer the question: IT WAS HARE! But
the same question again returns, *who* taught Hare, a person of the very
same country and class with Burke? This is a point to be resolved by the
Public Prosecutor alone; and we adjure him [&c., &c.].

The *Caledonian Mercury* was as anxious as the convicted Burke to
see Hare get his deserts, and hence readily accepted the argument for
Hare as the originator of the device. The *Mercury* differed from
Burke, however, in seeking to bring home guilt also to Dr Knox and
his associates. The accusation that Knox and his men had prompted
the murders is a wild one, and need have no place in our later discussion of Knox's guilt or innocence (and of what): it is in fact self-
defeating. Knox was hardly likely to start offering instructions on
how to murder a subject so that on anatomisation by him later he
would think it had died by natural causes. The use of the anatomist
witnesses is also self-defeating: they, with crimes of receiving
resurrected bodies on their consciences, were anxious to stress that
doctors had no motive for looking suspiciously at corpses — which in
fact is also, and even more strongly, an argument for Knox's
innocence. (In that instance, however, the anatomists were dubious
witnesses.) And the class — and indeed racial — prejudice assuming
Burke (or Hare) could not have of themselves thought out such a
method is self-defeating; but our evidence certainly gives it the *coup
de grâce*. Burke had had the opportunity to learn such methods. And
the lower classes knew far more about the middle classes than *vice
versa*, although it was a literary conceit that the converse was true.

The one point at which the question is still moot is if Hare had had
some converse with doctors. We need not take seriously the notion
of some person in Knox's outfit saying on arrival of the first corpse
that if the gentlemen, hitherto unknown, wish to produce more
corpses, the method of murdering them is as follows. The stories of
how the murders started are far too reasonable to warrant a hearing
for the melodramatic rival theory, which in any case would have
involved somebody putting his own life in the hands of two
murderers whom he did not even know. But it is a possibility that
Hare had encountered surgeons in the same way that Burke had.
And, while we must realise that such theories are pure conjecture,

they would explain something about him.

Hare is described as being a Roman Catholic, of the labourer class, and born in Derry or Newry. Newry, co. Down, seems more likely; it would occur less readily as an error, and it is the useful Maclean who mentioned it. This, however, complicates matters. Derry is clear enough — it would mean that Hare was one of the Catholic poor settling outside the walls in what is now the Bogside. But Newry is in a far less urbanised part of Ireland, and the reference might mean that Hare's people lived in the town, a substantially Catholic one, or that they lived in the adjoining very desolate hills, which look as though they would have made ideal hunting-grounds for highwaymen against travellers on the Dublin-Belfast road. Certainly Ireland had its share of highwaymen with, as we have noted, some touch of romance and a clinging of shadow political, religious and agrarian legitimacy to them. Agrarian secret societies flourished there — the frightful burning alive of a family named Lynch in their house, described by Carleton in "Wildgoose Lodge", took place a short distance from Dundalk on the other side of the mountains, in 1818. The crime of the victims was that the father of the house was supposed to have informed against the Ribbonmen, as the society was called, for some other agrarian outrage. The Ribbon confederacy was a secret society and enforced its will with the utmost zeal, when it could. Its origins lay in an effort to protect the weak and vulnerable Catholic tenants from victimisation, but its oath-bound rituals, elaborate forms of self-insurance, conviction of near-theological righteousness and capacity for employing a variety of sanctions against its enemies from warning to cattle-maiming, arson and murder, easily led it into becoming a sort of protection racket. It would have justified itself by its appeal to agrarian social justice, coupled with forms of patriotic and religious rhetoric. We have noted its relevance to Burke; but in point of geometrical proximity "Wildgoose Lodge" was far nearer to Hare.

It may be argued that Dundalk is still a score of mountain miles from Newry. But the Ribbonmen did employ the technique of bringing in their fellows from other lodges, out of the district, to cut down the possibility of recognition and vengeance. In fact the many hangings for the Lynch murders were primarily of local people. Yet outsiders might have been involved, especially to provide the hard core of support on which the hardening of the loyalties of a large group depended; Carleton seems to imply some strangeness in some of the ringleaders, although the prime agent was certainly a local. So that Ribbon brothers might have been drawn in from the Newry country. And while the authorities hanged "25 or 28" of the murderers, and persuaded themselves and their subjects that all the guilty had been slain, it seems to have been Louthmen only who were executed. County-consciousness was important administratively as well as in terms of local patriotism, and the Ribbon tactics of importing strangers would certainly have meant that the county border could well be crossed for such a dangerous quest, while the authorities were less likely to think in those terms, at least by that date. If there had been Newry involvement, however, a natural reaction from the parties concerned would be to fly the country when the trials and executions took place in Louth. And it is somewhat ominous — although the shot remains a very long one — that Hare is described at the time of Burke's trial, by Maclean, as coming to Edinburgh "about ten years ago". That would have been in 1818.

It really is the purest speculation. All that supports it, apart from the date — and even that, as we shall see, is not absolutely certain — is that Hare's savagery, moroseness, secretiveness about his past, and apparent conviction of his God-given right to inflict grievous bodily harm on anyone he chose would be consistent with an apprenticeship in the "Wildgoose Lodge" affair and similar affrays. It certainly does explain both his readiness to use violence and his seeming certainty of his justification for it, and that does take a little explaining. It must be stressed that Hare's vengeful character and nature as a predator on human beings is not the same thing as the local feuding and party fights Carleton describes elsewhere. That, for all of its ugliness, was an open business. "Wildgoose Lodge" was secretive violence and so, outside of pub-brawls, was Hare's. It might, too, explain Hare's solitude. An emigrant Ribbonman might be expected to bring organisational techniques to his comrades in exile, as did the founders of the Molly Maguires in Pennsylvania in the 1870s. But a man with a notorious and horrifying crime behind him, for which scores of his confederates had hanged, would very understandably keep as far away from the taint of Ribbonism as possible. And it would help account for his pitiless nature, both in relation to his victims and to Burke. It is true that while Burke seems to have repented, that was appropriate for him in his situation and most inappropriate for Hare in his, since his life depended on not admitting anything for which to repent. But Hare's whole demeanour throughout suggests no particle of pity. His evidence was undoubtedly perjured, and he lied to have Burke hanged for crimes of which he was equally guilty, but it is deficient in any kind of hypocrisy. He acted throughout like a man who was entitled to do whatever he may have done. This certainly would hold good of someone who had connived at a mass murder by fire, and who heard the screams and pleas of burning children without flinching.

Had Hare been active as a Ribbon agent in Newry it accounts for the missing years of his life. He was described as being of the same age as Burke. What was he doing while Burke was in the militia? We do not require "Wildgoose Lodge" or some equally radical explanation to account for emigration in 1818 or a little before: the post-Waterloo economic depression with the enormous mass of soldiers, including militiamen, thrown on the country, led naturally to the search for means of subsistence in an industrialising area. And while Dublin and its environs were in Liverpool's catchment area, Newry and Ballina, remote by hundreds of miles though they were from one another, both fell into the catchment area of Scotland. On the other hand it seems unlikely that Newry would have held Hare for so long on its own basis. Burke's statement in jail — his most solemn, in the presence of a priest, and his last — went out of its way to state his ignorance of any crimes of murder for dissection other than those committed by Hare and himself, and of any other crimes committed by Hare save those already mentioned, "and if any persons have disappeared anywhere in Scotland, England, or Ireland, he knows nothing whatever about it, and never heard of such a thing till he was apprehended". Now, we know that Burke had never been in England, unless for some peculiar military adventure of which we are ignorant. But Hare might have been, especially if before 1817-18 he had followed a well-beaten Irish track to the hop-fields of Kent as a seasonal labourer.

"Wildgoose Lodge" has to commend it that it gives us atrocious murders at either end of Hare's years in Edinburgh. It also suggests, unlike the England theory, that Hare kept to his home. And against the theory of a nomadic background Hare genuinely seems to have been far more interested in settling down than was Burke. Burke could not keep a family together, as we will see, but Hare very seriously tried to, even if his methods for providing for it was homicidal. It suggests a less nomadic pattern, and indeed nature, than for the former militiaman. But this may be deceptive. After all, Hare's domesticity arrived with the acquisition of a wife whose family he had, to be sure, cultivated before her husband's timely death. The possibility exists that Hare, like Burke, had been in the Irish militia during part of those missing years.

If so, why did he not speak about them? He needed to establish

credibility as a witness and a little "old soldier" work would not
have been out of place, especially in one regarded as an alien in birth
and religion. It was true that Burke's "old soldier" status was doing
him no good, but it may have militated to some extent in feeling for
him and against Hare. If the card was also Hare's, why not play it?

My speculation here would be that if Hare had served in the army
or the militia he, unlike Burke, was very anxious to forget it. It
would account for the understanding which drew the two of them
together. And they are, on the face of it, an unlikely partnership, save
for the attraction of opposites. The demon theory of Burke and Hare
more or less invites us to contemplate a conjuncture of Dylan
Thomas's "devils" or Hugh Douglas's "fiends", who recognise a
common whiff of sulphur from one another and immediately begin
to drool for blood. But a common origin as old soldiers is a rather
sounder basis for partnership. Failing that, the most likely
explanation is that Burke was not particularly censorious about his
acquaintances and Hare could hardly afford to be choosey about his.

What Hare's regiment would have been takes us a further leap
into guesswork. Remembering that Burke did not join the Tyrones,
Hare, despite the hostility to extra-county recruitment, might have
profited by Newry's being something of a frontier town and joined
either the Louth or the Armagh militia. The fact that he was a
Catholic and that the South Down militia acquired an unenviable
and somewhat exceptional reputation for sectarianism might have
induced such a decision. We can be fairly certain that in Newry the
young Hare would have encountered sectarianism, and it seems
reasonable to suppose that its iron entered into his soul — which
certainly consumed iron enough from some quarter — to leave him
with very different attitudes from those of the ecumenical Burke. As
we will notice when we turn to the women in the case, Burke's last
love was Protestant whereas Hare's wife was Catholic: a minor
point, perhaps, but a suggestive one. Hare's — and possibly Mrs
Hare's — notion of killing Helen MacDougal again suggest that the
killings as far as he was concerned may have had sectarian
undertones. That is not to say that he was not ready to murder
Catholics, and did murder them, but that Protestants really did not
"count" in his framework. A Catholic comrade — as distinct from a
Catholic acquaintance — might be immune from destruction but a
Protestant clearly was not, although Helen MacDougal had shared
many of their adventures (if not necessarily the homicidal ones).
Ironically the advantage which Irish as a first language gave to Burke
made Gaelic-speaking Irish Catholic immigrants his most natural

prey: Hare probably spoke little, if any, Irish. Once again, the exclusivist thinking with respect to the religion of comrades is reminiscent of Ribbon attitudes; even if Hare had not been involved in "Wildgoose Lodge" or other Ribbon outrages he would have been hard put to it to avoid imbibing Ribbon attitudes or the mentality of those more open fighters, the "Defenders".

What happened to Hare in the militia, if he was there and wished to remain silent about it afterwards? The most probable explanation is that his natural characteristics of surliness and bad temper were greatly strengthened under the severities of army discipline; that he was unduly conscious of bad feeling with Protestant fellow-militiamen and, perhaps, resented the requirement of parade for the Protestant service before the time allotted for Mass; and that, at some point, he fell very badly foul of the authorities such that he did indeed suffer the penalty of cat-o'-nine-tails with several hundred lashes. The point here is that Hare's moroseness and savagery would be consistent with having experienced such a fate; whereas Burke's cheery temperament militates against his having done so. The most likely charge on which Hare would have been punished would be fighting or drunkenness or some combination of both. Attempted desertion would also be consistent with what we know of him; it is even possible that he did desert, sometime near the very end. Volunteers were often admitted with oaths for the duration of the war. It was true that the war was officially over when Louis XVIII returned to Paris and Napoleon settled down in Elba but although the war was not formally resumed with Waterloo it was expected until Napoleon's surrender that it would be. The trouble about enlistment for the duration of the war was that the war appeared to be constantly changing its duration.

Seldom, it may be thought, has the Irish term "chasing hares" been so amply justified. Have we, then, ended up with three Hares to match our three Burkes, with the additional annoyance that the Burkes are real and in one place whereas all of the Hares may be imaginary — Ribbonman, migrant worker in England, embittered militiaman? In fact the three possible points of earlier career for Hare may not be mutually exclusive — although, of course, birth in Derry and birth in Newry are. (And even there he could have been born in one of them and brought up in another, in which case, were Derry a point of any continued residence, he might have been a speaker of Irish in infancy after all.)

But if we put aside the birth with a presumption in favour of Newry, then he could have grown up in a strong atmosphere of sectarianism, he could nonetheless have joined a militia for pay, security and improvement of his status as a labourer, he could have been the recipient of a cruel and brutalising punishment — which would have given him at least some association with a surgeon, if only to the latter's supervising his punishment and announcing what more he could take of it without a reasonable likelihood of death. And he could then have got out before 1816 or during it, either by leaving legitimately or by desertion: in the latter event that would be the point of departure for Scotland, which would make 1818 the date of arrival in Edinburgh, but not of Scotland. If he simply departed in the normal way and returned to Newry, he would have had some time in which to try his luck in seasonal migration to Kent. And if he had had such hideous experiences in the army, they might well have fed his soul toward revenge against the world in general and the Protestants in particular — thus assigning a motive for the participation in adventures like "Wildgoose Lodge" with the necessarily hurried departure following it.

It all remains totally shadowy, though shadows may be suggestive as well as confusing. I would still argue that even if Hare had some contact with surgeons the suggestion to sell their first corpse came from the resourceful Burke. And I would also feel very strongly that whatever human forces had brutalised William Hare, it was Man's doing and not God's. And it would certainly be the case that if, as seems likely, the process of brutalisation had been very thoroughly set in motion, if not actually perfected, by the time he set foot in Scotland, the work of a navvy on the Union canal would have played a very fair hand in completing it. It would have left its mark very powerfully on Burke also, but he retained a sunny nature in appearance, and he was, at bottom, not beyond redemption.

Having made sure that we have made sure of nothing, as Sherlock Holmes so unkindly remarked of the investigation of Inspector Stanley Hopkins, let us turn to the guidance of Sir Walter Scott to open our analysis of the next phase.

CHAPTER
4

Burke, Hare and the Industrial Revolution

Give me your tired, your poor,
Your huddled masses yearning to breathe free,
The wretched refuse of your teeming shore,
Send these, the homeless, tempest-tossed, to me:
I lift my lamp beside the golden door.
—Emma Lazarus, "The New Colossus"
(Inscription for the Statue of Liberty, New York Harbor)

"YOU are very sorry I am sure that these things have happened in Edinburgh & I am sorry that two of the murderers are Irish" wrote Maria Edgeworth to her friend Sir Walter Scott on 10 January 1829. "I fear the immediate effect must be dreadful for all my poor countrymen now seeking shelter in Scotland — God help them — no one else can or will I fear."

Sir Walter Scott deeply admired Maria Edgeworth, yet his reply made it very clear that her sympathy for the Irish immigrants into Scotland could not be thus bisected, and that Burke and Hare were part of the tragic multitude for which she mourned; they were, in fact, the natural result of the immigrant process, however terrible in their specific achievement.

The great number of the lower Irish which have come over here since the peace is, like all important occurrences, attended with its own share of good and evil. It must relieve Ireland in part of the excess of population, which is one of its greatest evils, and it accommodates Scotland with a race of hardy and indefatigable labourers, without which it would be impossible to carry on the very extensive improvements which have been executed. Our canals, our railroads, and our various public works are all wrought by Irish. I have often employed them myself at burning clay, and similar operations, and have found them as labourers quiet and tractable, light-spirited, too, and happy to a degree beyond belief, and in no degree quarrelsome, keep whiskey from them and them from whiskey. But most unhappily for all parties they work at far too low a rate — at a rate, in short, which can but just procure salt and potatoes; they become reckless, of

course, of all the comforts and decencies of life, which they have no
means of procuring. Extreme poverty brings ignorance and vice, and
these are the mothers of crime. If Ireland were to submit to some kind
of poor-rate — I do not mean that of England, but something that
should secure to the indigent their natural share of the fruits of the
earth, and enable them at least to feed while others are feasting — it
would, I cannot doubt, raise the character of the lower orders, and
deprive them of that recklessness of futurity which leads them to think˙
only of the present. Indeed, where intoxication of the lower ranks is
mentioned as a vice, we must allow the temptation is well-nigh
inevitable; meat, clothes, fire, all that men can and do want, are
supplied by a drop of whiskey; and no one should be surprised that the
relief (too often the only one within the wretches' power) is eagerly
grasped at.

As Raymond Williams has underlined, there are certain kinds of
conservatism, specifically in the age of the industrial revolution,
which supply a highly constructive critique of the destruction of
humanity and the environment by the alleged march of progress, and
in doing so raise precisely the questions which the Socialist historian
should be asking himself.

Burke and Hare came to Scotland in response to the call of the
industrial revolution. A personal factor probably played a larger part
in impelling emigration than earlier historians were prepared to
concede. In these two particular cases, William Hare could, as I have
suggested, been motivated by some personal involvement in
activities which made it wise for him to get out. In the case of
William Burke, the story is both more explicit and less credible. He
argued in his final statements that he had a disagreement with his
father-in-law about land, and it is worth stating that the Irish
adulation for land and the hereditary significance of making a claim
for agrarian proprietorship may have prompted Burke to
romanticise himself by asserting social status he did not have. Irish
folklore is full of legends of the good man done out of his rights, that
land and position might have been his had those who should have
been closest to him not shown themselves to be treacherous to his
interests. But Burke had been born a landless labourer; he died a
landless labourer; the balance of probability is that he lived as one all
his life. He may conceivably have married into a family with more
wealth than his but it is doubtful whether he had any real
expectations from it. He had no apparent reason for doing so. But he
had motives for leaving which probably turned on the collapse of his
marriage. And it is worth adding that while many Irish marriages
ended with a migrant labourer going abroad and losing contact,
marital shipwreck was probably the cause rather than the effect of

migration in many cases.

Irishmen were coming in to Scotland, particularly to Edinburgh, from the time of Waterloo with hopes of navvy work in mind. The Report of the Committee for affording Relief to the Labouring Classes in Edinburgh complained in June 1817: "There is no doubt that a very undue proportion of labourers, particularly Irish, have been drawn to this place during the last two years and kept hanging about the town from the hope of the commencement of the Union Canal and the agitation which that question has occasioned." However, neither Burke nor Hare would have been among them. It was the date of 1818 that saw Burke's arrival, and if by any chance Hare came to Scotland earlier, he did not come to Edinburgh itself until the same year. Burke told the *Courant* in his confession that "he came to Scotland to work on the Union Canal and wrought there while it lasted", which assigns to his service all, or almost all, of the four years of its construction. The evidence is, then, that Burke heard in the West of Ireland that the long-promised El Dorado was at last becoming reality; Donegal, Sligo, and Mayo itself were — and to some extent still are — natural recruitment areas for migrant work in Scotland, seasonal or permanent. The same areas remained agriculturally as barren as ever. The pressure of population to the harsh square mile continued to increase at galloping rates and the plethora of returned soldiers and demobilised militiamen made the competition for the few miserably-paid, back-breaking jobs in casual agricultural labour acute to the point of desperation. Agricultural depression after the war meant labour cutback; men near the point of starvation were walking miles in the forlorn hope of a few hours' work at miserable pay. Scotland at least promised steady employment. Burke was one of a throng who thankfully succumbed to the canal fever.

We have no such certainties about Hare, beyond the fact that the Irish north-east no doubt responded to the lure of the Union canal with some of the same enthusiasm as the north-west. Newry was a little remote from the axis of labour interchange which grew in these years between Belfast and Glasgow, and the growth of the linen industry in Belfast was beginning to offer an alternative point of immigration to its hinterland. But apart from Hare's possible need to get out of Ireland, Belfast was still an overwhelmingly Protestant town. The traditional Irish search for ethnic and religious companionship is less likely to have been a motive for the misanthropic Hare than for the gregarious Burke, but ethno-religious resentment could have militated against Belfast in his case.

Where Hare left from is a mystery; the persistence of a story of
Derry origin may arise from actual emigration from Derry, and if he
wanted to cover his tracks a move from Newry to Scotland via Derry
might have seemed less dangerous than a sojourn in Belfast, where
the forces of law and order were likely to be strong and well
informed.

The probability is that Burke arrived in Glasgow and went
rapidly to Polmont, not far from where the Union Canal was to link
up with the Forth and Clyde Canal. Hare's associations with the
canal are around Edinburgh. Even after the end of the canal-digging,
in 1822, he was still engaged as a labourer at Port Hopetoun, in
Edinburgh, where the Union Canal commenced. Hare certainly
went as far as possible from Ireland — and, it would seem, as quickly
as possible — in choosing his destination for Union Canal work.

The three great events in the history of Western Europe since the
birth of Christ were the Roman Empire, the Reformation and the
Industrial Revolution, and Ireland missed them all. She looted the
decaying Roman Empire, thereby acquiring plunder, slaves and
Christianity; she obtained the Reformation by the back door, in the
persons of largely venal Protestant episcopalian officials, placemen
and land acquisitors, and vigorously Presbyterian immigrants of all
classes to the north; she had a minor, local episode in the industrial
revolution in the Lagan valley in north-east Ulster, but here her
great contribution was not immigrant but emigrant. The industrial
revolution transformed the North Atlantic economy, and for most of
the nineteenth century Ireland supplied it with the bulk of the lowest
and most menial element in the labour force.

The Irish navvy became one of the main staples of the canal era.
Increasingly the advent of the Irish provided a labour pool from
which managers and foremen could apparently draw endlessly,
regardless of the collapse and death of individual exhausted navvies.
The Scottish canal boom was in fact nearing its end: the Union Canal
was its Indian Summer and since all that was involved was a
collateral cut linking the Forth and Clyde Canal to Edinburgh, it
would be a short season. The Caledonian Canal, open for limited use
in 1822, would only provide a few years' more of navvy work (but
the linking of Lochs Linnhe, Lochy and Ness must have seemed
remote indeed in the view from Polmont and Edinburgh). Moreover,
there would have been reason to believe that where the Irish had
been strong enough in numbers to give a good account of themselves
in the competition of rival ethnic work-forces on the Forth and
Clyde, and on the Union, on the Caledonian they would be heavily

outnumbered by their rivals, the Highlanders. This was not
absolutely true; many Irish did obtain employment on the
Caledonian. But the proportions were not comparable. The Forth
and Clyde established the settlement of the Irish in Paisley, and in the
Pollokshaws district of Glasgow; the Union ensured the much
smaller Irish settlement in Edinburgh; but the Caledonian has left
few permanent traces of an Irish incursion to Inverness. In any case,
by the end of the work on the Union Canal, Burke certainly, and
Hare probably, had reasons of a personal and amatory nature to
militate against their taking chances as far afield as Inverness.

Apart from the women in the case, the lifestyles of Burke
and Hare retained the contrast in gregariousness and misanthropy
which their environments had hitherto induced. Paradoxically, the
large town, Edinburgh, decreased a sense of community: Hare, with
quarters in Edinburgh, would have had less propensity to respond as a
member of a corps. Burke, near Polmont, residing in villages like
Maddiston, would have had far more incentive to win back again a
sense of being one of a group united in itself against a rather alien
native population. The navvies worked hard, fought amongst
themselves, drank together, and marched to and from work across
the farmlands of bitterly complaining local agriculturalists. The
distance from work to bed was often long, and the navvies had no
interest in making it longer out of commiseration for the wheat and
barley of local curmudgeons who noisily grudged the mere presence
of any of them, however much they were to benefit from the increase
in marketing opportunities as a result of the canal. No doubt Burke,
as a countryman, did appreciate the fact that his activity, however
industrial, took place among rural surroundings; even if the clear
country air offered its plenty of mist, drizzle and pelting rain.

Ethnic hostility dogged much of the canal construction, and
elicited patronising reproof from the middle classes but, as appears
many times during the Burke and Hare story, the only distinction
between the ethical conduct of the middle and working classes was
that the former had more money. From its earliest conception, at the
end of the eighteenth century, until it was finally closed in 1965, the
Edinburgh and Glasgow Union Canal was dogged by bitter
controversies. The canal was vital for the city's economic health —
yet special capitalist interests haggled so long and so selfishly over its
provisions that it seemed it might never come into being at all. The
Edinburgh magistrates held out against it for years, at the bidding, it
was said, of local coal monopolists, who would lose when the canal
brought in coal, until finally in 1814 an infuriated mob broke the

windows of the Lord Provost's house, in the correct belief that his
stand was preventing the working people from getting cheap coal
and fuel, an increase in the supply of what had hitherto been a very
scarce commodity in Edinburgh — water — and a large extension of
employment prospects. Even then the wrangling continued, and the
supporters of the canal scheme were accused of stirring up a
"Jacobinical" mob in a city "where the religious and moral
principles of the population were perhaps better than any town in
Europe". The *Edimbourgeoisie* has never had the need to pray God to
be given a good conceit of itself.

Raising the money proved difficult enough. It needed five Acts of
Parliament to authorise the raising of loans for the canal company
and the weary repetition in the titles (*"An Act to enable the Edinburgh
and Glasgow Union Canal Company to borrow a further Sum of Money"*
&c) told its own story of improvidence, baseless optimism and
nearsighted planning. The termini of the canal, Port Hopetoun in
Edinburgh and Camelon, Falkirk, are 25 miles apart, but by the time
the canal had accommodated the problems in terrain, of which much
the most time- and space-consuming arose from the rapacity of local
landlords, the full distance had swollen to thirty-one-and-a-half
miles. Landlords not only used every device to wring the uttermost
farthing from the company, but also introduced innumerable
irritants to force the company to swither the canal-route this way
and that in response to some invisible necessity invented by the
landlord that his spleen might be gratified. The company was in no
position to reveal a dauntless breast in the withstanding of the petty
tyrants of the fields: only the navvies were prepared to undertake
that task. But sharp practice proved contagious. By the end of the
1820s the company's secretary had been proved to be trading on the
canal himself under a false name and shares had plummeted to nearly
a quarter of the value they had reached after the canal's completion.
Henry Cockburn embodied these latter points in an opinion of
counsel on the grievances of several shareholders which he signed
only two days after the execution of Burke, for whose mistress he
had appeared in the previous trial.

As with most canals, much was made of the opportunities it would
offer for local employment, contractors being told to give a
"reasonable preference" to "natives of the place". But the incomers
from Ireland and the Highlands fairly rapidly swamped the natives.
Hare, in Edinburgh, probably saw more of the native force; Burke,
at the other end, would have had more experience of the
Highlanders.

The most serious affray between the Irish and the Highlanders took place nearer to Burke's area of activity than to Hare's, although there is no record that he ever worked on the section of the canal involved in it. Some sixty Irishmen employed around Broxburn attacked the Highlanders on the site and drove them out. The Highlanders brought in reinforcements, counter-attacked and were driven out again. They are then said to have sent the fiery cross to their fellows at some considerable distance and the next day 170 of them rallied at Winchburgh. The Irish pulled in 150 of their own number and took up their stance opposite. The offensive weapons ready for use were those relevant to their employment — scythes, spades, hedgebills, pickaxes and the like. The local inhabitants lined up on a hillside to give themselves the pleasure of seeing the two bands of invaders wreak havoc on one another, but the sheriff substitute managed to achieve a temporary truce which became permanent when a troop of soldiers arrived and arrested the leaders of the Irishry.

There is something peculiarly tragic in this. The two groups were both refugees from dying Gaelic worlds, for the most part, and their sense of alienation caused by the harsh conditions, exhausting work and grim modernity must have been decidedly similar. They were, undoubtedly, lonely and lost. Granted, they came from societies which had long honoured the tradition of the faction-fight whose vigour might well increase in proportion to the vagueness and antiquity of the original cause of hostility; and they had the incentive of acute job competition between the two ethnic groups as a basis for combat. But the conflict was in fact a mindless but symbolic expression of what lay in common between them — they were square pegs being thrust more and more harshly into the roundest of holes.

Drink was given the lion's share of abuse in accounting for these situations. The Pharisee is always ready to blame the publican. And drink certainly has the faculty of organising inchoate and uncomprehending anger into hatred of a specific target. Burke, the authorities agreed, only became really violent (apart from the requirements of his military and civil occupations) when he was drunk. We would not expect to find him in an affray of the deliberation of the Broxburn-Winchburgh engagements, unless, of course, he was drawn in for reasons of corps loyalty. But there would have been other motivations. Any sight the navvies might have of the wealth of the local lairds on the canal-bank, or of the ladies and gentlemen who might amuse themselves by strolling down to

observe the progress of the enterprise, might very naturally breed a
fierce resentment against a system which so nakedly sweated them
with little in return while the watching idlers luxuriated in wealth.
As they aimed their pickaxes at each other's skulls they were,
ironically, really fighting on the same side in bitter protest against a
clearly revealed system of class exploitation.

Living conditions did nothing to increase their sense of stability.
Hare was an exception here: it seems probable that during his stint on
the canal he came to live as a lodger in the house of the woman whom
he would later marry. Her house in Tanner's Close was a mere five
minutes from the commencement of the canal at Port Hopetoun.
Burke is spoken of as residing at Polmont, and in the village of
Maddiston. But Burke may also have been drawn, along with many
of the immigrants from Ulster and north Connacht, to inhabit the
temporary shelters thrown up by the workers when their
assignments went far from towns and villages. James E. Handley
quoted the *Glasgow Herald* of 16 December 1822 on the situation:

> Along the banks of the Union Canal certain edifices have been
> erected which strike the traveller with no little astonishment. These
> are huts erected by Irish labourers upon some few vacant spots of
> ground belonging to the canal proprietors, and are pointed out to
> strangers on the passage boats as great curiosities. Each, of course, is
> more wretched than another, and presents a picture of squalid poverty
> which is new to the people on this side of the Channel. [James Handley
> remarks that the writer seemed unaware of Highland conditions.] One
> of them, with the exception, perhaps, of a few sticks, is composed
> entirely of rotten straw; its dimensions would not suffice for a pig-
> stye, and its form is that of a bee-hive, only it is more conical. The
> smoke which does not escape at the door presents at all times the
> appearance of a hayrick on fire. A Hottentot kraal in comparison with
> it is a palace. In the midst of so much misery the children appear
> healthful and frolicsome, and the women contented and happy.

The navvies were simply dehumanised in the view of the well-to-do
observers. If Burke and Hare became like predatory beasts at war on
their own kind, in the end, they had been assigned the role long
before they took it up. To have one's poverty pointed out as a "great
curiosity" adds a spiritual degradation to the social and economic
ones. Inmates of the zoo obtain similar reactions except that they are
not expected to do the work which will make their viewers more
wealthy.

The work itself was hard in the extreme. It must have been
particularly taxing for William Burke, who was undersized far
below the usual proportions of a navvy. Under it his muscles would

develop, acquiring exceptional strength in the neck, shoulders, arms and — to his advantage in his final career — fingers. It was digging, picking, blasting, hauling, cutting, loading. Great stones had to be manoeuvred into place to supply landing-stages and securer canal-banks. Getting stones from quarries produced their fatalities and injuries as did the deep digging of reservoirs. A frayed rope put the lives of men dependent on it at terrible risk. Various industrial diseases took their toll during the excavation of tunnels. Men driving horses during the making of embankments could be crushed to death when adverse weather made the ground slippery and accidents occurred. Many cases of scurvy were reported — it was highly likely to affect the potato-dependent Irish. Typhus outbreaks became more frequent as the century advanced.

Burke and Hare were around twenty-six years of age when they began work on the canal; they were thirty when they finished. This was characteristic enough. Neither they nor their contemporaries would have been good for it very much longer, and by the time they took up murder they were beyond the age when navvies' work was still open to them. They might find themselves working ten hours a day, and the chance of an increase in hours obtained — and was often seized on — when the contractor was under pressure. Relations with the labour contractors were mechanical enough: it was one firm signal that they had stumbled into the world of the industrial revolution. There was little enough actuality to the myth of benevolent paternalism as far as the strolling labourer had been concerned, but at least the relationship between the farmer and himself had been a personal one. As a navvy, he confronted the inanimate in the person of the contractors. There were occasional instances of navvy subscriptions for a kindly contractor, but the very suggestion of exceptionalism about it indicates that such a situation was regarded as surprising. In general, the contractor got what he could get out of his navvies with scant regard for their health or dignity. He was merely at a higher point in the chain of employment. Williams and Hughes, for instance, who had answered the canal company so tartly in the matter of possible weekly wages, ultimately lost their contract because they were believed to have allowed the work to go forward too slowly. Naturally the replacing of contractors made the relationship more mechanical still, and put the navvy's employment at risk. Williams and Hughes seem to have had some humane instincts — Ms Lindsay credits them with having led the company to have the Glasgow Infirmary admit men in need of medical attention without application from the parish minister, and the committee subscribed annually to the infirmary for the duration of the canal-digging. This, especially from the point of view of Irish Catholic workers, was an important concession: yet the choice had its ironical side, for Glasgow was considerably distant from any point on the Union Canal. Burke may well have required treatment. He had a medical history going back to his militia days and may already have been suffering from the complaint of a schirrous testicle for which he was seeking assistance in his final years. (Indeed the original incidence of this may account for his attendance at the Ballina infirmary.) But if he was a patient during his navvy days, the curious choice of the Glasgow Infirmary meant that he would have some time to wait before commencing his fruitful acquaintance with the Edinburgh medical profession.

If the work was back-breaking there is little evidence that the navvies grumbled at their lot. They fought, got drunk, even indulged in private bouts of prize-fighting, but they were extremely industrious. The Irish in particular were demons for work and proved conclusively that the national reputation for indolence was wholly unjustified. They were thankful for their regular wage — it seems to have been half-a-crown a day. And while the navvies' reputation was always very low in the eyes of the locals among whom they worked, the Irish, noted Carlyle some years later, had the best image of all. That was in 1846, when the fear of famine had sent them in flight from home; the earlier migrants may have been less circumspect.

Probably the most unwelcome work would have been the all too frequent assignments for drainage, bridge-building and road-making in fulfilment of concessions gouged out of the company by the rapacious landowners. Here the navvies would encounter not merely mechanical cash nexus operation, but active hostility, and the task of working for the advantage of their enemies was uncongenial. The converse, of course, applied. To the public at large the navvies could be terrifying figures, huge, foul-mouthed, brawling, ugly, disfigured, known above all for their shouting and noise on the Sabbath when they were off work, and while one might have little sympathy with the enmity to the navvies expressed by the profiteering landowners or the patronising visitors, the quiet poor people in the villages on which they descended had even more reason for fear. One of the things that seems most to have frightened the locals — it is a point suggestively made by Eileen and Rhoda Power in their *Boys and Girls of History* — is the roughness and brutality of the women in navvy encampments. Ordinary countrywomen in

Scotland had little means to preserve beauty, figure and grace, but they remained gentle and feminine amid hardship and physical degeneration. The navvy women had to be as good with a word or a blow as their men. For it was not only a hostile environment with a work-force involving competing and warring elements from Highlands, Ireland and the canal country itself: Highlanders brought their own feuds with them, Irish showed extreme county-consciousness, religion fed flames of conflict. The navvy asked for no mercy and gave none.

Burke and Hare had been paid off by August 1822, and the canal was fully in operation such that sightseers could travel the more easily to Edinburgh for the revolting sight of George IV in kilts. Extra boats and horses were laid on for the occasion, and Sunday operation was permitted "to prevent disappointment to the public". It was blasphemous that the navvies should so noisily relax on their one free day; it was permissible that the Sabbath be violated when what was in question was a sight of the bloated, corsetted, Royal debauchee. A little more work did remain to be done on the Union Canal, but this was simply the making of a cut to Port Maxwell at the Falkirk end, and was quickly achieved in 1823. Few men were needed, certainly not Burke or Hare. Hare found casual labour work in Port Hopetoun itself: in a sense this occupation and its sequel, that of being a slum landlord, were natural spin-offs from his career as an Edinburgh navvy. He is also reported as working for a time as a hawker, initially with a horse and cart and later with a hand-barrow. It was ironic that he, physically much more the navvy type than Burke, found himself pushed into the position of a parasite, having been up to now very much the producer. Burke, on the other hand, seems to have thrown himself into a whole variety of occupations; having adapted his small body into the daunting trade of navvy work, he learned a variety of other skills and put them to work. His confession published in the *Courant* implies that after the Union Canal work was over he went across the Pentlands to Peebles and worked there for about two years as a labourer. The point is of some interest, in that it shows how much the migrants had to retain their options open, and oscillate between their old agricultural work and their new industrial activity; but in practice canal-work was transitional from agriculture rather than directly industrial, carrying with it much that lay in common with the tasks of an agricultural labourer. So Burke reverted and, indeed, would continue to do so: he turned his hand to casual labour in places like Carnwath, Peebles and Penicuik while finally settled in Edinburgh. But he preferred to retain his old calling simply as something on which to fall back. After his two years in Peebles, he worked as a weaver for eighteen months, according to his account, and as a baker for five. He also learned how to mend shoes from a man with whom he lodged for a time in Leith, probably about 1826. All of this suggests something more than a struggle for survival; there is evidence of attempt after attempt to break out of the labourer's straitjacket, to which his story about the land quarrel with his Irish father-in-law bears witness. This was not mere shiftlessness of occupation; it was much more an attempt to adjust to a society which had provided a labour market and then took it away again. Buchanan's edition of the trial summed it up as "Like most of his countrymen, he seems to have turned his hand to anything"; but the acquisition of these skills took more than merely turning a hand. He does not seem to have been disappointed. Maclean, for instance, remarked on the rarity of his violence even in drink, "without considerable provocation", his manner being in general "rather jocose and quizzical". At the time when his enterprise with Hare came into being he had been contemplating migration to the west of Scotland. He knew what he was about. Edinburgh had no future as a labour market, and indeed looked as if it had little as an economic centre of any kind. After all the effort Burke, Hare and their fellow-navvies had put in to raise the economic prosperity of the city with the opening up of the canal, Edinburgh was bankrupt in 1833.

CHAPTER 5

Burke, Hare, and Sex

" 'Journeys end in lovers meeting'," said Allen Uttershaw, in his
mild and ingratiating way. "Or would you prefer the other one —
'Journeys end in death'?"
                    —Leslie Charteris, *The Saint on Guard*

PROFESSOR T. C. Smout has penetrated what has hitherto been
largely virgin territory for modern historians in his seminal
article "Aspects of Sexual Behaviour in Nineteenth-Century
Scotland". As he so justly remarks, it is "sad (but currently
inevitable) that research into sexual history should generally appear
to be either prurient or trivial: if social history aims to reflect what is
important in people's lives, sexual history deserves much more
serious and central attention from social historians than it has had so
far". And since the first facet of the careers of Burke and Hare of
which we possess detailed, as opposed to minute, information is their
sexual behaviour in the 1820s, it is clearly desirable to give it some
attention. Up to now I have been using extraneous historical data to
provide clues to their lives. Now, at last, it is their turn to do some of
the work and enable us to see whether they throw additional light on
the past.

Professor Smout very properly devotes some attention to the
sexual behaviour of the Irish in Scotland. Given the great
transformation of Scottish society caused by the massive Irish
immigration of the nineteenth century, this may seem an obvious
proceeding, but in fact Scotland — like Ireland — is all too
frequently discussed in monocultural terms. Presbyterian spokesmen
in Scotland resemble their Roman Catholic opposite numbers in
Ireland in the regularity with which they identify their faith and
historical tradition with the country as a whole. This is as dangerous
as it is discourteous. At the same time the danger of stereotyping the
incursive alien is the next pitfall that awaits the historian who avoids
the monocultural trap and this, when one is dealing with an entire

century, can have serious consequences. Professor Smout may be
open to some criticism here, although he may well retort with his
characteristic blend of firmness and courtesy that a sample of three
— we must include Mrs Hare — is open to even more. But of course
we cannot construct alternative positive theses from our sample of
three. We cannot even claim it to be representative in that wholesale
murderers — again we must include Mrs Hare — are, one trusts, not
particularly   representative   of   the   Irish   immigrants   in
nineteenth-century Scotland. But it does raise some doubts which
may open up constructive lines of investigation in the long run.

Professor Smout observes that "the Irish had, in their native land
at least, an exceptional respect for premarital chastity", in which
connection he cites the late Kenneth Connell's essay "Illegitimacy
before the Famine" printed in the latter's *Irish Peasant Society*. This, he
feels, is confirmed by Irish immigrant behaviour in Britain, but not
by the habits "of the unaccompanied males. The men, uprooted from
their families, priests, and culture and herded into navvying teams
under brutalised conditions, behaved notoriously badly." And
Professor Smout effectively cites testimony from the great Irish
navvy writer of Scotland, Patrick Macgill, that "experienced men
would go with Scottish prostitutes but condemn with horror a young
girl of their own band who had been seduced by a farmer's son", an
attitude Professor Smout sees as "precisely the same double standard
as the middle-class Scottish male". (This is immigrant adjustment
with a vengeance: it is tempting to see in its origin certain cultural
parallels, but in fact both the Irish and the Scots were responding to
the same process of bourgeoisification.)

Professor Smout notices the low illegitimacy "where immigrant
Irish families were thick on the ground", associating it with "the
nature of nineteenth-century Catholicism in Ireland, with the great
strength of the priests and the emphasis on the worship of Mary and
the holiness of the virgin state". He follows Professor Connell in
reminding us of the high illegitimacy rates in Austria and Portugal as
a caution against equating "nineteenth-century Catholicism with
universal chastity" (or, more accurately in syntax, with a universal
chastity belt). "In the post-famine situation, with late marriage for
the males and few holdings to go round, the teaching of the priests
was reinforced by a quite separate economic sanction. For immigrant
industrial workers into Scotland the economic situation was
obviously of another kind, but the cultural and moral habit formed in
Ireland would not immediately collapse."

We may comment on the last point first. What Professor Smout terms "the great strength of the priests" (and any courting couple finding itself at the wrong end of a parish priest's blackthorn would heartily agree with him) derives — in its more intangible form — from Catholicism in Ireland being a popular and, in the eighteenth century, a proscribed religion, as opposed to a state and official establishment of the type laid down in Austria and Portugal. Clerical power initially derived from the hostility of the state. But it also greatly strengthened its organisational powers as the nineteenth century advanced. It found it much easier to rule four million than eight, especially when the agency of that fall in population — the great famine of 1845-1850 — induced a powerful mood of seeking increased spiritual reinsurance. Again, the impact of middle-class values on the Irish asserted itself most clearly through stronger links in the chain of Catholic organisation. This was as true of the Irish diaspora as it was of the Catholics remaining on the island itself.

The problem we have is that Professor Smout's evidence (although not Professor Connell's) is entirely post-famine. Certainly much of what he has said holds true for the earlier period, as readers of the previous chapter will acknowledge with respect to his remarks on the brutalised conditions under which the navvies sweated. But it does assume a more static world of emotions and attitudes, with much more potent social control. Even the Pharisaical attitude of the male chauvinist navvies, as described by Patrick MacGill, refers to the more conventional world of the late nineteenth century rather than the looser structures of behaviour and belief in the early nineteenth. Immorality had acquired its conventions no less than morality by that time. The working-class acceptance of middle-class values was a thing of tangible reality, and Catholicism ensured that acceptance in a peculiarly dynamic form. To say this is not to agree with Professor Emmet Larkin that there was a "devotional revolution" in the third quarter of the nineteenth century, but it is to accept the evidence presented by him as showing a marked increase in outward piety as a form of social behaviour. And sexual orthodoxy became the great foundation of this new conformity.

Professor Kenneth Connell was sure that it had been established from the beginning of the nineteenth century and as he admitted he based himself on "evidence collected by the Commissioners for inquiring into the Condition of the Poorer Classes in Ireland, and published in 1835-6". This is indeed a mountain of testimony and despite its initial dependence on public officials and social leaders it ultimately went far beyond elitist ranks for information. Curiously enough, it is Professor Smout himself who emerges as a formidable

witness against it, although in the context of Gaelic Scotland rather
than Ireland. He point out that evidence of surviving Gaelic songs
speak of very different social attitudes to sexual morality than those
implied in, say, "the remarks of Free Church commentators".
Precisely the same points exists for Ireland. The liberated sexual
language of Brian Merriman and the even more liberated sexual
behaviour of Eoghan Ruadh O Súilleabháin in the late eighteenth
century speak of a different world from that described in Professor
Connell's pages. And those two worlds were not merely separate by
sixty years; they were separated by an abyss between their cultures.
The evidence Professor Connell examines certainly shows that the
Irish knew what they wanted the British authorities to think; they
knew, in particular, that Protestants did insist that Catholicism bred
sexual immorality and they were very sensitive on the point. But
what the Gaelic and post-Gaelic world said and sang to itself is a very
different matter from what it told authority. They knew enough to
say that they saw illegitimacy as a social as well as a spiritual stigma,
and sexual licence as wholly reprehensible; but did they believe it?
They might say that they would shun the unmarried mother, but did
that in fact mean they shunned her? As nineteenth-century
respectability cast its dark shadows farther and farther over the
once-Gaelic world, profession of sexual respectability deepened in
that region into belief. But in 1836 Irish Gaelic and post-Gaelic
testimony to a Government commission and its itinerant Assistant
Commissioners had no more force than testimony of an American
Negro slave had to the authorities, civil and personal, at the same
date. The commission is, in the last analysis, more reliable on the
future than on the past; attitudes that people felt it would be thought
they ought to have would ultimately become the attitudes they chose
to have.

Burke was of Gaelic origin, though he was by now literate in
English. Hare we assume not have been Irish-speaking and was
definitely not literate: to judge from the pattern of signature he
dictated he pronounced his name "Willam" which again suggests he
had not in the past been in the habit of calling himself "Liam". Mrs
Hare's maiden name — the term has a certain incongruity in her case
— was Laird which again suggests non-Gaelic origins.

Our first known incident in the sex-lives of Burke and Hare is
shadowy, for it is that of Burke's first marriage. Of course it might
have its precursors in casual sexual encounter. Something of the kind
is to be expected with an army or a militia quartered on the country.
Patterns of sexual behaviour induced by the presence of the militia

make a marked contrast between the Napoleonic era and its sequel, and more ordered times. Burke is stated as having suffered from a schirrous testicle in later life, but what caused it, or how early it received medical treatment is unknown to us; but those visits to the hospital could be the first sign. The most likely cause of the complaint would be syphilis, which implies that Burke's first sexual adventures were with women of previous experience. In a word, the whores follow the army and the pox follows the whores.

The pre-famine Irish marriage-pattern was in total contrast to that of the post-famine Irish. As Professor Smout remarks, the later period reflects few and late marriages; but before the holocaust the peasantry and labourers married early and extensively. If their economic prospects were meagre, they yet settled for feeding two or more mouths with a cheery readiness to make do with the same sparse resources on which hitherto they saw to the wants of one. Many of these young marriages must have followed sexual experiences resulting in pregnancies. Where marriages in the Irish militia were concerned the probability was very greatly increased.

It is likely that Burke's first marriage was the result of a pregnancy. He was an attractive young man who had a way with ladies. Indeed he was to make great use of his sexual attractiveness in luring even the oldest of his female victims to party and death; an old and ugly woman is as grateful for gallantry as a young and pretty one, perhaps more so. And this was not hypocrisy in Burke. The only woman whom he loved of whom we have a physical description, Helen MacDougal, is nowhere represented as attractive. He seems quite genuinely to have been far less of a male chauvinist in that respect than his critics, such as Christopher North who seemed to feel that for him to have loved an ugly woman increased the sum of his sins. In the militia he would have been additionally enhanced by the smart and expensive bandsman's uniform, and he would have been one of the cynosures of all eyes when marches were being played before appreciative crowds, occasionally even at stately evenings. The fact that he was small would have singled him out among his fellows: Irish soldiers generally ran to some size, as the father of Frederick the Great, who doted on giants in uniform, readily acknowledged. We have, then, a polished, youthful drummer-boy and/or fifer, his youth and charm greatly increased by an offitial dress which underlined an appealing immaturity, and we have, it may be, certain initial advantages arising from shyness and lack of confidence in the English language. These latter would disappear, but it is credible to assume them. We could rely on him to draw the attention of a lady perhaps with a little greater sophistication, possibly slightly older, and even of superior social status.

It could be that Burke's wife was a Protestant. Her name was Margaret Coleman, which has more of a Protestant than a Catholic ring to it. To be sure the process of Irish Anglicization did some strange violence to names — the Irish hero Fionn Mac Cumhaill, or Finn MacCool, might very well find himself rendered as Phineas Coleman by a nineteenth-century notary. But one piece of evidence which seems to lend substance to the thesis of Protestantism is that the local curate at Kilmore, Mayo, near Ballina, was written to by a correspondent in Edinburgh (presumably a co-religionist and probably a fellow-cleric), and replied: "After the receipt of your letter, I sent for Margaret Coleman, Bourke's wife . . .". This may mean that he was not in the habit of seeing her at Mass; or that he would not have found it natural to call at her house. In such circumstances the boys would have followed the religion of the father, the girls of the mother, and the curate might well have been in the habit of "sending" for the family to make sure the boys were receiving Catholic education, but the alien religious affiliation of one marriage partner would make a priest a little chary of visiting the home, a proceeding which might appear to show respect to the hearth of a heretic. His manner of phrasing also suggests that she had resumed her father's name, which might indicate that she and her children had returned to his protection and support.

Burke's story about his quarrel with his father-in-law again might have behind it an annoyance that he could not himself get more support from a source of some wealth. If this were the case it makes it very likely that the marriage followed discovery of pregnancy; neither Catholic nor Protestant fathers of any pretensions to wealth, however small, would look with favour on the suit of a labourer's son from many scores of miles distant.

If Mr Coleman did enjoy some economic advantages it would seem probable that Margaret did not see the romance of her military courtship crumble into poverty and drudgery as swiftly and brutally as happened to many others. If she obtained no assistance from her father during Burke's years in the militia then her experience was unpleasant. Sir Jeremiah Fitzpatrick, M.D., Inspector of Health for the Land Forces, described the fate of Irish soldiers' wives as "itinerant beggary". The Duke of Wellington put it more bluntly still: when their husbands enlisted, wives went "not 'upon the parish' but upon the dunghill; to starve". Under the legislation of 1811

Margaret Burke would have been deprived of all benefits, being the wife of a volunteer who married her while in service. When the Regency authorities became concerned about economy, nothing could equal their public spirit against the profligacy of the poor.

Because the Donegal was quartered in Ballina for much of Burke's time of enlistment it is very probable that Margaret Burke was able to remain near her husband without following the travels of the regiment. She may have had quarters of her own; more likely, she remained under her father's roof, until Burke left the army. If in fact she and her children did choose to pass their lives with the militia, or were forced so to do, the experience was a foul one. Overcrowding, utter lack of sanitation, high propensity for contagious diseases, little and polluted air, filth, stench, refuse, were all the accompaniments for the quarters of women and children in the Irish militia. Frequently dogs and poultry were maintained there; legislation prohibited them from the men's rooms, which gives us a clue both to their presence and to their inevitable domicile. And most of the militiamen did get married or were already married. Even in camp women and children had to be provided for; the Donegal on one such occasion assigned nine tents "for the use of the women". When the militia marched the women and children marched too, unless they were lucky enough to get lifts for part of the time. As for sexual intimacy, it was probably a matter of making the most of what opportunities there were. The situation certainly did not make for privacy or delicacy, and even if Margaret Burke was lucky enough to be spared experience of it, her husband knew it, and so did his mates. To argue that graduates of the Irish militia would have had strong taboos against sexual promiscuity is, in Mencken's phrase, to spit boorishly into the very eye of the known facts. It also seems likely that the conditions would lead to a ready expectancy of adultery among married women. If Burke's wife were at home and he sought sexual outlet one of the most obvious ways of obtaining it would be with the wife of a comrade, especially if his medical history had given him a distaste for the professionals in the game.

Father Anthony Corcoran, the curate of Kilmore, is our only witness to Burke's life between demobilisation and emigration. His Reverence was a trifle melodramatic, but then the occasion reeked of melodrama, with the execution of his most celebrated former parishioner scheduled for three days thence. It would seem that Corcoran had not in fact been the curate during the Burke residence at Ballina—he is an unlucky ecclesiastic who is given a twelve-year stint as an underling in one place—but as a witness to the name that

Burke left behind him, his evidence is suggestive. "I have minutely inquired into the conduct of the unfortunate Bourke," he wrote. (The spelling is not ignorance; variants are to be expected given that the name itself had been Anglicized from "de Búrca". Every signature of William Burke that has come down to us has the spelling "Burk" — as one might expect from a native speaker of the Irish language in which the final "e" mute is unknown.) "I feel much pleasure in assuring you that there was not a blot on his character for the time he lived in Ballina." He sent, as we know, for Margaret, "to whom I communicated the sad news of the awful death that awaited her ill-fated husband. She was prepared for the shock for some time. She was acquainted with her husband's criminal intercourse with the notorious M'Dougal".

To Father Corcoran, as to many another priest in Ireland, emigration meant loss of faith. Patriotism and clericalism dictated the thesis that the stay-at-home saved his soul: the unknown world meant damnation. If Irish popular attitudes to sex were less constricted than they would become, Father Corcoran clearly had no truck with such looseness. His letter does not mean that Margaret Burke knew her William to be murdering people in collaboration with Helen MacDougal; it meant that she knew he was living in open adultery with her which, from Father Corcoran's point of view, was as bad as murdering seventeen people. Whether Margaret Burke really regarded it as only a matter of time until her husband would be hanged once she had heard of his liaison with Helen MacDougal is quite another matter, but Father Corcoran clearly thought such a sentiment appropriate and edifying for her. There are several other points of interest to the historian of Irish sex. The priest is automatically ready to blame the woman and pity the man; indeed in his reading of the matter Burke would have been as right as rain had it not been for Helen MacDougal (whose entry in his life was, however, inevitable with emigration). The fact that Helen MacDougal was Scottish made the matter worse, but even without this, Irish clerical anti-feminism, on sexual matters, is standard. The man is half pardoned as being "misled"; the woman is by implication the devil's agent. (There are strong grounds for suspecting that many Irish priests in the depth of their hearts believe that what really happened in the Garden of Eden was the sin of fornication.) Again, the genuine pity and sympathy for Burke is in remarkable contrast to the howls of execration with which his name was being generally greeted. Father Corcoran may have been anxious to point the contrast between a virtuous life in Ireland and a descent into Scottish damnation, and no doubt had a point or two to make against emigration in forthcoming sermons, but the underlying picture is still important. Burke left a good name in his locality. After all, if the local boy goes abroad, kills seventeen people — many of them Irish — and is about to be hanged for it, it is curious that some wiseacre did not surface to announce that he had told his familiars time and again that, mark his words, that boy would be hanged some day. But nobody did. It says a good deal for Burke. And it also indicates that his wife preserved the greatest love for his memory. After all, whoever else Father Corcoran spoke to, he certainly spoke to her, and if Burke had been a bad husband in Ballina she was not prepared to say so.

There were, according to Burke's confession to the *Courant,* two children by his marriage in Ballina. We know nothing more of them. The conception of one as the cause of marriage and of the other after Burke had left the army would seem plausible enough; and in that event the existence of a babe-in-arms would have increased Margaret Burke's refusal to emigrate. "She would not come to Scotland with him," declared the *Courant* confession. "He has often wrote to her, but got no answer." Presumably it was from one of these letters that she learned of the existence of Helen MacDougal — the alternative being that the news came to her from Con Burke, but this is less likely. The initial failure to answer letters could well have arisen from an autocratic father who had resented her forced marriage with a labourer and now thought it well to have her make an end of a bad bargain; once she heard of Helen MacDougal that could well have supplied the final touch. Writing was not easy in that world — Burke was unusual in his command of it — and it would be a work of great pain for a wife to write to her husband about his adultery whereas she could express herself forcibly enough about it when they were together. Emotion was a matter for the tongue, not the pen.

One point in Father Corcoran's vindication of Burke has to be gainsaid, however. Burke did abandon his wife, and his remarks about her seem curiously cold, for him. There are various reasons for this. Firstly, from the time of Adam, men have found it easier to blame women than to accept responsibility. Secondly, Burke may never have been deeply in love with his wife. With all due respect for the nomadic propensities of his lifestyle he abandoned his marriage after a remarkably brief period following demobilisation. If the marriage had been a forced one he may never have possessed anything for her but an appreciation of her sexual charms. And thirdly, his confessions were made after he had gone through a terrible ordeal of trial together with someone with whom he really was in love, and that at the end of it his first thought was not of his doom but of her preservation. Margaret Burke may have seemed very shadowy in comparison with that. As to the children, it is a part of the nomadic existences of Burke, Helen MacDougal, Hare and Mrs Hare that so little is made of their children in the story. Helen MacDougal is reported by Maclean as having had two children "by her husband" (although in court she denied ever having been married). Nothing more is heard of them. Mrs Hare is described by Maclean as having a child by her first husband, Logue, and it is notorious that she made her grand entrance during the trial with an infant who was also to be useful in saving her from especially violent attack after her release. (It seems the appropriate origin for the tag "Hit me now with the child in me arms".) Christopher North, with his customary charity, referred to the child as a "yellow, 'yammering' infant (the image of its father)". Venom rather than accuracy is North's long suit, but it seems difficult to see how he could confuse a babe-in-arms with a three-year-old, which is at the very least what the Logue child would have had to be. (Of course it is not absolutely impossible, and the resemblance to Hare might be coincidence, or else a proof that Hare was the father of a child born to his future wife in the lifetime of her first husband.) But if the infant was Hare's child, what happened to Logue's?

Infanticide is one possibility, and it needed no wholesale murder firm of the Burke and Hare type to set in motion. As Professor Connell notes, it was an answer many Irish Catholic women took, certainly in preference to abortion, which was felt to be just as morally reprehensible and much more personally dangerous; in any case infanticide is well known in post-natal depression, and the economic circumstances in which Helen MacDougal and Margaret Hare lived were likely enough to increase such feelings. Abandonment of the children to the care of authorities was a well-known proceeding. Most likely of all is infant mortality. The conditions in which the protagonists operated were anything but hygienic. Helen MacDougal's children might have been placed with her own family, with whom she retained connections. The only actual reference to infanticide in the literature which I have seen was with regard to Mrs Hare, and the story in the *Courant* where it appeared on 1 January 1829 compels no respect for its reliability: it is not a date on which Scottish journalists are at their best. It was said that she had a child by Hare when married to Logue and murdered it to escape detection. This really seems to be another addition to the brood, since everyone is agreed that one child was at least accepted as Logue's, and the infant in court, if not actually the Logue child, was admitted even by the most hostile witness to be alive. In summing up it seems fair to suggest that children held much less central a position in this nomadic world that in the settled, pre-emigrant condition. The one point when children enter the story — apart from the Hare Madonna — was when Burke gave his nephews, the sons of Con, some of the clothing of the murdered "Daft Jamie" Wilson, apparently out of·compassion at their ragged and near-naked condition — an act of more generosity than wisdom, as the subsequent identification of the clothes would show.

Our suspicions that Burke did not at any stage care deeply for either wife or children are decidedly increased by what we know of the chronology of his sex-life after he left them. At the time of the trial, in December 1828, he, Helen MacDougal and Maclean all stated separately that he had lived with her for the past ten years, which is to say within a few months of his taking up work on the Union Canal. On the other hand once taken up the connection proved endurable under the greatest of strains. It was, for instance, much more long-lasting than his marriage. It is one of the great mysteries of the case, but it is also one of its most unmistakable features. Burke's love for his Nellie seems to have been as passionate and intense as his respect for human life in general was small. It was as though Love had to receive so powerful an affirmation to answer the huge offerings given to Death.

Professor Smout is, I think, justified in drawing some generalisation from MacGill's testimony about the Irish navvies' readiness to use rather than to respect Scotswomen. But Burke entered on a relationship which, for him, proved to be permanent, and he seems to have leaped the barriers of ethnicity and religion with the greatest of ease. It seems to have been decidedly atypical. In this uncertain, formative period of immigrant adjustment we could well assume the development of sexual alliances, transient and permanent, between representatives of the immigrant and of the host culture of a proportionately larger kind than would be evident as prejudices and tribalism hardened later in the century. Nevertheless the Irish Catholic navvies as an invading army did look with suspicion on the concept of sexual alliance of a permanent kind with the locals. Mrs Hare underlined the point when in the middle of the murder partnership she advised Burke to murder Helen MacDougal. Mrs Hare, according to Burke's *Courant* confession, made the suggestion not because of any immediate shortage of potential corpse material but because of the potential untrustworthiness of Burke's love. "The reason was, they could not trust to her, as she was a Scotch woman." Burke refused. The Burke-MacDougal relationship would not be unacceptable to Burke's fellow-Irish in normal circumstances, but in the tension of murder conspiracy tribalism sprang into active response. Later in the century we might expect that tribalistic reaction in a normal, as opposed merely to an emergency, situation.

A nice point arises as to whether Burke's love for Helen MacDougal permitted him to trust her with the terrible secret of the murders. Although he would not have her murdered, did he in fact conceal the murders because of her ethnic alienation? Or did she know? The jury found her not proven, the mob and the great mass of subsequent commentators have been satisfied that she was guilty, and Burke himself went to his grave insisting on her innocence. None of these three points are particularly conclusive. The one point on which Burke's confessions are really valueless as evidence is on the question of Helen MacDougal's guilt. The principle that spouses cannot testify against one another was one he intended fully to vindicate in the matter of his common-law wife. She had been found not proven on one murder; he must do nothing which might place her in peril on counts which could be brought in relating to others. The views of the mob are also worthless, and none of the subsequent commentators have brought in firm evidence. They jury's verdict seems an eminently sensible one, and it is difficult, with a trail as cold as one hundred-and-fifty years later can make it, for a historian to go far beyond it. Certainly there is less evidence connecting Helen MacDougal with the crimes than exists against Burke and the Hares, which may have influenced the jury. If it seemed somewhat questionable justice for Burke to hang while Hare went free, it would have been outrageous for Helen MacDougal to die while Hare lived. Whatever she was guilty of, it could have been no more than being an accessory before or after the fact. Yet she would have hanged if found guilty. The indictment charged her with actual participation in murder but no evidence was ever forthcoming of that. The jury may have come to its conclusion on those grounds, with the further justification that the indictment had absurdly overreached itself in her case. Henry Cockburn had made the most of the psychology of this situation in his speech, which is acknowledged to have been powerful in its impact.

What does stand in her favour is that as the story unfolded her behaviour seems much more consistent with ignorance than knowledge. She was physically unattractive, and may therefore have lived in fear that she would lose Burke. As we know she was in no danger, but love cohabits very easily with baseless jealousy. The account of her violent reactions to Burke's apparent interest in the attractive Mary Paterson seems highly genuine. William Roughead, who takes Helen MacDougal to be guilty, reached the conclusion that MacDougal knew Burke was about to murder Mary Paterson, but was furious at the thought of his showing any appearance of sexual interest in her! The story of what happened before the murder rests in this instance on the testimony of Mary Paterson's friend, and she was in no doubt as to the real violence of Helen MacDougal's jealousy. In fact the episode makes far more sense if Helen MacDougal was innocent. As Roughead remarks it was certainly not a "put-up job", the kind of sham fighting in which Burke and Hare elsewhere indulged to distract their victims.

There is the possibility that at some later stage Helen MacDougal guessed what was happening and that her love for Burke — and also her fear of him and Hare if she came to the conclusion they were murderers — prevented her informing on him. Mrs Hare's anxiety to get rid of her seems less a precaution against a potentially weak conspirator than of an intimate who might discover too much. But Helen MacDougal consistently seemed to act as though the murders were outside her cognisance. Her very conduct after being found not proven in returning to the West Port and going to a pub for a drink is much more suggestive of bemused innocence than brazen guilt. She does not seem to have been intelligent, and her wanderings until her disappearance all seem suggestive of acute shock. Her main anxiety was to see Burke again. This was denied. At one point Burke did say in the *Courant* confession that she "might have a suspicion of what was doing".

This raises the question of why Burke so carefully exempted her from complicity, if indeed he did. One answer would be the ethnic argument. For all of his years with her, this would say, he trusted her less well than he would have done an Irish Catholic. If so, he was badly mistaken. For one thing, as the sequel would prove, he obtained from her the loyalty he gave her, and he was thoroughly betrayed by the other representatives of his ethnic group, the Hares. Whether guilty or innocent she stood in peril of her life and made no move to save herself by dissociating herself from him. And as we know he seems to have been singularly free from ethnic prejudice, in emergency or otherwise. It is probable that he took a somewhat male chauvinist line. She worked as reaper and hawker along with him and did her day's stint with the toughness of any man; she drank and fought with him as well as loving him and when they did quarrel Burke could shower her with blows and missiles as he would do in a quarrel with a man; but he genuinely believed in protecting her in a crisis, even if his method of protection was to cut her forehead open with a glass when her jealous scene was preventing the commencement of homicidal operation on Mary Paterson, rather than tell her what was toward. It seems, then, that he kept her in the dark as much as he could, and did so, not because she was a Scot, but because he loved her.

Why he did is his business. Contemporaries united in giving an unflattering account of her appearance. In part this arose from the belief that bad people ought to look unpleasing, but not all the sources are wholly hostile. The odious Christopher North might be expected to dredge in the lower depths of his considerable vocabulary when it came to speaking of Helen MacDougal and Margaret Hare: "Poor, miserable, bony, skinny, scranky, wizened jades both, without the most distant approach to good-lookingness, either in any part of their form, or any feature of their face — peevish, sulky, savage, and cruel, and evidently familiar, from earliest life, with all the woe and wretchedness of guilt and pollution — most mean in look, manner, mind, dress — the very dregs of prostitution." North's remarks gave him some status as an authority on meanness of another kind and in fact the ladies could show in the history of their lives that their appearances followed lifetimes of hard, physical work in field and on canal bank, with small returns for labour much greater than he expended on anything save food, drink and character assassination. But Maclean described Helen MacDougal as "of a dull morose disposition, either when sober or intoxicated" and believed her life with Burke to have been most unhappy, with perpetual quarrelling, often physically, sometimes with grievous bodily harm to her.

Maclean's evidence is somewhat self-defeating in that elsewhere he argues that Burke quarrelled little save under provocation, but no doubt Helen MacDougal's readiness to flare up in a jealous rage offered him much of that. But it seems likely that these quarrels and fighting actually formed part of the basis of their sexual attractiveness to one another. They worked off their frustrations against their demeaning and debilitating working conditions by fighting, much as their fellow-Irish and fellow-Scots on the canal brawled in larger numbers, and then — unlike the embattled navvies — they turned their battles into reconciliation and renewal of love. The Hares had something of a comparable relationship, save that Mrs Hare differed from Helen MacDougal in often emerging the victor when she took her man on. Many primitive societies exhibit such forms of love, and primitive figures confronted with the constriction of a more advanced and more impersonal society revert in some ways more strongly to their original instincts in inverse proportion to the extent to which occupational modernisation is being forced on them in their economic activity. The difference between the battles is that the Hares seem to have been ready to fight about anything, whereas love or jealousy always seems to have been at the root of fisticuffs in the Burke *ménage*.

As to North's remark about "prostitution", Helen MacDougal's life reflects the exact opposite. So far from seeking to recruit her income in such a fashion she seems to have fallen very violently in love with two and possibly three men and to have lived on devouring their affection of which she could never have too much proof, if we are to judge by the last case. She told the court in 1828 that she was thirty-three, had been born in Stirlingshire, and was unmarried. One of the strangest things about her is that we may not know her real name. Scottish courts are normally careful to the point of pedantry in referring to women's names, with all variations in nomenclature throughout life being accounted for, *vide* Burke and Helen MacDougal being indicted for murder of "Madgy or Margery or Mary M'Gonegal or Duffie, or Campbell, or Docherty", but Helen MacDougal was only indicted under that name, and our information is that MacDougal was in fact the name of the first man with whom she had lived. Buchanan's edition of the trial asserted that her name was Dougal, possibly arising from further confusion. MacDougal was a sawyer, and apparently had a wife living, and Helen's children of him were therefore doomed to remain illegitimate without even the cover of a subsequent marriage of parents. MacDougal ultimately died, after which Helen may have entered on another common-law marriage. If so, she left that man for Burke. She had not moved far from her birthplace in Redding, near Polmont, save for a brief period in Leith during which MacDougal died of typhus; Helen then returned to Maddiston, near Polmont, where Burke was at work on the canal. She would then have been about twenty-three. And from Maddiston they travelled together to Peebles, Leith and ultimately Tanner's Close, under the friendly roof whose proprietors were William and Margaret Hare.

The local priest at Maddiston is said to have told Burke to leave

Helen MacDougal and return to his wife in Ireland; that Burke
refused and was therefore "excommunicated". But there was no
local priest in Maddiston. Edinburgh, with 14,000 Catholics, was
then served by only four priests. If Burke really was told to choose
between the church and Helen MacDougal, it must have been there,
and probably happened in confession. Burke, having removed to
Edinburgh, is said to have lodged in a house known as "The Beggar's
Hotel" under the proprietorship of one Mickey Culzean, when it
was destroyed by fire with the loss of all the possessions of Burke and
Helen MacDougal. These possessions apparently included a number
of books acquired by Burke, among them Ambrose's *Looking Unto
Jesus*, Boston's *Fourfold State*, Bunyan's *Pilgrim's Progress* and Booth's
Reign of Grace, and commentators assumed that these originally
emanated from Helen MacDougal "for they are all of the kind
affected in most Scottish homes of the period". But it was Burke who
would have read the books — Helen MacDougal was illiterate and if
the books came from her they must have been the property of the
deceased sawyer which she simply acquired with the rest of his
personal possessions at the time of his death. Burke seriously seems to
have sought a further basis for unity with Helen by looking closely at
her church, perhaps because his own had been closed to him. Once
bereft of the books, he took to attending services in a house near
Culzean's new premises in Brown's Close, off the Grassmarket. He
also did some lay preaching on his own. Burke was ecumenical, but
to have been so fully cut off from his own religious roots could have
been productive of tensions and sense of personal guilt, which gave
more incentive to both his religious search and his private fighting
with Helen MacDougal. If Burke had been driven to the conviction
that he was certain of damnation for continuing to live with the love
of his life it might partly account for his acceptance of the role of
murderer. He had only one soul to lose, and if it was lost, it was lost.
In one respect Burke's ecumenism and attempt to enter the
theological world of Presbyterianism from which his Helen had
originated may have had serious side-effects for his peace of mind.
He had enjoyed attending Protestant services when in the militia, but
a harder look at Calvinism, coupled with the Irish Catholic
propensity to Jansenism, could have deepened in him a sense of being
predestined to damnation.

Meanwhile Burke was supporting himself largely as a cobbler and
Helen MacDougal was playing her part by hawking his wares on the
streets with such success as she could find. In summer, 1827, they
went back to work as agricultural labourers in the harvest at

Penicuik and were contemplating a move to the west when at the beginning of November they met Margaret Hare on the street. Burke had known her before. She suggested that they move in to her house in Tanner's Close, in the West Port, and that there was a cellar where he could work. Her husband, whom Burke did not know, kept his donkey in it, he now being a hawker. And thus at last Burke met Hare. Their acquaintance, outside of the courtroom, did not extend beyond a calendar year.

The person of Margaret Hare was in the fullness of time to be handled as roughly as that of Helen MacDougal by the literary talents of Christopher North and others; they were well advised to keep their violence to literature, for the lady had long shown her capacity to give more than as good as she got. North himself had a whiff of it in remarking that in comparison to Helen MacDougal, Mrs Hare "has most of the she-devil". Of the four she is perhaps the hardest to invest with dignity. Burke's gaiety and charm, Helen MacDougal's tortured love, Hare's bleak misanthropy give them individual tragic aspects, of which in a way Helen MacDougal's tragedy may be the greatest. "Let her live," said North viciously. "Death is one punishment, Life another." It certainly was, for her. Her guilt was the least of all, her love who had stood so gallantly by her had gone to his death to the yells of execration of 25,000, she herself was driven from Edinburgh to her home country in Stirling and thence back again and finally forced out of Northumberland. We last hear of her being stoned in Gateshead. Apparently Burke had hopes that his *Courant* confession would gain her some money but there is little indication that she ever got it. Charles II might hope that his attendants in his final hours would let not poor Nelly starve; Burke had no such reason for optimism.

But Margaret Hare introduces a freak note of black humour into the whole business which sets her apart from the others. There is pathos enough in her departure pursued by the mobs, bewailing her misfortune in having met Hare and demanding only a quiet retreat to her native place. Yet however unfortunate her situation it was preceded by attempts to save her own skin at the expense of everyone, to say nothing of holding her child at the ready "as if it were a bundle of rags", sneered North, "but now and then looking at it with that species of maternal fondness with which impostors sit on house-steps, staring at their babies, as if their whole souls yearned towards them — while no sooner have you passed by, than the angry beggar dashes its head, to make it cry better, against the pavement". (It is hardly surprising that North assumes anyone confronted with a beggar would pass her by.)

For all her efforts at pathos and her undoubted ill-treatment at the hands of the mob, she comes across from the first as a lady definitely knowing her own mind. Like the other three she was considerably given to drink, but the reasons for it are less obvious. Sir Walter Scott's point about the value of whisky to the poor labourers does not exactly apply. Margaret Hare was good for a heavy bout of labouring work, wheeling her barrow of stones with the best of her first husband's employees during the Union Canal days, but she acquired somewhat more means than they by her marriage to Logue. She was sensitive about her drinking. Hare at one point came from a day's work to find her far advanced in her cups and, said the reporter of Maclean's account, lay down on the bed from which injudicious point he commenced "remonstrating with her on the subject". She thereupon threw the contents of a bucket of water over him. He got up, knocked her down and they were off. But "as usual with her, she had the last word and the last blow". During her cross-examination she spoke "with an affectedly plaintive voice, 'gentle and low, an excellent thing in woman' ", jeered North, but she dropped it momentarily when the Lord Advocate somewhat tactlessly enquired, "Were you the worse of drink at the time?" "No, sir," shot back the lady, "I was not; I had a glass, but I was not the worse of it." The Lord Advocate retreated from the point somewhat hastily. Water may have been within reach of the witness, and there was, of course, the baby.

When Hare was working on the canal he first took up lodgings with James Logue who with his wife Margaret (often referred to by her intimates as Mary) kept a house "at the back of the well in the West Port". Logue is occasionally referred to as a labourer but in fact he seems to have been a capitalist in a small way, setting up a lodging house and getting labour contracts on the canal as far afield as Winchburgh. Logue was probably decidedly older than most of the actors in the drama and Margaret may also have been a little older. Certainly she behaved like it. Maclean was quoted as crediting her with "being a desperate character, and a most boisterous disposition, tyrannizing over those under her sway, or control — completely given to drink — often brutally so, and seldom without a pair of black eyes". The latter adornment seems to have been less likely in Logue's time, but there are grounds for suspicion that in his later years the lady found consolation among the lodgers. Logue seems to have been of a quiet disposition — which may account for so many of the authorities giving his name as "Log" — but at some point he quarrelled with William Hare to such an extent that that lodger took his departure. In view of the speed of Hare's marriage to Margaret after Logue's death it is reasonable to suppose that the husband may have been objecting to payments by the lodger in kind as well as in cash.

Logue's next action known to us is a decidedly suspicious one. He died. He may not have been young, but he was active. At this point Hare reappeared with a speed which suggests he had remained in touch with Margaret, and they were married. The question which nobody seems to have asked is whether Logue's decease was in fact a natural one. In the circumstances there must be doubt about the matter. Oddly enough the general readiness to throw every possible and impossible crime against the Hares after their arrest and, still more, their release, did not extend to the raising of questions on the manner in which Hare won his kingdom, and a kingdom it was, with seven beds and a fixed, regular income from an unceasing supply of tenants. Hare must have found it a pleasant change from his hawking. Despite the statements of MacGregor, Roughead and others, it is clear that he continued working: the donkey in the cellar is one proof of this, and the journey with Burke, Maclean and Helen MacDougal to the sheep-shearing is another. But it certainly made his life a more agreeable and secure one. Logue's death, so short a time before Hare began murdering on a wholesale level, seems curiously fortunate. It would also mean that Margaret can hardly have been innocent in the matter. Hare, exiled from his Eden, could only obtain access with the connivance of the lady. It certainly would explain why Hare turned so readily to murder in 1828 if he had already used it to considerable advantage two years earlier.

Suspicion becomes strengthened by the fact that a very large body of evidence swirls against Margaret Hare in the matter of the Burke and Hare murders themselves. It is true that Burke, in his most formal confession, sought to clear Margaret Hare as well as Helen MacDougal from complicity in and even knowledge of the murders, and that he put that confession as superior to the *Courant* one in point of reliability, but there is too much in the other direction. After all, while Burke had far less motive to exonerate Margaret Hare — she had certainly testified to the effect that he was a murderer and had also sought to throw suspicion on Helen MacDougal — he was a gentleman. Her own evidence, for a start, certainly suggested knowledge of what was going on. In particular when she was asked what she thought had become of the old woman Campbell, or Doherty, she replied: "I had a supposition that she had been

murdered", and added, to the great excitement of the public, "I have
seen such tricks before". Secondly, the *Courant* confession of Burke
makes some casual references which seem hard to imagine would
have been misunderstood by the reporter making notes, and which
seem consistent with a clear statement of recollection. The usual
Burke and Hare victims were down-and-outs and prostitutes, but the
most notable exception was "Daft Jamie", the West Port's version
of the village idiot. Village idiots usually have relatives, and he was
no exception. Moreover, he was well known. It was Hare's wife
whom Burke described as introducing him to the house — in his
original confession he says nothing as to who did it. The story is
reasonable. The selection of such a victim seems likely as the action
of someone who was not a normal protagonist in that matter. Burke's
account was that he was having a drink and saw her bring the boy to
the house, where he would have been left in Hare's charge. Then she
entered the shop where Burke was drinking, asked him to buy her a
dram "and in drinking it she stamped him on the foot. He knew
immediately what she wanted him for, and he then went after her".
It may have been the *Courant*'s man who improved Burke's account
with the words "Mrs Hare led poor Jamie in as a dumb lamb to the
slaughter, and as a sheep to the shearers", but it may not. Roughead,
accepting the authenticity of the lines, describes them as an example
of "the devil's ability to quote Scripture" and cites Burke's interest
in revivalist meetings in the Grassmarket; but in any case Burke had
been taking part in sheep-shearing as little as a few months before
Daft Jamie was murdered in October 1828.

Burke also explained in the same place that he was in the habit of
giving to Mrs Hare £1 of his half of the takings for the corpses "for
the use of the house, of all that were murdered in their house". He
could have simply told her that they were receivers of corpses as
opposed to murderers and an indignant landlady might need a *douceur*
because of the inconvenience and bad name which traffic on the
premises in human remains might give rise to. He maintained that
that was the story he had told Helen MacDougal. But the final
damning charge in his *Courant* confession was that Margaret Hare
often helped him and Hare pack the bodies in boxes. "Helen
MacDougal never did, nor saw them done; Burke never durst let her
know."

Why did Burke at first exonerate Margaret Hare and then tell a
series of stories which incriminated her almost casually? He may
have acquired some animus against her on reflection about her
testimony against him and her gratuitous references against Helen

MacDougal, and might have noticed how closely the stories of Hare, whom he now execrated as a traitor, agreed with those of his wife. So much had happened in the previous twelve months that it would take a little while for all of it to come back, and he might not at first have remembered Mrs Hare's murder suggestion against Helen MacDougal; this would now return as a reminder that there may have been a stronger undercurrent of personal hostility than he had allowed for. And he was strongly affected by a sense of particular guilt over Daft Jamie. He stated firmly that the principal agent in that murder was Hare. But Hare's account specifically made Burke the prime mover. Burke had little hope of any charity towards his memory, but he was anxious to do what he could to have that case given its proper perspective. Roughead, no friend of Burke's, accepts his version above that of Hare, and it does account for a murder so alien to Burke's normal methods of operation. Accordingly, he implicated Mrs Hare, but without signs of the deep anger he felt towards her husband. He had liked her. That earlier acquaintance between them does not mean that Burke, too, had enjoyed her sexual favours during Logue's absence or after his decease. But Margaret Hare may well have found him attractive. She may have invited him to live in the house with thoughts of an alternative to Hare, as she had previously found Hare an alternative to Logue. From this standpoint she had every motive to resent Helen MacDougal's possessiveness towards Burke. There may have been more at stake than mere security in that suggestion of murdering Helen: Margaret Hare was much less security-conscious than either Burke or Hare, as the line about seeing such tricks before goes to show. Indeed, had Burke complied Hare himself might not have been immune. Margaret Hare might well have contrasted the charm and consideration of Burke with the morose brutishness of Hare; and her affections were changeable. (There even seems to have been another, unnamed lodger, who took over the courtesies required by her between Hare's quarrel with Logue and his formal return to marry her.)

It can be argued that Hare, if not his wife, did show consistency in his affection towards her, although their years of married life together were to be few. But the case is much less clear-cut than that of Burke and Helen MacDougal. Hare had an economic stake in marrying Margaret, just as he had a security stake in defending her in his evidence. Were he to betray her, she would betray him, and he had far more on which to be betrayed. Certainly their conduct towards one another after release was very different to that of Burke and Helen. When they were separated Burke prayed for Helen, hoping that God would help her to turn away from evil — or so his auditors rendered it, his meaning being most likely evil temptations and an evil environment. And she clamoured to see him to say goodbye. But Hare, once he had made his escape, set forth on the road from Carlisle without another thought for his wife and family that anyone knew. And Mrs Hare set sail for Ireland in the hope that she might never see him again. Lonsdale's *Knox* alone assumes that the Hares both returned to Ireland together, but since they most certainly did not, the possibility of a later reunion can be discarded as far as credence of that authority is concerned. It deserves notice only as a clue to Lonsdale's own reliability in dealing with evidence, and as he is the foremost of Knox's defenders, the point is of some importance. His assurance that Helen MacDougal later lived in Australia (no doubt as a potential partner for Ned Kelly) can likewise compel little respect.

Margaret Hare was everything the Irishwoman in Scotland was supposed not to be. She was licentious, drunken, grasping, promiscuous, reckless and exploitative. The wife of the Irish emigrant is traditionally maternal, oppressed, pious and a model of sexual propriety. It is much less easy to make any case for Margaret Hare's defence than for those of the other actors. Even William Hare can claim to have been brutalised. We have little evidence suggesting she had been. But if she cannot be defended, it can at least be said of her that in a brutally male-dominant world she fought her corner and held her own. If she did little that was good, her strength of character, and her insistence on her rights and more, merit respect. Irishwomen had shown themselves models in endurance and submissiveness, and much good it did them. Margaret Hare summed up the realities of male rule, and fought it for all she was worth. In that sense she was a pioneer in women's liberation

Burke, Hare and
Immigrant Enterprise

"Glory be, whin business gets above sellin' tinpinny nails in a brown
paper cornucopy, 't is hard to tell it fr'm murther."
—Finley Peter Dunne, "On Wall Street",
Mr Dooley's Opinions

WE naturally tend to assume a majestic economic progress over
the vastness of centuries from nomadism to settled farming to
urbanisation; Burke and Hare remind us that nomadism continued
into the industrial revolution, was in many respects intensified by it,
and was part of the process of early nineteenth-century urbanisation
itself. The very nature and psychology of navvying and the
movement of location it induced meant that the bulk of the migrant
industrial work force would be encouraged to maintain a nomadic
outlook in any event. But the lives of Burke and Hare and of their
victims within Edinburgh all point to nomadic life and outlook
within the city. Hare's establishment was more than a mere
flophouse, but tenants seem to have been highly mobile; when Burke
himself obtained a house — for what was legally to have been a brief
period but one which nevertheless exceeded the remainder of his life
— the same thing obtained. Casual work might draw them away
from Edinburgh for months at a time, whether in the business of
canal transport — Hare did a little boatmanship in addition to his
hawking — or in the harvesting or shearing time. Social and even
blood relationships seemed to rise, intensify and vanish, only to
reappear after years of inactivity. Burke found his brother Con
before him in Edinburgh, complete with wife and family and
supporting them as best he could on earnings as a scavenger in the
employ of the Edinburgh police; the carter John Brogan whose
father's house was used for murder and subsequently taken over by
Burke, was described by Burke as a cousin of his; a cousin and a
daughter of the late MacDougal both appeared during the lifetime of
Burke and Hare business activity, the former to play the role of
victim (probably the twelfth) and the latter of witness in the last

murder; and to cap everything the rumour tore around Edinburgh during the trial that Hare's mother and sister had arrived in town to visit the head of the Scottish branch of their house only to learn that he was, in the fullest sense, helping the police with their enquiries into the most famous Scottish mass murders since the massacre of Glencoe, and the most famous outside legal auspices since Sawney Bean. No doubt Hare had a mother but her fortuitous appearance and her still more unaccountable disappearance (her son being in no position to offer Oresteian welcomes at that point) suggest yet another artefact of Ben Trovato, the most overworked contributor to the Edinburgh press during the trials. But the other cases are perfectly well attested to, and are instructive. In so nomadic a society ties of kinship were important when they came to notice. Burke would use them, notably in the case of the old lady Campbell or Docherty, his last victim, such that he might more easily draw her into the net. The old lady seems to have looked on the claim of relationship as a necessary form of legitimisation of so casual an acquaintanceship, however much of an obvious joke the claim might be. On the other side Burke was very quick to defend Brogan, who was briefly arrested with the others, and Brogan's evidence did nothing to incriminate his cousin (apart from agreeing with other witnesses that he was chucking whisky around in a manner that was afterwards to be identified with possible anxiety to dispel the odour of a concealed corpse). Brogan's father's earlier departure, possibly to Glasgow, and Burke's assumption of his house could have been because he had begun to have suspicions and wished to save both his neck from the law and his body from his cousin; but the son said nothing which would have given the jury that impression. The most notable assertion of the significance of kinship ties is that made by Burke in the *Courant* confession. He quoted himself as telling Hare "that he would have most to do to" Ann MacDougal "as she being a distant friend, he did not like to begin first on her". It is easy to sneer at the delicacy of this, a delicacy which was of little use to poor Ann. Yet it is worthy of the notice of the sociologist. You are entitled to hold down the legs of your mistress's deceased lover's cousin while Hare is stifling her unconscious and alcoholised person; but it is taboo to perform the stifling yourself. And Burke, of course, was not suggesting he was any the better man for not having done the major task; on the contrary he seems to have been grateful to Hare for obliging him. He just found it hard to do so personally. At least it merits notice in a thesis on kinship ties among nomads in urban structures during the industrial revolution.

The nomadic aspect is emphasised among the victims. After the murders had been disclosed the press was quick to speak of a long history of anxiety about mysteriously vanished persons but in fact there seems little sign of anything of the kind. It was important that at a time when Burke and Hare seemed to have shown the threadbare character of the garment called civilisation which men use to clothe the naked body of savagery, every possible attempt at self-reassurance be made. Hence it was better to say that the disappearances had not happened without remark. But, particularly where the nomads were concerned, little was heard of them. And most were nomads. The business of hawking was widespread and even old people came from long distances to get money from the city where the pickings would be better than in their own villages or hamlets. One of the earliest victims was staying in Hare's overnight having come down from Gilmerton — a good four miles even on today's roads. A curious case which will occupy much of our attention involved an old woman and her grandson both having come from Glasgow. The Hares were apparently their first, and certainly their last, port of call in Edinburgh. Points of origin often seemed to fix a victim in Burke's recollection in a way a name did not.

The murders present a picture of all sorts of people wandering in and out of Edinburgh, in many cases with nobody to know whether they were dead or alive and with anyone who might care, far away. The business of urban growth meant less, and not more organisation, and brought mankind nearer to, instead of farther from, the jungle. Class structures were hardening and the middle and upper classes found they had quite enough to do in protecting themselves without considering the protection of the lower classes. In any case, the industrial and living conditions to which the workers were reduced drew little interest from the better classes — save insofar as they won comments of ridicule or disgust — so why should their lives be? Health was a matter of concern when there was a possibility that contagious diseases might spread to the upper and middle classes, but not particularly in other circumstances. In fine, the industrial revolution had murdered so many workers that Burke and Hare might well murder a few more without exciting particular comment.

Where the two men did run into difficulty was when they selected victims who for certain reasons had attracted the attention of the "better" classes — specifically the reasons of prostitution and idiocy. Carnal knowledge and contemptuous amusement were both avocations of the well-to-do and hence, despite the nomadic

character of their existences, Mary Paterson and Daft Jamie were
unwise victims to have chosen. The nomad is normally faceless to the
better classes but where some sort of performance is involved, the
nomad gets a face. This last would be even more true of the more
settled members of the working-class population, but on the West
Port it was difficult to determine how far anyone was settled. Even
house ownership meant very little promise of long stay — as was
shown in Brogan's case — and even without Burke and Hare around
life expectancy was not good. We could sum the thing up by saying
the condition of the Edinburgh immigrants could be best thought of
if one compares them to tinkers trapped in an urban environment.
Most were illiterate—Burke was exceptional here—many were
bellicose, finding welcome solace and oblivion in drink, some were
not originally Anglophone and among themselves they evolved a
new and vigorous vocabulary of slang and cant. Burke himself seems
to have pioneered the word "shot" for a corpse — Hare said in
testimony, "He said this many a time when he had no thought of
murdering", so presumably it did not mean purely corpses initially
serviced by Burke and Hare — and of course it was from that
populace that the word "burke" itself roared into being.

The existence of these nomads naturally insured that the ethnic
origin of the victims would be as varied as a specialist in racial
theories of anatomy would desire. However, the special advantage
being Irish gave to Burke and Hare naturally ensured that pride of
place would go to their own countrymen. In this they differed only in
degree from the innumerable Irish who would infest ports and cities
throughout the nineteenth century there to leech on their gullible
fellow-Irish, whether as political bosses, con-men, slum profiteers,
sweated labour contractors, tommy-shop operators, paymasters
handing out wages in pubs, publicans paying paymasters to do so,
protection racketeers, and straight honest-to-God swindlers.
Certain priests, whatever their intentions, became little more than
exploiters. In the matter of Irish migrants growing wealthy by
trading on the bodies of other Irish migrants, Burke and Hare are
anything but an unrepresentative sample: they are the symbol for an
age. As a symbol, their work simply achieves a greater dramatic
force. If you were Irish you were particularly bidden into that
parlour, there really was a welcome there for you.

The houses of Burke and Hare throw useful light on the dwelling
arrangements among the nomads and there is no questioning their
representative character. Thomas Ireland's *West Port Murders*
described Tanner's Close as "dirty, low [and] wretched". "The

outer apartment is large, and was all round occupied by wretched beds; one room opening from it is also large for such a place, and was furnished in the same manner. So far from any concealment being practiced, the door generally stood open, and we have mentioned above that the windows were overlooked by the passengers in the close; but there is a small inner appartment or closet, the window of which looks only upon a pig-sty and dead wall, into which it is asserted they were accustomed to conduct their prey to be murdered."

Ireland's account is clear enough as to the tenement overcrowding where Burke lived.

> "The room is small, and of an oblong form; the miserable bed occupied nearly one end of it. . . . For some days after the trial everything remained in the position in which it had been when they were arrested, and presented a disgusting picture of squalid wretchedness; rags and straw, mingled with implements of shoemaking, and old shoes and boots in such quantities as Burke's nominal profession of a cobbler could never account for. A pot full of boiled potatoes was a prominent object. The bed was a coarse wooden frame without posts or curtains, and filled with old straw and rags. At the foot of it, and near the wall was the heap of straw under which the woman Campbell's body was concealed. The window looks into a small court, closed in by a wall."

It may be remarked that Ireland, and all later commentators, have chosen to assume that Burke and Hare were idlers who resorted to murder because of congenital laziness. As Sir Walter Scott pointed out to Maria Edgeworth, and as any sensible student of Irish migration will at once confirm, the Irish migrants showed enormous industry when they could get work, and Burke and Hare worked physically far harder in the course of their lives than any of their commentators can have done. Even when they embarked on the lucrative business of murder Burke was still regularly working as a cobbler — Ireland's evidence gives the lie to his own assumption of idleness — and Hare was certainly working as boatman or hawker up to very near the end, the murders happening when he had returned home after his diurnal labours. Maclean makes it perfectly clear that the shearing at Carnwath, on the farm of one Mr Edington, took place during the summer of 1828, and it featured Burke, Hare and Helen MacDougal. The problem is of course that Ireland, like all subsequent commentators, found his socio-economic ethics offended by the thought that Burke and Hare were actually members of the deserving poor, particularly that they were industrious, enterprising and assiduous in their pursuit of honest work. After all, it is not an easy thought that Burke and Hare resorted to murder, not because they were economic wastrels and dodgers, but because they were economic activists, innovators and producers. They were, in fact, excellent examples of immigrant enterprise whose ultimate business diligently answered the needs of the host culture and who adapted their own skills to meet the demands which the host culture let them know existed.

The outlines of the story are clear enough. For reasons that will become clear it is necessary to rely largely on the two confessions of Burke for they contradict one another very little. At the beginning of November Helen and he met Margaret Hare and had a dram with her — in alcoholic matters the speech of Burke and Hare had readily adapted itself to the host culture — and had become the Hares' tenants in consequence. Burke lived there continuously, being at work as a cobbler; Hare was out most days hawking or in boatman's work on the canal; Helen MacDougal was also out, hawking Burke's shoes. On November 29, an aged pensioner, Donald by name, departed this life by natural causes on the premises of Mr and Mrs Hare. (Burke put the event later, as being near Christmas, but Lonsdale's *Knox* opts firmly for November 29 and, as Roughead says, Lonsdale may have had Knox's records on which to base himself.) The deceased died of "a dropsy", according to Burke, and, in the way in which lodgings were let in that kind of nomads' world, he had been living on credit, for he drew a pension quarterly. Hare — or, more likely, Margaret Hare — had been generous to the old man: the sum owed was as much as £4. Clearly, he had been lent money in addition to being put up rent free until quarter-day — with beds at 4d. per person £4 would have taken care of his rent from the previous Christmas, which is incompatible with quarter-day payments. It is fair to the Hares to say that their kindness really looked like costing them dear. They were trying to carry on a business on humane terms, and now they were to pay for that economic sin.

It was none of Burke's business, but he liked to be on good terms with people, he was friendly with Margaret Hare, and he was at least prepared to leave his cobbling aside to lend a sympathetic ear while Hare made moan about how near they were to quarter-day and that if Donald had only been able to hold out until then, all would have been well. In his official confession Burke says that it was a day or two after Donald's death that Hare and himself had what proved to be the most momentous conversation to date in either of their lives. In proof of this was the fact that the coffin was about to arrive —

Donald was being buried "on the parish". It is important to notice that Hare's initial action was to inform the authorities so as to get the expense of a funeral, at least, off his hands. It is necessary to stress this as Burke and Hare are so widely associated with resurrectionism. Parish after parish in the lowland regions has its stories of graveyards plundered by Burke and Hare. Watch-towers are described as being erected near cemeteries after the revelations during the legal proceedings in the matter of Burke and Hare. At the time not only the newspapers but the magazines filled their columns with the fruits of rumour: thus the *New Scots Magazine* of January 1829 explained that Burke had been "engaged in the trade of a resurrectionist" while employed upon the canal "and practised it more or less". But Burke in his *Courant* confession explained that he had told Helen MacDougal that he was buying dead bodies and selling them to the doctors in partnership with Hare during 1828 "and that was the way they got the name of ressurection-men", and in his final official confession, in the presence of the sheriff-substitute, the procurator-fiscal, the assistant sheriff-clerk and Father William Reid, he declared that "neither he nor Hare, so far as he knows, ever were concerned in supplying any subjects for dissection except those before mentioned; and, in particular, never did so by raising dead bodies from the grave". He had absolutely no reason to lie; he did want Hare to receive punishment for what he had done, and if he could justly have fixed the crime of resurrectionism around his neck, he would have done; and he had, after all, confessed to fifteen murders, so why on earth should he deny activity in a lesser crime? Yet the legend has persisted, error even invading the awful majesty of the printed manuscript catalogue of the National Library of Scotland where he is identified as "resurrectionist".

So far was the thought of resurrectionism from the minds of either Burke or Hare that the opportunity of recouping Hare's losses by the sale of Donald's body was nearly let slip. The coffin was at the door. Then, and only then, did the idea of selling the body come up. Burke attributes it to Hare. Hare in his lost confession may have attributed it to Burke — Sheriff Duff and Sir Walter Scott, both of whom saw that document, mention that Hare attributed to Burke much that the latter in his post-trial confessions ascribed to Hare. The balance of probability seems to rest with Burke, given his acquaintance with the medical fraternity in Ballina; this certainly was the reason why he undertook the negotiations with the doctors from the first, taken together with his literacy and superior address over Hare. But of course Hare could have heard gossip about the resurrectionist traffic which at this juncture was reaching roaring heights. Both of the Irishmen would have been interested in the stories of importation of corpses from their native land. Boats from Dublin were being evacuated by the passengers at the first opportunity because of the stench. The poverty and over-population of Ireland resulted in a system of export to Britain tacitly permitted by the authorities. Burke may well have heard of the resurrection business as a boy growing up on the Tyrone border.

The resurrectionist business was associated with every form of crime and blackguardism as any reader of Stevenson's "The Body Snatcher" or Mark Twain's *The Adventures of Tom Sawyer* can bear witness. As Dr Robinson found out to his cost, and Huck Finn and Tom Sawyer to their horror, the illegality of the business left the medics open to extortion, assault and even murder; and Stevenson raises the ugly question that so active an association with criminals could lead a blackmailed sawbones to do a little burking on his own account. But even if Hare had previously been a murderer he gave no sign of any personal knowledge of resurrectionism. Whoever had the idea, had it belatedly. Recollection of gossip would take a little time to surface, especially if it was a matter of Burke remembering childhood stories or anecdotes in the Ballina hospital eighteen years before.

They stood by as the parish representatives delivered the coffin and nailed down the subject, after which Hare started operations on the lid with a chisel. Burke in his *Courant* confession says that it was he who removed from the coffin what was from Hare's viewpoint the very dear departed, and the body was then hidden in the bed. Burke and Hare then ran out of the house, got tanner's bark from behind it, brought it in, put it in the coffin and nailed it down, inserting a sheet over the bark, and the coffin was taken away and interred in the West Church Yard with such solemnity as the parish accorded to these affairs.

"Hare did not appear to have been concerned in anything of the kind before, and seemed to be at a loss how to get the body disposed of," said Burke in his first official confession. So Burke let his good nature take him further, and Hare would seem to have made an arrangement that if Burke took command of the affair, he would get a generous cut. They "went in the evening to the yard of the College" — that is to say, Old College, around which thousands would fight to get a look at Burke's own dissected corpse in little more than a year. They "saw a person like a student there". Burke asked the boy "if there were any of Dr Monro's men about, because

he did not know there was any other way of disposing of a dead body
— nor did Hare". Where had Burke heard of Dr Monro? Or did he
simply ask for the Professor of Anatomy? It was the action of a
person of intellect rather than of experience, at all events. Great
ironies turned on the next exchanges. Had the young man been
content to give Burke directions, Professor Alexander Monro's man
would doubtless have taken delivery. Monro might have been
something of a fraud battening on the reputations of his father and
still more of his grandfather but he needed corpses as urgently as
anyone else. He had no chance of maintaining an intake of students
without subjects for dissection. And had Monro been the recipient,
he would no doubt have been the receiver for all of the future output
of Messrs Burke and Hare. There were reasons, which we will
explore, as to why Knox did not ask questions; but Monro would
have been silent out of sheer stupidity. It was pure chance — and an
ironic testimony to Knox's and the Professor's contrasting
reputations among students — that Monro was not cast for the
villainous role which Knox was afterwards to sustain in the mind of
the public and the mob. Yet if the law were to treat him as it treated
Knox, no power could have prevented his receiving Burke's hanged
body for dissection and by law he, and only he, would have had to
dissect it. At that point Old College would be lucky to remain
standing with a mob fighting, not only for admission, but to add the
dissector's corpse to that of his subject. The unknown student must
have thought himself to be doing Knox a minor favour; he was in fact
wrecking Knox's career, prolonging Monro's and possibly saving the
University from the worst crisis in its existence.

   "The young man asked what they wanted with Dr Monro, and the
declarant told him that he had a subject to dispose of, and the young
man referred him to Dr Knox, No. 10, Surgeon Square." Burke and
Hare continued their travels and reached the address where they saw
"young gentlemen". Burke would later learn that these were Knox's
assistants Thomas Wharton Jones, Alexander Miller, and William
Fergusson, who would ultimately obtain a knighthood. Again, he
explained that he had a subject. They became very businesslike in one
direction, and very reticent on another. They "did not ask how they
had obtained it" which Burke was, of course, perfectly ready to
answer truthfully; he may not have adverted much to this at the time,
but he would remember it later. No doubt it confirmed his earlier
observation of low medical ethics. What they did tell Burke and
Hare was to "come back when it was dark" and said that they
themselves would find a porter to carry it. Whether Burke and Hare

felt that all this running between the West Port and Surgeons' Square was becoming tedious, or whether they did not want a porter in the employ of such fine young gentlemen to see their wretched quarters, is difficult to determine: but they gave the porter no work at this juncture. They returned with the body in a sack. Uncertain about delivery arrangements, they left it discreetly at the cellar door and returned to their new friends. However, they were invited to introduce the late Donald without further ceremony, did so, laid him out on the dissecting table, and awaited comment. Again, Burke then or later was to be struck by what was not said as much as what was. Donald still had a shirt on his back "but the young men asked no questions as to that", simply requesting that it be removed. This Burke and Hare did, the young men apparently leaving matters to them on the ground that it was still legally their corpse. At this point the doctor made his entrance, looked at the remains, named £7 10s. as a price and told Jones "to settle with them". As with the men, so with the master: the intellectual, Burke was realising, did not concern himself with irrelevancies. Knox "asked no questions as to how the body had been obtained". The money seems to have been given to Burke — Hare would say in court that he never received money directly and though we know that that statement was untrue for the one instance where he would act alone, there is no reason to assume that Burke would not otherwise remain the active agent in all negotiations. They may or may not have divided the money in the presence of the doctors, but it seems more likely that they waited to do so until they had left. In the presence of so much medical discretion it would have been tactless to start discussing the bases of their individual claims. In any event Hare got his £4, and an additional 5s., and Burke received the balance which, while smaller, gave him a clear profit of £3 5s. It was not a bad return for what had begun as an exercise in gratuitous psychological support. The Hares made hardly anything from the transaction, apart from collecting a debt that had looked irredeemably bad. Nevertheless, there was no doubt a wild time in the West Port that night. It is reasonable to assume that Burke talked pretty freely of his adventures to Helen MacDougal, and this would be consistent with any later stories he told her about becoming an entrepreneur in the resurrectionist business. Mrs Hare also would have to be told of her swain's cleverness in sparing her the loss of their loan to the deceased. And Burke would remember that Jones bade him farewell with the interesting words "that they would be glad to see them again when they had any other body to dispose of".

Burke had noted the urgency of demand, and his quick mind could contrast the transformation of the corpse from the incubus of the morning to the purveyor of golden eggs at night. There is no reason to believe that he went farther at that time than the reflection that Donald's fate might in the course of nature overtake others enjoying the amenities of the Hare hostelry. What seems to have struck him forcibly, though, was that where Hare and himself had reason to believe the doctors might take the corpse off their hands with some compensation, the reception they had obtained had surpassed their wildest expectations. The doctor himself had been businesslike and generous; Jones and Co. had been positively voracious in their anxiety to welcome both it and any possible successors. It seems likely that the thought occurred to Burke that the doctors might have taken them to have murdered Donald. It is always somewhat annoying to suspect that a legitimate transaction is interpreted as having an illegal origin about which everyone is remaining politely silent. Burke and Hare do not seem to have volunteered the information that their behaviour had been strictly legal; in all fairness Hare really was owed the money and was entitled to the proceeds of the Donald estate, and since the only asset in that proved to be the unwitting testator himself, all was in order. But both Burke and Hare came from a part of Ireland where the tradition was to "pass no remarks" which might produce unwanted complications, and they came from a caste which had bitterly learned the dangers of undue loquacity under the weight of an uncertainly enforced savage penal code.

Why did Jones, Miller and Fergusson make such a display of their hunger for corpses? Sir Walter Scott explained part of the problem in his great letter to Maria Edgeworth:

> ... the horrors which you have so well described ... resemble nothing so much as a wild dream. Certainly I thought, like you, that the public alarm was but an exaggeration of vulgar rumour; but the tragedy is too true, and I look in vain for a remedy of the evils, in which it is easy to see this black and unnatural business has found its origin. The principal source certainly lies in the feelings of attachment which the Scotch have for their deceased friends. They are curious in the choice of their sepulchre, and a common shepherd is often, at whatever ruinous expense to his family, transported many miles to some favourite place of burial which has been occupied by his fathers. It follows, of course, that any interference with these remains is considered with most utter horror and indignation. To such of their superiors as they love from clanship or habits of dependence, they attach the same feeling. I experienced it when I had a great domestic loss [Lady Scott had died in

1826]; for I learned afterwards that the cemetery was guarded, out of goodwill, by the servants and dependants who had been attached to her during life; and were I to be laid beside my lost companion just now, I have no doubt it would be long before my humble friends would discontinue the same watch over my remains, and that it would incur mortal risk to approach them with the purpose of violation. This is a kind and virtuous principle, in which every one so far partakes, that, although an unprejudiced person would have no objection to the idea of his own remains undergoing dissection, if their being exposed to scientific research could be of the least service to humanity, yet we all shudder at the thought of any one who had been dear to us, especially a wife or sister, being subjected to a scalpel among a gazing and unfeeling crowd of students. One would fight and die to prevent it. This current of feeling is encouraged by the law which, as distinguishing murderers and other atrocious criminals, orders that their bodies shall be given for public dissection. This makes it almost impossible to consign the bodies of those who die in the public hospitals to the same fate; for it would be inflicting on poverty the penalty which, wisely or unwisely, the law of the country has denounced against guilt of the highest degree; and it would assuredly deprive all who have a remaining spark of feeling or shame, of the benefits of those consolations of charity of which they are the best objects. If the prejudice be not very liberal, it is surely natural, and so deeply seated that many of the best feelings must be destroyed ere it can be eradicated. What then remains? The only chance I see is to permit importation from other countries. If a subject can be had in Paris for ten or twenty francs, it will surely pay the importer who brings it to Scotland. Something must be done, for there is an end of the *Cantabit vacuus*, the last prerogative of beggary, which entitled him to laugh at the risk of robbery. [*Cantabit vacuus coram latrone viator*. — Juvenal. The empty traveller — i.e. the traveller with empty pockets — will sing in front of the thief.] The veriest wretch in the highway may be better booty than a person of consideration, since the last may have but a few shillings in his pocket, and the beggar, being once dead, is worth ten pounds to his murderer.

It is in fact Scott who reached the heart of the next problem: what led Burke and Hare to move to what Professor Philip Curtin has termed "more direct methods" than those of the resurrectionists and the work of nature which had rewarded them in Donald's case? Hare's confession, made to the authorities on 1 December 1828 in order to form the basis of turning King's evidence against Burke, has since disappeared. But Sir Walter evidently saw it and his comment gives the best explanation yet offered as to why Burke and Hare took up murder at all. He had been sent a copy of the *Edinburgh Advertiser* with the first published text of Burke's official confession and he wrote to his friend, John Stevenson, who was assisting in the preparation of the report of the trial he subsequently co-published with Robert Buchanan. Scott had probably been shown the Hare document by one of his friends, most likely by Sir William Rae, the Lord Advocate, who had stayed at Abbotsford shortly after entering office; Stevenson, with much lower official connections, would not have seen it. Scott was kindly advising in the light of his own special knowledge. Buchanan, Hunter and Stevenson would print the letter as a footnote to their text without indicating its authorship. Sir Walter wrote on 7 February 1829:

> Dear John—I return the paper. There is a slip in which Burke's confession differs from that of Hare. They give the same account of the number and the same description of the victims, but they differ in the order of time in which they were committed. Hare stated with great probability that the body of Joseph, the miller, was the second sold (that of the old pensioner being the first), and, of course, he was the first man murdered. Burke, with less likelihood, asserts the first murder to have been that of a female lodger. I am apt to think Hare was right, for there was an additional motive to reconcile them to the deed in the miller's case — the fear that the apprehensions entertained through the fever would discredit [the house], and the consideration that there was, as they might [think], less harm in killing a man who was to die at any rate. It may be worth your reporter's while to know this, for it is a step in the history of the crime. It is not odd that Burke, acted upon as he seems always to [have been] by ardent spirits, and involved in a constant succession of murther, should have misdated the two actions. On the whole, Hare and he, making separate confessions, agree wonderfully.—Yours, W. Scott.

We can take the point slightly further. The murder Burke assigned to the first position was in fact that of the first victim who was not dying or dangerously ill; hence to a man facing death it was the first really heavily on his conscience. Therefore he thought of it first. Then in adding up his totals he had to account for seventeen, and Joseph the miller and the other ailing victim, the Englishman from Cheshire, slipped in at an early stage. He was to contradict himself slightly on the point of their deaths in the succession of murders, as between his official and his *Courant* confession. Burke and Hare did not jump into the murder racket on the apparent hint from the Knox boys; they drifted into it through grey moral areas.

There was plenty of danger of fever in Edinburgh — indeed Carlyle noted a bad outbreak of it coincident with Burke's execution. Ironically, as it continued to rage in the early 1830s the famine in subjects ceased, and the doctors no longer needed so much dubious assistance — fortunately for them in that the Burke and Hare revelations had very depressing effects on the resurrectionist

market. Joseph was well known to Hare and had apparently been
lodging with him for some time when he went down with fever. "He
had once been possessed of a good deal of money," Burke told the
Courant, and "was connected by marriage with some of the Carron
Company". But now, in the early weeks of 1828, they were far from
him. In the official confession Burke said that they had given Joseph
drink, but he was not "tipsy". Joseph was clearly dying, and at times
could not even speak. The Hares were definitely worried because the
fever case was being rumoured abroad, with the likelihood of
adverse effects. It was at this point that they seem to have told
themselves that Joseph was doomed in any case, that the
prolongation of his life would only give him unnecessary pain and
possibly risk economic injury to the Hares, and that he was better
dead. They may well have worried that his continued existence
might imperil theirs, or that of their womenfolk. One curious point is
that, on this logic, they did not murder Joseph for gain either; they
expected him to die, and were prepared to get their money then. The
first murder was motivated not by gain but by fear. It was
presumably Burke who realised the vital importance that death
should show no signs of violence and accordingly Burke obtained a
"small pillow and laid it across Joseph's mouth, and Hare lay across
the body to keep down the arms and legs". This again points to
Scott's being absolutely right about the order: later, they would
resort to stifling with the open hand, but the use of the pillow
suggests that the work at this point was new to them. The old woman
of Gilmerton, Burke's candidate for first murder victim in his
confessions, was murdered by hand alone. In any event there they
were with their corpse. But this time the porter was used, met them
at some point such as the back of the Castle — by arrangement made
by Knox's assistants — and took charge of the body, Burke and Hare
accompanying them to Surgeons' Square where they received £10.

A second infection scare arose with an Englishman from Cheshire
who was staying with Hare for a few nights and proved ill with
jaundice. "He was very tall," Burke told the *Courant,* "had black
hair, brown whiskers, mixed with grey hairs" and "used to sell
spunks in Edinburgh". Burke never discovered the man's name, but
said he "was about forty years of age". Presumably the man was very
debilitated with the jaundice; no other of their victims was a figure
of such size, or so obviously redolent of masculinity in its prime.
Who did the murder is unclear. Burke's official confession speaks of
the two of them getting "above him" and holding him down, "and
by holding his mouth suffocating him". The pillow was no longer

needed. They could do the job with less danger of losing hold on their victim, simply by getting the thumb under the chin and drawing the first two fingers quickly and firmly down over the nose, thus blocking the entry of air through the nostrils and keeping the mouth firmly closed. Burking had been invented. Knox once again gave them £10.

And now, at last we reach the old woman of Gilmerton. In his *Courant* confession Burke assigned her death to 12 February, which, if Scott is correct and inferences are sound, argues that the first two murders had happened in January or very early February. Abigail Simpson was her name. She was a pensioner of "Sir John Hay", thought Burke, which the *Courant* believed should be "Sir John Hope", but in fact her journey seems to have been made to sell salt and camstone, and not to collect the pension as Roughead supposed. As Burke recalled it the Hares "decoyed her in" — again, an action which suggests practice in the murder business before this case. "She had one shilling and sixpence and a can of kitchen-fee. Hare's wife gave her one shilling and sixpence for it; she drank it all with them." She was a "stranger", noted Burke's official confession, adding that "she and Hare became merry, and drank together"; the *Courant* version elaborates on this by saying that the old lady mentioned having a daughter so "Hare said he was a single man, and would marry her, and get all the money amongst them". This actually sounds more like Burke than Hare, and we have to allow for the possibility of transposition of their roles; Burke's anxiety to underline Hare's guilt might have resulted in such an action. But if Helen MacDougal were anywhere around during the time when the old lady was growing gracious with her hosts it would have gone very hard with William Burke should he show signs of wanting to marry anyone else. For Mrs Hare to stand by and accept it implies that she knew there were reasons for the declaration of matrimonial independence. In any case it is more likely that the Hares would have brought an intended victim home at this early stage in the partnership, and the lady would have played up to the person who had invited her in. So let us accept Burke's account and acknowledge that Hare could give some passable imitation of geniality when he put his mind to it. Well he might have done, given the generosity of the old lady to him. In any event, she agreed to stay the night "as she was so drunk she could not go home".

In the morning "she became very sick and vomited; and as at that time she had not risen from bed" Hare proposed terminal action. She was given "some porter and whisky" which "made her so drunk that she fell asleep on the bed. Hare then laid hold of her mouth and nose, and prevented her from breathing." Burke meanwhile "laid himself across her body, in order to prevent her making any disturbance — and she never stirred; and they took her out of bed and undressed her, and put her into a chest". An embassy was then sent to Knox's rooms in Surgeons' Square where "they mentioned to Dr Knox's young men that they had another subject" and it was on this occasion Alexander Miller took command. The porter was sent to meet them, and they accompanied him to the classroom with the chest. "Dr Knox came in when they were there; the body was cold and stiff." It was at this juncture that the doctor made the most memorable contribution among his occasional discourses to them: he "approved of its being so fresh, but did not ask any questions". He gave them £10 and sent them on their way, leaving them in no doubt that another nice fresh body from Burke's and Hare's emporium would find comparable pay and a happy home. The old lady "had on a drab mantle, a white-grounded cotton shawl and small blue spots on it. Hare took all her clothes", said Burke to the *Courant*, "and went out with them; said he was going to put them in the canal". Having dug it, he might as well put it to some use. Yet another point had been added to the methods of Burke and Hare: alcohol, which devoured so much of their profits, was now deployed into the business of providing the material whose selling price it would afterwards consume.

At this point the order becomes problematic. The confessions of Burke give up any real attempt to assign an order, and indeed retail events of a date anterior to those of other cases described previously. But one of the next cases, if not the next case, was one of the most celebrated. Mary Paterson was afterwards to be made a count in the original indictment against Burke but the count was dropped in circumstances to be noted later. Burke himself was very brief about it in both of his confessions, but there was an important witness to the origins of the murder. We will take Burke first. In his official confession he declared: "That in April 1828, he fell in with the girl Paterson and her companion in Constantine Burke's house, and they had breakfast together, and he sent for Hare, and he and Hare disposed of her in the same manner; and Mr Fergusson and a tall lad, who seemed to have known the woman by sight, asked where they had got the body; and the declarant said he had purchased it from an old woman at the back of the Canongate. The body was disposed of five or six hours after the girl was killed, and it was cold, but not very stiff, but he does not recollect of any remarks being made about the body being warm." The *Courant* confession adds little. She:

> "was murdered in Burke's brother's house in the Canongate . . . by
> Burke and Hare, in the forenoon. She was put into a tea-box, and
> carried to Dr Knox's dissecting-rooms in the afternoon of the same
> day; and got £8 for her body [the porter said it was £10]. She had
> twopence halfpenny, which she held fast in her hand. Declares that the
> girl Paterson was only four hours dead till she was in Knox's
> dissecting-rooms; but she was not dissected at that time, for she was
> three months in whisky before she was dissected. She was warm when
> Burke cut the hair off her head; and Knox brought a Mr ——
> [Oliphant], a painter to look at her, she was so handsome a figure, and
> well shaped in body and limbs. One of the students said she was like a
> girl he had seen in the Canongate as one pea is like another. They
> desired Burke to cut off her hair; one of the students gave a pair of
> scissors for that purpose."

And the note in Burke's own hand at the end of the *Courant* confession
adds "Burk deaclars that docter Knox never incoureged him, nither
taught nor incoregd him to murder any person, nether any of his
asistents, that worthy gentleman Mr Fergeson was the only man that
ever mentioned any thing about the bodies. He inquired where we got
that yong woman Paterson." Oliphant drew Mary Paterson's corpse
before dissection in the manner of the Rokeby Venus of Velasquez.

Burke had, perhaps, hesitated between business and pleasure when
he commenced the seduction of Mary Paterson. But he had made a
cardinal error. Her profession was older than his, in the words of the
cliché; it was the oldest in the world (Cain, presumably, being
relegated to amateur status). And her clients were much more
widely dispersed beyond the social barriers than he had realised.
Burke had failed to allow for the egalitarianism induced by sex. On
his showing in the confessions as many as three of the assistants and
students may have had previous carnal knowledge of Mary Paterson,
among them the future Sir William Fergusson. Stevenson, adapting
the scene for use in "The Body Snatcher", employs one of his
happiest euphemisms: "By a dozen unquestionable marks he
identified the girl he had jested with the day before". Yet for reasons
we will investigate in the next chapter Burke was able to rely on his
medical acquaintances' continued discretion. Lonsdale's account
states that "Burke on his next visit was confronted with his
questioner in the presence of two gentlemen" — presumably one of
the latter was Fergusson and the other may have been "the tall lad"
while the questioner seems likely to have been the student who said
she was as similar to the girl he had "seen" in the Canongate as one

pea to another, unless the enthusiast for horticultural analogy (in the *Courant* confession) was in fact the "tall lad" (of the official confession). In any event Burke dealt with the matter smoothly, retrieving his mistake as best he might; he "declared that he bought the corpse from an old hag in the Canongate, and that Paterson had killed herself with drink. He offered to go and show the house if they doubted him. His explanation was feasible; it rested on the whisky tendency of all such women — and Paterson's body smelt of liquor when brought in — their reckless life and exposure, and their frequent abandonment when at death's door." As we will see, the capacity of Knox and his associates to allow prejudiced generalisations to influence their judgment on the classes whence the victims of Burke and Hare came, was to prove one of the strongest cards the Irishmen held in their hands.

The evidence of Mary Paterson's friend Janet Brown was to have been given at Burke's trial, but when that count was set aside it remained for her only to communicate it to Ireland for his *West Port Murders*. Inevitably it thereby tended to show wisdom after the event. But the main contours are clear enough. Burke picked up both the girls and supplied them with whisky, one bottle each. Mary Paterson fell asleep at the breakfast-table, but Burke got Janet Brown away to a tavern. After they returned, Mary Paterson being still unconscious, they continued to drink when Helen MacDougal burst in, denounced Burke and Janet, and when Janet made it clear she had not known that Burke was "married", turned on Burke who finally threw a heavy glass at her with a resultant injury above her eye. Janet Brown left, Con Burke had gone to work, Mrs Con had hurried out to find Hare to soothe the disputants down, and Helen MacDougal disappears from the story still violently abusing Burke. As has been indicated, he was in no position to plead that faith unfaithful kept him falsely true, but that was in fact the position. The time was now about 10.00 a.m. When Hare appeared, he and Burke performed the murder. Janet Brown had sought refuge with a former landlady, Mrs Lawrie, who advised her to go and reclaim Mary Paterson. She found Burke gone — to make the preliminary arrangements at Surgeons' Square — and talked with the Hares unaware of the near presence of the corpse of her friend, whom her hosts represented as having gone out with Burke. Helen MacDougal was also present, cursing Burke for his dalliance with Mary Paterson. Roughead takes this to be duplicity; to me it seems that she believed what she said, and was also unaware of the presence of the body. Roughead's scenario assumes a genuine tirade to have been delivered by Helen MacDougal in the first instance, and a pretended one in the second. Janet Brown was not very bright, but Helen MacDougal hardly seems to have been an actress capable of dissimulation to such an extent. Eventually the Lawrie maidservant was sent to bring her back, and when she returned to the Con Burkes' once more, Mrs Con was there alone with no further news. Roughead believes that Mrs Lawrie's action may have saved Janet Brown's life; it seems perfectly reasonable. Mary Paterson's clothes were ultimately found at Hare's, when the four were arrested. When all was known Janet Brown voiced some suspicion of Con Burke but his behaviour is consistent with having been told a credible story by his brother, to wit that Mary Paterson "had gone off to Glasgow with a packman". Con Burke himself had other casual meetings with Janet Brown, but they were not of an erotic nature. When she enquired for her friend, Con replied, in her version, "How the hell can I tell about you sort of folk? You are here today and away tomorrow", and "I am often out upon my lawful business, and how can I answer for all that takes place in my house in my absence?". Janet Brown took this as proof of complicity, which she also ascribed to Mrs Con because of her behaviour on the day of the murder. But in fact their conduct is consistent with innocence. Con Burke had every reason to be annoyed with his wayward brother for inflicting quarrels with his womenfolk upon his own stable family. If Will was to pick up prostitutes in addition to flaunting a mistress, it would be well for the peace of the Con Burke household if he could arrange to have the resultant scenes elsewhere. Mrs Con was apparently told by William Burke to get Hare, on the occasion when she hurried from the house; this again would be natural as a means to stop the violent scene being caused by Helen MacDougal. And Con's remark about his own business and "you sort of folk" sounds more like a hardworking Irish husband's complaints about prostitutes than a guilty man's attempts to shuffle off his dark secret. Above all, Burke and Hare were intelligent, and knew perfectly well that the wider their terrible secret was spread the less chance there was of keeping it. In this connection it may be asked what Con ever gained from any complicity he might have had, apart from old clothes and perhaps some free drinks. And it is significant that when Burke was seeking, in his confessions, to exonerate his Nelly — who had, after all, been indicted and found not proven as distinct from not guilty — as well as seeking to clear Knox and his associates and, more vaguely, Mrs Hare, he never mentioned Mr and Mrs Con. He had, of course, to mention Helen MacDougal; but if he was aware that his brother and sister-in-law had been involved in

any of the murders he would surely have said a word to save them,
when he was so industriously trying to defend not only his beloved
Nelly but also Dr Knox and his associates who were linked to him by
no ties at all, and when he was even saying a word or two in defence
of Margaret Hare, who had done her bit to help hang him. His failure
to mention them suggests he did not think of them as involved in the
murders at all. The most one can say is that Con, like the doctors, had
learned not to ask too many questions, but in his case this would be a
salutary doctrine about disputes involving hysterical women when
much drink had been consumed.

The next case may be dealt with briefly. "In May 1828," says the
official confession, "an old woman came to the house as a lodger, and
she was the worse of drink, and she got more drink of her own
accord, and she became very drunk, and declarant suffocated her;
and Hare was not in the house at the time; and she was disposed of in
the same manner." Despite the discrepancy, this seems to be the same
case as that appearing as follows in the *Courant* version:

> "an old woman who lodged with Hare for óne night . . . was murdered
> in the same manner as above. Sold to Dr Knox for £10. The old woman
> was decoyed into the house by Mrs Hare in the forenoon from the
> street when Hare was working at the boats at the canal. She gave her
> whisky, and put her to bed three times. At last she was so drunk that she
> fell asleep; and when Hare came home to his dinner, he put part of the
> bed-tick on her mouth and nose, and when he came home at night she
> was dead. Burke at this time was mending shoes; and Hare and Burke
> took the clothes off her, and put her body into a tea-box. Took her to
> Knox's that night."

We now come to what may as well be termed "The Case of the
Broken Back", and it will take a little time, as the reputation of
scholarship on Burke and Hare over the last century depends on it.
Initially, we will return to Burke's confessions, lacking any from
Hare as we do. Burke assigned the case to midsummer 1828.
Roughead describes it as "one of the gang's most cruel crimes, which
from information obtained by Leighton we know in greater detail
than usual". Burke's official confession simply says that "a woman,
with her son or grandson, about twelve years of age, and who
seemed to be weak in his mind, came to the house as lodgers; the
woman got a dram, and when in bed asleep, he and Hare suffocated
her: and the boy was sitting at the fire in the kitchen, and he and Hare
took hold of him, and carried him into the room, and suffocated him.
They were put into a herring barrel the same night, and carried to
Dr Knox's rooms".

The *Courant* confession is merely an elaboration of this:

> "In June last, an old woman and a dumb boy, her grandson, from Glasgow, came to Hare's, and were both murdered at the dead hour of night, when the woman was in bed. Burke and Hare murdered her the same way as they did the others. They took off the bed-clothes and tick, stripped off her clothes, and laid her on the bottom of the bed, and then put on the bed-tick, and bed-clothes on top of her; and they then came and took the boy in their arms and carried him ben to the room, and murdered him in the same manner, and laid him alongside his grandmother. They lay for the space of an hour; they then put them into a herring barrel. The barrel was perfectly dry; there was no brine in it. They carried them to the stable till next day; they put the barrel into Hare's cart, and Hare's horse was yoked into it; but the horse would not drag the cart one foot past the Meal-market; and they got a porter with a hurley, and put the barrel on it. Hare and the porter went to Surgeon Square with it. Burke went before them, as he was afraid something would happen, as the horse would not draw them. When they came to Dr Knox's dissecting rooms, Burke carried the barrel in his arms. The students and them had hard work to get them out, being so stiff and cold. They received £16 for them both. Hare was taken in by the horse he bought that refused drawing the corpse to Surgeon Square, and they shot it in the tan-yard. He had two large holes in his shoulder stuffed with cotton, and covered over with a piece of another horse's skin to prevent them being discovered."

Firstly, there is no discrepancy in these accounts. Secondly, there are two points reflecting the strongest proof of authenticity for the *Courant* account, which in general is more open to question than the official one: Burke reveals a superstitious fear arising from the refusal of the horse to proceed, with the implication that it did not do so being because it scented foul play, and then he applies a rational reassessment of his own baseless terror by showing, with the professional interest of an Irish labourer coming from a nation of horse-dealers and their observers, that Hare had been swindled as to his horse's health by the horse-coper. The horse had been an investment to improve the transport of the product of their labour, and it also symbolised Hare's rise in the world from donkey-owner to horse-owner. But his moment of pretension was ill-based. This was not callousness in Burke. It underlines that under his diplomacy he was shaken by superstitious, and perhaps spiritual, fear, and that he also retained the hard peasant reaction to social questions of agrarian origin. Under the penal laws Irish Catholics had been forbidden to own a horse of value over £5, and horse-ownership thence derived *cachet*. The joke Brendan Behan was so fond of telling, that an Anglo-Irishman was "a Protestant on a horse", underlines the point, as indeed does the modern propensity of Irishmen rising in the socio-economic scale to take up horse-riding and send their daughters to riding-school. We may deduce that Hare may have made something about his new status in keeping a horse, and that Burke, after he had seen the ludicrous reality behind his sudden terror, was grimly amused at the sudden descent of that grandeur.

A shrewd reader might also deduce that the detail in Burke's account showed that he had been shaken by the murder of the boy. It is true that children of that age were often fed whisky, especially when in the charge of nomadic parents or guardians, and it is therefore probable that he was yet another alcoholically stupefied victim. Such trappings of humanity as normally attached themselves to the principle of euthanasia under anaesthesia were not entirely absent. But he may have had two or three minutes of terrified consciousness of his approaching fate, or, if not that, at least of pain.

Burke's confessions were prohibited from publication by the Lord Advocate until Hare had been released from jail and sent from Scotland. But in the month that elapsed between the trial and execution the newspapers, highly conscious of the enormous increase in the circulations from the Burke and Hare case, were frenziedly printing any likely and unlikely addition particulars on which they could get their hands, and so, too, was Thomas Ireland, who had published the first two parts of his *West Port Murders* before New Year's Day 1829 and had to keep up his instalments until the accounts of the execution and the texts of the authorised confessions would be at his disposal. His text ultimately reached 15 parts. It was perhaps inevitable that bogus confessions of Burke were soon in circulation with claims attached as to their having been smuggled out of the jail, and that these should find print in pamphlet and newspaper form. But Ireland's inclusion of such matter gave it a permanent status with ominous results for the future. That Ireland's text of the trial was unsatisfactory in the extreme in comparison with the Buchanan edition has been universally recognised, but the obvious inference has not been drawn.

One of Ireland's unauthorised "confessions" of Burke added more details to this case, specifically that the little boy's back was broken by Burke in order to terminate his life. This was further embroidered in Alexander Leighton's *The Court of Cacus* (1861), the first substantial account of the case since the contemporary publications. In this version Burke is making friends with an aged and destitute drunk when he meets the old woman, with an attendant boy, who in addition to his dumb idiocy is also deaf and blind. She is Irish, has walked from Glasgow, and is wholly strange to Edinburgh. Burke decides her to be a better prospect than the old man (why is unclear, since the account implies it was not originally intended to do away with the boy, and Knox would not price the decrepit female corpse above that of a decrepit male. His rates had by now stabilised to £10 in winter and £8 — because of problems of preservation — in summer.).

Burke is indeed represented by Leighton as being pleased that the intended victim was a stranger to Edinburgh (not that he showed much restraint when they were locals). The old lady and the boy are separated, the one to drink and death with Burke and Hare, the other to whatever form of communication he might achieve with the "she-wolves" Margaret Hare and Helen MacDougal. Burke and Hare discuss the possibility of letting the boy loose in Edinburgh, and ultimately Hare goes off to find gift-wrapping for Dr Knox while Burke, in the phrase of George MacGregor's *History of Burke and Hare* (1884), remains "to consider the whole bearings of the important matter under discussion". MacGregor here cites Burke's *Courant* confession but adds, "Leighton, however, obtained some further information, and in the light of it the tragedy becomes even more horrible". Indeed it does. Over to Alexander Leighton:

> "The night passed, the boy having, by some means, been made to understand that his protectress was in bed unwell; but the mutterings of the mute might have indicated that he had fears which, perhaps, he could not comprehend. The morning found the resolution of the prior night unshaken; and in that same back-room where the grandmother lay, Burke took the boy on his knee, and, as he expressed it, broke his back. No wonder that he described this scene as the one that lay most heavily upon his heart, and said that he was haunted by the recollection of the piteous expression of the wistful eyes, as the victim looked in his face."

So far, so bad. And then, courtesy William Burke, we are back to the horse, together with sarcastic remarks about the horse's inability to furnish profits at its decease comparable to those offered by its human freight. But apart from the problems occasioned by portage Knox's boys take delivery in fine style, and there is an end of the adventure and, subsequently, of the horse.

MacGregor may have had some difficulty in adopting this, given his readiness to assign chapter and verse to Leighton precisely where the present account quotes verbatim. And MacGregor raised another point which shows a historical sense not wholly in abeyance: "But was it not strange that no questions should have been asked? or that

no suspicions of foul play should have been raised?" when the
students were having the labour of unpacking the consignment.
However, his context makes it clear that while the integrity of the
students may be intended to abide his question, Leighton is free.

Roughead was the next account compelling, or at least inviting,
scholarly respect, although nearly forty years have elapsed between
MacGregor's publication in 1884 and his contribution to the
"Notable British Trials" series in 1921. There are some
improvements. The lady is now not only Irish, but "hale", possibly
in order to emphasise the contrast in cash potential from the
old man who is left to "bewail the loss of his dram" — it really says
something for Roughead that he can attach an additional slur to
Burke for his meanness in failing to murder the old party. But there is
a bright side. "Had" the old man "known the price he must pay" for
the lost dram "he had been content to go dry for the brief remainder
of his days". (These were the great days of the "Had-I-but-known"
school of writing which moved the homicidal poetic fury of Ogden
Nash.) The child is apparently no longer blind, but has been "dumb
from birth", a fact which, in addition to his relationship to the lady,
"might have moved the pity of any but these human tigers".
Leighton's account ascribed a night's wandering in search of
packaging arrangements to Hare; Roughead sends Hare out on the
street next day. Then we are back to the back-breaking, once more
in Leighton's words, shrouded this time with the awful authenticity
of a footnote to source by title and page. And then, once again, bring
on the empty horse.

After this, there is no looking back. The one slight sign of dissent
appears in Isobel Rae's *Knox the Anatomist*, published in 1964. She does
not offer us a complete revival of Back-break House but explains
that after the murder of the old lady Burke and Hare "fell on the boy
as he sat by the fire in the kitchen". Their form of assassination is left
prudently open but Burke is given Leighton's line of being
perpetually haunted "by the appealing look in this boy's eyes".

Isobel Rae had entered the proceedings as a late advocate for Dr
Knox and hence she needed to exercise some discretion. Hubert
Cole's *Things for the Surgeon*, published the same year, needed none,
although he did follow MacGregor in seeing a problem while
drawing its implications against the wrong target — "The old
woman was suffocated and Burke broke the boy's back: the only
occasion on which they killed a victim in a manner which should
have been immediately recognised as violent". Norman Adams in
Dead and Buried?, appearing in 1972, was no less positive, assigning to

Hare as well as Burke complicity in the decision to murder the boy (of which, in the pre-Leighton historiography, there is no doubt): "Burke coldbloodedly broke the boy's back over his knee and later confessed that the expression in the youngster's eyes would haunt him to his dying day. That did not stop him from tossing the boy and the woman, possibly his grandmother, into a herring barrel . . ." etc. etc. What was so lightly tossed into the barrel, chez Hare, proved sardine-quality indeed when they rolled out the barrel for student practicals.

After all of which it will be no surprise to learn that Hugh Douglas, whose *Burke and Hare-The True Story* was published the year after Adams, likewise finds additional support for his basic thesis that his subjects were "fiends out of hell" by swallowing the broken back lock, stock and herring barrel.

What was the real basis to the suspicions of MacGregor and Hubert Cole? It is not enough to say that the complicity of Knox and what seems to have been a sizeable group of students has to be assumed without question given the state of the boy's corpse. It was one thing for Knox and Co. to accept corpses with minor marks of violence which would be consistent with pressure on the dead body in raising it from the coffin, packing it in herring-barrels, or otherwise. A corpse arriving with a broken back demanded an explanation. It had met death by violence; an explanation had to be given. The procurator-fiscal had to be informed. There was no comforting ambiguity about this case, such as might shroud Knox and his associates in any possible investigation. They would immediately be liable to arrest for concealment of a death by violence. Even if Burke had a plausible story about the child's death, Knox could not risk accepting it on his own responsibility. The run of Burke and Hare murders allowed him such an option, and he invariably took it, and his wisdom was supported when Professor Robert Christison — who had no reason to love him — agreed that any injuries were consistent with bruises after death occasioned by the actions of resurrectionists. But that argument could not be advanced in this case. Death by accident required reporting; back-breaking after death would need the substantiation of an immediate examination to prove it was an event *post-mortem*. The customary Burke fudge that the body was simply bought from persons who happened to have it would not obtain; those persons would have had to be identified to the procurator-fiscal. This matter was not one of inviting Knox — and God alone knows how many students — to shut their eyes and think of Science; this was inviting them to place their necks in halters.

But above all, why on earth *should* Burke break the boy's back? Let us pass over the fact that the form of death practised by Burke and Hare was, when all was going well, a singularly humane one; in the cases of Daft Jamie and others it certainly was not, in that they were not in deep, drunken slumber, however many had been. This child was probably murdered with as much consciousness of what was happening as it was capable of having about anything. Indeed a shrewd writer who picked up the humane quality in Burke might be pardoned for assuming that Burke might surprise an expression in the child's eyes just before suffocation, and that Burke might well be haunted by it. It is not certain. Burke does not say that the boy was asleep, but he may have been — one hopes he was. But it might not have been the deep sleep of the intoxicated.

Let us pass over, also, the physical problem. A man of six feet or over may find it a relatively easy matter to break the back of a child, but a man of five feet and a half or less would find it much more difficult, and one much less easy to have natural resource to, however homicidal his tendencies may have been. This factor again implies the work of an inventor and one who had momentarily forgotten what Burke looked like. He was strong, but he had not a wide reach. But this is only supportive evidence.

No, the real and the conclusive destruction of the story is one that is wholly consistent with the most hostile interpretation of the actions of both Burke and Hare. They had brilliantly perfected a means for providing corpses which showed virtually no traces of murder, and they knew how vital it was to maintain their business on those terms. On the Leighton argument Burke, for no reason under the sun, suddenly dispensed with his superb technique and resorted to an action as stupid as it was hideous. The cobbler — which Burke was — sticks to his last; the burker sticks to his burking.

Therefore on all grounds the story is proved a fraud. Once demonstrated, the real mystery becomes why so many writers should have countenanced this fiction in whole or in part having at their disposal every basis for discrediting it. MacGregor and Cole actually saw part of the fraud, but in their anxiety to throw nooses around the necks of the Knox seminar lost control of the material within their grasp. Isobel Rae could not bring herself to stand over the whole of a story which would have condemned her adored Knox not only to the status of accessory after the fact — and, therefore, before a whole series of subsequent facts — but to a level of imbecility which should have made him, not the intellectual giant of Edinburgh medicine but its intellectual pigmy; yet she did accept other parts of it, and in so doing lent further credence to the whole.

The clue to this century of credulity lies in a point at the outset of my own investigation. I have been struck by Burke's likeability, and have tried to discover why a decent man could have done what he undoubtedly did. They would seem to have had an inkling, again perhaps a subconscious one, that this pattern of homicidal brutality simply did not possess a character of the infernal blackness they wished to ascribe to it, for what they took to be dramatic or moral purposes. Therefore a story which revealed Burke capable of casual, almost infanticidal, sadism was grist to their mills. In so doing, they actually support my case. He was not evil enough to justify their rhetoric: so more evidence, however discreditable, had to be found.

What was happening was quite nasty enough without any improving from Leighton and his credulous disciples. By now any qualms of conscience had been burked as thoroughly as the victims. Roughead complained that the brevity of Burke's narrative was suspicious: on the Paterson murder he wrote: "The baldness of his account, in the light of Janet's statement, shows how partial and fragmentary are his versions of the several tragedies in which he and his associate played their fiendish parts." It is difficult to see where such a catalogue of self-accusation is to be charged with partiality, apart from its refusal to acknowledge breaking the back Burke had not broken; as often, an important fact has been observed by a commentator and has then been misinterpreted because of the need to make sanctimonious noises. As the confessions continue their taciturnity became more marked because, I suggest, Burke was finding it hard to stomach the recital. At no point does he sound as though he gloated over it, and rejoiced in his successes; it is reasonable to suggest he confronted what he had done for the first time coldly, in the official confession, and as his recital increased so did his self-disgust. As Sir Walter Scott pointed out the year must have been increasingly blurred by alcohol. Each event would have been all-important in itself. Then when it was over, it became forgotten as the next loomed on the horizon. Scott's point may be taken further. Neither Burke nor the Hares would seem to have murdered when they were wholly beyond the use of reason; one or two victims might have been murdered when the killers were drunk beyond the point of responsibility, but the great bulk died following sober conspiracy and relatively sober execution. But there is an analogy to modern murders by heroin addicts: the craving for the next "fix" dwarfs all other considerations. The very use of alcohol to

bemuse and render unconscious inevitably increased the amount that
Burke and the Hares had to consume. It is this which helps account
for one of the most terrifying aspects of the later phases —
inevitability. As Burke told the story they had reached a point where
it had become part of nature itself for them to murder. Desisting was
what now seemed unnatural — the detective-story writer's oft-
made point that even the most altruistic murderer becomes driven to
that resort, and more and more insensible to moral restraints.
Alochol craving exacerbated this tendency. So did the thrill of
excitement: they were taking pleasure in growing bolder:

> "When they first began this murdering system [Burke told the
> *Courant*] they always took them to Knox's after dark; but being so
> successful, they went in the day-time, and grew more bold. When they
> carried the girl Paterson to Knox's, there were a great many boys in
> the High School Yards [near Surgeons' Square], who followed Burke
> and the man that carried her, crying, 'They are carrying a corpse'; but
> they got her safe delivered. They often said to one another that no
> person could find them out, no one being present at the murders but
> themselves two; and that they might be as well hanged for a sheep as a
> lamb. They made it their business to look out for persons to decoy into
> their houses to murder them. Burke declares, when they kept the
> mouth and nose shut a very few minutes, they could make no
> resistance, but would convulse and make a rumbling noise in their
> bellies for some time; after they ceased crying and making resistance,
> they left them to die of themselves: but their bodies would often move
> afterwards, and for some time they would have long breathings before
> life went away."

Burke curiously referred to the situation towards the end much in
the way that an alcoholic, or a drug addict, cured by circumstances
beyond his control, looks back on the past.

> "Burke declares that it was God's providence that put a stop to their
> murdering career, for he does not know how far they might have gone
> with it, 'even to attack people on the streets', as they were so
> successful, and always met with a ready market: that when they
> delivered a body they were always told to get more. Hare was always
> with him when he went with a subject [save in isolated instances
> already attested to, such as the Paterson case; but it is clear that the
> whole thing became for Burke, in retrospect, a perpetual rondo of
> death, in which each case had grown as like its predecessor as possible],
> and also when he got the money. Burke declares, that Hare and him
> had a plan made up, that Burke and a man were to go to Glasgow or
> Ireland, and try the same there, and to forward them to Hare, and he
> was to give them to Dr Knox."

This last may have been pipe-dreaming, but on his own showing

Burke at least saw himself as having been trapped in an apparently unbreakable nightmare. We must remember that Burke had been cut off from drink for two months when he made his confession. The craving and the stupefaction would have arisen from his brain rather like a cloud of depression arising from the mind. And since Hare, too, would have been swiftly cut off from alcoholic sustenance, it is reasonable to see some reappraisal in his case also. We simply do not know what its results may have been. As it was, Burke and Hare were on the verge of important extensions of business when they were apprehended; they were also trapped like rats in a labyrinth constructed by themselves and their environment; they were also suffering serious psychological tensions which inevitably meant a breakdown of security as they themselves broke down. The case of Mrs Campbell or Docherty, described in detail during the trial, suggests a general pattern of disintegration. If Burke and Hare had trapped themselves in their own cycle of death, Nature was throwing obstructions into the working of that cycle with effects that would ultimately destroy it. Or, to accept Burke's phrase, "it was God's providence that put a stop" to it. It is noteworthy that he sounded genuinely thankful it was over — it was not only repentance, but relief. Repentance alone had merely added its horrors to the cycle: "Burke repented often of the crime, and could not sleep without a bottle of whisky by his bedside, and a twopenny candle to burn all night beside him; when he awoke he would take a draught of the bottle — sometimes half a bottle at a draught — and that would make him sleep."

He was stupefying himself even as he was stupefying his victims. Sometimes he knew them. There was, for instance, "a cinder-gatherer; Burke thinks her name was Effy. She was in the habit of selling small pieces of leather to him (as she was a cobbler), [which] she gathered about the coach-works. He took her into Hare's stable, and gave her whisky to drink till she was drunk; she then lay down among some straw and fell asleep. They then laid a cloth over her." Effy fetched £10 at Knox's with the best of them.

Sometimes the material seemed almost delivered into their hands by the process of society. Burke was on very civil terms with the police and in the last days at least was accustomed to giving a few glasses to a policeman when, presumably, professional business prevented his extending hospitality much farther than the next victim. The *Courant* confession mentions that Andrew Williamson, a policeman, "and his neighbour, were dragging a drunk woman to the West Port watch-house. They found her sitting on a stair." Burke entered into discussion with them. He suggested letting her go to her lodgings; they said they did not know where they were. Burke then said he would take her "to lodgings. They then gave her to his charge. He then took her to Hare's house. Burke and Hare murdered her that night the same way as they did the others." And she in her turn fetched £10.

This particular confession differs markedly from the official statement, where Burke does indeed bring a woman to the house but she is not described as getting drunk until "after some days". The police are not mentioned. The *Courant* pressed the matter further: did the police know Burke when they handed over the obstreperous female? Burke stressed that "he had a good character with the police; or if they had known there were four murderers living in one house they would have visited them oftener". This last statement is very strange. It looks like an accusation of Helen MacDougal as well as of Margaret Hare, and yet that is wholly contradictory of everything else said by Burke at any stage, including certain passages in the present document. It seems really odd that nobody took him up on it. The best solution I can offer is that Burke made some grim pleasantry to the effect that had the police known that four of the people in that house would one day be arrested for murder, they would have looked in more frequently; or else he was making a sarcastic enquiry as to whether the *Courant* man thought the police believed Hare's house contained four murderers. In any event it seems clear enough that Burke maintained good relations with the police to his profit, and that thereby he showed very sound business instincts. This is rather striking in one way. In a town where Irish immigration had progressed far enough to penetrate the police force one might expect such collaboration; but Burke had no difficulty in winning the confidence of a police force of almost wholly non-Irish composition. Despite the occasional fracas in which he figured, usually for business reasons rather than of accidental origin, he earned for himself the name of a desirable immigrant. In legal terms he would certainly have been much less of an immigrant than he would have been viewed in social terms. Since 1800 Ireland had joined England and Scotland within the Union, although each country preserved its own legal system — those of Ireland and England being cousins in kind and hierarchy while that of Scotland differed vastly from them. So Burke was entitled to claim the privileges of a native, and seems to have made the most of them. Williamson was simply unaware that Burke's services as an improver of the community's culture extended well beyond the West Port, as far as Surgeons' Square.

These may have been all the murders at the time of the quarrel of Burke and Hare (although it is probable that at least one of the Haldane women, whose cases we will take together, antedated it). As to the quarrel, it may have had its inception in Margaret Hare's bright suggestion to Burke that he murder Helen MacDougal during a visit to the country. As we know, Burke refused, but he may have been growing a little alarmed. A story grew that after Helen MacDougal's release she told the sheriff that the women had overheard Hare telling Burke that they could murder the women when times grew bad for corpses. Naturally it was reprinted by Ireland. It sounds like the artificial sensational glosses which multiplied like codfish during and after the trial. For one thing there was no shortage of corpses, and we know from Burke's revelations that towards the end they thought of opening up production in Ireland and Glasgow, so no shortage was anticipated. (They clearly had not considered the likelihood of a fall in demand, although the fever which had commenced them on their homicidal career might well have ended it had they still been in business when it struck in 1832 and provided corpses and to spare for all.) But there was a real danger that the habit of murder could grow on them to such a degree that they would end by devouring one another. Burke's need to drug himself with whisky before finding sleep could well be placing him in deadly peril; apart from his love for Helen MacDougal her presence beside him in bed gave him more insurance against an attack from the Hares. And the Hares may have had the same idea. Margaret Hare's testimony in the witness-box included a statement that Helen MacDougal and herself told one another that "perhaps it would be the same case with her and I" as they stood in the passage outside the room while Burke murdered Mrs Campbell or Docherty. This may simply be picturesque detail to lend substance to a version of the death which incriminated Burke while keeping the Hares in the clear; it certainly revealed that Margaret Hare was as much an accomplice as Helen MacDougal was, but made it clear that this in each case could be the result of fear, or even of love. What is important about it beyond all speculation, however, is that Margaret Hare had the idea of members of the quartette killing one another in her mind; and Burke, interestingly, associated her with a more active view of the same thing. In any event, Burke and Helen MacDougal went for a holiday to Falkirk, the official confession stating it was "to the house of Helen MacDougal's father", a gentleman of whom we otherwise know nothing — not even his name, if it was not Dougal — apart from the negative point that he seems to have been unwilling to shelter his daughter after her release from prison. The *Courant* confession supplies the interesting touch that their visit "was at the time a procession was made round a stone in that neighbourhood" and that Burke "thinks it was the anniversary of the battle of Bannockburn", which would put it at 24 June 1829.

While Burke was making such comparative analyses as might occur to him on the subjects of Irish and Scottish fathers-in-law and patriotic anniversaries, Hare had been occupying himself with some private study and research on his own account. He "fell in with a woman drunk in the street at the West Port. He took her into his house and murdered her himself". Burke in the official confession simply added that he himself "does not know the woman's name, or any farther particulars of the case, or whether any other person was present or knew of it", which may be a clue to a suspicion on his part that Margaret Hare did the work of securing the legs of the expiring victim on this occasion. It does not seem to have been a *sine qua non* for the murdering process when the party of the second part was feeble, female and very drunk — Burke himself acknowledged having later killed such a person on his own — but the possibility of Margaret Hare's involvement here cannot be excluded. In any case Hare sold the corpse "to Dr Knox's assistants for £8".

Burke's *Courant* confession represents him as doing a little detective work on his own account at this stage. "When Burke went away he knew Hare was in want of money; his things were all in pawn; but when he came back, found him to have plenty of money. Burke asked him if he had been doing any business, he said he had been doing nothing. Burke did not believe him, and went to Dr Knox, who told him that Hare had brought a subject. Hare then confessed what he had done." In the official confession, which did not mention this little investigation, the next paragraph simply says that "about this time he went to live in Broggan's house". It is reasonable to infer, as subsequent writers have, that there was a row after which Burke and Helen MacDougal left. But the row may not just have been about Hare's lie, or rather it may have had more to do with its future implications. If Hare was ready to double-cross Burke, might he not do so in a much more dangerous way resulting in loss of life to either Burke or Helen MacDougal? Indeed, the fact that Burke had taken a financial interest in Brogan's house *before* June implies that he had already decided to get out before Hare's first act of treachery furnished him with the excuse. It seems to have been legally undertaken in friendly circumstances; Hare had his signature transcribed and put down his own mark as a witness. But Burke now knew that Hare was not to be trusted; it must be remembered he had only known him a short time and that chance, rather than mutual confidence, had made them accomplices. There is also the point that if Hare, with his takings from hawking, from boatman's work, from bed-rents and from murder, was still destitute and forced to turn to the pawnshop, he was now getting through money very fast, and he could therefore have additional motives to speed up his collection of corpses. Burke said to the *Courant* that as it was, a lodger would now be tried by them as to whether he or she would drink, and if they did, their fate was normally sealed. Both he and Helen MacDougal certainly came into that category, and hence they were well advised in departing from the *pension* Hare.

The fact that the firm continued to operate is a further proof against any involvement by anyone else: Con Burke and his wife, Helen MacDougal or young John Brogan, all of whom had been variously charged by Roughead and others with probable complicity. Burke obviously knew all of these persons better than he knew Hare and had more reason to trust his life to them; but he nevertheless returned to Hare. It could be argued that this also militates in favour of Margaret Hare's continued ignorance, but Hare had no reason, as Burke now had, to end the relationship between the two men. Hare had been treacherous to Burke; Burke had merely been suspicious, and presumably annoyed, at Hare but had not in any way broken faith with him. It was also true that the partnership would do better with extra premises: the acquisition of Brogan's place, together with the occasional use of Con Burke's, gave them three. Hare's house was necessarily useless as a theatre of operations when it filled up to its full complement, with two and even three persons sleeping in one bed. Ironically the very thing that was best for the Hares' economic health before the beginning of the murdering time now was a barrier to real prosperity. Hare was not the only businessman to discover that factors which enriched him when his income expectation was small would now impoverish him when he was on a more lucrative line of activity. So a little murdering at other addresses might be necessary. During harvest the Hare hotel was at its most overcrowded and then Burke and Hare seem to have put their new profession behind them and returned to their old as agricultural labourers. It was harder work, but it was psychologically less exhausting and demanded less capital outlay. The alcohol which facilitated the murders was a legitimate business expense, but no claims could be made against it.

Mrs Haldane, however, must have been murdered before the

harvest, perhaps before Burke had left Hare's. She was somewhat
less nomadic a figure than the average client, being well equipped
with progeny in the vicinity. In general the nomads by definition
protected their murderers although luck in that respect would run
out with Mrs Docherty. However, Mrs Haldane, if not exactly
nomadic, was connected by parentage with the criminal classes,
having had a daughter transported in 1827 from the Calton jail for
fourteen years. She also had another daughter "married to ——— in
the High Street". Burke and Hare might be felt to be taking a
considerable risk. The lady was a lodger, and it was always possible
that her offspring might bestir either herself or ——— to make some
inquiry in the West Port, no great distance from the High Street, as
Burke had the opportunity of noting during his last hours.
Presumably the High Street address ensured that there would be
little pursuit of the prodigal parent. Mrs Haldane, "a stout old
woman", was left to her own devices, the last of which proved to be
staggering into her landlord's stable when she was drunk "and falling
asleep among some straw". It really was more or less meeting mine
host half-way, and no doubt Hare acknowledged as much when he
looked in to see to the livestock for the night. Burke and he had little
difficulty in their work; Mrs Haldane was left dead where she had
fallen, and transport to Knox's was effected the following day.
Burke omitted to mention the sum she fetched, but remembered the
fact that she "had but one tooth in her mouth, and that was a very
large one in front". Inconsequential detail does impinge in the mind
at such times, perhaps as a distraction from the reality of what had
happened.

Burke's recital of Mrs Haldane's errant relatives omitted one
daughter, but he had every reason to remedy the fact later in his
account. It was after Burke had gone to live in Brogan's house that a
third child of Mrs Haldane appeared. She seems more to have
resembled her mother and, it may be, the sister who was enjoying His
Majesty's policy in peopling his remoter possessions with persons
involuntarily detained in his keeping; she, too, had little in common
with that sister in the High Street so respectably married to what
Burke, in the official confession, referred to as a "tinsmith", one
Clark. (He doubtless did give Clark's name to the *Courant* but that
sapient journal deleted the name.) Burke remembered Peggy
Haldane coming into Brogan's but could not recall why. Had she
been seeking her mother it would no doubt have been remembered
by him. The most likely thing would have been that Peggy recalled
an earlier acquaintance with Burke, whose agreeable manners made

quite an impact on many who met him, and hence she was vaguely in quest of hospitality rather than of her missing parent; but she followed rapidly in her footsteps. She would seem to have got drunk, or rather drunker, rapidly, and was sleeping it off when Burke murdered her. The time was the early morning. In both accounts Burke, with every motive to incriminate Hare, went out of his way to stress Hare's non-complicity with this crime. "Hare was not present," stresses the official confession; "Hare had no hand in it," agrees the *Courant* statement. This is further evidence in favour of the credibility of both documents, and it is welcome, given the network of falsehood with which the subject was enmeshed by the contemporary press and the publication of Ireland's and Leighton's works. There is a pleasing irony in the thought that all those authorities who spilled so much ink in stating how heinous in Burke it was to have murdered must now be set aside in his favour where veracity is in question.

Hare seems to have come into the second Haldane case for transport up to Knox's. Brogan was still occupying his own house but neither he "nor his son knew the least thing about" the murder "or any other case of the same kind". The *Courant* account mentions that Peggy was a lodger of Hare's, though it is hard to see that even what he terms her "idle habits" and her being "much given to drinking" would have prevented her setting some inquiry afoot for her mother if she had been there when her mother disappeared. Burke described how it had been possible to do the murder without assistance. "She was so drunk at the time that he thinks she was not sensible of her death, as she made no resistance whatever. . . . This was the only murder that Burke committed by himself, but which Hare was connected with. She was laid with her face downwards, and he pressed her down, and she was soon suffocated." Delivery to Knox was effected by tea-box; proceeds £8 which, if contract was then in existence, argues death fairly early in July.

But the fact that victims increasingly become recognisable in identity now becomes a stronger and stronger feature. James Bridie's note to his *Anatomist* happily ascribes the ultimate discovery to "the incaution of their race". It will hardly do. What does seem to be involved is an increasing inability to pass up any opportunity for murder; what had begun as deliberate search for nomads now becomes a voracious battening on whatever swings within their reach. And it seems also as though Burke is almost risking exposure from a subconscious desire to be discovered and the nightmare ended. One could suggest that Bridie made the mistake to be expected of his times in attributing the "incaution" to race; it may have been much more connected with religion. Burke was born into a faith in which confession was an inbuilt structure and his actions seem from now on almost in search of a declaration. The exception is that of Daft Jamie if we accept, as I believe we should, his assertion that Mrs Hare initiated that encounter. And it is not wholly an exception. Burke knew the appalling risk that was involved in taking on Daft Jamie. Yet when Mrs Hare's heavy foot conveyed what was on, he walked into the episode as though unable to stop himself. It was not only Daft Jamie who seems driven unconsciously as a lamb to the slaughter; Burke in retrospect knew that he himself had walked blindly towards his own doom as well as Jamie's.

Sir Walter Scott and the sheriff had noted that Burke attributed primary responsibility to Hare where Hare had often assigned it to him; but in the last cases other than Daft Jamie, Burke fully accepted the responsibility for having initiated matters. There was, for instance, the washerwoman Mrs Hostler "who had been washing in the house for some time" and who was suffocated by Hare and himself "one day in September or October 1828". The *Courant* as usual is fuller in details. Mrs Hostler had returned to finish up the clothes after which they gave her whisky, got her drunk, persuaded her to go to bed — Mrs Brogan being out and it being in daytime — and when she was alseep, murdered her. They put her in a box, put the box in the coalhouse in the passage, and uplifted her to Knox in the afternoon, getting £8. "Mrs Hostler had ninepence halfpenny in her hand, which they could scarcely get out of it after she was dead, so firmly was it grasped."

This was certainly close enough to the normal tenor of life to elicit comment; Mrs Hostler was no doubt engaged in casual labour, but she seems to have been relatively well established in the neighbourhood and her disappearance much more likely than those of the nomads to elicit enquiry. The next victim (if she was not, in fact, a little earlier) was even closer to home. Ann MacDougal was young, married and a cousin of the late MacDougal; she had come on a visit to see Burke and Helen. It is not absolutely clear that she was staying at the Brogan house — the official confession speaks of her "coming and going to the house for a few days". If this were true it would really be incredible if her lodging had been with other relatives and they had made no enquiry. The assumption must be that she put up in some place where she was not known, or where there would be no particular interest in her fate. Even so it seems strange that she had said nothing to her husband about her intention of calling on her late cousin's mistress and the gentleman presently consoling her; it is possible, of course, that her marriage was on the rocks and that the visit had arisen because of this fact. But when all due allowances have been made, it still seems enormously risky. In any event Burke and Hare got her drunk and when she was asleep Hare did the murder at Burke's request: although Hare was stated as having done it, Burke went out of his way to make it clear to the *Courant* that it had been at his instigation. Helen MacDougal was presumably out of the house during all of this — possibly at her work hawking Burke's shoes. No doubt she was led to assume that Ann had made a final call and said she was returning home, or going to some other town. She obtained no mention in the account, other than in mentioning her relationship to Ann. But danger came from another quarter — Brogan.

> "One of Dr Knox's assistants, Paterson, gave them a fine trunk to put her into." [Paterson was the doorkeeper, not an assistant, and as we will see later seems to have seen means of turning his acquaintance-ship with all parties to his financial advantage.] "It was in the afternoon when she was done. It was on John Broggan's house; and when Broggan came home from his work he saw the trunk, and made inquiries about it, as he knew they had no trunks there. Burke then gave him two or three drams, as there was always plenty of whisky going at these times, to make him quiet. Hare and Burke then gave him £1 10s. each, as he was back in his rent, for to pay it, and he left Edinburgh a few days after. They then carried her to Surgeon Square as soon as Broggan was out of the house, and got £10 for her."

If the contract were by now operative, this puts the murder after that of Mrs Hostler, and probably well into October. "Hare was cautioner for Broggan's rent, being £3, and Hare and Burke gave him that sum." Presumably Hare undertook the role before Burke invested in property and Hare's name, as a man of property intimate with Burke, had been needed to guarantee the debt of Burke's cousin or cousin-in-law. "Broggan went off in a few days, and the rent is not paid yet. They gave him the money that he might not come against them for the murder of Ann MacDougal, that he saw in the trunk, that was murdered in his house. Hare knew that the rent would fall upon him, and if he could get Burke to pay the half of it, it would so much the better; and proposed this to Burke, and he agreed to it, as they were glad to get him out of the way. Broggan's wife is a cousin of Burke's. They thought he went to Glasgow, but are not sure." It was, as the Duke of Wellington, now Prime Minister, had said in another context, a damned close-run thing. But Burke retained a friendship with Brogan's son, who would be among those present on the day of the party for Mrs Campbell or Docherty and was therefore arrested and later released.

And now we come to the case which excited the most horror in the public mind, even in the heyday of Leighton's fable of the broken back: "Daft Jamie". It occasioned the bitterest attacks on Burke, Hare and Knox; it excited popular comment and scurrilous lampoon alike; it became the centrepiece in any popular dramatic representation until the end of the nineteenth century. Daft Jamie's name was among the yells into the ears of Burke on the scaffold during his last minutes on earth. *Noctes Ambrosianae* reached the zenith—or nadir—of its envenomed discussion of the case when it was mentioned, the unfortunate novelist Hogg being assigned such lines as "for whilk last murder, without ony impiety, ane may venture to say, the Devil is at this moment ruggin that Burke out o' hell-fire wi' a three-pronged fork, and then in wi' him again, through the ribs — and then stirring up the coals wi' that eternal poker — and then wi' the great bellows blawin' up the furnace, till, like an Etna, or Mount Vesuvius, it vomits the murderer out again far ower into the very middle o' the floor o' the infernal regions". Society and Daft Jamie's family had done little enough to provide for him in his lifetime, but both were loud in becoming his champions once he was dead. Burke himself was more shaken by it than by any other murder in which he had been involved (as we can now assert, given that his greater penitence for the broken back has of necessity been proved as mythical as its occasion).

Joseph Forster, in an otherwise undistinguished and inaccurate essay on Burke and Hare in his *Studies in Black and Red*, grounds the cult of Jamie in Scottish national character: "In Scotland a peculiar tenderness to people belonging to the afflicted class of 'Daft Jamie' exists, much to the credit of the national character."

It can hardly be said that the form in which contemporaries revealed their "peculiar tenderness" for Daft Jamie is anything short of nauseating: it seemed to combine the cold-blooded cynicism of the eighteenth century with the patronising condescension of the nineteenth. After the discovery of the murderers a whole variety of scribblers leapt into print concerning him — indeed he proved to have infinitely more capacity for economic re-use than any other of their victims. After reading some of these effusions it is hard not to feel some prejudice in favour of Burke and Hare: they merely murdered the poor wretch, as opposed to wallowing in a series of unctuous jeerings at evidence of his mental inadequacy coupled with virtuous declarations of sympathy at his fate. The public, secure in the superiority of its own intellect, revelled in such gems as Jamie composing a quarrel with his equally deficient friend Bobby Awl with the sentiment, "Ou, what could ye say to puir Boby? He's daft, ye ken", or, alternatively, told itself that wisdom came from the lips of children and fools as Jamie replied to the query "why do the ladies in general not carry Bibles to church?" "Because they are ashamed of themsel's, for they canna fin' out the text". These and similar utterances were scrutinised for their unintentional droppings of human wisdom with all the industry of an American annotator of La Rouchefoucauld. Scotland had not had her enlightenment for nothing.

The whole phenomenon seemed hell-made for Thomas Carlyle, and he was appreciative enough of it when writing to his brother John on 13 January 1829. "There has been a dreadful piece of work at Edinburgh, with Irishmen decoying people into houses, and there *murdering* them to sell their bodies to Dr Knox! One unspeakable miscreant is to be hanged for that crime in a few days. They killed *Daft Jamie* in that way; the poor purblind creature that went about with a show-box on his back; said to be a brother of Peter Nimmo's." What Carlyle in fact meant was that Daft Jamie was of the same kidney as another Edinburgh character well known for his mental illness — i.e. they were both daft. Peter Nimmo's form of insanity led him to attend lectures at the University of Edinburgh medical school for some ten years: if Dr Knox heard of him, and he undoubtedly must have done, it is hard not to accredit him with the remark to his pupils that such an action was proof of insanity indeed. Carlyle was forever finding matter for amusement in Peter Nimmo, and even wrote an article for *Fraser's* a couple of years later extracting the maximum hilarity for his readers from the eccentricities of the idiot. It was the literary version of that form of eighteenth-century recreation which consisted of going to view the inabitants of the local Bedlam.

Most accounts of Daft Jamie are drawn from *A Laconic Narrative Of The Life & Death Of James Wilson, Known By The Name Of Daft Jamie, To Which Is Added, A Few Anecdotes Relative To Him And His Friend Boby Awl, An Idiot Who Strolled About Edinburgh For Many Years*, published by W. Smith at Bristo Port for threepence (the price of a night at Hare's lodging-house), and so likely a candidate for fictionalisation compels rather less authority than has been assigned to it. But it is very firm in asserting that Jamie was born on 27 November 1809. His relatives' unsuccessful legal proceedings against Hare after the death of Burke

make it clear that his parents were John and Janet Wilson, of whom
the father was dead, and that there was at least one sibling who also
bore the name of Janet. The mother was illiterate, but the younger
Janet was not. The *Laconic Narrative* explains that the older Janet was
a hawker, much as Hare himself and Helen MacDougal were, and
that Jamie having pulled down a cupboard with all the household
crockery was beaten for it with sufficient savagery that he ran away
from home and thenceforward supported himself by the charity
elicited by the amusement arising from his idiocy. Maternal, and
indeed sororal, affection seem to have concealed themselves well
until Jamie was beyond the further expression of it: at the same time
it is hard to blame poor Mrs Wilson for despair at finding chaos at
home in the wake of an exhausting day's hawking. Jamie's amusing
traits were much less funny for a family which had to cope with the
results.

We have already examined the probabilities of Daft Jamie's initial
approach to the Hares' domicile, where he was killed. And everyone
agrees he was killed there, including the indictment where his death
formed a count, subsequently set aside, against Burke. This militates
again in favour of Burke not having been the active agent in drawing
Jamie into the net which Hare testified him to be: when Burke found
victims he was by now bringing them to his own house, and calling
Hare in. The indictment also places the murder between the 5th and
26th days of October (it allows for the remote possibility that it could
have happened in September or November, but that is merely a
matter of legal form) which leaves it far beyond the time when
Burke brought his prey into Hare's. When Burke reached Hare's on
this occasion Mrs Hare said to him, "You have come too late, for the
drink is all done; and Jamie had the cup in his hand." This would seem
to have been a formula for the provision of more drink, together with
the occasion for it. Incidentally, Burke himself "had never seen"
Jamie "before to his knowledge". Perhaps not, but it seems hard to
see how he would have been ignorant of the folklore surrounding
him; there was far too much of it to have originated in posthumous
manufacture.

"They then proposed to send for another half mutchkin, which
they did, and urged him to drink; she took a little with them." At this
point a discovery seems to have been made which should have led
Burke and Hare to drop the matter, were they not now too enslaved
to murder by habit: being daft, Jamie was not particularly fond of
whisky. It is a little difficult to square this with some of the stories
about himself and Bobby Awl and their arguments about getting it,

but Jamie was as vulnerable to journalistic fiction as Burke. What Jamie really liked was snuff; he was believed to have come to the Hares in hopes of some. He drank the whisky courteously, but there seems to have been disagreement about his consuming more: as Sir Walter put it grimly to his son Charles, "Having in that respect more wit than wiser folks he refused the liquor they tried to forc[e] upon him". "They then invited him into the little room," continues the *Courant* confession, "and advised him to sit down upon the bed. Hare's wife then went out, and locked the outer door, and put the key below the door. There were none in the room but themselves three. Jamie sat down upon the bed. He then lay down upon the bed, and Hare lay down at his back, his head raised and resting upon his left hand. Burke was standing at the foreside of the bed." It is almost as though Burke were describing a painting, one which he clearly found it difficult to forget.

"When they had lain there for some time, Hare threw his body on the top of Jamie, pressed his hand on his mouth and held his nose with the other. Hare and him fell off the bed and struggled. Burke then held his hands and feet. They never quitted their gripe till he was dead. He never got up nor cried any." But the official confession, although much briefer, is actually more explicit on this point. "Hare was lying alongside of Jamie in the bed, and Hare suddenly turned on him, and put his hand on his mouth and nose; and Jamie, who had got drink, but was not drunk, made a terrible resistance, and he and Hare fell from the bed together, Hare still keeping hold of Jamie's mouth and nose; and as they lay on the floor together, declarant lay across Jamie, to prevent him from resisting, and they held him in that state till he was dead."

No doubt Jamie had remained quiet because of some hypnotic tension in the atmosphere — Burke's own account seems to suggest he felt it. Whether Jamie entertained any apprehensions as to his own safety before Hare attacked him we cannot know, but his failure to maintain his usual routine of chatter and laughter adds its own chill to the story. In any case the terrible thing had now happened. Other than the dumb child — who may have been asleep — Burke and Hare had killed their first victim who knew what they were doing, was neither unconscious, near-unconscious nor ill; and Jamie, as though into his clouded mind had come the blinding realisation that in him was the life principle at war with death, fought for all he was worth.

Jamie was strong and wiry: his body was that of a vigorous nineteen-year-old even if his mind hardly reached that of an infant one-third of his age. But in the degrading manner of a class-obsessed rhetoric, the heroism of the struggle was no sooner seen, and its symbolism responded to, than it was vulgarised into ludicrous exaggeration or else transformed into banality. The latter is evident in the road shows which turned that awful grouping, broken at last by Hare's murderous assault, into exchanges such as:

> *Burke:* We're going to kill you, Daft Jamie.
> *Jamie:* If ye kill me, I'll tell my mither.

Attack and defence in the law of the jungle do not speak, even when the results are for the benefit of scientific research. As for the improvement of the combat, the most repulsive example of it was the story, current at the time and solemnly quoted for many decades afterwards, that in the course of the struggle Jamie bit Burke in the testicle, which induced cancer and would have killed him had he not, in Forster's words, "been disposed of in a much more satisfactory manner". It was of course Burke's longstanding complaint which had produced this gloss.

Hare took a brass snuff-box and a copper snuff-spoon from the body, gave the latter to Burke and kept the box, which he later said he had thrown away "in the tan-yard". Burke's indictment mentioned a brass box in Burke's possession which it was insisted had derived from Daft Jamie, but in fact, said Burke's *Courant* confession, the box was Burke's own. It was an interesting lesson to him that where formerly he had walked undisturbed from one murder to the next, sharing jokes and drams with policemen on the way, evidence was now descending from empty air to convict him: in those days the vital thing was to escape suspicion — or it was for him. Jamie was dead by noon. Summing up, Burke recalled Jamie having evidently been sensitive to danger from the earliest, continually asking for his mother (and being told "she would be there immediately") — Burke doubted if Jamie drank more than one glass of whisky the whole time, but of course Hare may have made his assault in the drunken conviction that one glass of whisky would dispose of Jamie's few senses. Jamie's body was put into a chest Hare kept clothes in, and taken to Knox's, where it fetched £10 and elicited some comment and special action, of which more later.

"And the last was the old woman Docherty, for whose murder he has been convicted." We will set her aside until the trial, for the event was very fully traced there. There was little enough time between Daft Jamie and herself. It may have been as little as a week, for she died on 31 October. Burke and Hare had by then known one another for a calendar year.

In one sense, obviously, we have been looking at a dreadful recital, all the more hideous if one takes its practitioners to have been men of decency and sensibility, in one case, and of at least industry and affection, in the other. The transformation of a man such as Burke into the mass murderer that he had become is a tragedy, and Hare's may be as great did we but know what it was. As for the victims, the fact that they had been reduced to such hopeless straits by the jungle that was industrialising Scotland such that they became natural prey for Burke and Hare does not gainsay their claims on life and dignity. They too had been brutalised, in many instances not by vagrancy, but by work. They had taken their places on the labour market, been used up and thrown aside. Posterity, when it heard of them at all, was happily ready to condemn them as incorrigibles when in most cases their lives had been far harder than posterity could in its pampered surroundings envisage.

Burke and Hare met all the finest specifications which sociologists and historians of the migration process have been speaking about for years. They reached a new country. They studied the situation. They saw an economic need, a demand, an ability to furnish supply. They maximised their own skills and particularly used their advantageous position among those of their own class and ethnic origin. They assimilated enough of the ethos of the host culture to show themselves acclimatised, as they slotted into the Scottish tradition of initiative, invention and enterprise.

Burke, Hare and the Scottish Enlightenment

At first we all with one accord disbelieved the story conceiving it to be a newspaper invention fitter for the days when children were frightened with stories of Jews making them into *mutton* pies, than for our enlightened and civilised times.

—Maria Edgeworth to Scott, 10 January 1829

Scholars, unhappily, must yell
In torment on the hob of Hell;
While louts who never learned their letters
Are perched in Heaven among their betters.

—Ancient Irish gloss, translated by Frank O'Connor

THE Scottish Enlightenment was one of the wonderful moments in the history of human intellect. From time to time a generation or two in the history of a country will produce a galaxy of intellect such as throws all the surrounding terrain into contrasting darkness. Its own activity, the controversies among its actors, the effect of its luminaries on their pupils, the stimulus of actor upon actor, all combine to perpetuate its glory for a season; and in the end it falls, leaving its admirers to bewail the new darkness in which they dwell. Periclean Athens is conceded to be such a generation and its glory is extended to the commencement of the next century with perhaps an Indian summer extending to the achievements of Aristotle, Demosthenes and Aeschines. More narrowly Rome from Sallust to Ovid may be conceded some of the same magic. Elizabethan England surely has such a claim, from its antecedents in the time of More to the afterglow in Jacobean drama. The Americans of the Revolution, the true Revolution of the Intellectuals, established their credentials from the prime of Franklin to the Report on Weights and Measures by John Quincy Adams. The so-called Irish Renaissance was another such event, from its commencement in exile with Wilde and Shaw through the heroic achievements in Ireland itself before the Easter Week Rising of 1916 to the final death in exile with Joyce, O'Casey and Samuel Beckett. And among these rare emanations the Scottish Enlightenment takes its proud place.

It differs from its European counterpart in being more academic and more long-living. Universities were the breeding-ground of the Scottish Enlightenment and even where major figures failed to gain university chairs, as David Hume failed and Robert Knox failed, the activity of university controversy and the competition and inspiration of university contemporaries maintained the primacy of the university in the story however much the foolish conduct of the institutions might have merited otherwise.

In one sense to think of the Scottish Enlightenment as alive and well in the first quarter of the nineteenth century comes as a shock to students who have allowed themselves to become unduly parochialised by absorption in Europe while failing to extend their horizons to contemplate Scotland. The European Enlightenment is generally conceded to have been swept underfoot in the chaos of the era of the French Revolution. The American Enlightenment, if only because so many of its practitioners became major figures in the American Revolution and the new federation it brought into being, is admitted to have had a much longer survival potential: romantics will at least permit it to have lasted to the Fourth of July 1826, the day on which Thomas Jefferson and John Adams both died on the fiftieth anniversary of the Declaration of Independence. The Scottish Enlightenment had continued without the intervention of revolutions either to preserve or destroy it. But a case can be made that a mortal blow was struck in 1828-29 and that it was the last of the victims of Burke and Hare.

That the Scottish Enlightenment still was very much alive when Burke and Hare went into practice can be seen by a glance at the remarkable man for whom their homicides were carried out. But one guiding star does not make an Enlightenment. For all his brilliance Knox could hardly sustain the claim for its survival on his own. However, he was not alone. The Edinburgh Medical School might appear to be declining, as one contrasted the sorry spectacle of Professor Alexander Monro *tertius* in the chair of anatomy with all the triumphs of his father and grandfather who had preceded him, and it was natural to make such a contrast in that the lecture-notes were the same and the present inheritor very decidedly dependent on the past. But Knox had rivals who were his equals in brilliance and his juniors in age, among them Robert Liston, James Syme, Robert Christison — and among his own pupils William Fergusson would one day achieve a remarkable name. The Enlightenment had given

up the ghost in certain other places — the chair of Philosophy at
Edinburgh having descended from Adam Ferguson to Dugald
Stewart was now disgraced by the blatantly political appointment of
the Tory John Wilson, otherwise Christopher North, an entertaining
lecturer but otherwise adding nothing to his subject. Indeed it could
be maintained that Wilson was in his way the ironic coda to the
Enlightenment: in its heyday the Enlightenment in Scotland — and
in America and France — had been distinguished for the capacity of
its stars to shine over many fields in addition to their own, whereas
Wilson could shine, but not over his own field. This very matter of
versatility can be extolled too far. While it bred a wholesome mutual
nourishment it could also make for superficiality and flightiness. But
at its finest it showed the spectacle of a mind grown disciplined and
deep in one set of disciplines transforming the understanding of
another by the subjection of it to a set of techniques tried and proven
in another sphere.

By 1828 the Scottish Enlightenment was no longer producing a
range of men who were masters in several disciplines at once. If the
medical scene looked fresh, original and vital it was no longer with
figures who would shine far beyond their own fraternity. The
nineteenth century would prove Edinburgh's greatest epoch of all in
the production of original discovery, but as Hugh MacDiarmid was
to point out in *Scottish Scene*, such triumphs as there were receive little
recognition outside the field of medicine proper. The great men of
the Enlightenment had a hold over the communications media in the
polite world which ensured that success in one branch of scholarship
received its celebration by the *literati* in others. Specialisation was
now tightening its grasp over learning, and one of the results would
be that the sciences stopped talking to one another and to the public
at large. In this way Knox was unique: Syme, Liston, Christison and
Fergusson have little claim on scholarly attention outside the world
of medicine. But Knox was to shine in a field far beyond the medical,
even if the origins of his interests in it are to be found in the study of
anatomy.

A nice point exists, in any case, as to how far the term "Enlightenment" may be used to cover the persons whose attitudes were so
strongly critical of the whole concept of scientific investigation and
discovery at any cost. Of the most interesting writers at this point,
Scott, Carlyle and Christopher North were all bitterly anti-
enlightenment and indeed the reflections of Scott and North
pronounce the obsequies for the Enlightenment ethos after Burke
and Hare had become known. Professor Smout finds the term

"golden age" serves his purpose better. But of course the Scotts and Norths had their role to play in the Enlightenment: they were its critics and gadflies who forced it to more constructive self-defence and more drastic attempts to justify itself. Certainly the energy of most parties had become dissipated in literary exchanges rather than in scientific advancement. Yet Robert Knox himself, until his ruin, took strength and comfort from his critics. The intellectual arrogance of the Enlightenment was never more strongly asserted than in him. What brought it and him down finally was the proof that the superiority of Science to the common prejudices of Society broke before the exposure of the sins of Science itself. The Enlightenment alternately sneered and thundered at the barbarism of men and their laws; Burke and Hare proved the Enlightenment guilty of barbarities from which even a judge such as Lord Braxfield would draw back in horror. Science had pronounced itself the superior of Social Ethics; now it came tumbling down from its throne to the dust. Ironically the circumstances in which it fell robbed it of the only defence it could have and the only justification it could still maintain.

The background may be stated simply enough. The University of Edinburgh had its resident professoriate, good and bad, but around it were what were then called "private lecturers". (Oddly enough, the term was apparently destroyed by Wilson alias North who made some insulting reference to how private many of them were when asked to toast them at a public banquet: the more cumbersome usage whence the term "extra-mural" devolved dated from that time.) As the performance of Professor Alexander Monro *tertius* declined the students flocked to the dissecting-rooms of Dr John Barclay at Surgeons' Square. Well they might: there were over 400 of them, yet neither in inspiration nor in practical experiments had they any means for self-advancement. At the time the Burke and Hare murders broke, Monro was being bitterly lampooned in the *Lancet* for his lack of system, his dullness, his evident indifference and his low standards. It was becoming a case of deficient teaching compensated for by deficient examination. The *Dictionary of National Biography* lists the number of distinguished names who studied under Monro, but neglects to point out that the result was that almost all of them made haste to study under Barclay too. John Bell, the elder brother of Sir Charles Bell, stated in 1810 that "In Dr Monro's class, unless there be a fortunate succession of bloody murders, not three subjects are dissected in the year. On the remains of a subject fished up from the bottom of a tub of spirits, are demonstrated those delicate nerves, which are to be avoided or divided in our operations;

and these are demonstrated once at the distance of one hundred feet". The increase in subjects in the event of the "fortunate succession of bloody murders" required, of course, that the murders be detected as the hangman was the chief means by which Monro, under the law, obtained his corpses — though, despite the hideous range of offences for which hanging was still the penalty, murder alone got the Professor his corpses. There is a pleasing irony in the thought that Knox's large supply of corpses was equally to benefit from a "fortunate succession of bloody murders", with the difference that in his case the supply could only be maintained when the murders were undetected.

Barclay's achievement was an impressive one, and in 1817 an attempt was made to create a Chair in Comparative Anatomy within the University of which he was intended to be the occupant. Monro bestirred himself with a vigour on this point which he never showed in teaching or research; and the Chair was prevented from coming into being. But Barclay's reputation grew even greater, and by the time he retired at the age of sixty-five it was his, and not the University's, school of anatomy which maintained the lustre of Edinburgh medicine. As Dr James Moores Ball sums up: "He had built up a large and valuable museum; he had assembled an extensive library; he had framed a new anatomical nomenclature; many of his pupils had attained eminence in the profession." And from the latter he chose as his successor Robert Knox, who gave his first course of lectures on anatomy and physiology in the winter of 1825-26, thereby proving his own superb intellectual quality, inspirational discourse and vast range of knowledge. It gave the final touch to the happiness of the last year of John Barclay's life. Knox in his view had been his best pupil.

Robert Knox was born in Edinburgh probably in 1793, but possibly a year or so earlier: it put him about the same age as William Burke and William Hare. Knox lacked the fortune of familial connections: no Alexander Monro *primus* or *secundus* was to be found among his progenitors to guide his succession to a chair, nor did he have the advantage, like Christison, of having a father in academic life even if in a very different faculty. But the Scottish "democratic intellect" was at his disposal; he won his education in the Edinburgh High School, as Walter Scott, John and Charles Bell and Henry Brougham also did, and in a much less elitish society than London, he could have hopes of sure rewards were he to maintain his standards of industry and inquiry. But under the teaching of Alexander Monro, Knox met his first failure; it may have been that the indulgent examination

system with which Monro tried to compensate for his indifference as
a teacher could pull the mediocre through while destroying the
brilliant but ignorant. In despair he fled to Barclay, and Barclay
launched him as an anatomist. His examination performance now
proved one of the most memorable triumphs of the era: "Anatomy,
described in the choicest of Latin words, seemed to ooze from his
fingertips," commented Moores Ball. From graduation in 1814 he
entered the army as an assistant-surgeon. Like William Burke he also
missed being present at the battle of Waterloo, but he reached
Brussels quickly enough after it to have his hands full with the
wounded and dying. He was never to obtain subjects with the same
ease again.

It was some two years after this experience that he made his way
to the Cape of Good Hope, where his anatomical investigations took
him into anthropological and sociological fields. He published some
of his conclusions, and it is clear that it was the work he undertook
then which laid the foundations of the racial theories with which he
later became associated. This is an important point in the light of the
events of 1828. Knox was not to publish his major work, *The Races of
Men*, until 1850, but it is noteworthy that it was founded on
observations and conclusions made some thirty years before, and that
the views expressed in it would have been held by him with little
change at the time of the Burke and Hare murders. After his African
experience Knox studied in Paris where he advanced his
investigations in ethnology and placed his anatomical expertise on a
footing with the latest advances and most progressive theories. In
fact he eclipsed his master, adding the inductions of Cuvier, then
crowning his career in the making of palaeontology, and the
revolutionary and as yet widely ignored anatomical theories of
Geoffrey St Hilaire, to the excellent foundation Barclay had
established in comparative anatomy. Knox's student intake broke all
previous records. They came because he was so brilliant, and
expounded his subject so well; but it was also vital that there be no
shortage of subjects and this, in a year such as 1828-29 when he had
504 pupils, was a daunting task.

One point is fundamental to our understanding of him. Bridie,
Dylan Thomas and others have looked on the private life of Knox —
his taste for agreeable female society, his apparently sexual
attractiveness despite a blasted eye, falling hair and an almost satanic
smile, his marriage to a woman of the lower orders and his bitter
defensiveness on the subject. But the clue to Knox lies not in his
private life but in his scholarly world. His pupil Fergusson may have

touched the world of Burke and Hare — or at least that of Mary
Paterson — in a private capacity, but Knox, for all of his
eccentricity, does not cross the barriers in that manner. His home in
Newington Place, his work in Surgeons' Square, his visits to the
fashionable drawing-rooms and his walks with colleagues across the
Meadows are the even tenor of his way. Burke and Hare were
essential to his public life, and his relations with them can only be
accounted on that basis. He may have married into the lower classes;
for that reason, perhaps, he did not frequent their society. The lower
classes might send their driftwood to him and he would make that
driftwood the firm supports of his house of intellect; but the journey
must be theirs.

It was a professional association, but it was one of outstanding
emotional quality. Knox's brilliance, his wit, his embattled snarl
against his rival in the University, his tremendous sense of teamwork
and military organisation of his officers — all of this made Burke and
Hare even more inevitable. The chief could not let the students
down. The students could not let the chief down. The subjects had to
be found, and hence the urgency of the twenty-year-old Fergusson
and his fellows. Knox was a hard taskmaster, but he praised and
promoted brains, and industry, and resource, and loyalty. They fled
to do his bidding before he even bade. The symbolism of the whole
thing was noteworthy even in its staging. Burke, who had an eye for
the dramatic and the poetic—several phrases in his confessions read
more like Gaelic imagery than repertorial improvement — set up the
entrances and exits at Surgeons' Square with fine precision. The
interview with the assistants would first take place: then Knox
would make his entrance, look over the corpse, say his piece, name a
price, tell the boys to see to it. In a word, he went to some trouble to
ensure that he did not go to some trouble. More by example than by
instruction he gave his pupils their priorities and their sense of the
overriding importance of the main business.

Knox was an actor and a showman — any good lecturer must be
— but there was no falsity to his expertise or to his identification
with students. He took their fees, but he gave them value, perhaps
much better than value. The resultant mutual admiration went far
deeper than an ordinary love affair. They exulted in his latest sally,
his most recent exposition, his finest barb against the absurd Monro,
his superb and lightening elucidation, his assured and lucid references
to the latest scholarship of Paris, his firm, clear and relevant citation of
his African discoveries. And he, knowing that it was, at bottom,
his mind and voice that they were applauding, revelled in their

applause. His was no vulgar pandering to them; his was a hold on their loyalties for the best of reasons. And when the crash came, his class — the largest he had ever had — rallied to him as never before. After all, it had been for them that he had done what he had done, and had shut his eyes to what he had shut his eyes. It was before them that the finest displays of his terrific courage were given; his contemptuous ignoring of the howls of rage from the mob outside the lecture theatre, his grim and well-known readiness to sell his life dearly in the event of a murderous attack, his unflinching countenance against threats while loyal students opened paths in hostile crowds before him by well-chosen blows. That class overbore his protests and presented him with a gold watch. But though the students he had would stand by him, the students he had yet to obtain did not, and the numbers began to fall. Those students who had been in their mid-teens in 1828 might still come to him; by the time of the crisis they had made their commitment to medicine. They knew that Knox was charged with providing a market for murderers but that it was in the cause of the students he had incurred such a charge. The generation that fell away from Knox was those who had been young enough to be frightened by the story of Burke and Hare. Numbers began to fall in 1835, and by 1844 he had been driven to go to Glasgow, where his intake was smaller than ever.

But the bond between students and Knox was as real and as intellectual as that between students and Socrates, as different from Monro's dishonourable indulgence to cover his inadequate teaching as gold from dross. And it was this bond which prompted so much enmity to Knox. It is a nice question whether Christopher North, whose relaxation consisted in roistering with congenial companions and whose lasting work was agreeable but ephemeral journalism, was quite as secure as Knox himself in his comments about students. After all, Knox won his unenviable notoriety because of his desire to serve the students: North won his reputation in time spent away from them. Student loyalty becomes another charge against an academic when his critics have done little to win such applause themselves. North, in his capacity as Professor Wilson, could win the just applause of a good lecturer, but this was little more than the applause which would go to a popular actor. Knox won the reverence given to the great teacher and director of scholarly destinies. Accordingly, when the crisis broke, North assailed the loyalty of Knox's students in terms seldom directed towards students, for all of the violence of anti-student rhetoric in recent years. There is a certain charm in the thought that North pilloried students who did go to lectures in terms

he would never have applied to those who did not. As to his
vindication of the howling mob watching Burke's execution in
contrast to his execration of the students' loyalty to Knox, it must
make for one of the most striking examples of ferocious anti-
intellectualism to have emanated from the holder of a university
chair:

> ". . . But for the accursed system he and his assistants acted on, only
> two or three experimental murders would have been perpetrated, —
> unless we must believe that other — nay, all other lecturers would
> have done as he did, which, in my belief, would be wickedly to libel the
> character of our anatomists.
>
> "*Shepherd.* Is't true that his class received him, in consequence of
> these horrid disclosures, with three cheers?
>
> "*North.* Though almost incredible, it is true. But that savage yell
> within those blood-stained walls, is no more to the voice of the public,
> than so much squeaking and grunting in a pig-sty during a storm of
> thunder. Besides, many of those who thus disgraced themselves and
> their human nature, were implicated in the charge; and instead of
> serving to convince any one, out of the shambles, of their own or their
> lecturer's innocence, it has had, and must have had, the very opposite
> effect — exhibiting a ruffian recklessness of general opinion and
> feeling on a most appalling subject as yet altogether unexplained, and,
> as many think, incapable of any explanation that will remove from the
> public mind, even in its calmest mood, the most horrible and damning
> suspicions. The shouts and cheers at Burke's appearance on the
> scaffold, were right — human nature being constituted as it is; but the
> shouts and cheers on Dr Knox's appearance at the table where so many
> of Burke's victims had been dissected, after having been murdered,
> were 'horrible, most horrible', and calculated — whatever may be
> their effect on more thinking minds — to confirm in those of the
> populace the conviction that they are all a gang of murderers together,
> and determined to insult, in horrid exultation, all the deepest feelings
> of humanity — without which a people would be a mob more fierce
> and fell than the concentrated essence of the Burkes, the Hares, and the
> Macdougals."

One point raised by North is noteworthy: the question of whether
Knox's ethics and precautions were those of the other anatomists.
Now, in one respect Knox was certainly guilty of exacerbating the
situation. His own proud and arrogant personality, his love of
offensive reference to rivals, his delight in turning his students into a
cadre of embattled admirers as against those attending other classes
— all inevitably increased rivalry among the anatomists and heated
up the competition for subjects. It was but one minor incident in the
story that one of Knox's admirers should have been quick to turn
Burke and Hare away from Monro's door. Monro himself was no

match for Knox, save in that he had the chair and Knox did not. The trouble was that Knox was not only venting his spleen against the incompetent and unworthy professor, but against any of his rivals, be they older or younger, richer or poorer, well-connected or of obscure origin, brilliant or bovine. His savagery in reference to his juniors forced them on the defensive, and in order to hold their following they in turn had to whip up the corpse market and improve their standing with resurrection men.

Admittedly, Knox was not the only one creating a market. His friends and disciples were bitterly to complain that he was made a scapegoat, and perhaps he was. In fact, one of the doctors was obliged to make an investigation, and his questions to Knox illustrate some of the problems of the common predicament. Robert Christison was then in his thirtieth year, having obtained at the age of twenty-five the Chair in Medical Jurisprudence and Police at the University of Edinburgh. The police did much for the University's pursuit of research; Monro got the hanged corpses of criminals, and Christison got the victims. The problem for Christison was that when the Burke and Hare murders first broke, the police recovered a body from Dr Knox's and arrested Burke, Helen MacDougal and the Hares, and at this point it looked as though everything might turn on Christison's own investigations. We will deal with the case of Mrs Campbell or Docherty under the trial: suffice it to say now that the body contained bruises, and it fell to Christison to work out whether these had been produced after death (in which case they might have happened in the business of packing), before death (in which case they might have nothing to do with the fact of death itself at all), or during some act of violence which was the cause of death. In fact, Christison neither in the witness-box nor elsewhere could come to satisfactory conclusions on the point, and his investigations only resulted in definite conclusions when Burke and Hare came to his assistance, the latter by turning King's evidence and the former by producing his confessions. Christison had been publishing a series of "Causes and Observations in Medical Jurisprudence" in the *Edinburgh Medical Journal* and in vol. xxxi (April, 1829), he discussed his problem in detail, under the head *"MURDER BY SUFFOCATION.—Injury of the spine after death imitating an injury during life—Experiments on the effects of blows given after death."* (The propensity of almost all parties to perpetrate new myths on Burke and Hare even extended to the *Medical Journal*, whose clerical staff unconsciously testified to the inaccurate gossip about Burke's and Hare's methods by listing Christison's article in the table of contents as *"Murder by Strangling, with some Remarks on the Effects of External Violence on the Human Body soon after Death"* – strangling, of course, would have been instantly detectable but it was often mentioned in place of the correct "suffocation". Christison's experiments were detailed and were cold-blooded enough to repel a future generation. (Conan Doyle remembered his days as a medical student in the Edinburgh of the now aged Christison when he ascribed that experiment to Sherlock Holmes in *A Study in Scarlet*.)

Christison, then, might have had his doubts about Knox, but his own delicacy was not at the forefront where scientific research was concerned. So when he called on Knox to see whether he could obtain further information he was not in any position to adopt a weak-stomached approach, nor probably would he have wished to. Christison summed up their conversation with the words "Knox, a man of undoubted talent, but notoriously deficient in principle and in heart, was exactly the person to blind himself against suspicion, and fall into blameable carelessness. But it was absurd to charge him with anything worse." Christison's problem was that while he himself was making his investigations, rumours were flying around that Knox had put up the money for Burke and Hare to murder; and that was very awkward from everyone's point of view. Once this suspicion was entered against one doctor, it would be entered against all. Moreover, the question existed as to how many others would have fallen into "blameable carelessness". Knox was cavalier; but would Monro, or Syme, or Christison himself be particularly quick to subject the delivery-man to cross-examination on the arrival of a corpse? Given the fact that most cadavers were obtained by resurrectionism, which was in itself illegal, doctors were accustomed not to ask questions of the vendors. By definition they were winking at one kind of illegality: why should they then be so careful to work out at which kind of illegality they were winking?

Christison was officially making one investigation in support of the police inquiries but he was, simultaneously, committed to a defence of the medical profession. There was a limit to what he wanted to discover and where enquiries were to go. It is clear that he did not like Knox — the bullying manner of the elder man would be at its very worst in confronting the young professor. The notorious deficiency "in principle and in heart" would have been all the more pointed in Christison's mind by the repetition of what Knox had said to his class about Liston, about Syme and no doubt about himself. (Leighton insists that Knox once accused Liston in a lecture of accidentally killing a patient, and added for good measure that Liston had originally been a butcher's apprentice but had been dismissed for stealing a sheep's head and trotters.) But Christison knew that if things turned strongly against Knox investigations might become more widespread as to the origins of certain cadavers. The recipients of official corpses, such as Monro and himself, might be relatively immune, but Syme and Liston would be in grave difficulties.

Christison was, if anything, disposed to cut down on the sensational aspects of the case where he could. He is the only person whose writing I have seen which actually questions whether Burke and Hare killed as many as sixteen people ("villains of his [Burke's] rare stamp are apt to indulge in the strange vainglory of exaggerating their actual wickedness"). But he says he did think that Knox "must have found it very difficult to supply" his class "with sufficient materials for dissection" and that he had therefore "rather wilfully shut his eyes to incidents which ought to have excited the grave suspicions of a man of his intelligence". This was a nice point. If Knox was so clear as to his own intellectual superiority to that of his contemporaries his professions of ignorance were curious.

It must have been a strange and unpleasant conversation. On the one hand the younger doctor was trying to ascertain any suspicions the older may have had, and the older was seeking to explain he could hardly be blamed for not having them. On the other, there is a touch of the older man impliedly snarling that they were all taking meat where they could get it. What Knox actually did do was to hand Christison a story so improbable that Christison clearly thought it was manufactured for the occasion. Christison said that the Campbell or Docherty body removed by the police from Knox's rooms "must have been delivered there while warm and flexible, and consequently never had been buried. He made very light of this suggestion, and told me that he had ten or eleven bodies brought the previous winter to his rooms in as recent a state". That statement, of course, was certainly true, though Christison — this was before the confessions of Burke and Hare — can hardly have expected that its veracity arose from all of them having been murdered. The corpses, said Knox, "were got by his providers watching the low lodging-houses in the Cowgate, Grassmarket, and West Port, and, when a death occurred, purchasing the body from the tenant before anyone could claim it for interment". But Christison apparently did not believe him, though if he said he did not he has concealed it (also concealing what must have been Knox's explosive rejoinder). Knox, thought Christison, "could scarcely have been so little aware of the habits of the low populace who frequent these dens, as not to know that a death in one of them brought a constant succession of visitors to look at the corpse, and keep up a series of orgies till they saw it carried off for burial; and consequently, that no such arrangement with the lodging-house keeper as he described was practicable. In fact Professor Syme" — who, of course, was not then a professor — "told me that, when he taught anatomy a short time before, he had tried to organise such a system of supply, but that he found it impossible, for the reason given".

But was Knox lying, and was the scheme he spoke of an impossible one? He may well have convinced himself he had such a system, with Hare, who was, after all, a lodging-house keeper. The system of wakes, which is what Christison meant by his reference to "a series of orgies", is likely to have been employed by Irish and Highland immigrants, but Christison is making the error of assuming that proceedings which would be held for people who were known to the community would be extended for those who were not well known. On what we know from Burke and Hare, Joe the miller and the Englishman from Cheshire died with no reason for anyone to think it was not from the progress of their respective illnesses, yet no mention of a wake arose nor any need to prevent one. Joe — as the reference to his family indicates — was a Lowlander; the Englishman is agreed to have been English. Hence wakes did not obtain in their cultures. Christison was somewhat vulgarly generalising for all of the lower classes on the basis of Gaelic usage, and even there the wake would be less likely to apply when the deceased were so nomadic as to be unknown in their new surroundings. As to Syme's experience, he was probably unable to command the fees Knox could pay and hence no business resulted although he was given an Irish — or a Highland — "pleasant answer" as a reason for non-performance. If Syme had put up such fees his "lodging-house keeper" acquaintances might well have thought about a little Burking and Hareing on their own account.

Knox's peril became much more acute when Hare confessed and put an end to Christison's uncertain speculations. Because of the notoriety of the cases the Procurator-Fiscal decided to proceed against Burke and Helen MacDougal in the matter of Mary Paterson and Daft Jamie, in addition to the corpse in hand. Had this happened, Knox, who was subpoenaed but not called, would have had to explain why he was so convinced that they had not been murdered. Knox had indulged himself in the matter of Mary Paterson by inviting fine art-work on the corpse, so he could not plead that the cadaver had made no impression on his mind; and the decease of one so young might well have elicited more enquiry than it seems to have done. Fergusson was also subpoenaed, and he would have to account for his acceptance in his professional capacity of the decease of someone whose vitality in hers he had remarked but a few days before. Knox's trouble in preserving the body is interesting: Lonsdale indicates he wished to have it preserved from some time as an excellent specimen of the young female form. And there would have been the delicate question about Daft Jamie, whom Knox's porter said was ordered for dissection out of its natural turn when the students insisted the corpse was that of Jamie and Knox insisted that it was not. The head was rapidly removed and Fergusson took charge of the malformed feet. It is difficult to be certain whether any rumour of Jamie's disappearance was then in circulation; Roughead speaks of a "hue and cry" but these things tend to be arisen in retrospect, and it is a little hard to see Knox, Fergusson and the rest of them being convulsed by an agitation as to the whereabouts of an idiot vagrant from the West Port. What is much more likely is that they knew nothing about Daft Jamie being missing (and at the time they took delivery neither may anyone else), that Paterson the porter and one or two others who knew their West Port may have announced it was Jamie, that Knox somewhat testily took the line that a cadaver "wasn't anybody" on the ground that if cadavers were thought of as people it would stand in the way of scientific investigation, and that Fergusson and his associate removed identifiable features in that such marks could lead to trouble whether the body had been murdered *or resurrected*. Certainly neither Knox nor anyone else would have wished to find themselves trading civilities with the relatives of some dear departed who was now in the doctor's possession, whether via the grave or otherwise. Thomas Hood's contemporary ballad "Mary's Ghost" discussed the effects of medical dissection on the tender passions:

> The arm that used to take your arm
>   Is took to Dr Vyse,
> And both my legs are gone to walk
>   The hospital at Guy's.
>
> I vowed that you should have my hand,
>   But Fate gives us denial;
> You'll find it there at Mr Bell's
>   In spirits in a phial. . . .
>
> The cock it crows, I must be gone.
>   My William, we must part;
> And I'll be yours in death although
>   Sir Astley has my heart.

After the trial and execution of Burke, Knox asked a committee to investigate the allegations against him. On 23 January Sir Walter Scott was asked to be on it, and declined, on the ground that he was being asked to "lend a hand to whitewash this much to be suspected individual. But he shall ride off on no back of mine"; Scott had already strongly protested on the 14th about Knox being allowed to read a paper on some dissections to the Royal Society — it was "very bad taste to push himself forward just now". The committee was formed without him, initially under the chairmanship of the Marquess of Queensberry, who withdrew after a month: the committee reported on 13 March. The Marquess's reasons remain unknown to this day, but we may be very safe in doubting that objectivity and integrity had much to do with them. In the childish fashion of British society, he owed his place on such an enquiry to his rank rather than to his attainments, which were those of patronage of the boxing-ring. He had known Byron, and had cut something of a figure in the Regency, although eclipsed by the famous Duke, "Old Q", from whom his Marquisate had collaterally descended. He was not the Marquess of the Rules and the Wilde scandal, but his great-grandfather. But it was not exactly a family to produce models of probity and mental stability.

Those who did report were Mr (afterwards Sir John) Robinson, that secretary to the Royal Society to whom Scott had made his protest in the matter of the projected essay. It may be that Scott's objection had led Knox and Robinson to have an enquiry set on foot. Otherwise the personnel was unexceptionable — a couple of advocates, four professors of whom two were in surgery, the heir to a baronetcy, and a banker. The committee forthrightly stated that they knew of no evidence "that Dr Knox or his assistants knew that murder was committed in procuring any of the subjects brought to his rooms, and the Committee firmly believe they did not". They agreed that suspicion might have been aroused by the brevity of the interval between death and delivery, the "absence of external marks of disease" and the views of Knox and other anatomists that most people engaged in the body traffic were of a "generally abandoned" character. (This, incidentally, suggests that all resurrectionists were embryo Burkes and Hares, which raises an interesting point about public ethics — were Burke and Hare, as so often stated, unique in their infamy, or were they potentially two of thousands? The committee, in its aside, was opening up a fear which may have been widespread.) But since nobody knew that Dr Knox or anyone else had ever had suspicions excited by Burke and Hare, the committee found no evidence that they had been. No marks on the bodies were known to have given a presumption of death by violence as against disease, and dissection naturally made further investigation difficult. Knox was recorded by nobody as telling visitors, assistants or his hundreds of students that he had suspicions of murder (granted that Knox's *obiter dicta* in his otherwise excellent lectures were peculiar at the best of times, especially when discussing absent colleagues, it still seems a little bizarre to have him remark in mid-incision that he wondered if this particular corpse might not have been a product of murder). The committee noted that nobody had ever disfigured a corpse to prevent recognition (this made no mention of the swiftness with which Daft Jamie was dismembered, but it is true that he was not, in any exceptional way, "disfigured"). The committee did feel Knox had been "incautious" in leaving himself open to be imposed on by Burke "who appears from all the evidence before the committee to have conducted himself with great address and appearance of honesty, as well as in his conversations with Dr Knox as in his more frequent intercourse with his assistants", and also in leaving the bulk of the dealings to his youthful assistants and his doorkeeper. "It appears also that he directed or allowed these dealings to be conducted on the understanding (common to him with some other anatomists) that it would only tend to diminish or divert the supply of subjects to make any particular inquiry of the person bringing them as to the place and mode of obtaining them." The committee felt this procedure had been "very improper in the case of persons bringing bodies which had not been interred. They think that the notoriously bad character of persons who generally engage in any such traffic in addition to the novelty and particular nature of the system on which these men professed to be acting, undoubtedly demanded greater vigilance". The objection to this is that the "notoriously bad character" was conceded as applying as much, if not more, to persons with disinterred corpses to hand as to persons with uninterred ones. And the "bad character" argument is the usual class-conscious begging of an awkward question. In fact, nothing is known against Burke's character until he took up murder, and anything about Hare's before that time remains the merest speculation.

The committee concluded by stating that the extent to which Knox could be blamed in the matter of Burke and Hare "is, that by this laxity of the regulations under which bodies were received in his rooms, he unintentionally gave a degree of facility to the disposal of the victims of their crimes, which under better regulations would not have existed, and which is doubtless matter of deep and lasting regret, not only to himself but to all who have reflected on the importance and are therefore interested in the prosecution of the study of anatomy. But while they point out this circumstance as the only ground of censure which they can discover in the conduct of Dr Knox, it is fair to observe, that perhaps the recent disclosures have made it appear reprehensible to many who would not otherwise have adverted to its possible consequences." The last crack was well taken. Burke and Hare had enlightened Scotland in no uncertain way, and the result of their proceedings was that much which people had preferred not to think about was well and truly under their notice.

Those who knew Knox might wonder about his "deep and lasting regret", save in so far as what happened was likely to inhibit his own work and career. They were given little time so to wonder, because on 17 March 1829, Knox broke silence on the subject for once and once only. There is a bleak dignity in the document which conveys some of the character of its author. It was addressed to the editor of the *Caledonian Mercury*, whose reports had hitherto done little to discourage the inflammation of the public mind against him:

> Sir—I regret troubling either you or the public with anything personal, but I cannot be insensible of the feelings of my friends, or of the character of the profession to which I have the honour of belonging. Had I alone been concerned, I should never have thought of obtruding on the public by this communication.
>
> I have a class of above 400 pupils. No person can be at the head of such an establishment without necessarily running the risk of being imposed upon by those who furnish the material of their science to anatomical teachers; and, accordingly, there is hardly any such person who has not occasionally incurred odium or suspicion from his supposed accession to those violations of the law, without which anatomy can scarcely now be practiced. That I should have become an object of popular prejudice, therefore, since mine happened to be the establishment with which Burke and Hare chiefly dealt, was nothing more than what I had to expect. But if means had not been purposely taken, and most keenly persevered in, to misrepresent facts and to inflame the public mind, that prejudice would at least have stood on right ground, and would ultimately have passed away, by its being seen that I had been exposed to a mere misfortune which would almost certainly have occurred to anybody else who had been in my situation.
>
> But every effort has been employed to convert my misfortune into positive and intended personal guilt of the most dreadful character. Scarcely any individual has ever been the object of more systematic or atrocious attacks than I have been. Nobody acquainted with this place requires to be told from what quarter these have proceeded.

I allowed them to go on for months without taking the slightest notice of them; and I was inclined to adhere to this system, especially as the public authorities by never charging me with any offence, gave the whole attestation they could that they had nothing to charge me with. But my friends interfered for me. Without consulting me, they directed an agent to institute the most rigid and unsparing examination into the facts. I was totally unacquainted with this gentleman, but I understood that in naming Mr Ellis they named a person whose character is a sufficient pledge for the propriety of his proceedings.

The result of his inquiries was laid before the Dean of Faculty and another Counsel, who were asked what ought to be done. These gentlemen gave it as their opinion that the evidence was completely satisfactory, and there was no want of actionable matter, but that there was one ground on which it was my duty to resist the temptation of going into a Court of law. This was, that the disclosures of the most innocent proceedings even of the best-conducted dissecting-room must always shock the public and be hurtful to science. But they recommended that a few persons of undoubted weight and character should be asked to investigate the matter, in order that, if I deserved it, an attestation might be given to me which would be more satisfactory to my friends than any mere statements of mine could be expected to be. This led to the formation of a Committee, which was never meant by me to be anything but private. But the fact of its sitting soon got into the newspapers, and hence the necessity under which I am placed of explaining how that proceeding, in which the public has been made to take an interest, has terminated.

I have been on habits of friendship with some of the Committee, with others of them I have been acquainted, and some of them I don't even know by sight. I took no charge whatever of their proceedings. In order that there might be no pretence for saying that truth was obstructed from fear, I gave a written protection to every person to say what he chose about or against me. The extent to which this was in some instances taken advantage of will probably not be soon forgotten by those who witnessed it.

After a severe and laborious investigation of about six weeks, the result is contained in the following report, which was put into my hands last night. It is signed by every member of the Committee except one, who ceased to act long before the evidence was completed.

I cannot be supposed to be a candid judge of my own case, and therefore it is extremely probable that any opinion of mine on the last view adopted by the Committee is incorrect and theirs right. If it be so, I most willingly submit to the censure they have inflicted, and shall hold it my duty to profit from it by due care hereafter. My consolation is, that I have at least not been obstinate in my errors, and that no sanction has ever been given in any fair quarter to the more serious imputations by which it has been the interest of certain persons to assail me. Candid men will judge of me according to the situation in which I was placed at the time, and not according to the wisdom which was unexpectedly been acquired since.

This is the very first time that I have ever made any statement to the public in my own vindication, and it shall be the last. It would be unjust

to the authors of the former calumnies to suppose they would not
renew them now. I can only assure them that, in so far as I am
concerned, they will renew them in vain.

I have the honour to be, &c., &c.,

R. KNOX.

A detached view of this document might lead to the conclusion
that Knox was making a great fuss about his own broadmindedness in
accepting the adverse conclusions in a report which was extremely
favourable in its general remarks, and that there was a touch of
cunning in making so grand a gesture out of this receptivity. No
doubt many contemporary witnesses may have allowed some such
reflection to cross their mind. But in fact Knox was an incredibly
proud man, who had allowed no man to be his master or be
admitted to the right to criticise him since the death of John Barclay.
If there was art in the matter, there was conviction also. It must also
be said that Knox continued his long career as his own worst enemy
in personal relations, however acute his competition for that honour.
Knox's opinions were progressive and his enemies likely to be
Tories; yet he deliberately dragged Burke's own counsel, Moncreiff,
the Whig Dean of Faculty, into his discussion, and considering that
some persons were hinting he paid for the defence of Burke and
MacDougal (an allegation neither truthful nor sensible but
revelatory of the paranoia of the times) he was being rash in the
extreme to introduce his name. This alone would be likely to fuel the
fires of an embattled Tory such as North, as indeed the April number
of *Blackwood's* would make clear. Again, Knox himself seemed to
reveal a paranoid streak with his ominous but vague references to the
sources whence attacks were coming: did he mean the Church of
Scotland, the University establishment, the medical rivals or some
other unspecified area? In fact Knox's charges of conspiracy against
him were as wild as the allegations that he had instructed Burke and
Hare in murder or paid for their defence; the screams of rage in the
popular press and in broadsheets had nothing of an artificial
campaign about them. We may be very safe in doubting if Professor
Alexander Monro, for one, regretted to hear of his formidable
enemy being hanged in effigy, cursed by the mob around Burke's
gallows, or vandalised by window-smashing crowds in Surgeons'
Square or Newington Place, but he would have been even less
capable of getting up such agitation as he would have been of giving a
good lecture. Other errors in the document again reflected temper
and not guilt, but they did not help the author. The "months" for
which Knox held silence coupled with the six weeks of the

investigation and the enquiries of Mr Ellis all offer a time-span incompatible with the time available, but this is of little account. Knox's argument that his innocence was attested by the failure of the authorities to prosecute him was so ridiculous that it really creates the assumption of innocence: as everyone was prepared to remind him, the Hares were not prosecuted either. In fact the letter is a good indication of how stupid a brilliant man can be.

"No case ever struck the public heart or imagination with greater horror," wrote Henry Cockburn, Helen MacDougal's defence counsel, in his immortal *Memorials*.

> And no wonder. For the regular demand for anatomical subjects, and the high prices given, held out a constant premium to murder; and when it was shewn to what danger this exposed the unprotected, everyone felt himself living in the midst of persons to whom murder was a trade. All our anatomists incurred a most unjust, and a very alarming, though not unnatural odium; Dr Knox in particular, against whom not only the anger of the populace, but the condemnation of more intelligent persons, was specially directed. But when tried in reference to the invariable, and the necessary practice of the profession, our anatomists were spotlessly correct, and Knox the most correct of them all.

The last line might be taken as an oratorical flourish; Cockburn was a generous man and Knox had been destroyed, whereas Liston, Syme, Christison and even the wretched Monro had all survived the furore. But his argument is still a reasonable one. We have no reason to assume that what Knox did or did not do was out of keeping with the methods of the day.

Yet the question of his guilt remains, and with it the more interesting question, of what was he guilty? It is the perennial of the controversy, writers self-indulgently trying Knox again and again. Knox himself seems to emerge as some sort of Prometheus or Faust, eternally seeking the advancement of humanity against the prejudices of prevailing ethics — or prevailing superstition. But in fact the entire controversy is absurd.

Knox simply did not regard the Burke and Hare murders as criminal: on the contrary, he looked on them as an enlightened method of disposing of worthless derelicts with ultimate betterment to the more deisrable segments of humanity by reason of the benefits conferred to the study of anatomy.

Professor Philip D. Curtin has provided the clue to Knox's thinking in his *The Image of Africa*: Knox, he remarks there, was "the real founder of British racism and one of the key figures in the general Western movement toward a dogmatic pseudo-scientific racism". He quotes Knox's *Races of Man* to effect — "Race is everything: literature, science, art — in a word, civilisation depends on it." The history of the world was an evolutionary struggle between the races "especially between the light and the dark races. ... The later, light-skinned peoples were destined to ... wage a war to the death against the rest, until the dark races became extinct". Knox's opinion of the Irish was perfectly simple: they were to be eradicated from the face of the earth.

> "The really momentous question for England, as a *nation*, is the presence of three sections of the Celtic race still on her soil: the Caledonian, or Gael; the Cymbri, or Welsh; and the Irish, or Erse; and how to dispose of them. The Caledonian Celt touches the end of his career: they are reduced to about one hundred and fifty thousand; the Welsh Celts are not troublesome, but might easily become so; the Irish Celt is the most to be dreaded ... the source of all evil lies in *the race*, the Celtic race of Ireland. There is no getting over *historical facts*. Look at Wales, look at Caledonia; it is ever the same. The race must be forced from the soil; by fair means if possible; still they must leave. England's safety requires it. I speak not of the justice of the cause; nations must ever act as Machiavelli advised: look to yourself. The Orange club of Ireland is a Saxon confederation for the clearing the land of all papists and jacobites; this means Celts. If left to themselves, they would clear them out, as Cromwell proposed, by the sword; it would not require six weeks to accomplish the work. ...."

***

> "I am no believer in the extreme degree of improvement to be derived from the advancement of science,"

continued Sir Walter in his letter to Miss Edgeworth on 4 February 1829:

> "for every study of that nature tends, when pushed to a certain extent, to harden the heart, and render the philosopher reckless of everything save the objects of his own pursuit; all equilibrium in the character is destroyed, and the visual force of the understanding is perverted by being fixed on one object exclusively. Thus we see theological sects (although inculcating the moral doctrines) are eternally placing man's zeal in opposition to them; and even in the practice of the bar, it is astonishing how we become callous to right and wrong, when the question is to gain or lose a cause. I have myself often wondered how I became so indifferent to the horrors of a criminal trial, if it involved a point of law. In like manner, the pursuit of physiology inflicts tortures on the lower animals of creation, and at length comes to rub shoulders against the West Port. The state of high civilisation to which we have arrived is perhaps scarcely a national blessing, since, while the *few* are improved to the highest point, the *many* are in proportion tantalised

and degraded, and the same nation displays at the same time the very highest and the very lowest state in which the human race can exist in point of intellect. *Here* is a doctor who is able to take down the whole clock-work of the human frame, and may in time find some way of repairing and putting it together again; and *there* is Burke with the body of his murdered countrywoman. on his back, and her blood on his hands, asking his price from the learned carcass-butcher. After all, the golden age was the period for general happiness, when the earth gave its stores without labour, and the people existed only in the numbers which it could easily subsist; but this was too good to last. As our numbers grew, our wants multiplied — and here we are, contending with increasing difficulties by the force of repeated inventions. Whether we shall at last eat each other, as of yore, or whether the earth will get a flap with a comet's tail first, who . . . will venture to pronounce?''

It will serve very well as the envoi to the Scottish enlightenment.

CHAPTER 8

The King and William Burke

Part I—CHRISTMAS EVE

Macheath
The Case is Arraign'd, the Lawyers are Met,
The Judges All Rang'd—a Terrible Show.
I go undismay'd, for Death is a debt,
A debt on demand, so take what I owe.
                                        —John Gay, *The Beggar's Opera*

BURKE, Helen MacDougal and the Hares were arrested in consequence of information laid with the police by two married visitors of theirs, the Grays. The authorities worked on the matter for a month before deciding that their only firm hope of any conviction lay in persuading Hare to turn King's evidence. In the interim some investigations were made, of which the fullest record we possess is that by Christison: but his scientific researches and private inquiries proved inconclusive and in one ancillary line of investigation, as we have noted, he drew certain incorrect conclusions owing to the clouding of his mind by race and class prejudices. The Crown's case ultimately depended on the Hares. Burke was found guilty on that, and Helen MacDougal found not proven. Burke then confessed, once to the authorities, once to a reporter from the Edinburgh *Courant* in the presence of authorities, once at least to his confessor, Father William Reid (without possibility of publication). These confessions must not be confused with bogus counterparts or with the statements made by Helen MacDougal and himself before trial.

The final murder, of Mrs Campbell or Docherty, was the only one for which he was tried, and hence the only one for which we do have other substantial evidence. The Hares certainly lied in their evidence; other witnesses are not always trustworthy and their evidence at best only partly covers the events of the murder; Helen MacDougal's statements are both fragmentary and at certain points false, however little real guilt may actually attach to her. As for the contemporary accounts, with their heavy dependence on rumour, and the secondary sources, with their heavy dependence on Ireland and Leighton, they simply increase the need to turn to Burke as the one sure repository of truth in most respects.

The arrests of Burke and Helen MacDougal took place on All Saints' Day, 1 November, Mrs Campbell or Docherty having been killed on a day more associated with the power than the vulnerability of old women, to wit Hallowe'en. The body was picked up from Knox's rooms on November 2, All Souls' Day, when the Hares were arrested. Judicial examination of the prisoners took place on the 3rd.

Burke was to give two very different versions of events in his two statements made before trial, and these divergent narratives were read to the jury as the conclusion of the prosecution's case. (The fact that Helen MacDougal's second declaration — made, like Burke's second, on November 10 — supported her first may well have weighed well with the jury in the presence of the forcible change in his two stories. His second statement meant that he had lied in his first; and this left the second equally — and justly — open to question.) Burke's statement of November 3 began by certain truthful biographical data: he was Irish-born, thirty-six, resident in Scotland for ten years, a shoemaker, domiciled in the West Port for over a year and in his present house there for "about two months", and living with Helen MacDougal for about ten years but not married to her. We will continue with Burke's statement directly, its lies being sufficiently obvious in the light of his confession, but it is worth responding to the curiously haunting and compelling tone of his narrative. The compulsion has nothing to do with its credibility, but it is manifestly the work of a good story-teller at a wake speaking to a people who have never rejected the supernatural. Indeed Burke comes very close to telling the Sheriff-substitute, George Tait, Esq., that he got the body from the fairies, which in his birthplace would not have met with total incredulity, as an incident on Hallowe'en, when fairies are particularly interested in shoes:

> James Gray, with his wife and child, came to lodge with the declarant about a week ago . . . on the night of Thursday last, the 30th October, no person was in the declarant's house, except Helen MacDougal, Gray, and his wife . . . on the morning of Friday last, he rose about seven o'clock, and immediately began his work by mending a pair of shoes: . . . MacDougal rose about nine o'clock. . . . Gray rose about six o'clock, and went out . . . Gray's wife rose soon afterwards, and lighted the fire; and the declarant then rose, as before mentioned . . . he went out about nine o'clock to get some tobacco, and he returned in a few minutes, and they all four breakfasted together about

ten o'clock, and the women were occupied through the day in washing
and dressing, and sorting about the house; and Gray was going in and
out, and the declarant was working; . . . on Friday evening he told Gray
that he and his wife must go to other lodgings, because he could not
afford to support them any longer, as they did not pay for the
provisions which they used; and they went away, and the declarant
accompanied them to Hare's house, to which he recommended them . .
. . . he thinks Gray and his wife went away at five o'clock.

. . . about an hour afterwards, when he was standing at the mouth of
the entry, a man came forward to him dressed in a great coat, the cape
of which was much up about his face . . . he never saw the man before,
and does not know his name . . . the man asked if the declarant knew
where he could get a pair of shoes mended; and the declarant, being a
shoemaker, took him home with him, and got off the man's shoes, and
gave him an old pair in the meantime: . . . while the declarant was
mending the shoes, the man walked about the room, and made some
remarks about the house being a quiet place, and said that he had a box
which he wished to leave there for a short time and the declarant
consented: . . . the man went out, and in a few minutes returned with a
box, which he laid down upon the floor near the bed, which was
behind the declarant, who was sitting near the window with his face to
it . . . the declarant heard the man unroping the box, and then making a
sound as if he were covering something with straw; and the declarant
looked round, and saw him pushing the box towards the bottom of the
bed, where there was some straw on the floor, but he did not observe
anything else than the box . . . the man then got on his shoes, paid the
declarant a sixpence, and went away . . . the declarant immediately
rose to see what was in the box, and he looked under the bed, and saw a
dead body among the straw; but he could not observe whether it was a
man or a woman . . . soon afterwards the man came back, and declarant
said it was wrong for him to have brought that there, and told him to
put it back into the box, and take it away . . . the man said that he would
come back in a little and do it, and then went away, but he did not
return till Saturday evening about six o'clock; and when he did not
return on Friday night, the declarant took the box into the entry, but
allowed the body to remain under the bed.

. . . on Saturday morning about ten o'clock, he went out to the shop
of a Mr Rymer, in the West Port, and when he was there, a woman
came to the door begging, whom he had never seen before: . . . the
people in the shop refused to give her anything; and the declarant
discovering from her dialect that she came from Ireland, asked her
from what part of it she came: she said it was from Innishowan, which
is a small town [this is clearly a reporter's error for "a townland in
Innishowen which is in the north of Ireland"] in the north of Ireland,
and he then asked her name, and she said it was Mary Docherty, and the
declarant remarked that his mother's name was Docherty, and that she
came from the same part of Ireland, and that they might perhaps be
distant relations; and as she said that she had not broken her fast for
twenty-four hours, if she would come home with him he would give
her breakfast; and she accompanied him home, and got breakfast, at
which time the only other persons in the house were Helen

MacDougal, Gray, and his wife . . . she sat by the fire till about three o'clock in the afternoon, smoking a pipe, the declarant going out and getting a dram, because it was Hallowe'en, and they all five partook of the dram, sitting by the fireside . . . at three o'clock Mary Docherty said she would go to the New Town to beg some provisions for herself, and she went away accordingly. . . . he thinks Helen MacDougal was in the house when Mary Docherty went away, but does not remember of any other person being in the house. . . . a few minutes before Mary Docherty went away, William Hare's wife came into the house, but went away into the house of a neighbour, John Conway, immediately before Docherty went away; and he thinks that Hare's wife or Conway's wife may have seen Docherty go away; and Mary Docherty never returned. . . . Helen MacDougal and Gray's wife then washed the floor and cleaned out the house: . . . there was no particular reason for doing so further than to have it clear upon the Saturday night, according to their practice, and the declarant continued at his work: . . . soon afterwards Gray and his wife went away, and Helen MacDougal went to Conway's house, leaving the declarant by himself, and the declarant had not mentioned to any person about the dead body, and had no suspicion that it had been discovered.

. . . about six o'clock of the evening, while he was still alone, the man who had brought the body came, accompanied by a porter, whom the declarant knows by sight, and whose stance is somewhere about the Head of the Cowgate, or the Foot of Candlemaker Row, and whose Christian name is John . . . the man said he had come to take the away the body; and the declarant told him the box was in the entry, and the porter took it in, and the man and the porter took the body and put it into the box and roped it, and the porter carried it away . . . when the man came with the porter, he said he would give the declarant two guineas for the trouble he had in keeping the body, and proposed to take the body to Surgeons' Square to dispose of it to any person who would take it; and the declarant mentioned David Paterson, as a person who had some connexion with the surgeons, and went to Paterson's, and took him to Surgeons' Square, where he found the man and the porter waiting with the box containing the body: . . . the body was delivered, and Paterson paid a certain number of pounds to the man, and two pounds ten shillings to the declarant: . . . he then went straight home, and was informed by some of the neighbours that a report had been raised of a dead body having been found in the house, and in particular by Conway's wife, who told him that a policeman had been searching his house; and he then went out in search of a policeman, and he met Finlay and other policemen in the passage, and he told them who he was, and they went with him to the house, and found nothing there, and they took him to the Police-Office.

. . . he yesterday saw in the Police-Office the dead body of a woman, and he thinks it is the dead body which was below the bed; but it has no likeness to Mary Docherty, who is not nearly so tall. And being interrogated, Whether the man who brought the body, and afterwards came with the porter, is William Hare? Declares that he is. And being interrogated, declares, That the porter's name is John McCulloch, and declares that the box in which the body was contained was a tea-chest. And being specially interrogated, declares, That the woman above referred to, of the name of Mary Docherty, was not at his house on Friday; and he never, to his knowledge, saw her till Saturday morning at ten o'clock: That she promised him to return on the same evening; but she did not, and he does not know what may have become of her. And being interrogated, declares, That he sprinkled some whisky about the house on Saturday, to prevent any smell from the dead body. Declares, That Hare did not tell him, nor did he ask, where he got the body. Declares, That he did not observe whether there was any blood upon the body. And being specially interrogated, declares, That he had no concern in doing any harm to the woman before referred to, of the name of Mary Docherty, or to the woman whose body was brought to the house; and he does not know of any other person being concerned in doing so. Declares, that Docherty was dressed in a dark gown. And being shown a coarse linen sheet, a pillow-case, a dark printed cotton gown, and a red striped bed-gown, to which a label is affixed, and signed by the declarant and Sheriff-Substitute as relative hereto, declares, That the sheet and pillow-slip are his, and he knows nothing about the dark gown and bed-gown: That the blood upon the pillow-slip was occasioned by his having struck Helen MacDougal upon the nose, as is known to Gray and his wife; and the blood upon the sheet is occasioned by the state in which Helen MacDougal was at the time, as is known by Gray's wife. — All which he declares is true.

The deletions in the above document are purely the repeated uses of the words "Declarant" and "That" from the main body of Burke's story, a deletion policy undertaken out of respect to its literary quality.

There are some particulars in this document which show qualities of that sureness of touch with which Burke's account of himself so impressed Dr Knox, his associates, and other witnesses. It contains some plausibilities. Gray and his wife had been the informants to the police, and Mrs Gray had spoken of seeing a dead body under some straw beside the bed, and to have recognised it as that of Mrs Docherty who had participated in jollifications the evening before, Friday. What Burke was doing was separating the two quite truthful parts of the same story, the presence of the body, and the visit of Mrs Docherty. His version of the arrival of the body had decidedly outré features but was not incompatible with a world where a poor man knew he could gain a few pounds by assisting in a resurrectionist delivery. The statement would square with the story apparently told to Helen MacDougal, that he was trafficking in resurrectionist corpses, acting as middleman. But having the wit to see what Christison had by that time already observed, that the body was far fresher than would be consistent with actual digging up, he carefully did not suggest that he took the corpse to have been resurrected. He simply said that he asked no questions, which was again compatible with the lifestyle of the West Port at that time. He used a trick similar to those invoked against the law courts in his native Ireland. Coming from an environment where to fall into the hands of a hostile law meant very probable disaster, he could doubtless draw on stories current among the militia and the local fireside of means by which the law had been successfully deceived. It should be stressed that in this respect Burke's Irish origin was important, such as fiddling with weekdays as against calendar dates.

He had hinted prejudice against him on the part of the Grays, and is said to have impressed the police by this. He might be able to confuse Rymer as to the date of meeting Mrs Docherty. But he then dragged in an incredible number of people who were most unlikely to support him. He does not seem to have cleared any common story with Helen MacDougal — which again points to the absence of any conspiracy between them — and Helen MacDougal in fact testified on the same day as Burke did, in her case to the effect that Mrs Docherty had left earlier in the day but that the day of her visit was that preceding her murder, not, as in Burke's version, the day after it, that she went away at 2.00 p.m. to Saint Mary's Wynd to inquire for her son as opposed to going to the New Town to beg, that Burke was not present in the house when she left, and so forth. She was later in her statement of November 10 to amend this slightly, admitting that she had had a row with Mary Docherty who had been very troublesome and difficult and that it had ended with the old lady being driven out of the house by her. It is of course quite possible that Mrs Docherty did leave or was thrust out of the house in the afternoon, and that she later returned or was induced to return. Burke might have some confidence that he would get some sort of corroboration from Helen as to the story of departure in the afternoon; what she was bound to demolish, in the absence of prior collusion, was the Burke thesis on the date.

But Burke's impulse for self-destruction went far beyond this. The Conways were almost bound to be questioned, and so some role could reasonably be ascribed to them, and Mrs Hare might be allowed to wander in and out, as indeed during the day she was to do. But why bring in Knox's porter, unless Burke regarded him as such a ruffian that he was bound to stand over any story (and how would he know what story he was to stand by?). John McCulloch could testify to a story similar to that he had told, but he was bound to add that the person who obtained his services was neither a mysterious stranger and/or Hare but Burke himself — and indeed he did so testify. The strangest thing of all is the sudden change of the identity of the unknown stranger into the far from unknown Hare. Taken in its totality, Burke's story invited the authorities to believe that before 31 October 1828, Burke and Hare had never met in their lives. And if there was one thing about them on which a mountain of evidence could be produced, beginning with the Grays, Rymer, Paterson and McCulloch, it was that Burke and Hare had been well acquainted for some considerable time.

Burke's initial statement simply tells a narrative of a quiet man at his work, his day being broken only by a little difficulty with the lodgers and the arrival of a customer sequacious of repair for his shoes and storage for his corpse. The next day involved a little drinking in the hours around noon, but after that it had been all business, with house-cleaning and body-removal. But other witnesses testify to large amounts of drinking being done over the two days, and the policeman Fisher would later testify to Burke's "insolent tone of voice" in their initial encounter which led to arrest of Burke and Helen MacDougal, a significant variant on those excellent relations which had supplied material for Burke and Hare in the past. Mrs Conway would testify that Burke immediately before arrest was told by her husband "that there was a noise abroad, that it was reported, he had murdered the woman" to which "he laughed, and said he did not regard what all Scotland said about him". Lord Meadowbank, one of the judges, was interested enough to lead her to admission that the laughter was "very loud": "he said that he defied all Scotland to say anything against him". This unexpected expression of Irish chauvinism was offset by Helen MacDougal, who while she also "laughed very loud", "said all the world could not say anything against him". Scotland and the world thus defied, he went out and met the police. In other words, they were drunk when arrested and had probably not been sober for 24 hours. Burke may therefore have said much that incriminated him to the Superintendent who questioned him on arrival at the station: Alison, second string for the Crown, asked Fisher at the trial whether he heard "any conversation between the Superintendent and Burke" at that point but was quickly cut off by the Lord Justice-Clerk with the cryptic utterance "Keep to *that*". As Stareleigh, J., would rule in *Bardwell v. Pickwick* some years later, what the soldier said isn't evidence, especially when the soldier, as in this instance, is drunk and being lured into making a statement. It is possible that part of the declaration of November 3 in fact came from the Superintendent's notes on November 1; in any event Burke by November 3 must have been suffering from very serious alcohol withdrawal-symptoms, in that he was not only recovering from an exceptionally heavy bout over Hallowe'en and All Saints' Day, but that his imprisonment meant a sharp end to what had clearly become a very heavy reliance on alcohol. He would later say himself that he needed half a bottle with which to sleep. By November 3, his nerves must have been in rags.

Yet drunk or sober, his conduct before and after arrest does suggest a subconscious urge for self-destruction or, more specifically, self-revelation, and some of his remarks in the post-trial confessions would bear that out. And, taken as literature, that first declaration of November 3 is remarkable. There is in it almost a touch of reversion to a boyhood effort to avoid punishment for some fault by appeal to an omnipresent praeternatural world. The "mysterious stranger" himself intrudes almost as a *doppelgänger*: the story divides between the undoubtedly pleasant initial encounter with, and hospitality to, his countrywoman, and the dark sequences with the hero alone, confronted by the man in the greatcoat with cape over his face. It was as though Burke was testifying to his own dual personality. The kindly but murderous host was indeed kindly as well as murderous; and now Burke in prison, cut off from the deluding and clouding effects of intoxication, found it psychologically necessary both to confront the murderous half of his nature and to thrust it into an alien form. His own researches into Calvinism could well have led to a mental hunger for the division of his own nature into two parts, one kindly and saved, one murderous and damned; and his Irish antecedents included a wealth of folklore about the effect on human nature of mysterious visitors of either benevolent or malevolent intent. James Hogg had only a few years before published his *Private Memoirs and Confessions of a Justified Sinner* which abounds in the images of damnation and *doppelgängern*, and should thereby have made much more of Burke than the nauseous and vindictive contemplation of his incineration in the infernal regions which John Wilson alias North, accurately or otherwise, ascribes to him in the *Noctes Ambrosianae*.

Elsewhere other statements were being taken, Helen MacDougal's on November 3 and the Hares' on November 4. As Roughead points out, our only surviving evidence on the line Hare took before he turned King's evidence is a leak in the *Courant* on November 6. "The parties in custody, two men and two women (their wives), and a young lad, give a very contradictory account of the manner in which the old woman lost her life. One of the men, not

Burke, states that it was the lad who struck her in the passage, and killed her." In other words Hare's first thought was to pin the thing on the unfortunate young John Brogan. The authorities showed what they thought of this by releasing Brogan shortly, but Hare had taught them a valuable lesson. He was ready to incriminate the innocent to save his skin: it was a reasonable presumption that with due encouragement he might in time agree to incriminate the guilty.

An attempt was made to get Helen MacDougal to inform against her lover: in the Lord Advocate's words, she "positively refused". In any event it is doubtful if she could have said much but whatever she knew, she was as faithful to her Will as he to his Nellie. This restricted the market to the Hares. The Lord Advocate a few days before Burke's execution stated that since King's evidence was needed "the choice, therefore, rested between Hare and Burke; and from the information which" the Lord Advocate "possessed, it appeared to him then, as it does to him now, that Burke was the principal party, against whom it was" the Lord Advocate's "duty to proceed. Hare was therefore chosen; and his wife was taken, because he could not bear evidence against her". And, *ipso facto*, Helen MacDougal, on any estimate the least guilty of the four, paid the penalty for her loyalty by being put on trial for her life.

Burke's articulacy and literacy singled him out for attack: murderers with some education are—not always necessarily correctly—believed to be a greater danger to the community. But the prime explanation is that Hare was prepared to talk and Burke was not and therefore it appeared to Sir William Rae that Burke was the principal party. Had Burke talked, it would doubtless have appeared otherwise to Sir William.

The second declaration (November 10) admitted that the first was "incorrect in several particulars"; neither Burke nor anyone else was likely to imagine this would be viewed by a jury as anything other than an admission of lying. The Lord Justice-Clerk would be very nasty about the matter in the trial, and most unwarrantably, linked the largely consistent statements of Helen MacDougal with the mutually contradictory ones of Burke. It must have been a matter of desperate anxiety to Burke that his impulses for self-destruction should have rebounded on the head of Helen MacDougal, against whom the Lord Justice-Clerk was later to deliver so damning a direction; it accounts for the heartfelt delight Burke expressed when she was found "not proven" in that apart from his love for her it released him from the guilt of her conviction resulting on his action after as well as before his arrest. It would have been a bitter irony had Burke saved Helen from murder only to be directly responsible for her death on the gallows. As it was the Lord Justice-Clerk must have done much to confirm the condemnation of her in the public mind which in turn led to her persecution, forced departure from Scotland and possibly even her death at the hands of an unknown mob.

Burke's second declaration did not seek to incriminate Hare, and indeed went so far to clear all the parties that it is clear he was anxious to withdraw from any suggestion of trying to extricate himself by laying the blame on his partner. Mrs Docherty had come to the house on Friday, and all the events ascribed to Saturday had happened on the Friday, and Mary Docherty was admitted to have returned after her initial departure.

Burke recounted a quarrel and fight with Hare and continued that after they had been separated they sat down by the fire for further consumption of whisky, and then missed Mary Docherty, asked the women as to her, found they did not know, made a search, found that she had crept into the straw, had vomited and had died. When all were satisfied she was dead Helen MacDougal and Margaret Hare "immediately left the house, without saying anything", Burke supposing they did not want to see a dead body. The neighbours were fairly noisy, it being Hallowe'en — this was a telling point in that Burke could rightly claim possible witnesses against him were themselves likely to have been drunk on the night in question. They stripped the body, and one of them — he could not remember which — proposed selling it to the surgeons.

So they decided to sell the body to David Paterson, "whom they knew to be a porter to Dr Knox, in Surgeons' Square, and who they knew received subjects". After this, said Burke, they kept the body where it was, Helen MacDougal and Margaret Hare returned. Next day Burke went out, got whisky and sprinkled it under the bed and on the walls to guard against any smell. He took a walk outside at noon, was away for two hours, found Helen and the Grays still at home on his return and called on Paterson at 5 p.m., but he was not at home.

Burke now made another error, and one which should have alerted the authorities to the fact that Mary Docherty was not the first body he had sold to Dr Knox, however innocent any such sales might have been; and equally, if there was a suspicion of murder in her case, it behoved the authorities to look into all other consignments sent by Burke and Hare to Knox. He stated at this point that he then got John McCulloch, took him to his own passage and left him there, found Hare in the house with an empty tea-chest and nobody else apart from the cargo, put the body in the tea-chest with Hare's assistance, roped it up with a clothes-line, called in McCulloch, told him to follow Hare "and put the tea-chest upon his back . . . but they did not tell him what was in the tea-chest, nor did he ask them". Hare then led McCulloch (whose evident strength would well invite the attention of an anatomist specialising in muscular development) to Surgeons' Square, after which Burke called on Paterson, found him at home, told him he had sent a subject to the Square, accompanied him there, met Hare and McCulloch and saw the tea-chest put into a cellar apparently without examination but with the payment to them of five pounds, whence they paid the long-suffering McCulloch. Now if Burke had never before sold a corpse and only knew of Paterson's relationship to Knox and Knox's readiness to take bodies, how could he be so certain Paterson would and could take delivery — yet he hired a porter and had the full journey accomplished before any confirmation had been obtained from Paterson? The authorities now had their hint, and it was up to them to make the most of it.

Burke had nevertheless pleaded guilty to nothing more than concealment of death. It was also arguable that he had lied in the earlier declaration to clear himself of the odium of having sold the corpse of a guest. But everything should have pointed to a thorough investigation of all the bodies to Knox and other anatomists in recent months. Undertaken properly this would have involved interrogation of Liston, Syme, Monro, William Pulteney Alison and Christison himself. Resurrectionists were certainly inclined to shop around for the best prices: why would not Burke and Hare? One anecdote of the time had a pair of resurrectionists who considered themselves underpaid by Liston robbing his dissecting-rooms and carting off the body for a resale to Knox.

Why such an investigation was not launched is a nice question. Instead, the authorities simply took further interviews with Burke (who went out of his way to exonerate Brogan at the end of the second declaration thus giving the lie to Hare), with the Hares and with Helen MacDougal. Presumably one problem about this was that, on the basis of his reply to Christison, Knox had worked out a good defence for himself, that his corpses came from lodging-house owners in poor districts who seized corpses with no relatives who had died on their premises; whereas Syme had said this was impossible. Therefore Syme must have had suspicions if anyone came to him with a fresh corpse: had anyone? Liston had been himself involved in body-snatching: had he met Burke and Hare? Syme's reply to Christison against Knox reminds us that he was to return Knox's dislike with interest and that their feud would enliven medical life during the 1830s: but meanwhile Christison must have realised that protracted investigation could ensure that if Knox went down he would take many others with him. Even if they were proven innocent of trafficking with murderers their credit would be shaken by the investigation. For, of course, they were all guilty of being accessories after the fact to the crime of grave-robbing, and enquiries about fresh corpses must elicit answers which would touch on less fresh ones. It was expedient that the case not turn on an investigation of the doctors.

In simple class terms the professionals had every motive to stand together. If doctors had, in the most literal sense, skeletons in their cupboards, lawyers had some insalubrious reminders of the origin of some of their own fees and researches buried far out of sight of their own consciences and their acquaintances' sight. But we can find harder evidence than this. Sir William Rae was of legal antecedents. But his senior depute, Archibald Alison, was the son of the eponymous divine whose *Essay on the Nature and Principles of Taste* (1790) was one of the celebrated investigations of aesthetics in the Scottish enlightenment, dedicated to Dugald Stewart, and much admired by Francis Jeffrey; and he in turn was son of Patrick Alison, provost of Edinburgh. And the advocate depute had for an elder brother William Pulteney Alison, Professor of Medical Jurisprudence and Police from 1820 to 1822, in which chair he was succeeded by Christison when he became Professor of Institutes of Medicine, or Physiology (but, significantly, also including pathology at that time). Professor Alison would be subpoenaed but not called at the Burke trial. His devoted work among the fever-ridden poor between 1815 and 1820 would have brought him training in circumstances where cadavers were more readily available to him; but like the others he also needed his supplies. The younger Alison was in the strongest position to advise Rae of the dangers which any detailed investigations among the Edinburgh medical fraternity might open up. For all of his youth — William Pulteney Alison was only 38 at the time of the trials — he was one of the most prominent influences in the development of the *Edinburgh Medical Journal* and would have been well conversant with the research work which could be impaired by too searching an investigation, to say nothing of the careers that might be blasted. Above all, like so many other members of the Edinburgh establishment, he feared the mob. An anti-resurrectionist crowd had broken the windows of Glasgow University as early as 1749, and Dr Glanville Sharp Pattison, of Glasgow, had been forced to emigrate to the United States in 1814, after an ugly scandal in which he and his associates were saved by the

eloquence of John Clerk and Henry Cockburn at their trial, and
saved by the strenuous efforts of the authorities from a mob evidently
bent on lynch action. The mob in Edinburgh had won notoriety at the
time and fame in Sir Walter Scott's *Heart of Midlothian* for the
lynching of Captain Porteous in 1736, and Scott's readers had cause
to know such a spirit was not buried with Porteous. Knox, the
stormy petrel and calumniator of his rivals could, and would, take
what was coming to him; but Professor Alison and his colleagues had
no desire to encourage investigations which would switch mob
attention to the profession at large. The nearest anatomist and his
rooms would be a target in that event.

The juniors whom Rae brought into the case were of less
consequence than he though even the least noteworthy, Robert
Dundas, of Armiston, came from a family which needed to be told
little about the dangers of mobs and of the investigation of scandal.
His maternal grandfather had been the famous Henry Dundas, who
ruled Scotland for twenty years; his father had been Lord Chief
Baron and *his* father had been the second Lord President Dundas. A
more important figure for the trial, Alexander Wood, was to
become a Lord of Session in 1842 with title Lord Wood and he, too,
had medical associations, his eponymous grandfather being one of
the most famous surgeons of his day, consulted by Scott's parents
about his lameness and even winning the estimation of Byron:

> Oh! for an hour of him who knew no feud,
> The octogenarian chief, the kind old Sandy Wood!

(Byron's scansion would seem to have degenerated in his few
moments of personal benevolence.) The old man, too, enlivened
family traditions for his descendants by being siezed by a mob during
the reform riots of 1792: it was the intention of his assailants to throw
him over the North Bridge (which would unquestionably have killed
him) on the inaccurate ground that he was Sir James Stirling, the
Lord Provost, but he saved himself by yelling "I'm lang Sandy
Wood; tak' me to a lamp and ye'll see". They agreed. But if the story
ended happily it did nothing to encourage his grandson to advocate
policies which might bring mobs about the heads of other surgeons.

Sir William Rae, as Lord Advocate, held responsibility for the
final decision, however much influenced he may have been — and
almost certainly was — by the opinions of Alison, whom he wished
to make solicitor-general, and possibly of the others. It is fairly clear
that the brunt of the affair settled on his shoulders. Alison, it was
said, "worked like a galley-slave" at his legal labours, but in fact

these were now suffering acute competition of the kind which would ultimately lead him to decline Rae's nomination for the Solicitor-Generalship when the Tories returned to power briefly in 1834. Alison loved literature more than the law, and on his return to Edinburgh in November 1828 after a walking and climbing tour he flung himself back on his refutation of Malthus, working on it "during every leisure moment" and "at length, on the 22d December 1828, brought it to a conclusion. . . . After a week's rest . . . I resumed my labours on a totally different subject, and on the 1st January 1829 the first three pages of my History of the French Revolution were written." It will be remembered that Burke and Helen MacDougal were tried on 24 and 25 December 1828, presumably the commencement of Alison's "week's rest". To do him justice he played his part manfully in that long day's journey into night, examining witness after witness and loyally supporting his leader. But it is clear from the foregoing that Burke and Hare held little of his attention beyond the mechanical, to say nothing of their unwanted evidence to him in support of Malthus's ideas on the checks on the growth of population by vice and misery. His memoirs recall but one moment of the trial.

Which brings us back to Rae, who was now in his sixtieth year and had been Lord Advocate for ten years. The apparently endless roll of Tory years from the accession of the younger Pitt in 1784, with the single exception of the year of "all the talents" (1806–07), had had its inevitable results. The Tories ran out of reliable lawyers for jobs and Rae, never in full practice since he had been called to the bar in 1791, became Lord Advocate when Alexander Maconochie went to the Bench as Lord Meadowbank. Maconochie had been promoted virtually to be got off the hands of the Liverpool government after a miserable performance in search of limelight for a Jacobin scare emanating from his own fevered imagination. Rae was no demagogue of that type. Nor indeed had he any claim to eloquence as a speaker at all.

The Peterloo massacre of 1819, the Six Acts of 1820, betokened a political sickness with which England anxiously sought to infect Scotland as well as itself. Rae kept a cool head despite incendiary placards from self-styled revolutionaries many of whom, in any case, were that gift of a paternal government, *agents provocateurs*. However, the Radical War or, as it has also been termed, the Scottish Insurrection of 1820, put considerable strain on him. He showed a good sense of public relations, took care to appear ready to temper justice with mercy, and made some shrewd bargains with prisoners

and counsel to have pleas changed from not guilty to guilty in the
hope — though not with the assurance — of gentler terms. Hence the
ease with which he would opt for the Hare solution. It was one legal
trick he knew how to turn.

The reign of George IV saw a movement from the politics of near-
violence to those of increasingly even constitutional confrontation,
coupled with literary warfare high and low. Rae's awareness that he
was far outclassed in quality as an advocate by the great Whig trio,
James Moncreiff, Henry Cockburn and Francis Jeffrey, led him to
back various journals of opinion which quickly brought him under
attack for the libels they printed. Jeffrey and Cockburn thundered in
the *Edinburgh Review* for the curtailment of the powers of the Lord
Advocate and Rae, who had started under such good auspices, found
himself bracketed with Maconochie for blunders leading to a want of
confidence in the office.

Moncreiff led for Burke, Cockburn for Helen MacDougal and
Jeffrey for the subsequent private prosecution by Daft Jamie's
relatives against Hare. Maconochie, now Lord Meadowbank, made
his view of the matter clear by coming the most impassioned
defender of Hare's immunity in his capacity as one of the presiding
judges: in his case the use of informers, and the firm establishment of
the principle of immunity to the very vilest of them, was a most
valuable defence of public order in his interpretation of that
institution. And Rae had been driven into taking up a position akin to
that of Maconochie on this and other questions.

The Whig triumvirate proposed to enjoy themselves by reminding
Rae where the real Scottish forensic genius lay.

The Crown's troubles began at the point where its problem
seemed to have been solved. Hare agreed to turn King's evidence.
And at this point he took a step either by his good luck or by their
inattentiveness: he elected to tell his version of the entire story in
response for a plea of immunity. We leave it to a later chapter to
examine the force of that promise; suffice it to say that had Rae and
Alison stopped Hare at the Docherty murder, there was some chance
of his being indicted for other murders without their breaking faith.
If, for example, Hare was allowed to say nothing about Daft Jamie,
then it would have been feasible at least to consider a prosecution on
that murder, and Burke's confessions after conviction would have
proved most valuable documents. Burke could even have given
evidence, and would at that point have been ready to. A stay of his
execution could have been arranged.

But Hare came out with all seventeen of the deaths, including the innocent blood of Donald, and Rae and his deputes found themselves faced with a surfeit of evidence. They faced the dreadful fact that by their own actions Hare was going to escape a just punishment for fifteen crimes. The mob would not like it.

Moreover, the situation committed Rae to lines of procedure lying farther and farther from simple justice. If he could hang Burke, that would clearly be justice; but what justice was it to let Hare go, and hang Helen MacDougal who was nothing but an accessory? Yet the mob, with its thirst for victims, was in no mood to make these distinctions among the accused. It was one for all and all for one, as far as the presumption of guilt was concerned, as soon as it had been fixed on Burke and his associates that some of them probably had been picking off casual ordinary people for the price their cadavers would fetch. Helen MacDougal was found not proven after the most careful trial, and even the prosecution never brought more than one count against her, yet she was assaulted by mob after mob, and possibly ultimately killed by one.

It was not only Hare whom they had to protect. Burke had murdered in Hare's lodging the drunk woman received from the policeman Williamson; so had Hare, but he could have argued that Burke smuggled her in and that he had entered the room to find Burke murdering her, or something of that nature. She was not one of his lodgers — it is doubtful if she ever knew where she was once she had departed from her pugilistic perambulation with Williamson, and a lodger, in law, does presumably have to take up residence voluntarily. But this case could not be touched. If it was aired in the open court that the Edinburgh police were supplying Burke (and Hare) with their potential corpses, there was an end of authority of law and order with a vengeance. So Rae blocked that case.

But why did Rae bring other cases into the indictment at all? It was perfectly open to him to have Burke tried on one offence and, if found not guilty or not proven, rearrested, and tried for another one. He had, after all, testimony from Hare covering at least fifteen. Yet if the Docherty case, the only one in which a body had been in the hands of the authorities, were to end in an acquittal it would be because the jury refused to believe the Hares, or declined to convict anyone on their testimony: and would not another jury be likely to do the same thing where Knox and Co., the only experts to have seen the other bodies after death, would have to testify that no marks of violence were present and that they had no reason whatsoever to believe that murder had been involved?

Hence Rae took the decision to indict Burke collectively for three murders, and he selected the best-known two in addition to the Docherty case. He had some basis for proceeding in the matter of Mary Paterson. He had the evidence of Mary Paterson's friend Janet Brown, who was now very clear in her mind — as she certainly had not been at the time — that her friend had been murdered and that she had had a very narrow escape. In the event, she was only to give her evidence to the press: her new-found assurance might not stand up well under cross-examination and might reveal signs of having been coached, by the thoughtful landlady Mrs Lawrie in the first instance and subsequently by the Crown lawyers and staff. And Rae must have suspected that he was likely to meet formidable opponents. How soon he learned that they would be the most formidable in the entire bar — formidable for anyone else, doubly so for him — we cannot say. Cockburn says in his *Memorials* that "Moncreiff and I were drawn into the case by the junior counsel", but such an event cannot have been unexpected. The splendid Scottish tradition of the rights of accused to have the best lawyers available has nothing in common with the grudging allotment given to English prisoners *in forma pauperis* at a much later date. In a murder case of this fame it was very much within the traditions that the Dean of the Faculty of Advocates might be briefed and Moncreiff had been elected Dean of Faculty in 1826. This in itself was symbolic enough; the Lord Advocate was a political appointment whose incumbent might well be chosen for political or social eminence rather than legal while the Dean was the choice of the profession. It was natural that junior counsel would turn to him, regardless of their politics: reputations could be won and lost on a case like this and it would be remembered what choices of leaders juniors had made. It mattered nothing that Patrick Robertson, the leading junior counsel for Burke, was a cheerful Tory of literary bent, friendly with Scott and Lockhart, and particularly close to Christopher North; or that Mark Napier, junior counsel for Helen MacDougal, should be a fanatical Jacobite happiest in the wake of the great Marquis of Montrose or Graham of Claverhouse, "Bonnie Dundee": they would turn to the best men, and if the best men were Whigs, so much the worse for the Crown.

For his third choice, Rae once more found himself limited. Once the disappearance of "Daft Jamie" had been established, public interest focused heavily on his case. It may have been possible to find evidence describing the arrival of "Daft Jamie" at the Hares', although if any were found it probably would do Rae little good, in that it would almost certainly disprove Hare's statement that Burke brought the boy to him (at a time when Burke was bringing all others he inducted into his own house) and focus unwanted attention on Mrs Hare. The medical evidence was, as in the case of Mary Paterson, restricted to Knox and Co., but it might be possible to treat them as hostile witnesses. After all, Mary Paterson might have died of the effects of alcohol, and Mary Docherty might have suffocated herself while under the influence of alcohol — Christison and the police surgeon, Alexander Black, were never able to swear absolutely that she did not — but Daft Jamie, on plenty of evidence, had never seemed physically better when last seen, so Knox and his merry men would have to give some explanation of what they thought him to have died of, and there might be some useful exchanges along the same lines as to why Knox had been sure it was not Daft Jamie, why Fergusson removed the twisted feet and so forth. Admittedly, these facts rested on the later testimony of David Paterson who may not at this date have been so forthcoming but who must have had some kind of story about Daft Jamie's reception, and very possibly this.

True, the murder had taken place at the Hares'; Jamie was not a lodger and so Hare's position was less vulnerable, but it did create the presumption that the Hares' role in the matter can hardly have been passive. Still, the hunt was up by now in the matter of Daft Jamie. Rae, with his usual eye to public reaction, felt he had better take his chances on it.

In the event, Rae's course proved to have the diametrically opposite effect of that he had intended. The mob was aroused in the case of Daft Jamie, but his hopes of profiting from its sentimental appeal were negated when he was forced to withdraw it from the indictment. He had called up the tempest without any means of controlling it. The mob made it very clear that it knew a principle was at stake somewhere which held that such persons were better dead; and against this it roared its rage. From this standpoint the mob attacks on Knox and his rooms and house read Knox's philosophy excellently. The rioters knew that his main use for them was as corpses, even if they did not see the ideological and pseudo-scientific apparatus which supported that view; and they rightly saw Daft Jamie as merely the thin end of the wedge. The other thing which lent wings to their fury was that Jamie, and to some extent Mary Paterson, were not unknown nomads whose murder might be objected to in the abstract but which meant less in the concrete. Jamie, and Mary Paterson, were recognisable human beings around whom sympathy and anger might most readily clothe themselves.

But Helen MacDougal was a human being too. And the course the Crown now took in her regard must lie as the greatest stain on the memories of Rae, Alison, Dundas and Wood. For having put themselves in the position of protecting two people of whom certainly one and one probably were guilty of far more than she, Wood drew up and Rae accepted, if he did not directly dictate, an indictment which went far beyond the limits of justice in an effort to hang her. Hare had no evidence to give which could implicate her in the murder of Mary Paterson: she had indeed made a violent scene against the entertainment of Mary Paterson and Janet Brown, had suffered injury, and had been thrown out. She was present at no point whatsover during the Daft Jamie affair. Yet the indictment against Burke and herself listed three counts to show that "*albeit* by the laws of this and every other well-governed realm, MURDER is a crime of an heinous nature, and severely punishable, *yet true it is and of verity* that you the said William Burke and Helen MacDougal are both and each, or one or other of you, guilty of the said crime, actors or actor, or art and part". Then came counts naming Burke only relative to Mary Paterson and Daft Jamie, and finally, in the matter of Mary Docherty:

> "you the said William Burke and Helen MacDougal did, both and
> each, or one or other of you, wickedly and feloniously place or lay your
> bodies or persons, or part thereof, or the body or person, or part
> thereof, of one or other of you, over or upon the person or body and
> face of" Mary Docherty when she "was lying on the ground, and did,
> by the pressure thereof, and by covering her mouth and the rest of her
> face with your bodies or persons, or the body or person of one or other
> of you, and by grasping her by the throat, and keeping her mouth and
> nostrils shut with your hands, and thereby, or in some other way to the
> prosecutor unknown, preventing her from breathing, suffocate or
> strangle her. . . ."

Not one word of evidence was ever given in court to support this charge against Helen MacDougal; the only evidence brought by the prosecution against her was in support of her having been an accessory before or after the fact. Yet by bracketing her with Burke in the indictment, and with its inclusion of counts with no reference to her, prejudice was bound to assert itself. In the event the jury would find Helen MacDougal not proven; but this indictment, for all the mauling it would sustain, fixed in the minds of the several mobs who persecuted Helen MacDougal after liberation, and of the subsequent commentators, that the verdict was unjust and that she should have been hanged. What Rae was about, of course, and what his depute Wood so clumsily executed, was a means to create the impression in the public mind that the two persons prosecuted were as guilty as any that were being permitted to escape.

The indictment was served on December 8. On Christmas Eve the court met at 10.00 a.m. and counsel for the defence at once made it clear they had studied it to advantage, together with the names of the fifty-five witnesses the Crown proposed to call. Rae appeared with Alison, Dundas and Wood. Moncreiff, Robertson, Duncan McNeill and David Milne appeared for Burke. Henry Cockburn, Mark Napier, Hugh Bruce and George Patton appeared for Helen MacDougal. The judges were David Boyle, the Lord Justice-Clerk; David Monypenny, Lord Pitmilly; Joshua Henry Mackenzie, Lord Mackenzie; and Alexander Maconochie, Lord Meadowbank.

The Lord Justice-Clerk, presiding, began by the customary, if normally unnecessary, adjuration to the prisoners to pay attention to the forthcoming indictment. Immediately Robertson was on his feet with an objection to its being read on the ground that the "libel" as it was termed should not be proceeded with "in this shape" and the objection to it should be stated now. The judges surveyed his rotund figure with sultry distaste. Robertson would become Dean of Faculty in some fourteen years' time and a year later would be elevated to the Bench as Lord Robertson in place of Meadowbank; but at present he showed few signs of the gravity of a future brother. His waggish manner was the delight of the bar, even if his appreciative audiences did not include the Lord Justice-Clerk.

"I am quite unaccustomed to this mode of primary objection to an indictment being read," snapped Lord Boyle. The grandson of the second Earl of Glasgow bore his fifty-six years with authority, having been in his present position for seventeen of them. He was in addition a former Tory solicitor-general, had been sworn of the privy council of George IV at the latter's coronation where he had cut a great figure in his robes, and was justly proud of his noble appearance. His somewhat bovine Toryism had made him a fairly stringent judicial supporter of Rae's activities during the "Radical War" in which he had done his bit in bullying merciful juries. He had little intention of taking much impudence from "Peter o' the Painch" (As Scott had nicknamed him). "The objection to the relevancy of the indictment is the proper time to state it," he intoned, "and not at this time."

"It is not necessary that it should be previously read, by the recent statute," replied Robertson sweetly. If the Lord Justice-Clerk thought he could teach him law, two could play at that game. "We have found very little advantage from not reading indictments," asserted Boyle, moving from recent law to his own custom somewhat rapidly. "The proper way," he added a little less weakly, "is to read them, unless they are uncommonly laid."

Henry Cockburn was on his feet, thereby demonstrating to Rae and his men — if they had any doubts about it — that the defence of the two prisoners would act in concert. "It is not necessary to be read. We object to the reading of it as it prejudices the prisoners. We think that the prisoners would be prejudiced by reading that which the Court will ultimately find no legal part of the libel."

This was telling the court its business with a vengeance and Meadowbank, always ready to have another performance in his ill-starred role of Strong Man, moved in. If the Lord Justice-Clerk was going to allow himself to be browbeaten, he would not. "What I hesitate about at all," he pronounced, "is against interfering with the discretion of the Court." This way well have induced private amusement in the ranks of the defence, Meadowbank's discretion having been one of the meanest allowances vouchsafed by Nature. But they would deal with him in their own good time, as the bar was by now more than accustomed to do. On his elevation he had taken the judicial title held by his late father, who had been venerated for his vast knowledge. Meadowbank the younger was more inclined to seek for knowledge as a cloak for the display of pendantry. An old Parliament House story current in his lifetime said that he asked an advocate pleading before him to explain the distinction between two words he had employed, viz. "also" and "likewise". "Your Lordship's father," said Counsel coolly, "was Lord Meadowbank; your Lordship is Lord Meadowbank *also*, but *not likewise*."

The shot had been fired across the bows. The Crown had been served notice they were in for a very rough ride, and the Bench that it would be ill-advised to try bullying tactics in the Crown's favour. Meanwhile, the defence let it ride. "If the Court wish the indictment read," said "Peter" pacifically, leaving little doubt as to his views of the objectivity of the Crown's wishes, "we do not mean to press the matter further." "I think that everything should be read," nodded Boyle, snatching back his dignity for the nonce, and directed a calm William Burke and an apprehensive Helen MacDougal to stand up to hear it. Following which, Duncan McNeill, a brilliant junior who would ultimately succeed Rae as Lord Advocate and Boyle as Justice-Clerk, declared on behalf of Burke that he was not bound to plead to so unprecedented an indictment, charging him with three unconnected murders committed in different times and places, and combining his trial with that of another "pannel" or accused who was not "even alleged to have had any concern with two of the offences of which he is accused". On the merits of the case, Burke pleaded not guilty, resting his defence on "a denial of the facts as set forth in the libel". Speaking for Helen MacDougal (although technically not her counsel) he went on to state that if obliged to answer, "her answer to it is, that she is not guilty, and that the Prosecutor cannot prove the facts on which his charge rests". And she was not, he stressed, bound to plead to an indictment naming two other crimes with which she was not charged.

Cockburn's remark in his *Memorials* about Burke — "Except that he murdered, Burke was a sensible, and what might be called a respectable man; not at all ferocious in his general manner, sober, correct in all his other habits, and kind to his relations" — suggests he met him outside the court, even though he was not Burke's counsel. It seems decidedly possible that Burke asked to see Cockburn and gave him very firmly to understand that Helen MacDougal was innocent in the actual as well as in the law-court-plea sense of the term; McNeill's different method of putting her case from that of putting his may be instructive here. He rested his defence "on a denial of the facts as set forth in the libel"; her answer was "that the Prosecutor cannot prove the facts on which his charge rests" in addition to her denial of them. Whatever else happened, she had to be saved, in Burke's view. Hence Cockburn and the other counsel may actually have been proceeding on a line of defence originating in part from Burke, although they themselves must have at once perceived the peculiarities of the indictment. But Burke would have been able to underline for them that Helen MacDougal was being framed in order to provide a judicial victim inflated to status commensurate with the now immune Hare. (With the names of the Hares as witnesses ten and eleven on the prosecution's list, their status was clear.) Cockburn's remark about "relations" of course alludes to Helen MacDougal, whom he regarded as Burke's common-law wife (though the earlier marriage actually prevented this from being the case).

Robertson outlined the case against the indictment, showering their lordships with precedents for his objections, and when he had finished Rae wearily replied. He was sure that their lordships would concur with him in thinking the objections and their authorities "entirely unfounded". He then promptly gave up the fight on the matter of a separate indictment for Helen MacDougal, adding lamely he was sure he could defend it: "my object in putting her in that indictment was, that she might derive advantage from being so placed". Hardly surprisingly, he said he would not detail advantages, which must be obvious to all. He merely added that if he had charged her in a separate indictment and had prosecuted Burke first and then her "adducing against her the same, or nearly the same evidence, which had been previously adduced against Burke; she could not have come here to this bar, in the same unprejudiced state, after the public had thus heard the evidence against her, which she would now appear in, if the case, as against her, was to go to proof". This might sound very well, but of course Rae had nothing like "the same, or nearly the same evidence" against Helen MacDougal that he had against Burke. He had a couple of witnesses, repulsive but real, to testify to Burke's murdering Mary Docherty, even if the fact that one of them was simultaneously murdering her meant that his statements on observation amounted to perjury. But he had no witness at all to Helen MacDougal's murdering her: indeed the Hares' evidence was that she did not.

The rest of Rae's statement makes sorry reading: "I thought it my duty, in justice to her . . . she, my Lord, makes the objection; she says that she will be prejudiced. God forbid, that any person holding the situation I do, should do any thing to prejudice a prisoner on trial. The very contrary motives guided my conduct in framing this indictment in the way I have done." He would take her case in ten days' time. "But if she shall suffer prejudice from the evidence in Burke's trial going abroad, let it then be remembered that it is not my fault. She and her Counsel must look to that — it is their proceeding, not mine."

In the event his generous anxieties were not to be put to the proof in that despite endless recrimination on his part the indictment fell, and only the final count, which did relate to the two prisoners, was taken. Moncreiff was shrewdly to raise the point at the end that the Lord Advocate had agreed to try her separately, which shows how little faith he placed in Rae's assumption that it would be more injurious for her to receive a separate and subsequent trial. Left to itself the Crown case against her would have been ludicrously thin, and if the terms of the original indictment had been persisted with, it would have contained nothing at all. But Rae, his good nature less in display, said testily, "now that I am to be restricted to the trial of one of these charges, I am entitled to try her and him together on the last of the charges exhibited". His choice of a charge may very well have been based on the fact that his chances might be very poor in a separate trial for her; had Burke been found not guilty or not proven, any further proceedings against Helen MacDougal would have been

absurd. And, had Burke been found guilty of murder on either the
Mary Paterson or Daft Jamie counts he would certainly have
confessed to the murder of Mary Docherty and appeared as a witness
in MacDougal's defence. He would have been devastating to the
Crown case. And, given the reactions to his joy at her acquittal, not
only from Cockburn but also from Alison, it is hard to see a jury not
being impressed by a man proclaiming his own guilt as a multiple
murderer, accepting his impending execution stoically, and fighting
for the life of the woman he loved. There might indeed have been a
reaction in his favour as well as hers, with quintupled fury against
Hare and a sense that the man being hanged was far better than the
one the Crown was protecting. It is doubtful if Rae realised this. But
from his standpoint — which was far from that of the best interests of
Helen MacDougal — he made the right decision.

Whether his decision to go ahead with the third count was best in
relation to the public weal given the choices in the search for a
conviction of Burke, is entirely another matter. As Roughead points
out, this prevented any examination of Knox and his associates, and
hence a great deal that had been aired was never sifted. The real
question was whether Rae's duty lay in clearing up the whole matter
with the best administration of justice possible, or whether it lay in
finding a couple of victims. Few prosecutors would have differed
from him in opting for the latter choice.

As to the legal argument, Cockburn summed up in *Memorials of His
Time*: "We carried two important points [the second being on Hare's
testimony], after a battle with the Court, which would probably
have been decided otherwise, if the leaning of their lordships had
been feebly resisted." Moncreiff now came into his own for the first
time. He was at the height of his forensic powers, and indeed would
leave the bar for the Bench some six months later: the Tories found it
expedient to retain a little Canningite ecumenism as they faced the
onset of the lean years; so popular a judicial appointment might be
expected to draw a little of the Whig sting. And a Whig James
Wellwood Moncreiff had been for all of his fifty-two years. He had
held a lighted candle at the meeting of 1795 in protest against the
continuation of the French war so that the great orator Henry
Erskine could see his notes; feeling ran so high at the time that as a
result Erskine was deposed by a large majority from his Deaconate of
Faculty in favour of the then Lord Advocate, our Dundas's father.
Boyle, and Meadowbank's father, were among the prime movers.
Moncreiff, for all of his enthusiastic politics, lacked the largeness of
literary interests so characteristic of the lawyers who matured in the

shadow of the *Edinburgh Review*, Jeffrey, Cockburn, Brougham and
their fellows. But if anything this made him the master of them all; as
Cockburn put it, "his reasoning powers and great legal knowledge
. . . made him the best working counsel in court. The intensity of his
energy arose from that of his conscientiousness. Everything was a
matter of duty with him, and he gave his whole soul to it. Jeffrey
called him the whole duty of man!" He wasted little time on style —
in which he differed greatly from his accomplished but affected
friend Cockburn — but took his unimpressive countenance into
action and held his audience by sheer force of personality. His speech
in rejoinder to Rae's concession on the separation of indictments and
obduracy on the multiple counts against Burke was the first time the
Court had heard the pleading of a virtuoso that day. It joined a
formidable restatement of the precedents asserted by Robertson to a
powerful denunciation of the general lack of fairness in the
proceedings of the prosecution. Moncreiff's presence in that court
was a vindication of the principle that whatever William Burke had
done he was entitled to the same treatment as anyone else. Sir James
must have been the first man Burke had seen who was prepared to
fight for his rights as a human being. There was an irony also in that
while Burke had taken the lives of others for money Moncreiff was
fighting to save his for none.

Moncreiff had begun by assuring his honourable and learned
friend opposite that he might rely on none of the defence
entertaining the smallest doubt "that he has brought this case to trial
in the manner that he thought best calculated for justice". As his
argument proceeded this became a very two-edged compliment. If
Rae had been operating in the manner that he thought best calculated
for justice, then his thought had little to be said for its calibre, and
their lordships would be ill-advised to lend much weight to his
reasoning. Moncreiff did not say this, of course, but it was implicit in
such lines as—

> let me say a word more of the prejudice that the pannel must suffer, to
> which I have heard no answer. There are three charges of murder, at
> the distance of six months, in different places — the prisoner is put to
> his defence *fifteen* days after receiving his indictment — he is examined
> and re-examined — five declarations libelled — perplexed and
> confused by these various charges and now called on to speak to a list of
> fifty-five witnesses: I ask your Lordships, is he not prejudiced in his
> defence by such a form of procedure?

But, as he says, his argument was not founded on that but on
precedent. Yet the humane philosophy of it, the assertion of Burke as
a person with rights, must have rung strangely in the ear of a prisoner

whose life had given him no reason to believe anyone had a right to live, let alone win a fair trial.

Lord Pitmilly gave his argument in reply first. Pitmilly was a judge of considerable experience — it extended, in fact, to having presided over the trial of the infamous Patrick Sellar for the clearances on the Sutherland estate where evicted crofters lost their lives, and Pitmilly's overbearing attitude to the counsel against the Duke's factor played a considerable part in securing Sellar's acquittal. He was long skilled in keeping a cool head between the various degrees of weight to be accorded to conflicting public interests. It had been the case in the past that pursuit of a pannel through a series of prosecutions on different indictments had led to public outcry; but here the pannel could not complain since the request had been his. "And, my Lords, since the prisoner himself states by the mouth of the very respectable counsel, on whose responsibility we take it, that he will suffer a prejudice by going to trial on an indictment which charges three acts of murder, unconnected with each other, I think they should be tried separately, and that the public prosecutor should proceed first with the one, and then with the others, if necessary." It is remarkable — although in view of the Sellar episode, not very remarkable — that Pitmilly founded his judgment so firmly on what public reaction might be. In the Burke case, it was clear that there would be outcry if a victim were not found. Had Rae invited a judgment against his own indictment by convincing Pitmilly a verdict of guilty was *more* likely if the demands of the defence were met?

Pitmilly had little learning, nor any great speaking power, yet his manner carried weight here. Inevitably such an initial opinion was bound to weigh with the rest. Meadowbank heartily commended the discretion of the Lord Advocate in his action which had left it to the prisoners to decide what course they wished to adopt. And the prisoner Burke had chosen trial on each count separately. This did not mean that Meadowbank entered "entirely into the views" the Dean and "Peter" had stated; but the responsibility would be theirs. Anyone would have imagined Rae had asked for that conclusion, so warmly did Meadowbank identify himself with the work of the Lord Advocate. But so long as Moncreiff and his men won the victory it mattered little to them how Meadowbank sweetened the pill of his treachery to Rae.

Mackenzie briefly and sensibly said that the indictment without objection would not have produced an illegal case but once a fair objection had been raised, it should be sustained.

Boyle supported the others, rather following Meadowbank's approach in claiming a decidedly Pyrrhic victory for Rae and finding precedents to support him. But he followed it up by declaring it was for the Lord Advocate to decide which of his three counts he would proceed with, while leaving him, as Rae bitterly told him "tied down". But if Rae scowled, and Cockburn claimed a victory in spite of judicial prejudice, and Robertson and Moncreiff had reason to pride themselves on their oratory, it all made no impact whatsoever on Alison. In his memoirs he happily explains that "I was one of the King's counsel who conducted the prosecution of the notorious Burke, who was tried on December 24, 1828, and convicted of three murders". Boyle handed down an Interlocutor of Relevancy, and Burke and Helen MacDougal pleaded not guilty to the third count.

Mary Stewart, or Stuart, in evidence now told Wood that Michael Campbell had come to her house last harvest, before Martinmas, and remained about two months leaving on the Monday "before the fast day, 30th day of October" (she was evidently a Catholic). Then a woman was in the house on October 30, leaving the next day; she was apparently Campbell's mother and was in search of her son. She never saw the woman again until she positively identified her body at the Police-Office. She identified articles of apparel as the woman's. The woman left in good health and, as Lord Meadowbank ascertained with an air of great importance, she had never seen her "the worse of liquor". As Mrs Stewart's acquaintance with the lady had been less than a day, the value of this contribution was open to question, but if Meadowbank wanted it, the defence was prepared to let him have it, and asked no questions.

Charles McLauchlan told Wood that "Marjory McGonegal", otherwise Mrs Campbell or Duffie, came to Mrs Stewart's house in the Pleasance where he was then lodging. She remained for some days at Stewart's (but Mrs Stewart was in the infirmary) and her son was there, but went away before her. She had then called on him at his own shop at the foot of St Mary's Wynd. She did not know where her son was, and was leaving town, she was in perfectly good health, was "of sober habits all the time" and had, he believed, no money, her son having paid for her lodgings — she had not breakfasted on the final morning, when he had gone (and she therefore had no money to be of any habits other than sober). Like Mrs Stewart, he identified her body at the Police-Office on Sunday, November 2, and credit is due to the police for the swiftness with which these witnesses were rounded up. It may have been that early, unsworn, questioning of Burke and Helen MacDougal revealed some recollection of names, of the Pleasance, or of St Mary's Wynd: Helen MacDougal in her statement of the 3rd said that Mary Docherty left finally with the intention of seeking for her son in St Mary's Wynd.

Given that in spite of all the publicity the Crown was unable to produce Michael Campbell it is hard to resist the conclusion that he had abandoned his mother. Stewart, the landlady's husband, was a labourer; they could not afford to keep her any longer without pay, and Campbell must have known that. The Crown had stumbled on an ugly story, and one which had many duplicates in migrant history, as the workers fled from unwanted dependants. It seems possible that Burke in his conversation in Irish realised that the son had abandoned the old woman and that this in fact sealed her fate.

The next witness, William Noble, shop boy to David Rymer, grocer and spirit-dealer of 107 Portsburgh, gave an account of her that might have been a completely different person. Witness knew Burke and Hare as callers to the shop, and recalled a woman coming in to ask charity on October 31. It was about 9.00 a.m. (which implies that Mrs Stewart and McLauchlan were early enough in getting rid of her). Burke was in the shop at the time. The woman was not dressed like a beggar and did not ask Burke for charity but he asked her name and on hearing it was Docherty (or, almost certainly, Doherty), said that she must be related to his mother, whose name he did not give. Burke took the woman away with him, saying he would give her breakfast; he saw Burke later in the morning when he bought some groceries. The next day, between 5.00 p.m. and 6.00 p.m., Burke returned and bought an old tea-box for which he did not pay and which Mrs Hare later took away.

There followed Ann Black or Conway whose husband John was a labourer; they lived in a one-room house adjoining Burke's. She saw Burke, followed by a stranger woman, going into the house. She said there was "nobody" with Burke, which under painful questioning from Wood became the woman and Helen MacDougal. The woman was sitting at the fire supping porridge and milk, wearing a short-gown and they remarked that they were washing at the time for her. Nancy Conway, probably with diplomatic intent, observed that they had a stranger. Helen MacDougal swiftly replied that it was a friend of her husband's — i.e. Burke's — "a Highland woman". This appears less a revelation of diabolical cunning to elude detection in any future homicide as a shrewd countermove from Helen to block any suggestion that Hallowe'en celebrations would then be in order in view of the arrival of an Irish guest. She seems in some respects to have had as much dislike for many of the Irish in general as did some of them for her, and she probably felt Burke spent far too much in hospitality towards them, getting very little in return.

But after nightfall Helen MacDougal felt the need of assistance from Nancy Conway. She had to go out, and asked Nancy to watch the door lest anyone should go in, until her return. Burke had gone out — whether observed by Nancy or not we do not know. As Henry Cockburn would point out in his speech to the jury this seems to tell in favour of Helen MacDougal's ignorance of any murderous intent on Burke's part. It was gratuitously bringing Nancy Conway's attention to bear on the Burke *maison*, where so much was shortly to be happening. Cockburn erred at one point (and, considering that he was addressing the jury about daybreak after a session since 10.00 a.m. the previous day, he is hardly to be blamed for it). He said that she told Mrs Conway "to look after her, as there was nobody else in the house, and she might go out". But Nancy Conway's evidence is that she wanted to prevent anyone entering. On this evidence the old woman might have left, for what Helen MacDougal cared; indeed, her open door policy indicates that it may have been exactly what she did want.

However, Nancy Conway, possibly still in search of refreshment, used her legitimate role as custodian to enter the Burke premises, fortified by a helpful if inaccurate suggestion by Mr Conway that he thought someone had gone in. She found her recent acquaintance there. When Nancy withdrew, so did the guest, by now "something the worse of drink", and told Nancy she was going to St Mary's Wynd to "see a person that had promised to fetch her word about her son, that she had promised to meet there", whence she would return here and stay the night as she had no money to pay for a bed elsewhere and had been promised bed and board by Burke. Indeed she proposed to stay with him for a fortnight. So what was the name of the "land of houses" she asked? Nancy Conway pointed out that there was no clear name of the land, the landlord owning three and the local name presumably deriving from him. This again counts in Helen MacDougal's favour, in that if the drunk old woman did wander out on the streets she might find it very difficult to get back, whatever her intentions. In any case, said Nancy, the police would surely take her in, given her intoxicated state. (As we know, they were open to offers of alternative accommodation, however.) John Conway, they now having reached his house, chatted with her about Ireland — the Highland thesis being now lost to sight.

Hare arrived, followed by his wife, and soon after, Helen MacDougal. The Hares would later imply that there were more people yet, and that Burke was among them, but Nancy Conway was very clear that he was not, and we have no reason to prefer the account of Hare — a liar in fear of his skin — to hers. Nancy Conway recalled that there was drinking and dancing in which Hare, Helen and the stranger woman all participated. However, Mrs Docherty hurt her feet during the dancing, and after a time the Hares and Helen MacDougal withdrew. But the old woman refused to go in with them until her alleged kinsman returned. Nancy Conway asked her to go; but Mary Docherty "bade me not to be cruel to strangers". The ironies were multiple by now. It may indeed be that the old woman had detected something in the Hares that frightened her — instinct can be strong at such a moment — and it is clear that Helen MacDougal had no very obvious expressions of affection for her, although this might have operated to the old woman's advantage rather than otherwise. It was hard on Nancy Conway, however, because John had to go to work at 4.30 a.m. and she needed to get up to make his porridge. Irish holidays were all very well, but they were not observed in Scotland, another misfortune for immigrant communities.

At long last Burke came home and Nancy Conway saw the old woman follow him to his own house "and I locked the door and went to bed". But it was no peaceful night that lay ahead of her. Soon after they had all gathered together, a disturbance became audible at Burke's: "they were fighting like". The next morning between 8.00 a.m. and 9.00 a.m. she heard Hare's voice calling Mrs Law who had returned to Nancy Conway's, but neither of them answered. Then came a girl called Paterson, in fact Elizabeth, the sister of Knox's porter, David Paterson, asking for "John" (the name by which Burke first introduced himself at Knox's), and then gave the name of Burke (which Paterson at least had since learned). Then came Helen MacDougal, saying Burke wanted her and on arrival she found Mrs Law and young Brogan before her. Burke had a glass of whisky in his hand, gave some to Nancy (and presumably had already given some to others), and then threw whisky from the bottle to the roof, his back being to the bed onto which, it seemed, the spirits would fall back. "He said he wanted it done, to get more spirits." Nancy inquired about the old woman, and Helen MacDougal "said Burke and her had been *ow'r friendly* together, and she had turned her out of doors: that she had kicked her out of the house". No time was given or requested for this event. Helen asked if Nancy heard it; she said no.

In their morning festivities Helen MacDougal sang a song, and

after 10.00 a.m. Nancy left, to return in the afternoon at the request
of Mrs Gray. She said nothing of what happened then, but late that
night Mrs Gray, who had previously told her "that a dead body had
been found in Burke's house", arrived about 8.00 p.m. "to take me in
to see the body; but when I went into Burke's house, I was so
frightened that I turned and came out". And Nancy Conway's fear
was still very evident: her voice was so low that the jury could not
hear it and had to have a slightly inaccurate transcription of her
words read by Boyle from his notes. Before Mrs Gray had mentioned
the murder, Helen MacDougal had said to Nancy Conway that Mrs
Gray had been stealing things from the house and once again asked
her to watch the door, which did not lock: that was about 6.00 p.m.

Moncreiff cross-examined, but the best cross-question was asked
by a juryman: "When you went into the house, what was the cause of
your alarm there?" "Hearing tell of a murder frightened me,"
whispered Nancy Conway. "I suppose we are to understand that that
referred to the conversation that Gray had with you, and nothing
else?" "Yes; and nothing else." It was a good point, and it should
have been Moncreiff who made it. But he, and Rae, and Cockburn
had learned one thing: there was both objectivity and intelligence in
the jury.

Mrs Janet Lawrie or Law confirmed. She seemed to think it was
six or seven when the Hares passed her door on the Friday evening,
and some time later she looked into Burke's herself to find the Hares
and the old lady there "merry, dancing and drinking". She was given
her glass, and remained about twenty minutes, returning home and
getting to bed about 9.30 p.m. The sound of dancing and singing had
ceased. But some time after she went to bed she heard scuffling or
fighting, with a great noise; Burke's voice was the only one she
recognised. The noise lasted for some time, and then she fell asleep.
Next morning Helen MacDougal arrived at 8.00 a.m. for a loan of
her bellows, and asked if she heard Burke and Hare fighting. Mrs
Law "asked her what she had done with the little woman" (to whom
her hostility may have been noticeable on the previous night's visit).
Helen MacDougal replied that "she kicked the damned bitch's
backside out of the door", for "using too much freedom with
William". She went away and returned about 9.00 a.m. She
borrowed a dram glass and invited Mrs Law across; Burke, Hare and
young Brogan were there. The Grays arrived before she left; asked
was she sure on that point she said she was. She described Burke as
sprinkling roof and bed with whisky, but she heard his explanation as
being that none of them would drink. (Burke's actions were

foolhardy: it was clear that having decided to give explanations to his neighbours coupled with peacemaking drams to get over the nocturnal disturbance, he suddenly worried about them picking up the smell of the corpse, and with characteristic boldness he staged a theatrical performance, half in mock-anger, half in mock-superstition, telling one of his hopes for more drink in return for the sprinkling — to the end he used his Irish folk-culture legacy to advantage — and another that it was disgust at people's failure to drink. It was also typical of him to have two explanations at hand, each with its own charm.)

Another neighbour, the grocer Hugh Alston, lived above a shop which itself was above Burke's "sunk flat", and now testified that on his way along the passage which led to his own house, at 11.30 p.m. on the Friday night, he heard "as it were, two men quarrelling and fighting, making a great noise; there was a woman's voice that attracted my particular attention, the cry of a woman, of murder". He went down and listened near at hand and heard "two men making a great noise, as if wrangling or quarrelling. I heard no strokes or blows — I heard a woman crying murder, but not in that way as I could consider her in imminent danger herself". The duration was thirty or sixty seconds: "she still continued to cry murder, — it was a very strong voice for a female voice; standing there a minute or two, there was something gave a cry, as if proceeding from a person, or animal, that had been strangled. . . . I could hardly distinguish it from that of a human being. . . . I heard these two men's voices. . . ." "No blows?" asked Alison. "No," replied Alston, "just a great deal of noise they were making by speaking." After it ceased the female voice still cried murder, striking the door with some implement "as if crying for the police and cried, 'murder here'." Alston went out in an unsuccessful search for a policeman; on his return he heard the men speaking, and the cries of murder had ceased. "I thought everything was over; — they seemed to have removed to a greater distance. . . ." He was about three yards from the door of the passage leading to Burke's house, the inner door being 15 feet away. Cross-examined by Moncreiff he recollected the striking on the door as being accompanied by the words "for God sake get the police, there is murder here". A question from Boyle established that the voice uttering cries "of a person or animal strangling, was different from that of the woman calling murder".

If we take this statement in conjunction with Burke's official confession after sentence, the cry of murder came from Helen MacDougal. The voice seems to have been far too strong for the old lady, and its sentences too clear and articulate for an elderly Irish immigrant happier in Gaelic than English. Despite her statement in her declarations, Helen MacDougal was on that showing the only person who could have called murder, and if she did so then she was not only innocent but actually tried to alert the authorities. It *could*, of course, have been Mrs Hare, but nobody including the lady herself ever suggested that. Through Cockburn at her trial Helen MacDougal would revoke her earlier denial of crying murder, and Burke in his official confession would support her.

It is possible that she knew of, or suspected, the intention of murder and that all of her actions earlier in the night and now — setting Nancy Conway as a guard on entry but not exit, being rude as she apparently was to Mary Docherty, yelling for the police when opportunity presented itself — would be consistent with clumsy but well-intentioned efforts to prevent the murder without alerting the others to that intent; and that a combination of love and fear prevented her breaking with them.

Elizabeth Paterson, only fifteen years old, then told Wood that she saw Burke when he came to her mother's house in the West Port at 10.00 p.m. on Friday, October 31, to see her brother David, Dr Knox's porter, who lodged with them. She told him David was out, he went away, and the following day her solicitous brother sent her down to inquire for Burke at his residence; Mrs Law showed her the way. It tells one a good deal about David Paterson that he would have sent his young sister on a mission for him to the residence of a person he knew to be a trafficker in human bodies and possibly a murderer.

"I am a keeper of the museum belonging to Dr Knox," began Paterson's evidence. It was fortunate for Paterson that Knox, and still more the loyal Fergusson, Miller and Wharton Jones, were not to give evidence although subpoenaed. A month later they replied in the *Caledonian Mercury* to various statements made by Paterson to the press: "It is amazing with what effrontery this person has contrived to push himself into the notice of the public under the feigned character of *'Keeper of the Museum belonging to Dr Knox', 'Assistant to Dr Knox', &c., &c.* . . . David Paterson was nothing more than *a menial servant, hired by the week at 7s., and dismissable at pleasure*; his duties being those generally and in other lecture-rooms performed by scavengers or porters . . . he had likewise to go messages, and *be ready at all times to receive packages*, and go for them." (Italics almost certainly the *Caledonian Mercury*'s, it being given to driving a typographical elbow fairly savagely into its readers' ribs.)

It is easy to deduce from this why Paterson, working with no job security for £18 4s. p.a. might envy Burke and Hare whose earnings had jointly totalled £143 10s. or £145 10s. (we do not know whether they got £8 or £10 for Mrs Haldane). Paterson or anyone privy to Knox's payment would deduce that each man obtained about £72 16s. p.a., or exactly four times his own takings for the year — and this not their professional work, but merely income on the side. Small wonder that Paterson might want to cut in on the earnings of Burke, Hare and the merchants of death in general. His intentions are a matter of great controversy, but at least it seems clear that he intended to profit from his special situation, and his methods may have involved blackmail. Knox's own letter of 11 January 1829 published by Paterson and not repudiated by Knox (who, however, only made the single public statement printed in our last chapter), seemed much more defensive than his assistants had been:

> David—From your not having come after that I have *thrice* sent for you, I fear that you feel satisfied in your own mind, of not having been faithful at all times to my interests.
> Still such is my good feeling towards you, that I wish to do every thing in my power to prevent your taking wrong steps — the public clamour is of course much against you, but *all such matters as these subside in a short period* [ital. *Cal. Merc.*, ironical], provided the individuals themselves do not adopt false steps.
> I think it would be prudent for you to come and see me this evening at nine — for you can have *no ground for believing*, since I have never said so, that *I am not concerned in your behalf, and ready to use my utmost exertions for you*. No *prejudice* shall ever be allowed to enter *my mind* against you, unless your own conduct give rise to it.
>
> R. KNOX.

There is some evidence that certain of Knox's rivals were hoping to short-circuit the doctor's flow of subjects by heading off cadavers through Paterson himself, and the porter's treachery was compounded by his later publishing a *Letter to the Lord Advocate*, implying that there were enough signs on the bodies for Knox to notice probability of death by violence, that Paterson was suspicious about the origins of the Burke-Hare cadavers, that Daft Jamie had his head and feet cut off on arrival, and so forth. It is quite likely that one of the doctor's professional rivals — most likely the one who was bribing Paterson to diver the Knoxward flow of corpses — was the author of this. Paterson by April had for these and other reasons become so assured of his welcome in high life that he pursued further literary glory. On 4 April 1829 Sir Walter Scott confided to his journal—

> I have a letter from one David Paterson, who was Dr Knox's jackal for
> buying murdered bodies, suggesting that I should write on the subject
> of Burke and Hare, and offering me his invaluable collection of
> anecdotes! 'Curse him imperance and dam him insurance' as Mungo says
> in the farce. Did ever one hear the like? The scoundrel has ever been
> the companion and patron of such atrocious murderers and kidnappers,
> and he has the impudence to write to any decent man!

Paterson was hired by Knox as porter, but also as something more:
he was not taken from 26 West Port for nothing. He was indeed
chosen as someone who could deal naturally and converse easily with
resurrectionists and other persons whose legal, and possibly moral,
status was unquestionably criminal. If, as his *Letter* implied, he really
had come to the conclusion that Burke and Hare were murderers, he
had determined to join them rather than denounce them — if only
the better to open up blackmail. Of course there were dangers in
dealing with such men, but things like that mean nothing to a man
who courageously sends his little sister to sound out the ground.

We have noted his perjury, then, at the outset, and it is clear that
the relevant Advocates Depute blundered in not checking on so
curious a claim instead of obediently inserting it in the particulars of
the witnesses at Paterson's command. But the defence also failed to
question it. Distinguished and industrious though counsel for the
defence in this case were, it is clear that their real hearts were in the
sections of the case where they were sending their rapiers hissing into
combat against Rae, and his team. The art of cross-examination in
criminal cases was still underdeveloped. Hare presented a challenge
and received special attention, though even there the work is not
masterly, and was restricted.

Paterson testified that on Friday night about midnight Burke
rapped at the Paterson door, asked him to come back to the Burke
domicile. At Burke's he confronted four people whom he dramatically identified as Burke, Helen MacDougal and the Hares, the latter
being separately brought into court for identification. Burke said he
"had procured something for the doctor", pointing "to a corner at
the head or the foot of the bed, I do not know which". There was
straw there. Paterson saw nothing at that juncture but understood
without proof that his allusion was to a "dead body, a subject". Then
Paterson, apparently quite happy to have walked across the West
Port in order to look at the head and foot of a bed with straw piled
around it, said "good-night, or so" to Burke and hied him homeward.
The following day he sent for Burke rather than making a return
journey with a possible prospect of actually discovering whether the

surprise package was just what the doctor ordered. He told Burke that "if he had anything to say or do with Dr Knox, to go to himself and settle with him". Burke "promised to do so, and went away". Paterson did not see Burke again until some time between noon and 2.00 p.m. when he saw Knox, Wharton Jones and Burke standing together in Knox's room in Surgeons' Square. Paterson was oddly vague as to whether Hare was present, yet he said that "one or other of them told" Knox they had a subject and Knox instructed Paterson that "if they brought any package, I was to take it from them", and on 7.00 p.m. along came Burke, Hare, porter and package. The package was identified as the "old tea box" as exhibited, or something like it. The cortège then put the box in a "cellar belonging to Dr Knox", Wharton Jones being present, and Wharton Jones and Paterson then walked to Knox's residence at Newington Place to tell him "what the men had brought" (which on Paterson's showing he knew no more of, on his own knowledge, than he had the previous night). Burke and Hare accompanied them with the porter at a discreet distance. Knox gave Paterson £5 for them, with orders to divide it and give each a share. Paterson got change, Burke and Hare got £2 10s. each and paid the porter; they were to return on Monday when Knox had examined the cargo, presumably to get more money. He saw no women with them. On Sunday, at 7.00 a.m., Police Sergeant-Major Fisher and Lieutenant Paterson called on him; they went to Knox's premises together and Paterson opened the cellar and gave them the package, still roped. In their presence he opened the box which proved to contain the body of "an elderly female, apparently fresh" and never interred; it was doubled up, all the extremities upon chest and thorax with head pressed down on breast apparently "for want of room". Paterson examined the body, stretching it on the table and said he "found the face a very livid colour" and "there was blood flowed from the mouth".

"You are a medical person," announced Wood, not even requiring witness to agree. "Did that appearance of the countenance indicate strangulation?" — "It did, my Lord; or suffocation, in my opinion." He found no other external marks or bruises; did he find any internal derangement, asked Wood, apparently by now under the illusion that he was cross-examining an anatomist not only enjoying Knox's regard but that of the police as well, since any such post-mortem would have to be under their direction. "I was not present at the examinaiton," replied Paterson. Meadowbank was not prepared to let so valuable an authority leave it at that. He ascertained by careful questioning that the eyes did not project, nor

the tongue hang out, nor did Paterson observe any marks about the
mouth, and that there was plenty of light. The Lord Advocate won
the admission that the lips and nose were dark-coloured and had
some spots of blood.

Of course porters do know a great deal that goes on not only in the
establishments under their care but often in the subjects taught, and it
was sensible to take the evidence of someone who had seen plenty of
dead bodies. The problem was that Paterson was being moved from
the status of broker in criminal operations to the sanctity of an
expert. Nobody seemed to ask questions as to the rigmarole which
Paterson had just produced. It may have been occasioned in part by
the fact that much drink had been consumed on the night of the
Docherty murder. It seems much more as though Knox and his team
were by now suspicious of Paterson, possibly suspecting that he was
contemplating a double-cross with a rival establishment, and he
knew they were, and that this accounts for what must have been
from Burke's standpoint Paterson's unexpected high-handedness; it
would also explain why Wharton Jones was so pointedly present
when Paterson took delivery.

As for cross-examination, Moncreiff firmly established that
Paterson had seen Hare act as principal as much as Burke, which was
a critical admission. "Did they frequently bring subjects that had not
been interred?" — "Frequently. . . ." A yelp from Meadowbank
elicited even more: Burke and Hare *and other persons* frequently
brought subjects who had not been interred. Moncreiff thus elicited
the fact that Burke and Hare *might* be legitimate body-traffickers and
that Knox certainly seemed so to regard them — although it was not
inconsistent with Knoxian indifference to the fact that they might
also be something else.

The younger John Brogan then gave evidence as to being in
Burke's house in the course of the evening of Hallowe'en from four
until seven. The prisoners, the Hares and the Grays were present, and
an old woman was there throughout. He did not return until 2.00
a.m. The Hares were lying in the bed; Burke and Helen were talking
together as they stood "out ow'r next the window". Eventually all
parties went to bed, John near the fireside with the women and
Burke and Hare in the bed. This begins to look as though the murder
was unpremeditated as to its time, although it clearly had been
intended all along. Drink was affecting matters and Burke and Hare
had taken a considerable risk on John Brogan's return. We now have
the possibility that what they had intended was to murder the old
lady when nobody was around, that having become very drunk and

very excited in their quarrel they murdered her regardless of
disturbed neighbours, the women's presence, the imminence of John
Brogan's return and everything else and that Helen MacDougal
now, for the first time, aware of the truth about the man she loved,
was commencing a desperate attempt at concealment for which she
was wholly unfitted by nature or training.

Brogan left the house at 7.00 a.m., returning at 9.00 a.m. where he
found the Grays, the Hares and Burke and Helen MacDougal. A
woman (Nancy Conway or Janet Law) had come in for "a light" —
inevitably reasons for joining a matitudinal bibulation would vary —
and asked "what had become of the spaewife". Helen MacDougal
said that she had been very *fashous* "during the night, and that in the
course of the night, Hare and Burke began fighting, and the old
woman called out murder . . . she gave her warm water, and then
cold water, and then she asked for a flannel clout and soap to wash
herself with, to make her white; and then the two men began
fighting, and she roared out murder, and she gave her a kick in the —
and set her to the door". (If Helen MacDougal was by now
determined on a cover-up, she might well choose to use her own cry
as an excuse for having thrown the old woman out.)

Brogan testified to the whisky-sprinkling, adding the interesting
detail that Burke poured the whisky to the roof, "on his own bosom"
and then under the bed. Burke left leaving Brogan sitting on a chair
near the bed, and told him to stay there and not leave the chair, until
Burke would return, but Brogan left fairly shortly leaving Helen
MacDougal and the Grays in the house. Nobody asked why, but
clearly John Brogan in his turn had become frightened of something
in the atmosphere — something other than whisky.

Ann Gray was the daughter of MacDougal deceased, which left a
wide range of psychological and economic possibilities open as far as
her relations with Helen were concerned. The family tie could
secure her a lodging briefly with Burke. On the other hand it is very
probable that she resented the destruction of her family life, and the
fact that her father's last years were spent with Helen made the latter
a natural scapegoat. Partly through the diversion of her father's
interest and income, in the direction of Helen, life had not been kind
to Ann MacDougal. Her husband James seems to have been worthy,
but he had all the problems of a migrant labourer with dwindling
resources. His health seems to have been very bad; he would be dead
within the year. It was not that he lacked employability; he was in
fact taken on the staff of the police after the case was over, and was
said to be giving satisfaction. But Helen and her Will were obviously

well-to-do, and throwing their unexpected wealth around on an
enormous amount of whisky. Ann Gray's economic suspicions may
have been aroused before Mary Docherty was dead at all.

She was businesslike enough. She knew the prisoners, had lodged
in their house five nights in October last, remembered on October 31
seeing a stranger there, a poorish-looking woman, dressed in a dark
gown with a red striped bed-gown below it and identified these
garments as produced in court. Burke had said he met the old woman
in a shop that morning. Burke wanted the Grays to quit
immediately — allegedly for fighting. But he then offered them
lodging at the Hares', and paid for it. Margaret Hare conducted Ann
there. Ann returned to pick up some of her child's clothes about 9.00
p.m. and found Mary Docherty there, singing and dancing with
Helen MacDougal and Margaret Hare. Ann left her at it.

Questioned, had Mrs Docherty seemed to wish to go out of the
house, witness assented: "in the course of the day" she had. "Who
kept here?" "Mrs Burke wished her to lie and take a sleep in the
house." (This point does suggest animus. Nancy Conway had
certainly shown that the old woman could have got out, and that
what finally kept her around was not Helen but Nancy herself — a
point on which, since it reflected marginally unfavourably on
herself, makes Nancy's evidence preferable to Ann Gray's.)

Burke drank, Hare drank, the women danced, and Ann went back
to the Hares', going to bed herself at 11.00 a.m. Hare and his wife
came home and ate supper and Helen MacDougal came in and had
some supper, and the Hares went out again, not to return that night.
In the morning William Burke was around early asking for Gray to
give him a dram, presumably in the general public relations drive
under way at that point. The Grays returned to Burke's shortly after
9.00 a.m. The old woman was absent; Ann inquired for her.
(Everyone seems to have done, which may be an attempt on
everyone's part to show more responsibility than everyone had at the
time.) Helen said the old woman was impudent, and she turned her
out; witness had thought the old woman's impudence might have
arisen from excessive drink, for "in liquor" she had certainly been.
Then, looking for her child's stockings, Ann went to the straw,
Burke asked what she wanted and on being told said "Keep out
there" with an oath. (This may be an embroidery: neither Janet Law
nor Nancy Conway remarked that sudden chill on the bonhomie of
the morning's geniality.) She gave a fairly vivid description of
Burke's asperges. Then some comment took place on potatoes which
were below the bed, and Ann Gray, by now smoking a pipe, went

below the bed, to which Burke sensibly commented that he would get them himself rather than have a lighted pipe near so inflammable a point, but in fact she got them.

On her own evidence she seems to have been a little ungovernable and from the first Burke adopted a most haphazard policy in her regard. Mrs Gray cleaned the house (presumably wanting to work her passage back); nobody told her to, and Burke said not to mind, it would do, only to be told by her "it would be better to be washed and sanded", at which point the instruction was given to Brogan to sit near the straw. Helen remained lying on the bed. Finally Ann Gray went out to look for Burke and found him coming up the street; he told her to "go home" while he had a dram, adding he would be back directly. She went back and found Helen and Brogan in the house, but not in the bedroom. She made for the straw and found Mary Docherty's right arm. Ann got her husband in to see. There was "not a stitch" upon the body. Gray lifted the "head by the hair, and saw the face a little over with blood about the mouth and on the side of her head". They threw back the straw on it, and got out, Gray before Ann. He held Helen in talk on the stair and Ann made her escape but as she did she observed her husband ask directly about the body. Helen "told him to hold his tongue, and she would give him a few shillings; and if he would be quiet, it might be worth ten pounds a-week to him". (This was surely sheer panic on Helen's part. Money on that scale was not only non-existent in the case; it would have given the Grays an annual income of £500, which was wealth far into the middle classes.) Ann went back in and spoke to Helen about the body "and she bade me hold my tongue". Ann said the body was the woman's "that was well last night, singing and dancing on the floor". Helen, whom she said did not know Ann had heard the conversation with Gray, offered five or six shillings to her if she would be silent, and added, "if I and my husband would be quiet, it would be worth £10 a-week to us; and I said, God forbid that I would be worth money with dead people". Gray then gave information. Ann did not see Burke again. She later identified the body at the Police-Office, and she recalled telling Nancy Conway to look at the body but did not herself see it at that time; as we now know, Nancy did not either.

This was bad, but it was not absolutely incompatible with the old woman's death from self-suffocation, followed by a decision on Burke's part to make money out of it by concealing the death and selling the body. Moncreiff did what he could. He took her over the story carefully, eliciting little that was new (apart from her assumption that since it was "Hallowe'en night, they did not wish me amongst them", an interesting revelation of the respect paid to ethnic exclusiveness where festivals peculiar to the individual groups were in question). Burke asked Gray on the Saturday morning that he and his wife should return to the house for breakfast. The Hares were not present; she had returned to her house before the Grays left. As to the conversation with Helen MacDougal on the stair, did she say anything else? Moncreiff was not Helen's counsel, but we can be very sure that his instructions from Burke were to do all possible to assist her, and he did succeed in getting a very remarkable admission from Ann Gray, something she had hitherto concealed. Helen MacDougal had said *"My God, I cannot help it"*. Gray had not heard the words. Had Ann replied? Yes, she had said "You surely can help it, or you would not stay in the house". Helen did not answer.

Gray's version of the interruption in the sleeping arrangements was less dramatic and less curious. Burke gave no reason for the expulsion of the Grays, save that it was no expulsion; he simply asked them to move to Hare's for one night and be back to breakfast next day, Burke being responsible for the cost at Hare's and taking them up himself. Mary Docherty had appeared with him early that Friday, Ann Gray had been making the breakfast and Burke asked for breakfast for her. A little later Burke told the Grays he thought the old woman to be "a relation of his mother's, as she was of the same name, and from the same part of the country". Gray also returned to Burke's at 9.00 p.m. following removal to Hare's, in order to get children's clothes, and there saw the "Burkes", the Hares and the "stranger woman". Next day Burke arrived with a renewal of the invitation to breakfast and thoughtful enquiries as to whether they had slept well, and Gray told him, very well. Gray testified that he had in fact been present when his wife found the body: she may have brought him along to keep guard against possible interruptions. The time was between 5.00 p.m. and 6.00 p.m. He recognised the body as that of "the stranger woman". He packed up their effects and was leaving when he met "Mrs Burke" and commenced a catechism in lieu of a bread-and-butter letter.

He confirmed the attempted bribe and the words about not being able to help it. Then the Grays left, pursued by Helen MacDougal, and they reached the street where they met Margaret Hare who "inquired what we were making a noise about" and, whether on being told or simply divining what the matter was, said "Can't we go into the house, and decide our matters there, and not make a noise about them here?". The "house" was evidently of the public kind, as

Dundas's last question implied: but that question and answer leave an interesting mystery about how that conversation began and ended:

> *Dundas:* And you went into a public-house and stopped there for some time?
> *Gray:* Yes; and I went and gave information at the Police-Office.

That would seem to have taken some time. Burke and Hare would have to have returned in the interval and moved the body by the labours of the porter McCulloch. Whether the Grays deceived Margaret and Helen as to their intentions or not, we do not know; they probably did. But the women had learned enough for them to want to inform Burke and Hare on their progress to Surgeons' Square. As the atmosphere was one of excitement rather than fear, it is likely that they were simply told the Grays knew about the body. At some stage Helen MacDougal had to find time to sow seeds of doubt about Ann Gray in the mind of Nancy Conway, having presumably conjectured that Ann would go back to her with some story about the body; and Helen was right, for Ann did, as we know, seek to recruit Nancy. During all of this time Gray must have been telling his story to the police, and considering that on any estimate he took over an hour to tell them about it, the whole thing suggests that the police were the least suspicious people in the entire story.

Alison then examined the porter John McCulloch who was treated with remarkable judicial offensiveness by Boyle although he had clearly done nothing save work hard for little pay. McCulloch identified Burke. Prisoner came to his house about 6.00 p.m. on Saturday, November 1, requesting him to come and carry something unspecified and to follow him now to his residence, which witness did. Burke came to the end of his bed and took some straw off it, taking the sheet and putting it into the box "like a tea-box". After some heavy prompting from Alison and Rae, McCulloch, who had hitherto been answering fairly leading questions in monosyllables, was got to admit that Burke put "something like the person of a body" into the box.

Pressure was needed to push the body down and fasten the lid. Hare was present. Witness could not say whether the head was uppermost. (These answers were delivered by the unfortunate McCulloch in response to questions variously fired by Boyle, Rae and Alison, with Meadowbank naturally poised for some dramatic intervention.) McCulloch was to go down the Cowgate, up the High School Wynd, and Burke was to be "immediately after me": on the Cowgate they would pass the place where exactly forty years later

James Connolly, the great Socialist theoretician from Burke's ethnic and class background, would be born.

Delivery was fittingly summed up by McCulloch in the words "and we went to the gate, and having put the burden off my back, I left it there". Bunyan's very words seemed to fall from his lips; but then Bunyan came from the same class as McCulloch and Burke and Hare.

And now there emerged the form of Police Sergeant-Major John Fisher to be examined by Alison. He remembered a man of the name of Gray coming to him about 7.00 p.m. "He was in before I came into the office." How long he had been waiting for the arrival of a senior officer nobody asked. Fisher went with Gray "to the West Port"; we know there must have been an hour's delay but Fisher was allowed to speak of making the journey as though it took place immediately upon meeting. This was not his fault, but Alison's.

His object in visiting the Burke demesne was, he deposed, "to inquire for anything to establish what had been said". "Was it to search for the body?" demanded Alison, coarsely sweeping this delicacy aside. "No," said the Sergeant-Major, "I understood that the body was removed before I went there. It was to see if I saw anything suspicious." Nothing in Gray's evidence indicated why Fisher knew that the body had gone, and yet Gray was the only person from whom he could have learned it. The reason for the *lacuna* will be found when we look at the relations between the Crown and Hare.

Fisher testified that he found Burke and his "wife" coming upstairs from the "sunk flat". Gray was with Fisher and so, too, was John Findlay, one of the police patrol. Fisher privately asked Burke "what had become of his lodgers". Burke at this stage must have realised everything was on the verge of total disaster, and he took a line with little precedent that we know of in his career — hard fighting back rather than a soft and ready answer. It may yet have been part of his diplomatic instincts; a line of hostility to Gray could be convincing and on one report actually was until Fisher talked to Helen MacDougal. "He said, that there was one of them, pointing to Gray; and that he had turned out him and his wife for their bad conduct." Fisher than asked him "what had become of the little woman that had been there on the Friday, the day before; and he said, that she was away; and I asked, when did she leave the house, and he said, about seven o'clock in the morning". Fisher said that Burke declared Hare had seen her go away and added "in an insolent tone of voice, there were a number more. I then looked round the house to see if I could see any marks on the bed, and I saw the marks of blood on a number of things there."

Fisher did not say so, but it seems certain that he now interviewed Helen MacDougal alone, with Burke probably being held by Findlay and Gray in confrontation. He testified that he asked her how the bloodstains came there, to which she answered that "a woman had lain in there, about a fortnight before that time, and the bed had not been washed since. . . . She alluded to the little woman, that I had asked where she was; and she said, the woman can be found; she lives in the Pleasance; and she had seen her that night in the Vennel, and that she had apologised to her for her bad conduct the night previous. I asked her then, what time the woman had left the house; and she said, seven o'clock that night." It is very clear that in her panic Helen volunteered far too much information, and that she had no capacity or training in telling a convincing story to cover guilt, in which she differed markedly from her lover. He probably wanted to say as little as possible to her, and simply have said that they must stick to a story that Mary Docherty had left at seven o'clock, and that in her panic, Helen, already trying to persuade herself and everyone else that the night had never happened, plumped for the previous evening as location for the seven o'clock in question while Burke boldly stood out for the more logical if apparently more perilous hour of 7.00 a.m. on Saturday. So it was that her desperate efforts to save her man resulted in Helen's putting the noose around his neck. He would have had ample leisure to realise she had doomed him, but he never held it against her. Poor girl, it is to be feared she may have realised it also, in which case her bitter grief when she was refused permission to see him after her release becomes even more poignant.

"When I found them to vary," continued Fisher to the court, "I thought the best way was to take them to the Police-Office." Burke still sounded convincing in his ears and in awkward recognition of the effectiveness of the suggestion of animus on the part of the Grays — an animus that may have been very obvious — "I told them that it was all personal spite, but that I must take them to the office, as I was sent down". But in fact he lied to them, and, given the likelihood that he was dealing with at least one desperate murderer, who can blame him? He was ready to drop it, had the stories matched. Then he was present during their examination, but his evidence was refused on that, and the superintendent who questioned them was not even listed among the original fifty-five witnesses subpoenaed by the Crown. He mentioned the marks of blood to the Superintendent.

The prison medical officer, Dr Black, the Superintendent and Fisher went back to Burke's house later, examined it, talked to Janet Law and found — possibly with her assistance — a striped bed-gown on the bed which they took away. He identified it; it was all they had taken then. There was what appeared to be fresh blood in the straw under the bed. He went to Knox's rooms the following day with Paterson: this must have been on information from Burke, since Gray would hardly have known of him. But Fisher did not say where the tip had come from, nor was he asked. The Crown was being very circumspect. There they "went down to the cellar, and he said 'Here is the box, I do not know what is in it'; and we opened it, and found the body of a woman in it". Gray identified the body. On a question from Boyle, Fisher confirmed that Paterson had at Surgeons' Square "looked at it, laid it out on the table, and examined it". Nobody enquired whether Fisher at any point sought an interview with the lessee of the premises or decided against doing so.

The body was brought to the Police-Office and shown to the prisoners. "They all denied it." "Denied what?" "Denied all knowledge of the body."

Counsel for the defence asked two questions, which gave ominous indications to Rae of where their investigations were going to go. "Did Hare deny all knowledge of it?" asked Moncreiff. "Yes," said Fisher helpfully. "He said he never saw it, dead or alive." Fisher at least was not going to restrict the proven lying to the two in the dock. And Cockburn, in the wake of Moncreiff, turned the screw almost casually: "His wife, the same, I suppose?" "Yes," said Fisher.

Part II—CHRISTMAS NIGHT

"Justice! There isn't enough to go round."
—A. J. Balfour

Ghastly in the candlelight, long, muscular, ungainly, his countenance smiling in what seemed almost idiocy, William Hare entered the witness-box. Meadowbank swore him, and thereafter brooded over him like a ponderous guardian angel.

Boyle in pointing out to Hare that his evidence was limited to the one case under trial threw witness into confusion by terming it "the death of an elderly woman, of the name of Campbell, or McGonegal". "T'ould woman, sir?" asked Hare in bewilderment.

Roughead is sarcastic about this — "he pleasantly rejoined" — but in fact he may never have heard, or at least never have taken in, either of those names. He had murdered an old woman who had called herself Docherty, and he could hardly be blamed for confusion when it turned out she was really called something else.

Well, if "*T'ould* woman" they wanted, "*T'ould*" woman they would get. He began by playing it very cool: native Ulster taciturnity stood his friend. Rae took him over the decade of his Scottish residence, his marriage, his year of acquaintance with Burke and Helen MacDougal, the nearness of their houses, the fact that he had been in Rymer's public-house on Hallowe'en and that Burke and himself had been drinking that day, that he drank a gill, that nobody was with him and that Burke told him about a person being in his house; and for the most part Rae got monosyllables for answer. However, to the question of the time he proved more forthcoming: could not say, it was "in the fore part of the day", Burke took him to the pub, told him to go to his house, said there was an *ould* woman there "that he was going to murder, and for me to see what they was doing". This assumption of Hare's natural interest in spectator sports was said to have been pointed by the offer of whisky, the more to enjoy the proceedings in comfort. Burke added that he had obtained the woman "off the street; and that he thought she would be a good *shot* to take to the doctors".

The invitation to murder and light refreshments having been accepted (Rae did not try his luck by inviting Hare to disclose his mental responses) Hare went down to Burke's, by himself, to find "a strange man and woman in the house, Nelly MacDougal, and the old woman — and she was washing her gown". Did Hare now know who the strange man and woman were? No. Was Gray the name, did he think? Yes, Gray. Witness identified the white and red gown as what the old woman was washing, and said then that he went away home, not calling on Nancy Conway until "after night". Then when he did go to Nancy's he found the Conways, Burke, Brogan and someone unknown to him. Burke went away with Brogan and the unknown man. "That old wife", Helen MacDougal and Margaret Hare were also present. Hare had "some drink" while there. He remained until between 11.00 p.m. and midnight. Then on invitation from Helen the Hares went to Burke's for whisky, leaving the old woman and the Conways. Later Burke arrived with the old woman. There was more drinking: "We were all pretty hearty." The old woman was, as Rae phrased it interrogatively, "that way too". There had been dancing and singing at the Conways. Did Hare "expect that any mischief was to happen to this old woman?". "Not that night."

Asked was there quarrelling or fighting with Burke, Hare said that Burke asked him what he was doing there, and Hare had said Nelly had asked him in. Burke struck Hare. Hare struck Burke. They had a fight. The women, said Hare, "were *redding* them", which Rae established as seeking to separate them. Burke then pushed Hare down on the bed twice and on the second occasion Hare lay like this for some time; how long he could not say. Meanwhile what Rae was now terming "this old person" was sitting at the fire, got up and asked Burke to sit down and said she did not want to see him "abused". Did she run out? asked Rae, fairly clearly "leading" the witness. "Yes," replied Hare, "she ran out twice to the entry, and cried out for the police." "She went out twice to the passage?" queried Rae. "Yes." "What did she call out?" "It was either murder or police, I could not say which, but it was some of them," an interesting implication of synonymity. "Well, how was she brought back again?" "It was Nelly MacDougal that fetched her back." "Both times?" "Yes."

Hare, of course, had heard nothing of the previous testimony and therefore did not know how much his version was in conflict with the evidence of Hugh Alston. It is impossible to think that Alston who heard much from a room from which he was separated by a passage and two doors would not have heard the sound of Helen MacDougal coming twice to bring the old woman back to the room. Alston did think the woman who cried murder had come along the passage and struck the door that gave on to the open air, but it makes no sense that he would not have heard the remonstrations and footsteps called for by the Hare narrative: he said he could not have been more than three yards from that outer door. Hare may have come to the conclusion that his immunity depended on implicating Helen as well as Burke. In the light of what else we know it is not altogether surprising that Hare, who was far less of a fool than he was trying to look, should have drawn that conclusion.

Hare continued with his laconic narrative, and Burke steadily watched him in the candle-rent darkness. He admitted that in the struggles he himself had pushed the old woman "over a little stool" and that the struggle continued while she lay there, drunk, calling on Burke to be quiet. Finally, when Burke had thrown Hare on the bed for the second time he "stood on the floor; he then got stride-legs on the top of the woman on the floor, and she cried out a little, and he kept in her breath."

Rae:	Did he lay himself down upon her?
Hare:	Yes, he pressed down her head with his breast.
Rae:	She gave a kind of cry, did she?
Hare:	Yes.
Rae:	Did she give that more than once?
Hare:	She moaned a little after the first cry.
Rae:	How did he apply his hand towards her?
Hare:	He put one hand under the nose, and the other under her chin, under her mouth.
Rae:	He stopped her breath, do you mean?
Hare:	Yes.
Rae:	Did he continue this for any length of time?
Hare:	I could not exactly say the time; ten or fifteen minutes.
Rae:	Did he say anything to you when this was going on?
Hare:	*No, he said nothing.*
Rae:	Did he then come off her?
Hare:	Yes; he got up off her.
Rae:	Did she appear dead then?
Hare:	Yes; she appeared dead *a wee.*
Rae:	Did she appear to be quite dead?
Hare:	She was not moving; I could not say whether she was dead or not.
Rae:	What did he do then?
Hare:	He put his hand across her mouth.
Rae:	Did he keep it there for any length of time?
Hare:	He kept it two or three minutes.
Rae:	Did she appear to be quite dead at that time?
Hare:	She was not moving.
Rae:	What was you doing all this time?
Hare:	I was sitting on the chair.

There it was, then, the evidence the Crown needed to convict, since nothing anterior to Hare's answers had proved more than concealment of a possibility of accidental death and sale of the body. It seems fairly certain that Hare had been thoroughly rehearsed in his account, even if Rae's syntax degenerated in his anxiety that the witness sound credible. The problem was that the witness had absolutely declined to assign any part of the act of murder to himself, and it was asking a lot of the jury to believe him. And if he was taken to be committing perjury on that, was it reasonable, was it even morally lawful, for the jury to accept the rest of his evidence?

On and on they went. Witness told how Burke stripped the body, put the clothes under the bed, took the body and threw it at the foot of the bed, doubled up with a sheet thrown over it, with head tied to feet and the whole covered with straw. As to the women, "when they heard the first screech, they left the foot of the bed and went into the passage", running. They did not return until all was over and the body secure in its temporary interment. They had previously been lying in bed with the rug over them. Hare observed no blood anywhere, nor did he hear the women cry out in the passage.

Burke went out after the ladies had returned, and remained out for ten minutes. The ladies asked no questions about Mary Docherty or anything else but simply returned to bed. Then Burke returned with the "doctor's man", whom Hare confused with Thomas Wharton Jones. Paterson was called for identification but did not appear. Presumably witnesses who had given evidence were in practice allowed to slip off as the clock ticked deeper and deeper into the night, although in theory they were supposed to remain on the premises. And if Knox and his assistants were in the witness-room, Paterson must have found his situation uncomfortable — and so, of course, did his former employer and professional staff. Hare said that Burke asked Paterson to look at the body and Paterson refused, saying "it would do well enough". The women were in the bed, and might have been asleep. Paterson left, but Hare had already fallen asleep, having known "well enough what I was about, though I was drunkish-ways".

He testified he awoke between 6.00 a.m. and 7.00 a.m., to find himself lying in the chair. Brogan had by now returned, and according to Hare was in the bed with both of the women.

Hare now turned to the Grays, with whose evidence his had small but significant conflicts. The Hares came home to find the Grays there; the Grays had fallen out with Burke and one of them "applied to my wife for a bed". This was cunning enough: to imply that it was Gray or his wife who asked lodging from the Hares suggested that Burke alone was making plans to clear out unwanted lodgers whereas to say the Burke made the arrangement sounded as though Hare was being directly invited as co-conspirator to help in clearing Burke's house of protagonists whose presence would get in the way of the murder. And it was so minor a point that if Hare was conflicting with Gray nobody would hold it against him, while if his story were accepted it fixed Burke as the ringleader much more firmly. When Rae — who, unlike Hare, had heard the Grays' evidence — asked whether Burke had not asked for the bed at the Hares for the Grays, Hare "could not say". He then described the ultimately successful quest for the box, and said that he helped put the body into it, but went out of his way to quote Burke as upbraiding him for not having done so when left alone briefly with box and body. Hare then got box, porter, Burke, women, himself and the court to Surgeons' Square without much difficulty: the women were in the street, not in the Square itself, "both coming and going" but they did not join Burke and Hare or enter the public-house to which they repaired after calling at Knox's house in Newington. Paterson — whom Hare called "the man" — gave the porter five shillings, Hare £2 7s. 6d. and Burke the same. It was important to have Paterson appear to pay the porter, although on his evidence the partners had done so: but here again if Paterson paid Burke, Hare and McCulloch it made Hare look less like a business partner. What Hare had done to earn so large a fee — and he agreed there was another £5 to be split between them — is a nice point. On his evidence he was paid incredibly high sums for viewing the murder and packing the body. On this showing Burke must have been either the most philanthropic or the most exhibitionist mass murderer in history. But Rae had no more rags to throw around the story. He closed his examination-in-chief by taking court statements from Hare to the effect that he "saw" Burke "apprehended that night" (and neither Gray nor the police represent him as a witness of it, but he may have observed from safety Burke and Helen being taken away), and also that he himself was arrested the following morning.

Although Hare had done nothing more to Helen MacDougal than to imply her to be an accessory before the fact, Cockburn took the full cross-examination and counsel for Burke did not cross-examine him at all. Moncreiff we know to have been in court at the time, because he intervened during the legal battle which broke out as to the limits of cross-examination open to Cockburn. So drastic a decision cannot have been made without consultation with Burke. And the effect were likely to be of symbolic significance. The whole refutation of Hare would be identified in the jury's mind not with the defence of Burke — who it seemed likely was guilty — but with that of Helen MacDougal; and if the jury were invited to contrast the probabilities of the guilt of Hare as against that of Helen MacDougal it was hard for it not to go to her advantage. Cockburn would make points helpful to Burke, but his main business and main effects must be on the side of Helen. And in his final speech this would involve his taking a very different line from Moncreiff and more or less accepting Burke's guilt.

Hell had broken loose before eight questions had been answered:

Cockburn:	Mr Hare, how long do you say you have been in Edinburgh?
Hare:	About ten years.
Cockburn:	What have you been employed at during all that time?
Hare:	Boatman and labourer.

Cockburn: You have not been boatman all that time?
Hare: Yes.
Cockburn: Where?
Hare: On the Canal.
Cockburn: Have you been employed in any other way?
Hare: I had a horse and cart, selling fish.
Cockburn: Any other way?
Hare: No.
Cockburn: Have you been engaged in supplying bodies to the doctors?
Hare: Yes.
Cockburn: Have you been concerned with supplying the doctors with subjects upon other occasions than that you have mentioned?
Hare: No, — than what I have mentioned.
Rae: I object to this course of examination.
Cockburn: I request the witness to be withdrawn.
(*Witness was withdrawn.*)

It was very nicely done, and it blew up in the face of the Lord Advocate the problem of Hare's being protected from justice for other misdeeds. The lengthy argument which followed featured Cockburn, Rae, Boyle, Meadowbank, Alison, Moncreiff and Mackenzie, but it relates to Hare rather than Burke and so it is set aside here. All that concerns us for the moment is to say it was the second time that, in Cockburn's words in his *Memorials*, the defence carried on an important point "after a battle with the Court, which would probably have been decided otherwise, if the leaning of their lordships had been feebly resisted", viz. "our right . . . to impeach the credit of the accomplices by questioning them about their accession to other murders or crimes". As any good defence counsel knows, questions which witness refuses to answer or is protected from answering may be lodged very effectively in the mind of a jury. The judges had backed Rae in protecting Hare, but had been forced to make concessions to Burke in so doing — concessions which would be even more important for Helen MacDougal.

When Hare was brought back he had retreated into a more wholesale denial than his earlier position. Witness admitted assisting in taking the body of the old woman to Surgeons' Square and then said he "never was concerned about any but the one that I mentioned". "Now, were you concerned in furnishing that one?" persisted Cockburn. "No," said Hare, rightly scenting a fluidity in the definition of furniture which should interest lexicographers, "but I saw them doing it." Boyle then told Hare that he was not bound to answer what would follow, adding in phrase of fine breadth of potential interpretation "If you have been concerned in raising dead bodies, it is illegal". Cockburn repeated the warning, very punctiliously, with one eye very firmly now on the jury. And then—

How often had Hare seen "them" furnishing subjects to the doctors? Did he decline answering? He did. And here was another question which he need not answer. Was this "the first murder that you have been concerned in?". It was a phrase with even wider powers of interpretation than that of Boyle, and it could hang pleasantly in the jury's mind as there was no way in which the term could be modified. Hare chose not to answer. Another question followed, with another warning. Had murder been committed at Hare's house the preceding October? This was having the cake and eating it with a vengeance. The defence had forced the prosecution to set that clause aside from the indictment, but it would do nicely as its own comment on Hare's insistence the Docherty case was his first association with body-traffic. "Not answer that," said Hare.

Burke had been reported by Hare as saying he had a *shot* for the doctors, and Hare understood this meant Burke "intended to murder that woman or somebody"? That, agreed Hare, "was his meaning". "Have you ever heard that phrase used by Burke before?" "Yes." "Frequently?" asked Cockburn quickly. "Not often," answered Hare, suspiciously. Hare understood that to mean Burke would murder somebody. "He said this many a time when he had no thought of murdering": Hare's emphasis suggested a little to much intimacy in this clairvoyance. "Then how did you understand that he was going to murder?" Burke told Hare. Gave the name of the victim, before noon on Friday. Witness was dancing at Conway's, the old woman being there, witness reaffirming he had no notion that mischief would befall, save from what Burke had previously told him. Cockburn went over and over this. So when had Hare "anticipated mischief that night"? "When he was on the top of her." Then, after some argument, Cockburn was allowed to ask about Hare's refusal to identify the body when Fisher showed it him. Cockburn firmly hammered Hare to his denial of knowledge of the body, again obviously to underline that earlier lies from Hare suggested his own guilt and the general untrustworthiness of any evidence from him. Once again he was warned before a question: had he had several transactions with Knox or his assistants "and Burke"? Did he choose to answer? He did not. Had he received money at various times from Knox. He never did. Had he received money from gentlemen claiming to be Knox's assistants? They never gave it to him. Did he get any money from Knox's assistants? Burke "might have had it paid to him by Dr Knox, and he could have given it to me". Cocky repeated it, did witness never receive money from

Knox's assistants? No. Who had got the money for the old woman's
body? Burke had, five pounds. The other five was coming on
Monday? Had he not said there would be another five? It was five?
Witness agreed. Cockburn began to bombard witness with
questions. Witness was positive it was to be paid? Was it three or
eight? Or did witness know anything about it? Witness did. Who had
said it would be paid? Dr Knox's man. What did he pay Burke? Five
pounds, four in notes and one in silver. That was all. Burke paid
McCulloch. Who paid witness? Witness could not say. Witness said
earlier he was positive? Burke paid witness. Was witness certain that
Paterson did not divide it between them? Paterson laid it on the table,
Burke lifted up half and "shoved the other over" to Hare. Witness
was positive Paterson did not pay him. Paterson did set the money
out in separate parts.

Having harassed and confused Hare to the point of self-
contradiction on a matter where the evidence of Paterson was
already on the record against him, Cockburn shrewdly moved the
questioning to allied ground which might prove treacherous for
witness. But Hare, for all of his earlier confusion, was ready for him.
Had not Hare had many quarrels or disputes with Burke about these
payments? "No, I never had any," answered Hare, sapiently adding,
"What payments?" Payments from Knox and Co.? "No, not about
that matter." No quarrels about money matters at all, in fact. This
prompted some questions on the admitted quarrel. The old woman,
asked Cockburn, had gone to the passage "and called out murder or
police"? Hare could not say which it was, it was one or other. Hare
pushed her over a stool? After that, witness replied, "she was leaning
on her elbow and sitting on her backside", a usage of corporal parts
which argued against her having deceased. It was before that she
went into the passage, a little before, being brought back by Helen
MacDougal. Hare had said that when Burke killed the old woman
she cried a little and moaned: was this like the moan of a person
suffocating? Hare agreed, though he denied it could be heard a good
way off, and heard nobody calling police or murder at the time of
that sound.

Cockburn's cross-examination ended in a fusillade of questions
under which Hare retreated once more into monosyllables, but he
could not offset the effects of this final restatement of his story at its
thinnest. He had been sitting in the chair in the same room as the
murder; Burke took about ten minutes to do it; Hare sat in the chair
"without stirring one hand to help her". The women went out but he
did not. He did not know whether the women's heads had been

covered with a rug when they had been in bed. Hare did not cover his head. He "stood" (Cockburn's slip, perhaps deliberate slip, for "sat") and saw it with his own eyes. He did not call murder or police. He called not a word. He did not go to the police next day and give information.He did take the body to Surgeons' Square, or rather followed the porter and took money — "part" — for it. And next day in the Police-Office he denied knowing anything about it. He had not been on oath in the Police-Office. And that was all, except that Meadowbank, with an eye to making a subtle support for Hare, established that his examination in the Police-Office had been when he was a prisoner and under that charge asked to identify the body. The prosecution let Hare go without another word.

The evidence of Margaret Hare was far less useful in bringing home the case for conviction. It has been argued, and there is no useful basis for disagreement, that Rae simply gave her immunity and the status of witness for the prosecution because Hare could not testify against his own wife. "Could not" in law, that is, and possibly in nature also. However, having got her, they might as well get something out of her, more particularly against Helen MacDougal if possible. After being sworn by Meadowbank, Margaret with infant in arms faced the wise men.

Her first answers at least gave promise of evidence more reliable than her spouse's. She gave Rae's leading questions monosyllabic answers in her turn. She was Hare's wife, she lived in Portsburgh, she remembered last Hallowe'en night, there were strangers sleeping in her house that night, Gray and wife by name. They were staying with Burke who had asked her to give them a bed for one night only, she could not tell what time of day when the arrangement was made, save that it was daylight. She remembered going out that night looking for Hare, say between 8.00 p.m. and 9.00 p.m., finding him at the Conways; at first she said Burke was there, and then retreated on the point. Helen MacDougal was there. Spirits were consumed. Witness could not say whether she had a great deal of spirits but said they were "not much" affected with liquor. She did not remember the old woman at the Conways' but after they had left for Burke's— following an unsuccessful attempt by Margaret to get Hare to go home — the old woman was there. "Was she there when you came in and went out?" "Yes." (This was contradicted by other evidence, but it was probably simple error as opposed to self-serving perjury.)

There was fighting between Burke and Hare, witness separated them. They started fighting again. The old woman called out murder and went into the passage, came back again, fell backwards, received a push, fell down on the ground, and witness could not say who pushed her. Witness saw Burke lying on top of her, could not say whether it was on her mouth or her breast, nor if she made a noise for "Mrs MacDougal and me flew out of the house and did not stop in it". They went into the passage, could not say for how long, perhaps a quarter of an hour, witness did not cry out nor did Helen. There was no sign of the old woman when they returned: witness had a supposition that she had been murdered. Witness had seen such tricks before. Witness asked no questions, nor did Helen MacDougal. Witness did not recollect lying down on bed. Witness had been standing between door and bed when Burke laid himself down on the woman. Witness could not say where Helen MacDougal was when murder began. Witness was not the worse of drink, had a glass but was not the worse of it. Witness went out before Helen MacDougal, both were alarmed and both flew out of the house. Hare was "near the dresser". Rae· got rapidly away from Hare who in his own evidence had been simultaneously on a chair and on the bed, but who certainly was not supposed to be on his feet.

Questioned about the origin of her suspicions, witness reported a conversation with Helen MacDougal in response to heavy prompting from the Lord Advocate. It had taken place during the afternoon, the female prisoner coming to the Hares and saying there was a "*shot* in the house". Female prisoner had said nothing more about the shot, did not mention about a woman, said that her husband had fetched her "in out of some shop", told witness "it was a woman" simultaneously with mention of the shot. Female prisoner did not say expressly they meant to make away with the woman, nor anything about the woman's fate that night, witness had understood the word *shot* having heard it employed on former occasions with that meaning, "the meaning of murdering a person, or making away with them". No word was said about giving the woman drink. Witness saw them give her drink, but they were not pressing drink on her, that witness saw. The woman was rather the worse of drink. Witness and husband remained there till between 4.00 a.m. and 5.00 a.m. Paterson and Burke entered, severally but with little interval. Witness heard nothing of what they said. Nobody else was in bed with her at this time. Did she know where the body had been put on that night? She did not, but from what she learned next day, it was lying under the bed. She knew a box was obtained for the body and that it was removed: Burke had asked her to get a box "to him" for storing old shoes, and one was obtained at Rymer's. Witness knew the body was put into the box. The women followed Burke and Hare later, finding them in the Cowgate, having followed them to "prevent them from fighting, in case they might be drunk".

Witness had made no answer that she recollected to the female prisoner when mention was made of the *shot*. She did not dissuade her from these things, saying neither "one thing nor another, that I mind". Witness had no recollection of talking the matter over with Helen MacDougal later "in your way to Newington" or elsewhere. "I have a very bad memory," said witness grimly, in the manner of an elder statesman reaffirming a long-hallowed foreign policy. Witness heard no expression of regret from Helen MacDougal "that this woman had been killed in this way": was the Lord Advocate expecting a touch of Lady Macbeth's "what, in our house?". Witness had a few words in the passage with the female prisoner, but could not recall content. Something was said concerning the woman, witness could not remember what. Perhaps witness could remember import of conversation, if not words? Witness thought she could. So what did witness think they were saying about the old woman? "We were just talking about her, saying, perhaps it would be the same case with her and I." Given the enormous difficulty with which this elusive topic of discussion was finally recalled, following several chariot-rounds over the course by Rae, one can hardly blame Meadowbank for spluttering "Is that to say you might be murdered; is that what you meant?".

Having now remembered that what worried her was the fear of being murdered, witness kindly confirmed it for Meadowbank: Rae's Herculean efforts to prompt her had at last won their reward. Meadowbank gallantly tried to put more sense on it. Did not witness know the proximity of Mrs Conway and Mrs Law and why not go there? "I dreaded to go there, as I had left my husband three times," replied Margaret. "The thing had happened two or three times before, and it was not likely that I should tell a thing to affect my husband." Meadowbank said hastily that he "thought you said" witness had left home three times; witness agreed she was proposing to "go away altogether". Boyle asked about the old lady going out. Margaret Hare, probably with a thought about evidence given in her absence, quickly said that it had only been as far as the inner door, not going out of it at all, nobody had brought her back. That, of course, counted against Hare's narrative; but it also left it unanswered as to who had beaten against the panels of the outer door and called murder in the hearing of Alston. Margaret Hare's readiness to move the old lady from her chief prominence in the indoor vocal and footrace championships was also consistent with what she must certainly have remembered, that the old lady was too drunk to have run or shouted to any effect. She was not prepared to bear witness to a call for the police from Helen: quite apart from any vindictive feelings she may have borne towards Helen, she wanted no awkward contrasts between Helen's cries and her silence. Neither did the Crown.

In fact, after Boyle asked if the old lady screamed, witness agreed she cried murder. When? During the quarrel of Burke and Hare. When Burke lay on her did she say anything? She was not saying anything or calling out. "I was afraid to see anything would come upon the woman."

Meadowbank underlined one of the least credible items in the story: "when you saw this", meaning Burke on the recumbent body of Mary Docherty, "was your fear occasioned or created by what had passed between you and MacDougal in the fore part of the day, when she told you of a *shot*, by which you understood this woman was to be murdered?". Margaret Hare looked at him in what must have been bewilderment, especially since that conversation had probably never taken place. "No," she said at last, "I passed no thought at the time." Well, she had gone there: she found the old woman: on her oath did she or did she not expect that night that the old woman was to be murdered? Meadowbank really had something there, although it comes oddly from him: his instinct up to now had been to protect Hare, yet the effect of his questioning, whether he realised it or not, was that either the conversation about the *shot* with Helen had been so commonplace as to be undeserving of mention — which meant that Margaret Hare was a long-standing accessory before several murders — or else the story of the conversation was a lie, entered into various reasons. Anyhow, witness denied any expectation of murder. Then, demanded Meadowbank, why did Margaret Hare think Burke would keep an old beggar woman in the house? The official reason had been that familial relationship had been discovered but presumably this cut but little ice with a pair of realists such as Margaret Hare and Meadowbank. "Why," said Margaret Hare, "I cannot swear what he was keeping her in the house for; I had no idea, sir; I just came round to spend the night of Hallowe'en, and I made a remark, that I did not wish to leave my own house that night." It sounds as though Meadowbank had really frightened her, although his purpose may simply have been to establish intention to murder on the part of both of the accused.

Moncreiff took the cross-examination. She could not indicate where the push the deceased got had come from: it could be either

Hare or Burke. Witness did not stop to see if deceased ever arose again. Then Moncreiff got her to agree that it was "instantly" after the pushing down that Burke "got above her", although Hare had argued for a continuation of the fight of Burke and Hare and its conclusion with his second and last fall to the bed. But Margaret Hare knew nothing of the evidence her husband had given, however much she might have known of what she had intended to say.

Witness remembered nothing of the way the door at the end of the passage was fastened. And nobody knocked on the door that witness heard when she was in the passage, nor did she then hear the old woman cry or make a noise. Witness had "no power" to go out when in the passage nor she nor Hare say anything after her return to the room. Burke and Hare were both standing "either standing or sitting I could not say which" when she returned to the room. Witness then went to bed and finally fell into a doze. Brogan came in and they had a dram. However, witness then said she out of bed when Paterson went out, which seemed something of a time-conflation. She deposed that after the departure of Paterson that Burke and Hare began fighting again — which, if true, indicates that for all of their successes the psyches of the partners were in rags — and "Burke lifted up a stick to strike Hare, and MacDougal took it out of his hand". Witness had no memory of the old woman being in Conway's. Witness was vague as to whether Burke entered his house after the others. Witness had a very bad memory, she reminded him. Moncrieff left it there, but Meadowbank, evidently still striving to make sense out of the story, asked why Margaret Hare did not go home "after all this transaction". Witness explained she was trying to take her husband with her. "I did all I could, sir, but I could not get him." Meadowbank left it there, with Hare's proprietary interest in the proceedings being for the jury to infer.

After that, the remaining witnesses were anti-climax. Margaret made her slow retreat, child to breast, and all Rae had left were the police doctors. Alexander Black, the police surgeon, gave a private opinion that the body he investigated on November 2 last had died by violence but medically could give no opinion. Death could have been caused by suffocation. His opinion was that "the woman had died a violent death, by suffocation". Witness proved quite incapable of separating this corpse from others who had in fact died of suffocation after drink. Nor could Professor Robert Christison, who succeeded Black, do much better. Christison was most excited by his own researches in the production of bruises after death, but while of scholarly interest this made the mystery greater rather than less. He stated that death could certainly have taken place after the manner described by Hare and his wife — which indicated that he at least was not confined to the witness-room. But suffocation after drink would produce comparable effect. Cockburn established Christison had, taking everything together, nothing more than a "probability" of murder on which to reply. What he and Black had succeeded in doing was to provide a justification for the Crown's dependence on the Hares.

The Crown then had read to the jury the two declarations of Burke, from 3 and 10 November. We know them, and their juxtaposition would have done him little good. There followed the declarations of Helen MacDougal issued on the same two dates. Much briefer than those of Burke, with the second a mere paragraph, they sounded much more plausible and less mutually contradictory. But their fateful time-flaw would oblige Cockburn to repudiate them, even if he were not by now under different instructions.

In her first statement she said she was thirty-three, Stirling-born, never married, had lived ten years with Burke with whom a year ago she moved to Tanner's Close, West Port, and three months ago to another West Port close, name unknown, occupied by John Brogan but left to them by Brogan some eight days ago. The Grays came to live there Sunday, October 26, and they, Burke and she were the only persons in the house on the night of Thursday, October 30, Ann Gray making breakfast for Burke and herself Friday morning at 10.00 a.m. during which process Burke went out saying he was going to the shop which she understood to mean "to get a dram" and he returned when breakfast was ready followed some five minutes later by a woman Helen had never seen before. The woman said her Christian name was Mary and seemed the worse of liquor, asked leave to light her pipe and obtained soap to wash her cap and short-gown and apron which she did, Ann Gray drying and ironing them. Mary spoke of coming from Ireland seeking her son and had said at an earlier stage she had had no meat for three days and was given some breakfast.

It was only now, in her version, that Burke began his conversation with her about her point of origin and made a claim of relationship. Then Burke brought in whisky and Mary went away to St Mary's Wynd after 2.00 p.m. Burke went out, said that Nancy Conway had wondered how they could keep the Grays in the house because of the noise of their quarrelling being so unpleasant to the neighbours, and Mrs Hare being present offered the Grays accommodation when Burke told them to go away and stay away and they left about 6.00 p.m. Burke went to Hare's about 7.00 p.m. Helen went there about

7.30 p.m. and not finding Burke there brought him from an adjoining "shop" and they had supper and drink and she went home followed by him with more whisky. The Hares came in and Nancy Conway joined them, and Helen went to Nancy's and had a dram, finding the Hares still at her house when she returned. They went away and then came back and Hare was very drunk and he and Burke lay down in the bed and Helen and Mrs Hare slept on the floor and the Hares finally left at 6.00 a.m. An hour later the Grays came in to get clothes they had left, and Burke got up at 8.00 a.m. and told Ann Gray to "sort the house and get the kettle boiled" and he went out for tea, sugar, bread and butter (the sobriety of his grocery-list no doubt producing a genuine sensation in the shop), and all save Helen then took breakfast together including the newly arrived young John Brogan, Ann Gray remaining to wash the floor and clean the house as Helen was poorly and in bed from hangover or other alcoholic effects.

Gray also remained in the house all day and Burke most of it, briefly lying down at one point. Helen sent Ann to Mrs Law to get clothes mangled about 5.00 p.m. and the Grays left at 7.00 p.m. and after that Mrs Law asked if Helen had given Mrs Gray "orders to get her gown" and Helen said she had not and Janet Law said "she was off with it". Then a girl came in to tell Helen a man was in the street with her gown, and Helen got the gown from Gray and then the Grays, Helen and Margaret Hare had yet another drink and Helen left the gown back with Janet Law to be mangled. Helen went home and kindled her fire and looked for Burke and having found him they went to the Conways, where Conway said Ann Gray had been kicking up a row and Helen and Burke were leaving when they were arrested by two policemen who said they had taken a corpse out of the house.

On "interrogation" Helen said she had not seen Mary since Friday at 2.00 p.m. and "in particular" had not seen her in the house on Friday night. Was shown body of woman in the Police-Office "yesterday" (i.e. November 2, All Souls' Day) but it was not Mary who had dark hair whereas the corpse's was grey. Had no knowledge or suspicion of dead body in house "and in particular" under the bed until after arrest, and there was only one bed in the house under which was so far as she knew nothing but straw and potatoes. Had no conversation with Gray about a dead body "and in particular" never promised him money to shut up about it. On being shown coarse linen sheet, coarse pillow-case, dark, printed cotton gown, red striped cotton bed-gown with label affixed and signed by Sheriff, declared the sheet belonged to one William McKim, who lent it to her, the pillow-case was used to hold dirty clothes and act as pillow, had never seen the dark gown before and the bed-gown was like Mary's but torn, which it was not, and hence Helen could not vouch for it. Stated that Burke had no money on Friday and had to borrow the money for Saturday's breakfast but that he gave her three shillings on Saturday night about 9.00 p.m. [a time by which they were almost certainly in custody] but did not know where he got it. "Being specially interrogated" Helen asserted she had "no concern" in killing or hurting Mary and knew nothing of Burke or Hare or anyone else being involved in such, or in hiding the body in the house, or in later disposing of it. Asked about bloodstains on sheet and pillow-slip she said Burke had struck her on the Thursday and her nose bled, and the Grays knew of that blow, and Ann Gray knew of the bleeding. Which with the usual assertion as to its truth and her own admission of illiteracy closed that.

The second document, that of November 10, involved initially her reaffirmation of the previous document which such of the jury as were still awake and alert could contrast with the opening of Burke's second declaration, also of November 10, repudiating much of his earlier statement. She then answered further questions to the effect that between 3.00 p.m. and 4.00 p.m. on the Friday Mary demanded salt with which to wash herself, became very troublesome, demanded tea at untimely moments frequently, and finally Helen took her by the shoulders, thrust her out the door and never saw her again. She expressly denied that Brogan brought any woman to the house — clearly while she was prepared to defend herself against the Grays' information to the police by counter-accusations of theft, she — unlike Hare — had no intention of implicating the innocent young John to save her skin. Finally she said that Burke and Hare had "a slight difference and a struggle together" on Friday night, but the noise was not great and there were no cries of murder that she heard. That was it.

Much discrepancy in them can be accounted for by drink, confusion, wish-fulfilment and an ostrich-like anxiety to avoid anything that looked productive of danger. Even with due allowance for drink Helen must have known that Nancy Conway, John Conway and (for a brief and perhaps unremembered period) Janet Law had seen the old woman in her company hours later than the time she assigned for the final departure. She even told Janet Law and Nancy Conway as well as Ann Gray that she had driven Mary out, but assigned a time far later than she would tell the police. Once again, nothing in this suggests a conspirator of any experience at all, but rather a desperate woman, terrified of what she has seen and of what she now believed her adored man to be. She told the police on her arrest that Mary had departed at 7.00 p.m. on the Friday and this had been enough to bring Fisher's suspicions to the point of making an arrest, yet once inside she contradicted what she had said to them by offering a new time which was less credible rather than more.

That done, the case for the Crown was closed. But the defence had no witnesses to call, so Rae was on his legs again. The subject of the trial was one of the most extraordinary and novel ever brought before this or any other Court and the public mind had been subjected to the greatest of alarm about it, and Rae was not surprised, because what was alleged was so atrocious that human nature shuddered and revolted at it, and even one such crime committed among us was calculated to produce terror and dismay. "The excitement naturally arises from detestation of the assassins' deeds, and from veneration for the ashes of the dead." (It was even more likely that it arose from fear of being murdered for the value of one's own cadaver. The jury, fifteen strong, would have fetched about £150 from Knox, and the Bench about £40 more.) But the discretion of the public officials had ensured that no improper disclosures had swollen the anxiety. (What this meant, of course, was that they had.) Rae then did much to dissipate feelings of terror by explaining that he was determined to tranquillize the public mind by bringing the parties implicated to trial and he would not be influenced in so doing by "collateral considerations, connected with the promotion of science" (except, presumably, the provision of corpses of convicted murderers for the delectation of Professor Alexander Monro).

The jury must banish from its mind all impressions from any source save the evidence. They must not think about other charges in the indictment (after which Rae then talked about his own motives in including these other charges). He summed up the evidence of Mrs Stewart, Charles McLauchlan and Noble. "Docherty" (very reasonably, Rae settled for calling her that) had left Mrs Stewart's house, and McLauchlan's premises, destitute but in perfect health, and then at Rymer's met Burke who induced her to enter his house. "This man, in all probability, thought that no human being would ever make any search or inquiry after this woman." Rae went over Nancy Conway's evidence, admitting, but not with any suggestions that he saw the force of it, that it was Nancy Conway who persuaded the old woman not to go away and that she had left the Conways not with Helen but later on, with Burke. He noted without

identification Alston's mention of "a woman calling murder, but not
as if she was in imminent danger".

Rae then turned to the case of Elizabeth Paterson and asserted her
evidence to be of major import. Burke had gone looking for David
Paterson at 10.00 p.m. while the Hares and Helen MacDougal were
all at the Conways. The search for Paterson meant that Burke
expected to have a dead body to dispose of and thus "he
demonstrated his predetermined purpose to put her to death".

Rae followed the time from the enquiry at Paterson's at 10.00 p.m.
to the noise heard by Alston at 11.30 p.m. and thence to Burke's visit
to David Paterson at midnight. Rae went over Paterson's arrival and
Burke's pointing to the straw with statement about a subject for the
doctor. The words proved time of murder and its "base purpose", to
wit to obtain £8 or £10 for the body.

Rae then took the Grays' evidence, making it clear he accepted the
assumption that Burke provided for their comfortable relocation and
return. Was it not apparent that the object was to prevent their
seeing, and doubtless preventing, this horrid deed? Rae ran over the
throwing of spirits and Helen's story of the expulsion of Mary
Docherty "using, at the same time, epithets, which it is unnecessary
for me to repeat". Burke's attempts to keep Ann Gray from the
straw, and her later discovery of its contents, followed. Then Rae
blundered, whether in bad note of the evidence or in some
discrepancy arising between depositions and evidence. He described
Ann Gray as calling on "her husband, and the neighbours, Mrs Law
and Conway, who are no less horrified than herself; and all these
persons identify the body as that of Docherty". Of course Janet Law
and Nancy Conway did no such thing; it was only after the corpse
had completed its overnight return trip to Surgeons' Square that they
identified it. Nancy had specifically declined even to look at it.

Then Rae briskly moved the box up to Surgeons' Square, got
Burke, Hare, McCulloch and Paterson to Newington, sent Gray to
the police and had the body back to the Police-Office to get
identification from Janet Law and others — this time accurately.
And then, significantly also very rapidly, the Hares' evidence was
dealt with by as little actual mention of those particular witnesses as
possible. On the other hand Rae pulled no punches in his presentation
of the crime, a recital he then termed "enough to freeze one's blood,
and excite our wonder that such monsters in human form should be
found in existence".

The fact of murder had to be established from the evidence. And
once again Rae had Mary Docherty alive and leaving Mrs Stewart's

in the morning, dancing and singing at the Conways near 11.00 p.m. and dead before midnight. Every appearance could point to strangulation. (At this point Rae seems to have blearily said strangulation for suffocation as others kept doing; or else the stenographer had difficulty in deciphering his own notes taken by candlelight.) Black could not swear to the deceased having been strangled, but he believed he would have done had he found the body at the time and in the condition the Grays had described it. (Suffocated was what he had said.) Christison had said that death by Burke as described by Hare would have produced results comparable with what he had seen. (So, of course, would death by Burke and Hare.) This should leave the jury without reasonable doubt of cause of death but "if your minds can be supposed to hesitate on that point, look only" on the Hares' evidence. "I may be prejudiced" — was there a smile around Rae's lips as he flirted with the remote contingency? — "but to me it did appear, that while the evidence of the wife was on many points exceptionable, Hare himself spoke the truth." Rae did not collect one particular on which he was led into self-contradiction or demonstrable falsehood under cross-examination. Perhaps even as he spoke Rae began to find his words turning against him in his mind, for he added hastily that whether an individual was sitting, standing or lying on a bed, or going out into the passage, were not differences which ought to vitiate the evidence. The jury would know how hard it was to find two would-be truth-telling persons capable of agreeing at all points about an interview two months earlier. If they had agreed, said Rae cunningly, the only conclusion would be that they cooked up the story in advance. (This may have been a slightly unfortunate idea to put in the jury's mind.)

Rae then made a very curious statement and one which could hardly have been an error by the stenographer:

> That both Burke and Hare were participant in this foul act, no one can doubt. And I need not state to you, that it matters not which was the principal aggressor in its execution. They are both, art and part, guilty of murder.

Now, this of course was true, save that it mattered a great deal who the principal aggressor was and, if Hare, why was he being permitted to escape? Indeed Rae at all times maintained in good season and bad that Burke was the ringleader although in fact Hare seems to have been the prime mover in the early murders. But Rae had just told the jury he thought Hare told the truth. And Hare certainly said nothing to imply he did anything but observe the murder. As Burke would tell the *Courant*, Hare perjured himself. It was seem that what Rae meant to say was "Burke and MacDougal", and was led into unintentional accuracy by what is widely known today as a Freudian slip.

If the jury accepted the statements of the witnesses, there was an end of the case, the murder was proved and by the hands of the prisoner. But Rae did not ask the jury to believe these witnesses' testimony without support. He looked back on the other evidence pointing to Burke's being the "leading instrument in this horrid deed". Burke brings her home, pays for the Grays to sleep elsewhere thereby selecting time and place of murder, journeys to Paterson before and after the event, negotiates sale of body, provides box and porter and goes to Knox for money. These facts substantiated the Hares' story that Burke was guilty, "the premeditated author, and leading instrument of this most hideous act".

But in mentioning Alston's arrival "at the very moment" of murder, Rae became a little uneasy. Discrepancies had to be admitted between his and the Hares' evidence "as to the calls of murder, and a doubt arises by whom these were made". His own impression was that the cries came from "the women when in the passage, incapable to resist the feelings which such a scene produced". (Here Rae supported Alston's impression as to the age and health of the person calling, save that in assigning the cries to Margaret Hare as well as Helen he did violence to the evidence. Alston had said nothing of *two* women, yet Helen could not be left looking more humane than Margaret Hare. It was also a somewhat sinister fact that both Hares had assigned the cry to the old woman, suggesting that Rae's remark on collusion may have been another Freudian slip.)

Burke's first declaration was false — "a proceeding not very indicative of innocence", added Rae coyly — but the second confirmed Hare's account in everything except, of course, the murder. Then Rae cited the passage from the second statement that when found Mary Docherty's body was partly on its back, and that her face was turned up, whereas it would have to be down for suffocation. (He was making little allowance for death-throes: but then he was right.)

He concluded by saying that if the jury did not find Burke guilty the situation of the "prosecutor, or rather of the country" would be most deplorable. Murderers were not going to commit murder before unexceptionable witnesses who clearly would lose their unexceptionability if they sat by and allowed them to do it. No more proof could be afforded that what obtained here and if it was deemed not to be enough "this frightful crime" must in future go unpunished.

As to Helen MacDougal, she was charged with being accessory. An accessory must know and be party to a murder without committing the act itself. The status could arise from acts committed before, during or after the deed. Helen MacDougal was accessory in all these respects. She knew Burke would commit the crime and took no steps to stop him but assisted by "alluring and detaining" the woman in the house until the murder had been done. She saw Burke bring the old woman in, saw the Grays removed for a night, not a week, which Mrs Docherty had calculated, and Burke paying the score for them at the Hares. (On the other hand, it made sense for Burke to limit his charity to one night, whatever Mary Docherty may have wanted or imagined she was getting: and she talked of a fortnight, not a week, to Nancy Conway, but there is no evidence that Helen knew of the old woman's assumption. Gray told the press if not the Court that much of Burke's conversation with Mary Docherty was in Irish, which almost certainly Helen MacDougal did not know nor would have wanted to learn. So neither we nor Helen would know what Burke promised his victim. Helen might simply have been told that the old woman really was some familial connection and the clannishness of the Irish migrants would supply obvious reasons for sheltering her. It is clear that Helen would not like it, but she would not be surprised at it. And, as we have seen, she did not "detain" Mary in the house, the whole design—if it had existed—having been left to the whim of Nancy Conway from time to time. Undoubtedly Burke thought Helen was looking after Mary Docherty, but she certainly did not take her duties to the extent of maintaining permanent custody, probably because she merely thought of the business as another example of her feckless helpmeet's deplorable charity. Burke's genuine warmth of nature was, here as elsewhere, his alibi. Also, Helen may have been thankful for any pretext which got rid of the Grays for a night. She was responsible for their presence, at least in kinship, but they seem to have been grating on her nerves by now, and the displacement might be the first step to departure.)

Was it possible she could see these things and not see something serious was intended? The proof that she did know was her statement to Margaret Hare (if true, and even Rae had just impugned the honesty of that witness — so in laying so much stress on her testimony on this point he was entering a very grey moral area himself). Helen had treated what she now knew to be a victim

kindly, set her to washing her clothes and gave her whisky. The
dancing at the Conways was clearly "for decoying the victim into
the snare, and making her fall the easier, by the state of inebriety into
which she was thus led" (he did not mention Helen then returned
home leaving the old woman after her, to the fury of Nancy
Conway). Could these proceedings be seen as anything else but
intended to assist the intended deed? Then Burke arrived and
brought the fight after him, and "if you believe Hare" (nice of Rae,
but a little belated) Mary Docherty sought to get out and was twice
brought back by Helen. If true, this was decisive not only of status of
accessory but almost of co-participant (if true, it was not, any more
than it was true of Nancy Conway when she prevented the old lady's
departure — and it probably was not true). Then as to accessory
status at the time of the death she did nothing to prevent it. (He had
just asserted that she called out murder and demanded the police.)
She had not assisted in the murder but presence was "substantially an
assistance" when no means were taken to prevent it. (It was not,
either in Scottish or English law: as Arthur Hugh Clough had pointed
out "Thou shalt not kill, but needs not strive Officiously to keep
alive".) "It encourages the murderer." (In fact Burke was decidedly
discouraged to find the women had fled, and may have been even
more discouraged to realise that in drink he had done what he never
did before, to murder someone in Helen's presence.) "It adds to the
terror, confusion, and danger of the deceased." (Who is, however,
dead.) The women had intervened to break up the fight but would
not do so to prevent the murder. They were stated to have run down
the passage unable to bear the sight. But why did they remain there?
Why not call the Conways or Janet Law or Alston who was outside?
In fact they were probably trying to prevent anyone coming in (by
roaring murder?). Could they have gone back in and lain down had
they not expected murder? (In fact, the combination of drink and
shock could have a very soporific effect. And it is interesting that
Helen did not sleep with her man after what he had done). Going to
sleep in the presence of a corpse was proof of real knowledge and
accession to the crime on Helen's part. (Rae rather hastily moved
from the women to the one woman, leaving the jury to work out
what was the justification for difference of treatment.) Her conduct
next morning was callous (or hysterical), singing a song and telling a
lie about the old woman's departure "in terms most unfeeling and
language so coarse as forbids my repeating" (in other words, revealing extreme tension). She was there for seeking to conceal the
murder and protect the murderer, and hence guilty of being an acces-

sory. She went further, trying to bribe the Grays to secrecy with the "truly enormous sum" of £10 "recollecting the price immediately paid for the bodies destined for dissection" (and also recollecting anyone's idea of a large unit of currency). "Strange as it must appear" the Grays' rejection of the bribe made little impact on the female prisoner (if in fact she knew it had been rejected). She and Mrs Hare went to Surgeons' Square and then to Newington "to take care that they had a share of the booty" (for which statement there is no evidence: actually Rae was arguing against his own case here in that Helen certainly went to warn Burke that the Grays were threatening to make trouble whether she believed them to be about to take a bribe or not). Counsel for the defence would separate these facts but the legitimate way to deal with them was to take them together (a reasonable means of avoiding close scrutiny of them).

Rae had a good point in stressing that the absence of a conviction meant much more in this case than in those of most murders. This really was an instance in which success could breed imitation. At the same time his argument was getting a little close to lynch logic, and in the special situation of Helen MacDougal, it deepened the case against Rae himself. One wonders if by the time he finished he had even succeeded in convincing himself of her guilt. He certainly had not convinced the jury.

And now it was the moment of James Moncreiff. At the beginning of his speech he said they had been sitting for some seventeen hours, which puts the time around 3.00 a.m., and the jury may have looked forward with little enthusiasm to a long oration — it would be considerably longer than the address of the Lord Advocate — in a voice which had become conspicuous for its shrill and harsh tones in cross-examination. But as his friend and colleague Henry Cockburn would record in his *Life of Lord Jeffrey* that voice would now change into "striking impressiveness" as it always did "whenever it had to convey the deep tones of that solemn earnestness which was his eloquence". His energy would supply what his absence of natural oratorical gifts had seemed to cut short. "He could in words unravel any argument, however abstruse, or disentangle any facts however complicated, or impress any audience with the simple and serious emotions with which he dealt. And, for his purpose, his style, both written and spoken, was excellent — plain, clear, condensed, and nervous."

Moncreiff at once came down like a hawk on any implication that because the crime, if proved, was one of the greatest atrocity, this should allow them to take anything less than clear legal evidence.

The case might seem without precedent; but there was plenty of precedent for murder. It was the motive which supplied the absence of precedent, yet this was murder for gain, and so were many other kinds. He then went on to argue that since it was agreed that Burke procured subjects for dissection people might assume that someone guilty of that could be guilty of any crime "however enormous". And he had another go against the wretched Wood's ill-fated indictment, on the good principle that ground where victory has already been won is worth revisiting: "we come into Court this day upon a charge of wilful murder, with this dreadful source of prejudice stamped on the face of the indictment, with the intent or motive so anxiously set forth in it".

And the indictment which was still before them, even if only its concluding section had been relevant to the proceedings that day, also prejudiced the situation by implying a habitual practice of murder to Burke. (The jury had not been chosen when the argument took place on the indictment, but forty-five jurors heard it, from whom the present fifteen had been chosen by ballot.) The jury must separate the counts not dealt with from the final and critical one and judge on that alone. And Moncreiff now turned to the ominous sign of Burke having already been condemned in the court of public opinion. "The great difficulty, therefore, which you 'have to encounter in this case, is to separate in your minds that which is truly matter of evidence before you from grounds of belief or suspicion received from other sources — from common talk — from newspapers — from handbills industriously circulated, though no doubt repudiated by my learned friends, and all the persons connected with these proceedings."

Moncreiff's anxieties were well taken. The association of ideas, even to the head of the English legal profession almost a century later, led to prejudgment of the case. "A man who was so dead to humanity," observed Birkenhead, "as to traffic in corpses and rifle graves was close to another and worse temptation. If a homeless wanderer when dead was worth money and while alive was naught but a nuisance, it might occur to such a man that, if the waif died before his time without undue marks of violence, business could be done. We do not know that in England anyone fell into that temptation. [We do — Bishop and Williams, the imitators of Burke and Hare, who were hanged in 1831 — but Birkenhead's contempt for his large readership was reflected in his indifference to research.] In Edinburgh, two men did, and their names have ever since been held in lasting detestation." Birkenhead assumed a progress from resurrectionism to murder whereas, as we know, the scientific innovations of Burke and Hare were perfected with no previous experience of the traffic. But Moncreiff's line of defence had to be Burke's own, apparently made initially to Helen MacDougal, that he was in the body trade with or without actual resurrectionist experience. And accordingly the tradition survived. What the error of Birkenhead shows is the manner in which the uninformed mind might make the association; in this respect Birkenhead seems perfectly to have mirrored the mind of the Edinburgh mob and gutter journalism, which Moncreiff struggled so effectively to prevent infecting the jury.

Moncreiff warmed to his work. The discovery of a dead body in someone's house with no satisfactory account as to the circumstances of its arrival invited suspicion of murder in most cases, but not in that of a man who trafficked in bodies. Then, such a man, fearing the fury of the mob as to his trade, would have ample motive for concealment and for false statement as to the body, without murder being the cause of his evasions. And Burke's use of a body he might have acquired by means of accident was simply consistent with his profession. "You have evidence that Burke and Hare acted together in this trade of procuring subjects for dissection, though William Hare, with his usual adherence to truth, chooses to deny this unquestionable fact. You have it proved by Paterson."

"Now, I put the case to you, that this woman died by intoxication, or by accident, or that she was killed in a fray, or killed on a sudden impulse, by this William Hare, without premeditation, or at any rate, without preconcert with Burke; and that *afterwards*, Burke having no *previous* participation, was willing, or was prevailed on to join in making booty of the subject." (What militated against this was the evidence that Burke's visit to Paterson before the murder, as Rae had stressed, really looked like intention: but Moncreiff was perhaps as anxious to bring home against his political enemies how contemptible the human evidence they were using as well as how unsatisfactory it might be. There was a natural temptation to make points more likely to show the guilt of William Hare than the innocence of William Burke.)

Moncreiff then took up the lifestyle of the parties involved — Burkes, Hares, Grays, Conways and so forth — and commented on the drinking "of ardent spirits morning, noon and night of the same day, to a great extent". A fight was admitted to have taken place in the room such that death of the woman by accident or unpremeditated violence would be very likely. And the case against

Burke rested on the necessity of showing premeditation. (Burke and Hare had been using a highly alcoholic environment to facilitate their homicidal activities and the fact that drink had become their Frankenstein monster operated both for and against them at the end — it created errors resulting in discovery but it also invited a presumption of accident where it had once been the most serviceable of agents to murder.)

Moncreiff then made the tactical point that the Lord Advocate would surely not have accepted the Hares as evidence, given the presumption of guilt against them, had the evidence against Burke and Helen MacDougal been conclusive. Therefore the whole case must turn on the evidence of the Hares.

Moncreiff now invited the jury to look at the case without the Hares' testimony. The Dean of Faculty accepted it that the old woman who had resided in the Pleasance, who had gone to the Burkes' house and re-entered there from the Conways', and whose dead body was found in Surgeons' Square, were one and the same person. But murder must be proven, and against Burke. Black had no opinion at all as to whether the body had died by violence, speaking in his medical capacity; and Christison, in his, could only have a suspicion of violence. The *corpus delicti*, therefore, was not even proven to have found its end by violent means. Suspicion and probability, such as Christison had testified to, were not enough.

Moncreiff reminded the jury they were still looking at the case without the Hares' testimony, on which evidence, he felt, there was no proof that the deceased had died of anything but intoxication. That she was intoxicated was certain, in support of which he somewhat unfairly added "if you believe one word of Hare's testimony, he tells you that she was so drunk that she could not stand — so drunk that she could not rise when down".

Moncreiff then moved to the hypothesis that violence had occasioned the woman's death: was there yet evidence of murder, and of murder by Burke? Neither was certain. Moncreiff asked the jury to consider the supposition, to which every prisoner was entitled, that Burke did not murder the woman — was an innocent explanation possible for the other circumstances, i.e. the meeting between Mary Docherty and Burke, the claim of relationship, the despatch of the Grays from the house for the night, the health of Mary Docherty in the evening and her being dead in the morning, the pains to conceal the body, its subsequent sale, Burke's arrival at Paterson's at 10.00 p.m. and at 12.00 midnight, "Mrs Burke's" offer of a bribe to the Grays for their silence? Moncreiff fastened at first on the discrepancy between Burke having said his mother's name was Docherty and the old lady might be related, and the old lady insisting he was a relation and that his name was Docherty — as though he had indicated a possible link through his father, not his mother. "The fact is," averred Moncreiff roundly, "that his mother's name was Docherty, and nothing to the contrary appears." The invitation was not proof of guilt. Nor were the arrangements made for the Grays' accommodation, which might have been simply to arrange for a night's lodging for the old woman — the other suggestions of bad feeling, or of leaving the Burke *ménage* to its Hallowe'en celebrations, did not need to be invoked. There was nothing sinister in any of this, unless one presumed the intention of murder before considering the acts. "This was a house which the lower Irish frequented," pointed out Moncreiff, thereby adding his own voice to what we have said about the nomadic labour force and its alien standards from the urban norm.

Moncreiff then moved to the death itself. It might have been sudden, it might have been violent, but that did not prove murder "especially considering the habits of Burke and Hare, unless it be combined with circumstances of a very different nature". (Here Moncreiff reached the crisis of his argument, which in essence traded upon sociological assumptions. The respectable middle class of most of the jury would have its stereotypes about drunken, brawling Irishry among whom violence might occur, but business operations involving careful organisation, meticulous contrivance and medical skill could hardly be expected to flourish in such a *mise en scène*.)

Moncreiff stressed that both the false statements, and the concealment, happened after the death and were consistent with the profession of a body-trafficker. So, of course, was the sale. And then the Dean of Faculty grasped the nettle of the 10.00 p.m. call on Paterson. What did it amount to? Rae had made much of it, but in fact Burke was in constant communication with Paterson "on matters of a different kind; and all that appears is, that he merely called at the door, did not find him, and there was no more of it".

Moncreiff fastened on the second call to Paterson, that of midnight, and argued that it testified for Burke's innocence "as it is a very improbable thing, that a man, conscious of murder so recently committed, should have brought *a surgeon* to the spot, and asked him to look at the body, so as to expose himself to instant detection". (The Crown had only itself to thank. It had been pleased to clap a surgeon's qualifications on the shifty Paterson, and once again respectability was being turned to Burke's account. There were two objections to the argument, however, one which even Rae should have got — that Burke was drunk, and went for Paterson in a bibulous recall that the possession of a body meant getting Knox's man without normal preparations to remove signs of violence, and that Paterson's refusal to see the body or deal beyond Knox's immediate command was probably because of his horrified realisation that a drunk Burke might insist on revealing the act of murder which Paterson had long suspected but was never mentioned; and the other nobody would have known, which was that Burke as a former internee in the Ballina military hospital would have assumed Knox, Paterson and all other "doctors" to have the morals of a schooner of pirates, and that hence he had nothing to fear from Paterson's visit.)

Moncreiff turned to Alston's evidence and conceded its significance. But he leaped on its damage to the Hares' testimony: it showed "that in whatever way the old woman may have lost her life, *they* were giving to you a tissue of mere inventions, on which it is impossible you can place the slightest reliance".

Moncreiff mentioned in passing the problem of the alleged bribe, offered by Helen to the Grays. He found the evidence of "these Grays" to be "extremely confused and contradictory" but, taking it as true, what Helen said was not evidence against Burke. In any case, stressed Moncreiff, the desire for concealment was as little a proof of murder than were the other circumstances explicable because of the need to cover up a traffic in bodies. (He said nothing about the sum of money supposedly offered, a sum which would certainly have swallowed up any profits from the corpse trade unless it picked up considerable speed.)

Moncreiff turned back, somewhat sardonically, to Rae's insistence that the proof be not considering each item by itself but putting them all together; "and, recollecting that, in the present view, you have no direct evidence of what took place in the room. And then I ask, whether, upon such slippery and doubtful circumstances, you could think it safe to pronounce a verdict of guilty? I apprehend that you could not."

Moncreiff then considered the prisoners' declarations, and dismissed them with the remark that their false representations were evidence of attempt to conceal the body-traffic, but not of anything more. Had they included admissions of guilt, it would have been "a different thing", but they had not. He also underlined that Burke had been got to make "no less than five declarations, relative to a variety of crimes, enough to perplex the wisest head, however innocent he may be; and if you find inconsistencies and contradictions in them, it is no more than might be expected, and really gives no aid at all to the evidence for proving the charge of murder".

Moncreiff then raised one of the most peculiar aspects of the entire case — the return of the Grays. Gray had shown that Burke had brought him back to the house

> "deliberately and intentionally, knowing that the body was lying in the house at the time. He voluntarily invites and calls upon these people to come into a situation where it was next to certain, that if a murder had been committed, it must be detected. This fact takes away all weight from the circumstance, that the Grays were sent out of the house the day before. They say there was some endeavour to conceal the body, throwing whisky about to prevent the smell, &c. I do not doubt it in the least. However, he does not seem to have been very anxious about that matter, for he desires the woman to put on potatoes, and she goes under the bed to search for them; and at last Burke goes out of the house, the Grays are left in the room by themselves, and then they immediately discover the body. The whole of that series of events may be accounted for, on the supposition that he was merely taking advantage of circumstances to turn the death of the woman to a means of profit; and that the Grays being probably aware of his occupation, he was under no great anxiety as to them. But you must suppose that the man was utterly bereft of reason, if, having committed a murder, and being desirous of concealing it, he acted in this manner. He just rushed wilfully into certain detection. It was by his own deliberate act, that these persons were called into his house, in order, as must be assumed, to see the state of it, and examine everything that had been done in it. This, at least, has little air of probability."

(The argument is an excellent one, but since Burke did in fact murder Mary Docherty, the question remains even more problematic. What Burke should clearly have done was to send Hare back to ask the Grays to stay there, or to detain them in conversation, until the body was at least parcelled up. But much of Burke's conduct on this entire day, from midnight onward, is not very rational. It is arguable that his peculiar behaviour in the morning may have been partly induced by light-headedness and trancelike responses which might arise from the amount he had drunk. But behind it all we seem to return to the impulse for self-destruction, driving him into action after foolish action — the invitation to the Grays to return, the message to Nancy Conway to come over, and probably to Janet Law as well, the chucking around of whisky involving exhibitionism of a highly memorable kind quite apart from air freshening, the somewhat obsessive calls on the Paterson home where a single, morning visit was all that was needed. Moncreiff was no intellectual, and certainly not a precursor of modern psychiatry. But he may have put his finger on it with the words "he just rushed wilfully into certain detection". And if, as I suspect, Helen was hysterically confronting realities for the first time, this would have increased Burke's desperation and subconscious wish to end it all.)

Moncreiff at last went back to the Hares, and pointed out that theirs was the only evidence of murder against Burke. But was it not the case that if murder had been committed, it might have been the work of Hare or anyone else? He went on to argue (rather tendentiously) that there was no evidence that the old woman was still alive when Burke returned to his own house, in that Burke might not have entered the house when Nancy Conway told the old woman Burke was passing and the old woman went back to the Burkes'. Indeed Moncreiff implied Nancy Conway might have been mistaken in seeing Burke or, more likely, that she told the old woman Burke had returned in order to get rid of her, although he did not spell this point out fully; and he suggested this might have been the cause of the fight. Then he examined certain other hypotheses: that the old woman had been killed in the fighting by Hare's action when Burke was present but not responsible. Burke might even have been lying in a drunken sleep when death took place. Without the Hares' evidence there was no "good legal evidence" of the old woman's having died by violence, and, if there were, there was none that she had been murdered, and, if there were, that Burke was a murderer or an accessory. After which, Moncreiff went on to deal with the Hares' evidence in very savage terms, making the case for its being treated as wholly worthless, ruthlessly confronting contradictions in the testimony of the Hares with one another, as well as with the evidence of Brogan, of Nancy Conway, of Janet Law, of Alston, and of Paterson.

Moncreiff finally took the obvious point which had indeed clearly animated the Lord Advocate's office, that since no clear answers were present Burke's guilt might be assumed as the most probable solution. But "this would be no safe rule of judgment". He did not demand all mere probabilities must be excluded but there must be no reasonable doubt of the pannel's guilt. But in fact Moncreiff saw no difficulty in finding an explanation to cover all the facts — Hare's last victims were to be William Burke and Helen MacDougal:

> What, if that ruffian, who comes before you, according to his own account, with his hands steeped in the blood of his fellow-creatures, breathing nothing but death and slaughter: — What if that cold-blooded, acknowledged villain, should have determined to consummate

his villainy, by making the prisoners at the bar the last victims to his selfishness and cruelty? What is there to restrain him? Do you think that he is incapable of it? It is impossible for any man that heard the trial to think so; and if so, what difficulty is there in accounting for the whole matter? The murder might have been committed by him, and all the means prepared by him, for exhibiting the appearance of circumstances to prove it against Burke. It will not do to say that this is a case of proof by circumstances; and, therefore, any probability, or any suspicion is enough. True it is, you must determine on the weight and conclusiveness of a proof by circumstances. But it is still by *evidence*, and not by mere conjectures, suspicions or probabilities, that your judgment can be guided. You must have *legal evidence* in this, as well as in all other cases, that the crime was committed, and that the prisoner was the person who committed it. Gentlemen, if it were otherwise, what would the condition of any man in this country be? If a man's life, or liberty, or character, were to hang on the breath of such witnesses as Hare and his wife, what security could any man have for his existence in society for a single hour? It is the easiest thing possible for such a base villain to destroy life, or the condition, or the happiness of any man.

The principles and rules of evidence, are among the most sacred rights of the people of this country: They have been much insisted on by all the best lawyers and judges, who have had to deal with such trials; — and any violation of them, under the influence of feeling, would break down the securities under which we all live in safety. I trust, therefore, that in this case you will do your duty to your country, and to the prisoner; and that, without clear legal evidence of his guilt, you will not convict him of the dreadful crime with which he is charged.

Moncreiff had done. He certainly had not closed with anything like a passionate expression of the innocence of his client. What he did do was to sum up the essence of Scottish Whig theory at its best and to make what had been a matter of political animus the basis for a splendid expression of political ideology. It was an affirmation of the rights of the accused against the immunity and credibility assigned to the public informer: Macaulay's great passages on Titus Oates and his school in his *History* were the outgrowth of these years and of the thinking of Francis Jeffrey, Henry Cockburn, Sydney Smith and the *Edinburgh Review* in general which Moncreiff was so competent to express in legal address if not in literary essay. But it also triumphantly asserted the rule of law against the mob. For where in the past autocratic rule and mob sentiment had been seen as polar opposites, it was now the fear of the mob that animated the government. Rae's capitulation to mass sentiment in Edinburgh over Burke was of a piece with Wellington's capitulation to mass sentiment in Ireland over Catholic emancipation. And it was for

good Whigs to resist the first and support the second. So Moncreiff
sheathed his sword. And at once Henry Cockburn was on his feet,
with rapier flashing in his turn.

Henry Cockburn was, is and always will be great fun. His early
years had won him the place of a Tory of reputable family, and an
education in Whig principles, a fact which was duly signalled by his
winning a post as Advocate Depute in 1807 on account of the political
opinions of his family and losing it some years later on account of his
own. His principles were indeed chosen on intellectual and
emotional grounds when the Whig cause had been darkest, but for all
of their strength he contrasted with Moncreiff in the wit, humour,
intellect, and worldly-wisdom with which they were held. Burke
became for Moncreiff a legal principle; it is doubtful if Cockburn
ever ceased to think of Helen MacDougal as a woman animated by a
fierce, devoted and illicit love, however couched in law his own
arguments were. As Karl Miller has pointed out, the defence of
Helen MacDougal fell in its way within his lifestyle. It was not that
he knew the *demi-monde* for reasons of licence so much as those of
adventure. Cockburn has been charged with occasional lapses into
coarseness and cynicism; but it would be truer to say that both as an
aesthete and as philanthropist he was peculiarly repelled by
hypocrisy, and wore his deeply held beliefs with a propensity to
laughter that disturbed an age moving deeper and deeper into a self-
important solemnity. Thus it became easy to charge him with a
lightness in conviction simply because, like Sydney Smith, he knew
how to mock himself as well as others.

If, as the close orchestration of the defence suggests, Burke had
made it clear to both leaders for the defence that closing ranks behind
Helen was the foremost consideration, it is possible to explain how
throughout the trial Moncreiff and Cockburn could simply alternate
their activities for the same end while now Cockburn was to open his
defence by presuming Burke's guilt.

Cockburn began by citing legal authorities to explain the doctrine
of accession but presented them in very practical terms. He cited
Baron Hume on accession before the fact: if John tells James he seeks
revenge on their common enemy who resides some distance away,
James lends him money or a horse to get him there, and some weeks
later James hears by common report that the man in question has
been killed, and how, but knows nothing of the circumstances until
that widely disseminated news reaches his ears — then James is
culpable but is not punishable capitally "as art and part of the
murder". Similarly he cited Hume again to show that assistance in

concealing the corpse, harbouring and furthering the escape of the murderers, committing perjury on their behalf in their trial or persuading others so to do or to conceal evidence in their interest, are immoral and criminal and inviting suspicion of graver involvement but are not even evidence of approval of the murder since such acts may be undertaken for love or pity of those involved to save them from consequences of what cannot now be undone.

He also cited a case with curious similarities to the present one. A woman had given birth to an illegitimate child. A man named Smith offered the child to a medical student named Taylor for dissection. Taylor agreed and went by arrangement to a garden to receive the body and found the child not dead, whereupon Smith, in Taylor's presence, killed the child, whose body Taylor then removed, concealed and refused to account for. Both men were tried for murder, Smith being found guilty but Taylor being acquitted, on the ground that presence at the crime, and removal and concealment of the body were not sufficient to warrant conviction although Taylor was to be the beneficiary of Smith's crime. Burnett had reported the case from 1807.

Cockburn continued by arguing that Burke and Helen MacDougal might well be married according to the law of Scotland, since they had cohabited conjugally for ten years, although neither seemed to have known it. (Burke really was married in Ireland, which did demolish the argument. However, Cockburn wished to show that psychologically Helen was as wife to her William, and on this he was certainly on sound ground.) As the wife of a resurrectionist to all practical purpose she was bound to see things "even where she is perfectly innocent, any one of which would be fatal to the idea of innocence in an ordinary case". And she was under his influence and had major interest in concealing his crimes.

As to the case, it was not alleged Helen MacDougal ever touched the old woman or urged anyone else to touch her, much less take part in any violence against her. (Except, of course, by Helen MacDougal herself, in her false statements to Nancy Conway, Janet Law and others that she had kicked Mary Docherty's backside out of the house; but as a cynical Irish policeman once remarked to the victim of an outrage, "they'll be a long time batin' your backside before they blow out your brains".) Secondly, it was agreed that Helen MacDougal had fled from the room with Mrs Hare when the murder was taking place "and Mrs Hare described herself as powerless". Cockburn suggested that this action of withdrawal during the crime by a wife was nearly enough to exculpate her from punishment for murder, if not proclaim her innocence. But he added to this the evidence of Alston, for whose respectability he in turn vouched. Alston had asserted the voice crying *"Police – Murder"* had been that of a woman. And who was this? It could not be the victim, whose gasps were attested to have coincided with the cry, nor Margaret Hare, since presumably she would have admitted to it in her evidence. Hence it had to be Helen. Surely this was enough to acquit her as guilty of murder. She was in the house, as it was "her husband's", and she was silent, not wishing to betray him. "But as soon as she saw what was going to be done, she fled in horror, and gave all the alarm that she could."

Like Moncreiff, Cockburn went on to ask the jury, in the initial instance, to set aside the Hares' testimony and see what else had been adduced against his client; and he made it clear he believed there was no case outside of their testimony, whence conviction must surely be impossible. He cited her statement to Nancy Conway that she herself was going out, that the old lady was alone in the house and to look after her. Rae had taken this to mean complicity in Burke's designs, but surely it indicated ignorance of them? (As we have noted, Nancy Conway actually said Helen MacDougal wanted her to keep an eye open in case anyone went *in*, which seems even more likely to suggest ignorance and innocence.) As to the false statements attributed to Helen after the crime, that Mary Docherty had been kicked out, and that she had apologised the following day when in the Vennel, Cockburn fully accepted that these were false statements. "But this is not only their explanation, but their defence." All this meant concealment of the crime from love of her husband, much as she had earlier concealed resurrectionism. "And, of all relations, how can it be expected that the wife, whose interest, as well as her affections, are involved in his, is, merely for the sake of justice, to become the betrayer of her husband?"

(It was characteristic of Cockburn's humanity that he could so clearly see how "mere" justice must appear when the love of wife for husband was to be set against it. Many advocates might have taken the point; but his detachment and sense of human realities gave him a perspective which the ordinary lawyer, above all else an acolyte in the sacred drama of the law, would not possess. On the other hand the absence of discussion or proof of Burke's earlier murders prevented Cockburn making another point. Helen's action in telling so many different stories which an investigation could easily weigh against one another suggests she had very little actual experience of lying for the concealment of crime.)

Cockburn took the story of bribes to the Grays on two levels: they were either attempts to hush up the presence of the body, innocently come by, or else efforts to conceal a husband's murder with no proof of personal implication. The first argument might have seemed the weaker, but Cockburn went further than Moncreiff on it, when he added how much she had to fear from public opinion if the Burke household was discovered to be a resurrectionist one. "She would have been equally injured in her circumstances, and equally urgent against publicity, although nothing could have been said against her, except that there was a subject under her roof."

He dismissed the story of her following the men to Newington as proving nothing one way or the other relevant to the charge. The whole thing turned on the Hares' evidence. Even more pointedly than Moncreiff, Cockburn turned the knife in Rae, citing him as witness that there was no case without the accomplices. "His Lordship has pretended, indeed, to argue otherwise. But his own conduct establishes what his real conviction is. It is always the duty of the public prosecutor to bring the guilty to trial when he can. He has no right to take culprits from the bar, and place them in the box unnecessarily; and, therefore, the very fact that an accomplice has been made a witness, is a proof that, in the opinion of the public accuser, he could not do without them. If the prosecutor's statement be true, these two accomplices were the property of the gibbet. Why, then, has justice been robbed of their lives? Because the Lord Advocate tells you, that their being made witnesses, was *a necessary sacrifice*.

"I hold these witnesses," asserted Cockburn, "who are thus represented to you, by the public prosecutor, as absolutely indispensable, to be not only unworthy of credit, but I hold them to be so abominable, that the necessity of claiming credit for them, pollutes all the other evidence in the case." (All of this going over ground so well ploughed by Moncreiff was necessary so that Cockburn could contrast the wifely devotion of Helen MacDougal with the guilty pair who were likely to escape by placing the noose around her far more innocent neck.) Yet supposing the Hares had told the truth, how effective against her was their evidence? Rae had singled out only two points. There was her reported statement about Burke having got a "shot in the house for the doctors". Yet, said Cockburn, all this proved was that she had known of an intention to commit murder and did not disclose it; he reminded the jury that he had cited authorities to show this was not equivalent to "being the murderer by accession". The failure by a near relation to disclose an

intended crime was not much worse than its concealment by the
same person after its committal. And Rae's other point had been that
she had not interfered to prevent the crime, which would fall on the
same grounds. But in fact, on the only reasonable deduction from
Alston's evidence, she had interfered. That was all that stood against
her, even on the Hares' evidence: prior knowledge and subsequent
cover-up.

But the matter could not be left there. The Hares had to come
under scrutiny. Cockburn wasted a little time by initially impugning
Hare as "a professional body snatcher . . . confessedly vitiated by the
habits of the most disgusting and corrupting employment which it is
possible to engage in", hence appealing to prejudices which
Moncreiff, at the commencement of his remarks, had been sensibly
seeking to answer. But he was on sounder ground in showing how the
Hares had given evidence which, made at the bar, would "have for
ever disqualified them from giving evidence in any Court of Justice".
He reminded them of William Hare's statement of how he had seen
the old woman die without intervening, how Margaret Hare had
spoken of "other tricks of this kind before" (actually "such tricks
before"), how William Hare had refused to answer about his
involvement in other crimes thus virtually confessing.

And now Cockburn approached his great climax, summing up the
whole case against the Hares' evidence against Helen, and showing
very clearly the motives they had for implicating her. It was a
triumph of rhetorical summation, and seldom has such work been
done in showing the interest of King's evidence in the conviction of
an innocent party, although it will be evident that Moncreiff had
prepared the ground for it brilliantly., Here again the splendid
teamwork of the two defences was powerfully evident. But it must
also be added that the argument has to be taken from the historian's
standpoint also. From this, too, it makes sense. Cockburn possessed a
historical sense, and in its discussion of evidence and bias it has much
to teach about this case in particular and about the historian's craft in
general:

> I know very well, that in spite of all this, they are admissible
> witnesses. But *why* does the law admit them? Why, just because, after
> they are admitted, it is the province of you, gentlemen, to determine
> how far they are to be believed. You are the absolute monarchs of their
> credibility. But, in judging of this, do not be misled by what juries are
> always told of those who turn King's evidence, — that they have no
> interest now but to speak the truth. In one sense, no man has any
> interest but to speak the truth. But it is notorious, that there is nobody
> by whom this is so universally forgotten, as by those who make a
> bargain for saving themselves, by betraying their associates. These

persons, almost invariably hurt the interests of their new master, by the excess of their zeal in his service. They exaggerate everything; — partly from the desire of vindicating themselves, and partly to merit the reward for which they have bargained. And you will observe, that in this case, these persons stand in this peculiar situation, that so far as we know, they are still liable to be tried for similar offences. There are other two murders set forth in this very indictment; one of them committed in Hare's house; and if we may judge from what these persons say, they have been engaged in other transactions of the same kind. They came from the jail to this place to-day; and they are in jail again. Do you think it is very improbable, that when coming here, they should feel, that if this prosecution failed, public indignation would require another victim, and that nothing was so likely to stifle further inquiry as the conviction of these prisoners? The worst feature, perhaps, of their evidence is, that it is necessarily given under the feeling of this *subsisting* interest.

The prosecutor seemed to think that they gave their evidence in a credible manner, and that there was nothing in their appearance beyond what may be expected in that of any great criminal, to impair the probability of their story. I entirely differ from this; and I am perfectly satisfied that so do you. . . .

It is said that they are corroborated. Corroborated! These witnesses corroborated!! — In the *first* place, I do not understand how such witnesses admit of being corroborated. If the prosecutor has a case without them, let him say so. But if he has not, — if something material must depend upon these witnesses, — it is in vain to talk of corroboration; because in truth, the thing to be corroborated does not exist. You may corroborate a *doubtful* testimony; but the idea of confirming the lies of these miscreants, is absurd. The only way to deal with them, is to deduct their testimony altogether. It is like corroborating a dream. The fiction and the reality may possibly be both alike; but this accidental concurrence does not make the one stronger than the other. But, in the *next* place, instead of being corroborated, there probably never was a case where suspicious evidence had the death-blow given to it by so many palpable contradictions. I won't attempt to go over these; because I will not impair the force of that most admirable analysis of the evidence which was given by my learned friend, the Dean. He collected — and contrasted — the various particulars in which Hare and his wife contradicted each other, and in which both were contradicted by all the credible evidence in the case. If you, gentlemen, can get the better of that fair and powerful contrast, you will do more than I can, and may convict; — if not, you cannot. My impression is, that these witnesses — who confessedly need corroboration — have not only not obtained it, but have been met by inconsistencies, sufficient to cast doubts on testimony otherwise pure. But the simple and rational view for a jury to take, is, that these indispensable witnesses are deserving of *no* faith in any case; and that the idea is shocking of believing them, to the effect of convicting in a case that is capital. The prosecutor talks of their being sworn! What is perjury to a murderer? The breaking of an oath to him who has already broken into "the bloody house of life"!

Cockburn worked with art and logic and it may well have been
here that the final nails were driven into the coffin of the case against
Helen MacDougal — here and in Cockburn's final words. But he in
his turn had to deal with the evidence of the prisoners' declarations
and like his learned friend the Dean he took a bold course, taking
Moncreiff's points farther so much as to call the whole examining
technique into question, and to testify to the want of civil liberties in
the Tory state established during the era of Revolution and Reaction:

> These miserable declarations are always the last refuge of the
> prosecutor in a doubtful case; insomuch, that whenever juries see that
> they are much relied upon, they may, from that one fact, be perfectly
> certain that the accuser is uneasy about his other evidence. You are
> aware what a declaration is. A person accused is taken, generally under
> all the agitation created by the first suspicion, into a room, where he
> finds a Magistrate, and a prosecutor, and two Sheriff's-officers, for
> witnesses; and there, deprived of all assistance or advice, he is asked to
> account for every circumstance, whether real or supposed, which
> seems to render his conduct suspicious. Happy is he if this operation be
> repeated only once, twice, — or even thrice. He is liable to have it
> renewed day after day, — *even after his committal for trial*, till his
> declarations, as here, may amount to five or six; and all this matter is
> accumulated against him, for the day of trial, when it is critically
> examined, and brought elaborately forward to fill up all the chinks of
> all the rest of the evidence. I assume everything to be quite fair on the
> part of the Magistrates and of the accuser. I know that the man is
> always warned not to criminate himself; and I know that he need not
> answer unless he likes; but I also know, that if he does not answer, his
> very silence is invariably construed against him; and that, although
> truth is always the safest course, it is one of which the safety is not
> always seen, even by innocent men. There is an irresistible temptation
> to account for present appearances, which makes either silence or
> truth extremely rare. A man of great firmness, or of courage to speak
> the truth, the whole truth, and nothing but the truth; — but, a man of
> any weakness, or who sees that he has been caught in ugly
> circumstances and who, from his very consciousness of innocence, is
> naturally burning for immediate liberation, has recourse, almost to a
> certainty, to any statement, whether true or false, which seems to be
> convenient at the moment. He thinks of nothing but the present
> instant, and never dreams of the curious web that is to be weaved
> round him, out of his declarations, at his trial. Whether this
> accounts for the fact or not, I cannot say; but I hold it to be an
> unquestionable fact, that the declarations of the innocent are very
> nearly as false as those of the guilty. I have no doubt, therefore, —
> though I must confess, that I have not been at the pains to study them,
> — that the declarations in this case are crammed with inaccuracies,
> and probably with lies. You, of course, will give what effect to this you
> think proper; but I submit to you, that there never was a case in which
> the circumstance was of less weight. Declarations are great favourites

with accusers; but I have long observed a growing disregard of them on the part of juries; and they are particularly useless in any question like this, where the maker of them, though he may be innocent of the crime for which he is tried, was unquestionably guilty of other crimes which made truth equally inconvenient.

It was again a lesson for historians, both in showing the social and psychological circumstances leading to the production of incriminating documents, and in illuminating the specific circumstances of interrogation in early nineteenth-century Scotland. It will be remembered that conditions under the much more barbarous criminal code of England would have been decidedly worse, and that no prisoner would have the services of an advocate, either of the stature of Cockburn or of the experience of the most "white-wigged" devil at the bar, to point out the dubious value of the documents produced. Cockburn's work here was a credit to the commonsense philosophy in which as an Edinburgh student he had been brought up; he who had listened reverently at the feet of Dugald Stewart was particularly capable of explaining how a lie under stress is not proof of a murder in cold blood, despite that which primitive Calvinism seemed to its votaries to assume.

Cockburn concluded by stressing again the powerful prejudice against the "revolting" body traffic and its probable effects on the justice of the case, especially when associated with suspicion of murder was involved. He alluded to the enormous dissemination of gossip and newspaper discussion of the case, with consequent overwhelming prejudice against the prisoners in the minds of the jury before a word had been said. He pointed out that the prosecutor must prove the case, and if any rational doubt be left it was to the prisoner's benefit. And then he struck home hard and true, not only in his client's defence, but in an indictment of the Lord Advocate for his conspiracy to further the judicial murder of Helen MacDougal:

> Can it possibly be said, that there is no rational doubt in this case? So far from it, that I am perfectly satisfied, that if MacDougal had been under trial for an ordinary murder, of which the public had taken no particular charge, no prosecutor would have seriously asked for a verdict against her upon this proof. But what she is endangered by, is, the cry of the public for a victim. I need scarcely remind you, that this is a cry to which you, who are set apart from the prejudices of the public, and are sworn to look to the legal evidence alone, must be completely deaf. Let the public rage as it pleases. It is the duty, and the glory, of juries, always to hold the balance the more steadily, the more that the storm of prejudice is up. The time will come when these prejudices will die away. In that hour, you will have to recollect

whether you this day yielded to them or not; — a question which you cannot answer to the satisfaction of your own minds, unless you can then recall, or at least are certain that you now feel, legal grounds for convicting this woman, after deducting all the evidence of the Hares, and all your extrajudicial impressions. If you have such evidence, — convict her. If you have not, — your safest course is to find the libel is not proven.

The end crowned the work, and Cockburn sank back in the knowledge that he had done his duty by Helen MacDougal with such success that the jury might yet do its. The sole question lies on the last word. His client had pleaded not guilty: why did he demand the verdict of not proven? The most obvious answers are, firstly, because he believed it to be the true verdict, and, secondly, because he believed it to be the verdict he was most likely to get other than guilty. The non-Scottish reader must not fall into the vulgar error of assuming not-proven to mean "we think you did it, but we can't prove it". An English verdict of not-guilty can be anything from a testimonial of innocence to an expression of personal conviction of guilt but a recognition of insufficient evidence; an English verdict of guilty often embraces much that would be a clear not-proven verdict in Scottish proceedings. No doubt the latter ought not to be so, but it is. The famous "reasonable doubt" can be made more real to a Scottish jury because it has its own verdict to inhabit and with which to illuminate its identity. But it means absence of proof of innocence as well as absence of proof of guilt. It is not a denial of innocence, but simply an admission of absence of any proof.

Cockburn's intensely political personality, particularly as a known contributor of some of the most bristling essays in political controversy in the *Edinburgh Review*, made him a natural target for Tory attack and if today the political background of the trial has been forgotten, it was not lost on the Tories after their defeat in 1830 as they licked their wounds and derived little gastronomic enjoyment therefrom; in the Burke and MacDougal trial Cockburn had verbally inflicted on Rae some of the same dreadful execution he had performed on him earlier in the *Edinburgh Review* in his articles on the Lord Advocate's office. So Tory rumours spread that the historic defence of Helen MacDougal with its highly moral indictment of the Lord Advocate for his efforts to throw a relatively innocent victim to the mob was conceived in cynicism and concluded in the same spirit. The story was that in the course of his address, and noting the effects of his utterances on the jury (a considerable feat by candlelight), Cockburn sneered in an aside: "Infernal hag! — the gudgeons swallow it!". Now this absurd fable deserves no notice of itself, were it not for the revelations in the rebuttal which Cockburn made in his *Memorials* (although Roughead fed his invective against Helen MacDougal by repeating it, with Cockburn's denial). To whom was Cockburn supposed to have said it, if not to the profoundly moralistic Moncreiff, who would have been appalled by such contemptible amorality? And how dared he say it in a small, silent court-room in the early hours without a certainty of being overheard by a jury who had to be convinced of his sincerity? Yet an idiotic Quaker writing a philosophic treatise on morality cited the case as an example of professional fraud, and, once he had swallowed that, the Tory *Quarterly Review* delightedly returned to its own vomit, wallowing in the alleged incident as an example of the hollowness of Whig moral principles despite philanthropic appearances. Moreover, the *Quarterly* was naturally happy to cite Cockburn as witness to the fact that Rae had indicted the right person.

But in his *Memorials* Cockburn said of the charge: "It is utterly untrue. No one could be more honestly convinced of any thing than I was, and am, that there was not sufficient legal evidence to warrant a conviction of Helen MacDougal. Therefore, no such expressions or sentiment *could* be uttered. At any rate none such, and none of that tendency, were uttered." But it is worth noting that Cockburn does not protest his client's innocence. With his view of the world, and his genuine sympathy with the love for one another of the Burkes, as he thought of them, to Helen he clearly assigned in his own mind as in his speech, a plea of diminished reponsibility. Whatever doubts Moncreiff might have about the Grays' evidence, Helen had tried some sort of cover-up, and the sum of money involved was much bigger than concealment of resurrectionism would have warranted. Cockburn may have given greater credence than he was prepared to allow the jury to do with regard to Margaret Hare's quotation of Helen as saying Burke had a "*shot*" for the doctors in the house. Even so, it did not weaken his conviction of her responsibility's being diminished, and his view of the evidence was absolutely correct. It came from a tainted source, it was unsupported, and any other evidence as to Helen's *a priori* knowledge and accession to the crime proved on examination to speak for rather than against her. It is, of course, quite possible that Helen did give such a message to Margaret Hare, that Burke had told her to leave such a word, and that she took it to be that he had got hold of a corpse, not connecting it with the old woman. But with such prejudice as there was in the case, Cockburn must have felt his strongest card to play was his clear proof that there was no proof, whereas the question of innocence would cause jury self-questionings on the meaning of diminished responsibility, the admission of guilt involved when bribes are offered and lies are told, the likelihood or otherwise of shots having been noised abroad, and so forth. By resting his case on a not-proven verdict, Cockburn made the jury's task a simple one.

Yet at the same time he ensured that Helen's sufferings at the hands of future mobs would be hard, and perhaps even mortal. It is doubtful if he considered the point, for all of his knowledge of his Edinburgh. But not-proven in a lay mind can induce assumptions of the escape of the guilty by legal contrivance and in the mind of Scottish mobs, always more contemptuous of the sacred trappings of authority than English mobs, it was for them to administer justice where their rulers had sold the pass, not for the first time. And in fact the English mobs, when Helen encountered them, would have the additional incentive that if their culture was more deferential, their suspicions as to a not-proven verdict would naturally be even greater. And so it proved.

And now the bright swords had returned to their scabbards, and the audience awaited the pleasure of the Lord Justice-Clerk, shivering in the cold and murky air whose evil wetness entered into the marrow of their bones, for Boyle shared the fashionable prejudices of the enlightenment on hygiene and had ordered a large window to be maintained open for the entire day and night of the trial. Lawyers by now had their gowns wrapped round their heads which, said the *New Scots Magazine*, "intermingled with various coloured handkerchiefs in every shade and form of drapery, which gave to the visages that were enshrouded under them such a grim and grisly aspect as assimilated them to a college of monks or inquisitors, or characters imagined in tales of romance, grouped and contrasted most fantastically with the costume of the bench and the crowded bar engaged in the trial". The candles flickered and guttered, and the Nonpareil of the Bench, glancing from white-faced prisoners, to nightmare audience, to exhausted jury, commenced his remarks.

It is fair to Boyle to say that his charge to the jury has come down to us only in part. It apparently involved a massive review of the entire evidence, and the shorthand-taker was no doubt tired, wet and weary. As Boyle had every intention of coming down very emphatically on the Government side, he got his feet clear at the beginning by a fulsome compliment to Moncreiff and Cockburn who were the most eminent counsel at the bar, and who had done their work with a zeal and consummate ability which the Lord Justice-Clerk had never seen surpassed. It was a trial in which compliments had been flicked from side to side in such forms as might do the maximum damage to the recipients, and this was no exception. After all, Boyle had a point: Burke and Helen really did have much better advocacy than did the King, and the jury might as well be reminded of that advantage. It was rough on Rae, but then everything was.

Boyle attempted to rescue the prisoners' declarations from the odium into which Henry Cockburn had thrown their provenance. And it was at this point that the warring philosophies between Tory judges and prosecutors, and Whig leaders of the defence, came clearly to the fore, and Boyle made his direction of argument implacably clear. He ordered the jury to take the declarations into account, declared them to be legitimate evidence in the eyes of the law of Scotland, pointed out that there could be no challenge to the certification of their voluntary emission under sobriety of mind and sense, and underlined the assurance to the prisoners that they need not answer. In fact, as between Boyle and Cockburn, there was a division which continues to our own day: whether the rights of the accused are to be protected in actuality as well as in appearance. The problem here was that Cockburn was only counsel, while Boyle was prepared to enforce his views, those of a former government prosecutor, with all the force his judicial eminence could give him. And he then impugned the lies, contradictions and absurdities in the declarations (a point already fully admitted by leading counsel for both pannels): "utterly incredible . . . beyond all human belief . . . absolutely false".

On the subject of the Hares, Boyle expounded a view of the law which might have won more support from the readership of the *Quarterly Review* than from a jury still recovering from the commonsense analysis of Henry Cockburn. Morally speaking it had to be conceded the Hares were as guilty as the accused, or more so, if possible, but this did not make their evidence inadmissible: they no doubt were guilty of murder *de facto* but they had to be already found guilty *de jure* for their evidence in this trial to be inadmissible. Otherwise, the evidence of informers could never be accepted and the whole fabric of society would break down, etc., etc.

Cockburn had hinted that the Hares' zeal might be self-serving in fear that they themselves would be called to account for the other two murders in the indictment (and he had, correctly, pointed to the murder of Daft Jamie at the Hares' own house as a likely pointer to their greater responsibility). But, said Boyle, the Hares were protected from prosecution on every one of the three murder charges in the original indictment, and hence any plea of interest on their part was without foundation. (Boyle was still gliding over the other twelve cases, on Hare's part, which might yet be taken into consideration, nor was he dealing with Cockburn's real point which was not what had the Government promised, but what did Hare think they might yet do?) Then Boyle inquired whether the Hares' evidence was credible, decided it was, felt different standards should not be employed in judging their evidence, didn't feel minor discrepancies called their accuracy into question, felt, if anything, they showed a story had not been concocted, agreed that no two people ever gave the same account of an occurrence and how much more difficult would it be to do so with "those agitating and horrid circumstances which have been the subject of our investigation at this time".

Boyle admitted that the version of the crime given by the Hares conflicted with the evidence of Hugh Alston, but would not the jury consider whether allowance should be made "for the state in which Mrs Hare and MacDougal were, when in the passage?". He made no other remarks on the conflicts between the Hares and the "other and unexceptionable witnesses" that have come down to us, beyond inviting the jury to reconcile them. His final point at this stage was to state that if Mary Docherty had come to her end by natural or accidental means, why should the Hares "lay upon themselves a load of guilt, by admitting their participation in the crime charged, which they must bear during the whole course of their future lives?". (Again, we will look later on how much of this guilt the Hares actually did admit, and how and why the authorities dealt with such admission or lack of it. But, although it is academic in view of Burke's actual guilt, it is fair to say that a resurrectionist in a panic, thinking he would be framed for murder when a death had been accidental, might well choose to swear away the life of an innocent associate if he believed that he himself, equally innocent, was nonetheless in mortal danger unless he could ensure his immunity. This would be all the more likely for an immigrant Catholic from Ireland with its stringent penal code against the lower caste. Boyle, like so many others in the case, neither had nor desired an insight on the minds of the undermen. But Cockburn's point is absolutely true: the innocent may very well lie in fears for their safety.)

Boyle then turned to the part of the case concerning Helen MacDougal, and as it happens we have his remarks in the first person, for the first time in the shorthand report. "Accession to a crime may take place before the fact, as well as at the moment the crime is committing. It may likewise be *inferred*, from the conduct of the party after the fact. And if you are to believe the evidence which you have heard, I am much afraid there are but too strong grounds for concluding that the female pannel at the bar has been guilty of accession to the crime under investigation, whether you consider her conduct before or after the fact, or while it was perpetrating." Boyle then entered upon an interpretation of the evidence which may well have staggered even Rae, and which would certainly have won him some sharp rebukes from a court of criminal appeal (an institution not to see life until the next century). It was impossible to believe "for one moment" that MacDougal did not know why Mary Docherty had been brought to the house. This permanent prohibition on credence arose from the "brutal and dissipated habits" of the prisoners which negated any question as to their having charitable motives. (The whole point was, of course, that the dissipation and, if one insisted, brutality of the nomadic way of life from navvy society to urban migrant labour obviously carried with it a ready hospitality which might be less easily offered by more settled households. Pre-famine Ireland abounded in such conventions at the lowest level of society, and what Boyle might term "brutal and dissipated habits" were to their practitioners an expression of love and conviviality. Burke offended cruelly against the traditions and practice of his people, but it was against an established social norm that he was offending. On Boyle's logic one would have to assume that every one of a carousing million Irish households to offer drink and a bed to a stranger had to have murderous intentions. No doubt a few did relieve unwary travellers of their purses and lives but it would ill become us to employ a Burke as a method of drawing up an indictment against a whole people.)

Boyle cited the evidence of Ann Gray as to Helen MacDougal's having "actually opposed the woman's proposal of going out of the house" (which was fair enough, but he said nothing as to what, if she were seeking to detain her, was extraordinary indifference about the matter as shown at other times). "The manner, too, in which she communicated the fact to Mrs Hare, of this poor woman being in their clutches, viz., that they had got a *shot* in the house, shows distinctly her complete knowledge of what was in view, and implicates her morally, as well as legally, in the guilt that afterwards ensued." (An entirely unsupported statement from a witness to whom, *pace* Boyle, suspicion had to attach, was simply presented as proven fact.) As to the murder itself, Boyle argued that the flight of the women into the passage "can in no respect be considered as substantially different from actual presence; or rather perhaps it ought to be viewed as making more strongly against this prisoner. In this way, at least, she must have been completely at liberty to call for assistance, and prevent the final perpetration of the crime; while it takes away the possibility of pretending, as might have been done, if she had remained in the room, that she was compelled to witness the deed, and dared not take measures to prevent it; as it is sworn that she and Mrs Hare had previously interfered to prevent Burke and Hare from fighting." (It is probable that in this blatant violation of the known facts Boyle here blasted his own credibility in the eyes of the jury: the whole tendency of the evidence was that Helen MacDougal really had tried to stop the murder and, on the evidence of Alston, she very nearly succeeded. As to her failure to stop a murder when she had previously stopped a fight, what he was suggesting was that she, a lone woman, should singlehandedly have taken on Burke *and Hare*. But of course the legal presumption, in stark defiance of all the probabilities, was that Hare had purely observer's status.)

Boyle then alluded to the subsequent conduct of Helen MacDougal, adding that it was "equally, and if possible, still more unequivocally established, because it does not depend on the evidence of Hare and his wife alone". (Boyle, like almost everyone else, found it convenient to treat the Hares as credible when it suited him, and in need of supporting evidence when he found that more expedient.) He alluded in passing to her "share in the concealment of the dead body" (presumably that she did not reveal it), "the part she took in its transportation and sale, by accompanying the other prisoner and Hare to Surgeons' Square and Newington" (she took no such part, and she did not accompany the men, but followed them), and her ill-fated essays in mendacity and bribery.

Boyle then looked at the *Smith and Taylor* precedent, said he disagreed with the verdict of the jury on that occasion, and added that the cases were in any case not analogous since Taylor certainly had no previous knowledge that Smith intended to commit murder. (This, of course, assumed that Helen MacDougal's prior knowledge had been proved: again, Boyle was not being very wise, since if the jury disagreed with him as to whether that had been proved, they would be ready to accept *R.* v. *Smith and Taylor* as a precedent on Cockburn's terms, and let the Lord Justice-Clerk dislike their verdict as fully as he did that of the jury in *Smith and Taylor*.) Boyle further cited Helen MacDougal's false statements in the declaration as making for a "totally different" case from that of Taylor (and here, again, he was presuming that his authority would outweigh Cockburn's realism in the matter of the value of declarations).

Boyle concluded, apart from the usual last formulae about reasonable doubts and satisfaction as to the prisoners' guilt, by advising the jury on Helen MacDougal that "if you believe the evidence laid before you, of the prisoner's whole conduct, you must, in my opinion, hold her to be guilty, art and part, along with Burke".

It was now 8.30 a.m. on Christmas morning and John McFie, Esq., Chancellor of the jury, merchant, James Trench, builder, John Paton, builder, Nicol Allan, manager of the Hercules Insurance Company, William Bonar, banker, Peter McGregor, merchant, Robert Jeffrey, engraver, David Hunter, ironmonger, James Meliss, merchant, James Banks, agent, Thomas Barker, brewer, Henry Fenwick, grocer, David Brash, grocer, William Bell, grocer, and William Robertson, cooper, retired to consider their verdict. It was close to 9.30 a.m. when they returned.

John McFie spoke the verdict. They found the pannel William Burke Guilty of the third charge in the Indictment. They found the Indictment Not Proven against the pannel Helen MacDougal.

What happened next has come to us in many versions, but it seems likely that counsel for the prosecution and the defence were in a better position to hear than anyone. No doubt those who remained swung round to watch the reaction of the prisoners in the new light of morning. And it made a powerful impression on at least two of them. It is to be doubted whether Archibald Alison, for the prosecution, based his version on that of Henry Cockburn, for the defence, although the latter had been published a few years before; for Alison, to whom, as we know, little of the rest of the case meant much, rendered the name of the female prisoner as Mary although Cockburn has it as Helen, and if Alison were simply drawing on Cockburn he would have had that part right. The incident haunted Alison; he even says elsewhere in his memoirs that he narrated it to Howley, the Archbishop of Canterbury, who was as struck by it as he. He says as he watched Burke's reaction "How many are there among his judges, his jury, or his accusers, who in similar circumstances would have done the same?". ("This is more flattering to Burke than to the tribunal," sneered Roughead.) And it stood in Cockburn's memory too, and he saluted the memory of Burke, in the terms we have seen.

McFie finished his verdict; counsel and audience swung round; Boyle, Meadowbank and Mackenzie (Pitmilly had left the Bench through illness when Hare began his evidence) looked down, preparing the form of their next addresses; and, however opposing their views — and indeed their degree of interest — in the trial,

Alison and Cockburn fully accord on the next words spoken. Generous though Scottish legal procedure was in most respects, the criminal would not be granted the right of statement before the sentence. But whether the right was granted or not, he took it. And what he said was better than any number of speeches from the dock.

He threw his arms around her neck and said: "Thank God, you are safe!"

William Hare
and the King

To hold with the hare and run with the hound.
—John Heywood, *Proverbes*, Pt. I ch. X.

CAPITAL punishment is an odious usage, as morally degrading to the state that employs it as is murder to the person who resorts to it, but the state which tried William Burke knew no better and it had, indeed, shown itself far more progressive than its neighbours in its dealings with him. However unfair Burke thought a result with execution for him and immunity for Hare, he was perfectly in agreement with the justice of his own fate. From his viewpoint it had certain advantages. It gave him opportunities, all of which he seized, to show the true magnanimity of his nature; it ended the nightmare spiral of murder in which he had become trapped; it ended his associations with a world for which his name, to judge by the voices of the 25,000 who saw him die, was forever synonymous with enmity to the human race.

Similarly, within the court if not beyond it, justice was done to Helen MacDougal.

But justice was not done in the case of William Hare, and probably not done in that of his wife Margaret. Both should have been placed on trial, and he at least deserved a verdict of guilty. Had they been indicted for the murder of Daft Jamie there would have been a case for finding her guilty of accession as strong as that against Helen in the Docherty matter was weak.

Why not?

The answer lies with Rae, and to a lesser extent Alison, Dundas and Wood (unless, like Cockburn on Helen MacDougal, we want to argue very diminished responsibility for Alison and Dundas, on the grounds of their lack of interest). And once the trial had commenced it also lay with Boyle and Meadowbank, each of whom played significant, though differing, roles in the preservation of Hare. As a result of their behaviour it was ensured that in the matter of Burke and Hare though the world might learn the truth, it did not learn the whole truth, and it did not learn nothing but the truth. It is therefore a matter of considerable interest how these eminent gentlemen became imprisoned in a conspiracy of their own making to defeat the course of justice. We have already seen the worst result of that conspiracy — the attempt on the life of Helen MacDougal. But there were other results. There was evidence which was suppressed, there were witnesses who were not sworn, there was protection of murder, there was protection of perjury, there was blatant acceptance by Crown and judiciary of statements under oath which were false and which they knew to be false. In fact, the result was a very singular one. If Burke, according to the generous Alison, proved himself the moral superior of judges and counsel in his reception of the verdict, Hare proved himself their tactical superior. On his arrest, he was a prisoner in the hands of the legal authorities; within two months, the legal authorities were prisoners in his. Would he lie? They must be his sureties in it. Would he deny murder? They must also deny it. Would he demand defence? They must supply it. Would he seek freedom? He should have it.

Now, how did this ridiculous comedy take place?

Hare's most odious action was to seek to throw the blame on the innocent young Brogan after his arrest. He had been brutalised, and rat-like he cared not what he mangled in his heat to escape. And then the authorities opened up the way in their interrogation. Burke and Helen MacDougal would not betray one another, nor Burke betray the Hares. Hare was made of poorer stuff, as the Brogan incident had indeed shown. It may well be that Hare's slowness in informing against Burke arose because of his fear that such an accusation would be close enough to the truth to incriminate himself. It is tantalising that we can guess so little of that duel between Rae and Hare, each trying to outmanoeuvre the other. And if Hare does not deserve moral respect, he should at least elicit some practical admiration of the kind all too readily accorded to equally immoral statesmen and generals, for the skill with which he consolidated the negotiations to his advantage.

It should also be said that Hare's moral position is not quite as destitute as might appear. We know that Burke had refused to turn traitor; Hare did not, and it would be nothing new had the authorities played the game of eliciting a confession by asserting the existence of one. If that happened, Hare could hardly be blamed for reacting against Burke with the anger with which Burke after the trial spoke out against Hare. Again, if Burke had Helen to protect,

Hare had Margaret. The promise of immunity covered her, and ensured that she at least would continue in possession of their child instead of its being left to an orphanage. Hare's very limitations of mind and spirit made him less capable of exhibiting fortitude than was the resourceful and accomplished Burke. A sense of humour is a great insurance during imprisonment; Burke had one, Hare does not seem to have had. We can see Burke cheering himself up with a song; but not Hare.

Macheath's famous remark in *The Beggar's Opera* "That Jemmy Twitcher should peach me I own surprised me" was applied, with thunderous enthusiasm, in reply to Lord Sandwich's attack on John Wilkes, but would it have been justified as a comment of Burke on Hare? Not from Hare's standpoint. The two men, after all, had been partners, but hardly friends. Hare might tell himself that he had dealt Burke in on a good racket, given him lodging, put up with the insult of his greater popularity, witnessed the signs of Margaret's interest in him, accepted his defection from the lodging-house and finally as a result of coming in with him on the Docherty enterprise found himself arrested through what was Burke's folly. And if he thought that one through, he might well feel aggrieved. Burke had let far too many people know about the old woman instead of smuggling her in, alive, and out, dead, as had been the custom when the firm was at its best. Helen MacDougal gave the alarm at the moment of crisis. The next day, what must Burke do when the body was still in the house to be discovered, but invite half the country to have a dram, including several who had seen the old woman and asked after her? It was not — presumably — the Hares who had insisted on the Grays being brought back to the Burkes. And finally Burke's own evidence suggests that Hare during the fight really had become murderous, and that by now something very close to hatred for his colleague was eating away at the misanthropic corpse-dealer. Hare may genuinely have felt he owed Burke no obligations, and if he was to get off by helping to hang him, very well, he would help to hang him.

To say this is not to gainsay the strength of Sir James Moncreiff's last point: that Hare's evidence might be crowning a career by an attempt to encompass the judicial murder of Burke and of Helen MacDougal. The point holds good whether Burke be innocent or guilty; for Hare's evidence had to cast him for the designer and shaper of the whole murder industry, and transform him from teammate to scapegoat. Burke might have had his deserts, but Hare's evidence still involved lies and distortions to make Burke — and if necessary Helen — suffer for a crime in which Hare had been co-partner. Despite the implication of contemporary and subsequent writers, there is absolutely no reason to believe that Hare ever held his position in the enterprise to be inferior to that of Burke. (The superstition developed over the years that he did accept an inferior status, to some extent arising from a repressed desire to seek reassurance that the chief miscreant had received his just deserts.)

Burke and Hare began as co-partners, with Hare, as landlord, somewhat before Burke as candidate for ringleader. The status of landlord is significant here. An Irish tenant simply did not inform the landlord what to do about others of his tenants. He might give advice, if asked, but that still did not make him a ringleader. In the case of the first murder, Scott established an urgent reason for encompassing the death of Joe the Miller — fear that the house would get a name for plague: but the motive was solely Hare's. If Burke took the lead, then it was purely as friend and mercenary acting under orders. But Rae and his associates were prisoners of their times, and in their world it was assumed that greater education ensured higher status. It was contrary to the enlightened Scottish ethic to countenance the notion that the more educated might be dominated and driven by the less. Hence, whatever the realities about the origins of the chain of murders, it was easy to assign them to Burke.

Again, the specific case in which Burke and Hare came to the attention of the authorities was one in which Burke most certainly had taken the initiative. It was also the case that Police-Officer Fisher and his associate were so impressed by Burke's diplomacy that they almost allowed the matter to drop, and then, having been led to make an arrest because of Helen MacDougal's blunder about the time, it would be natural for them to conclude after more evidence had appeared that the soft answerer who so nearly turned away wrath was a cunning person, and hence surely a ringleader. Admittedly, what they learned of other cases, especially Daft Jamie, should have thrown more suspicion on the Hares, but by then they were committed to Burke as leader.

William Bolitho in *Murder for Profit* remarks that "Hare would perform his informer's contract, with shameful loyalty. With Burke they will have to fear a faithful treachery. At the last moment, in court, he might play his betrayers false and his co-murderer true, and risk the freedom of the whole squad." Certainly Burke's evident intelligence, however slumbering from time to time in practical effect, must have been a little alarming. Hare looked more like someone who would take direction. The very appearance of the two men — Burke alert, Hare half-imbecilic — was a reminder to the prosecution that they were safer with the illiterate. Appearance, even at dead of night, would count for something with the jury, and surely Burke looked more like a ringleader than Hare? It is doubtful if they allowed for what actually happened — the appearance of Hare's lean, gangling, somewhat crazed-looking, vampirical form, nervously giggling in the Stygian darkness rendered more ominous by its interruptions of candlelight. To the jury Burke may have looked more like a leader than Hare, but Hare must have looked more like a monster than Burke. Still, Mary Shelley's *Frankenstein* had been published only a few years previously, and nobody ever suggested that the monster rather than Frankenstein had been the ringleader, however menacing he may have been.

Sir William Rae decided that if he had to choose, it would, for these reasons be Burke rather than Hare whom he would seek to hang. It is arguable that he may have been right for the wrong reasons. Burke's moral sense seems to have been much more strongly developed than Hare's, and education also seems to have given him more of a philosophic and reflective sense. From a moral standpoint, he was much more aware of what he was doing than was the brutalised Hare. But, of course, such a consideration was outside the purely legal arguments which should have been swaying Rae. And, it is not likely that this did have influence with him, if in fact he knew it. We may feel that Burke was the more responsible for *himself*; Rae held that he took the line he did as Burke was the more responsible for *Hare*.

Perhaps one notable silence in Rae's deposition is in itself worth a glance:

> The only matter for deliberation, regarded which of the four should be selected as witnesses.
> MacDougal positively refused to give any information.
> The choice, therefore, rested between Hare and Burke. . . .

The fact that *Margaret* Hare is passed over here when she certainly was an obvious and earlier choice, as being likely less guilty than either Burke or Hare, is suggestive. Rae then says, after Hare's agreement, "and his wife was taken, because he could not bear evidence against her". But in any reasonable order of lesser guilt she should have been taken first. The real point was that *she* could not bear evidence against *him*.

The selection of the Hares as King's evidence cut two ways: it rendered certain lines of investigation unnecessary, and in some instances — e.g. further research into the proceedings of the medical fraternity in general and the establishment of Dr Robert Knox in particular — Rae, Alison and their associates may have been very thankful that it did; and it also made it inadvisable to pursue certain other matters, in particular matters which would focus attention on the guilt of Hare rather than on that of Burke. Certain witnesses were never called; certain documents were not produced; certain questions were not asked; and of course certain murders were not investigated or, if they were, the results were not made known. As we have noted, Cockburn was to suggest that the Hares might yet be open to prosecution for their part in the Paterson and Daft Jamie murders mentioned in the indictment, but not proceeded with; and Boyle was pointedly to assure the jury that immunity for Hare extended also to those cases, an observation coming so pat as to lead to the conclusion he had been warned by Rae that immunity had been promised on those murders also; but it hard to resist the conclusion that the Hares had in fact been promised total immunity. Such an action would have been in keeping with standard procedure in political cases; Rae's experience of immunity was largely in political trials; and he may well have made himself so unpopular by giving only partial immunity earlier in his career that prisoners had since demanded that he spell out such immunity as he would give in return for King's evidence. Rae may also have discussed the matter with his predecessor, Meadowbank, which would account for Meadowbank's activity on the point, apart from his natural desire to protect the safeguards of the police state. And however much Hare did or did not know of Rae's record in the matter of partial immunity — possibly more than we might realise, since folklore travels and he may have been receptive to news about local social disturbances — we may be sure he would have given no list of his own murders or of murders to which he admitted being accessory without assurances of his own preservation.

It is also curious that Rae, in his deposition above mentioned, uses the words "On the 4th of November, William Hare and Margaret Laird were examined. . . . Hare and his wife were again examined by the Sheriff on the 10th of November. . . . They were a *third* time examined, on the 19th November", with no indication as to whether or not the examinations had taken place separately or otherwise. (They were, of course, confined to separate cells.) There must certainly be a suspicion that when — from the beginning of December — they had agreed to turn King's evidence, at least some of their confessions were made in each other's presence. After all, it was Sir William Rae's decision and he hardly wanted his hard bargain coming to pieces in his hands with major mutual contradictions in the open court.

Did Hare's lost confession acknowledge at least some participation in murder? Is that why it has disappeared? Did the Crown acquiesce in, or even initiate, an arrangement by which his evidence would lie on this point, given Rae's fear of encouraging the mob? Hare could have admitted his part in murdering, and been protected — but would public opinion have stood over such blatant denial of justice. The formula *socius criminus* permitted Rae to take testimony of Hare and his wife on the understanding that they must speak the truth. It may simply have been that William Hare had no intention of doing anything of the kind, and he somehow ensured his Margaret knew the story he was going to tell and would stand by him. Hare would have been long familiar with the assumption of many Irish Catholic labourers and tenant-farmers that perjury before a court of Protestant landlords was no crime. From Hare's point of view, with his memories of Orange magistrates and wholly partisan law-enforcement authorities, it may have seemed dangerous to trust completely in the promises of the state.

We go back to the moment in the trial when Hare steps into the witness-box.

The associate judges took their turn to swear the witnesses: Hare — and, interestingly, his wife — were sworn by the judge who would prove most concerned with protecting their rights, Meadowbank:

> Now, we observe that you are at present a prisoner in the Tolbooth of Edinburgh; and from what we know, the Court understands that you must have had some concern in the transaction now under investigation. It is, therefore, my duty to inform you, that whatever share you might have had in that transaction, if you now speak the truth, you can never afterwards be questioned in a Court of justice; but you are required, by the solemn oath you have now taken, to speak the truth, the whole truth, and nothing but the truth; and if you deviate from the truth, or prevaricate in the slightest degree, you may be quite assured that it will not pass without detection; and that the inevitable result will be, the most condign punishment that can be inflicted. You will now answer the questions that are to be put to you.

Meadowbank's assurances of "detection", of "inevitable result" and of "condign punishment", probably won less respect from Hare than the folklore of the banshee. If Meadowbank was in a position to "detect" any deviation from "the truth", he would not need Hare to be giving evidence in the first place. Where Hare intended to offer the lion's share of perjury would be over those episodes where his sole companions were his wife, happily squared, the accused, whom the authorities obviously did not want to believe, and Mary Docherty, deceased. Hare certainly would have been all too familiar with the place of the Crown informer in Irish society, and he would have known perfectly well that the authorities were sparing in the extreme in their analyses of the weak points in the credibility of the testimony of Crown informers. What Ireland had not prepared him for was the presence of the finest counsel in the bar to fight for the rights of his former friend Burke.

So, during his examination-in-chief, with or without Rae's certain knowledge, Hare coolly called Meadowbank's bluff by lying away. And in so doing he committed the wretched prosecution — and their allies on the Bench, Meadowbank and Boyle — to supporting his perjuries in the knowledge that any retreat on his credibility would place their case in an impossible position. Moncreiff, in his speech for the defence, was to sum up Hare's testimony as against that of his wife, and the evidence of both against other witnesses. Brogan had said he came in at 2.00 a.m. or 3.00 a.m. on the Saturday morning and lay down by the fire with the two women, Burke and Hare being in the ʰed; Hare said that the two women were in the bed and that Brogan lay down in the back part of the bed and slept there. Mrs Hare had the women on the floor, one man in bed, the other in a chair. Hare said that when Burke got Mrs Docherty on the floor the women escaped from the bed; Mrs Hare said she was standing near the door and did not get out of the bed. (It may be remembered that Burke, preoccupied with murdering Mrs Docherty, could not in fact remember the escape of the women at all, and no doubt Hare, having been murderer rather than observer, had difficulty in reconstructing an accurate account of events at the same point.) Hare said he sat on the chair during the murder; Mrs Hare, that he was standing by the dresser. Hare said the old woman was so drunk as being unable to rise after reaching the ground; Mrs Hare said little of the drunkenness, but, added Moncreiff, if she fell and suffered some injury, that could have produced death. Hare said the old woman ran into the passage and cried murder during the fight; Mrs Hare that the old lady never ran into the passage and that the door was never opened. Hare said Helen MacDougal went twice into the passage and brought back the old woman; Mrs Hare that this did not happen, the old woman not being in the passage and Helen therefore not bringing her back. Hare said all was quiet after the major events; Mrs Hare that there was a second fight.

(The Lord Justice-Clerk was later to say, it will be recalled, that these discrepancies were proof against any "previous concert or collusion". This is of course nonsense; they simply show that any such collusion had been too brief, that the two protagonists had not rehearsed their stories in the full detail necessary.)

Moncreiff continued to point out that Hare would insist that the old woman was brought to Burke's at 9.00 a.m. on the Friday. Nancy Conway and Janet Law both testified to the arrival of the old woman behind Burke at 2.00 p.m. Then he turned to Alston's evidence: the cries of murder had come from the passage, and in a "very strong female voice". Hare had said the old woman had called murder in the passage, and Mrs Hare that any such call would have been only in the room. Alston was clear as to the voice being different from the other, choking voice. On Alston's evidence, then, the Hares lied. And Moncreiff came back to the fact that they agreed on the main point — that the pannels were responsible for murder — "but on nothing else". Hare said he had no money from Knox's assistant; Paterson showed he did. Paterson said Hare also acted as principal. Paterson said he divided the money to avoid disputes. Surely Paterson, as opposed to Hare, was to be believed? And Moncreiff, like Cockburn, had a deadly point in arguing that the Hares had every interest in seeing the accused would hang for fear that they themselves would otherwise be made sacrifices to the mob's demands for blood. Their immunity *may* have extended to fifteen counts — or corpses — but their own backgrounds would still leave them with grave doubts on that score. They would have felt they were safe so long as somebody else was hanged.

Undoubtedly, the Hares were a desperate solution on Rae's part in another way. If, by any chance, Burke as well as Helen MacDougal was to have eluded the gallows, the howl for Hare's blood would have been enough to crack the firmament. Not proven for Burke meant an assumption of guilt by Hare; or at least a firm assertion by the jury that he was a liar, and if he were, the assumption must be that he lied because he was a murderer. In such circumstances Rae's problems in defending immunity would have been appalling. Boyle and Meadowbank had in different ways lent substance to his promises, but they also would have found their position a very difficult one. There would presumably have been another trial of Burke, this time perhaps over Daft Jamie, and the probability of Hare's guilt on that would have risen far higher in the public mind; yet Boyle had specifically stood over immunity on that charge. Hare had become a dreadful gamble for the government and, by the time they were finished with him, Moncreiff and Cockburn must have left so much doubt in the mind of the jury as to leave a decided possibility that the two jurors who allegedly wanted a not-proven verdict for Burke were partly led to that conclusion because of Hare's evidence. So that Rae's deal with the Hares, intended to ensure a certain verdict of guilty, ran the danger of causing the reverse effect.

The significance of what Hare had become to the prosecution's case was made all too clear when debate was opened up (after Hare had been removed) as to the admissibility of questions on Hare's having been concerned in other murders. "I am ready to admit he is not bound to answer," acknowledged Cockburn, "but I am entitled to put that question, let him answer it or not as he pleases. It will be for the jury to judge of the credit due to him, after seeing how he treats it."

"The caution that was put to this witness was, that he was not to speak to any of those cases, except the one under investigation," snapped Rae, "and how he can be asked with regard to them now, in this state of the proceedings, to me is inconceivable."

The Lord Justice-Clerk played for time. It was all very well to try to pull Rae's questions out of the fire, but it was dangerous to stand too firmly behind such a policy with Cockburn — and still more Moncreiff — out for blood. Rae's weakness of staff-work had already won a judgment against him from Boyle over the indictment; another was possible. "I do not think that the general question, if he ever supplied the doctors with subjects, ought to be put; at least, I am bound to tell the witness that he need not answer it unless he pleases." (In the event, the question slipped by Boyle after Hare's return, and Hare answered with so blatant a negative, against all the known facts, that prosecution and bench thereafter were virtually afraid to have a question as to the time of day to put to him, without a warning as to his right not to answer.)

But Meadowbank, as a former Lord Advocate much concerned with encouraging informers, particularly on political cases, leapt in where the Lord Justice-Clerk was being so cautious in treading:

> When we are gravely and imperatively called upon to tell the witness so, for what purpose is it that that question can be put, when the witness is told that he is not bound to answer it, I cannot discover; but, further, I have to state this, that the witness is brought here to be examined on the matter before the Court, and he cannot, in any circumstance that may be disclosed in that evidence, be examined on a cross-examination; he cannot be called on to answer other matters. And is he to be exposed to suppositions because he does not choose to answer that question? It would be subversive of every principle of justice, because the Court cannot protect him. . . .

Were Cockburn to carry his point, informers would be placed under notice that their careers might receive much more searching questions, whether they chose to answer them or not, than would be envisaged by the all-protecting mechanism as approved by Meadowbank. Hence informers might be slower to come forward, however much promise they might obtain of Crown protection. Meadowbank saw the same point, and was ready to fight like a tiger to ensure informers would be assured of a fair passage once they had told their all, and perhaps more than their all, to the Government authorities. Already it must have been clear to all that Hare had committed perjury, especially if anyone cared to juxtapose his examination-in-chief against Alston's evidence; and here, too, it was important from Meadowbank's point of view that future informers should not feel an undue pedantry would be involved in supervising their every utterance. But in his zeal, Meadowbank had over-reached his hand.

"Your Lordship will observe that I have only stated what the proposed question is, but that I have not been heard in support of it. . . Nevertheless one of your Lordships has not only formed, but has expressed an opinion, and a very clear opinion, against it." Meadowbank, thus manoeuvred into a position of the maximum peril to the side he supported, was left to writhe, and Cockburn continued. It was a matter of testing the witness's credit. The questions might be answered, and were they answered falsely the witness might be thus contradicted. The protection of a villainous witness by preventing any question about his own iniquities "humbly appears to us absolutely monstrous". Cockburn then said there were no authorities in Scottish law either way, and took the dangerous ground of citing English precedents for the discrediting of a witness by cross-examination on his own past behaviour, especially where it turned on the criminal.

English and Scottish procedure were nowhere more at variance than in cross-examination, replied Alison, or in the discrediting of witnesses. And he shrewdly pointed to the English hostility to the accused, whereas in Scotland safeguards obtained. The English prisoner, not being furnished in advance with a list of witnesses, naturally has a freer range in dealing with them than was the case in Scotland. To be shown iniquitous a witness in Scotland must first be shown to have been convicted of an infamous crime.

Moncreiff was on his feet. This needed rescuing. The authorities cited by Alison assumed the use of other evidence to discredit a witness; the defence would not call other evidence. Hare could testify against Burke on any other case; but Burke, or his advocates, could examine Hare on his past conduct to show the worth of his word. Boyle had warned Hare of the need for the truth, and Meadowbank had also; was not that evidence of his suspicious character? And with this situation already acknowledged, could not the real nature of such a witness be brought out into the open? The defence believed that if Hare answered truthfully with respect to his past, what he said would speak for itself; if he spoke falsely — i.e. if he denied previous involvement in murder — the law would afford "remedies independent of the effect of this trial" (which were, of course, frozen in the hands of the Lord Advocate). And if Hare declined to answer, the jury would draw its own conclusion.

Boyle observed succinctly that "we all know the course the Court follows in such a case, which is, to tell the witness not to answer the question unless he thinks proper". Pitmilly was by now gone. Much depended on Mackenzie. Fortunately, Meadowbank could be relied on to reiterate his own position, thus increasing the impatience of his colleagues and their natural disposition to examine the point of view for which he was prepared to hear nothing. He began by regretting having given his early reaction, and assured everyone, with little probable effect, that had the bar been able to change his mind it would have changed it. The witness must be particularly protected against questions as to things from which their Lordships could not protect him being questioned on other occasions. And surely Scots law permitted no question to be put which witness could not competently answer, or the jury take as evidence.

Were the prisoner to be asked about other murders, Rae might have to say more about other murders, and the jury would have to go through all of that evidence, and the prisoners might end being convicted on matters not at issue in the indictment! The Bench could allow no question which, if answered in the affirmative, would disqualify a witness. Suppose witness were asked "Have you committed ten acts of perjury?", and witness said yes, what would follow? Their Lordships must tell the jury witness's answer was either true or false. "If true, must it not also be added, that he cannot be believed upon his oath; and that, if it appears not to be true, then he is equally incredible." And, triumphantly flashing his syllogism in his colleagues' faces, Meadowbank sat back.

Henry Mackenzie spoke next, and at once fulfilled all of Cockburn's hopes. (Cockburn and he had become members of the Friday club, a literary, social and scientific body, from the year of its foundation a quarter-century before. Scott was in it, and Dugald

Stewart, and Sydney Smith, and Jeffrey, and Brougham, and Alison's
father the essayist on taste, but not the son — in fact, no other person
in that court. It was not politics that was at stake here, but
receptivity of mind.) Witness could not be protected beyond the
present case, nor could any admissions he might make as to other
crimes protect him against proceedings in their connection. But the
want of protection should not prevent questions being put, although
the court should warn him that he was not obliged to answer.
Protection of public prosecutor's witnesses did not differentiate
themselves from defence or private prosecution witnesses who might
also be so protected. He sustained Moncreiff on the matter of
questions to witness differing from the production of other and
unheralded witnesses against him.

Boyle reiterated his intention of warning the witness, and
specifically dissented from Meadowbank. And after some sparring
among counsel, with Meadowbank grumblingly enquiring whether
every other murder was now competent to be discussed, the witness
was recalled.

We may now look at some points in which the protection of Hare
led to questions not being asked, and to investigations not being
made. The most obvious examples arise in connection with the
evidence of John Fisher, which in turn raised questions about the
Grays'. This was not raised by the defence, as it was in fact evidence
for the prosecution, but the prosecution did not deal with it either.

Fisher had been sure that he would find no body at Burke's. Now,
he would only have had such an assurance from Gray; therefore Gray
knew the body had already gone up to Surgeons' Square. But he
spoke of nothing in his evidence between his and his wife's discovery
of the body, and his part in Burke's arrest, save that they and Helen
met Mrs Hare, and retired to a public-house, after which he gave
information to the Police-Office. But, on Fisher's evidence, Gray
knew when he came to the Police-Office that the body had gone,
therefore somebody else had told him something else in the interval.
Gray was not anxious to conceal anything, and it emerged from his
statements to the press that he had indeed seen someone between his
discovery of the body and his visit to the pub with Helen and
Margaret: William Hare, no less, who had also been present when
the disputants Helen and the Grays encountered Margaret Hare on
the street.

Gray was equally explicit about the next stage: Mrs Hare, rather
like Cassius before Caesar's murder, enquired why urge they their
petitions in the street, come into the capitol, or her equivalent

thereof, the public-house, but Hare did not accompany them. Gray (who said nothing to the press about his wife) left the pub after an interval, removed from the Hares' house his child's things (but not, apparently, the child, which in fact like so many other children in this narrative exists but never makes an appearance) and moved to new lodgings. It has to be inferred that Hare told Gray he was going to move the body, and possibly even mentioned Knox's name; or else that when a reasonable interval had taken place in the pub Margaret Hare, perhaps jeeringly, told Gray that if he did tell the police they would find no corpse in the house. Otherwise Gray would not have known about the vanishing corpse. Either of those inferences suggest that one or the other of the Hares behaved very stupidly; had they let Gray go without indicating the fate of the corpse, Fisher would have arrived in pursuit of a cadaver, found none, and had his already strong suspicions of Gray increased. As it was, Gray was in a position to give the police an expectation of what they would not find, and apparently an indication of its destiny.

It was the Crown's duty to supply all the pieces of the jigsaw in evidence, so that the total picture would be evident once the final addresses were made: Scottish procedure knows nothing of the English and Irish "opening speech for the prosecution" which often does so much to prejudge the whole trial in the mind of the jury. Why was this critical evidence concealed from the court? The body's removal from Burke's to Knox's was a focal point of the case. The inference is clear enough. Gray was not asked about it because to do so would be to exhibit Hare in an executive capacity. Hare — or Margaret Hare — had known enough to state on his or her own responsibility that the body would be gone when the police arrived, and all of this without reference to Burke. Hence all question of Hare's appearing purely as a sleeping partner, or at least a comatose one, would disappear. And Helen MacDougal's pathetic bribes suddenly would begin to look very innocent. She makes a ridiculous attempt to hush things up; the Hares, coolly and professionally, detain the Grays and remove the body. It is obvious from this recital who is the neophyte and who the tried and proven masters. With this evidence on the stand the contrast between Helen MacDougal in the dock and the Hares under immunity would become even uglier. So the Crown was suppressing evidence.

Rae had the excuse that the decision to take but one count in the indictment meant that the evidence of many subpoenaed witnesses would be irrelevant, but there were several persons who appeared on no prosecution list of witnesses and who must have had much of importance to communicate. There was the Police-Superintendent who examined Burke after arrest at the station, and whose remarks Boyle would not allow Fisher to report. There was Captain Stewart, who arrested William and Margaret Hare on the Sunday morning about 8.00 a.m.

Of the witnesses cited but not called by Rae, by no means all were irrelevant by reason of knowledge of the Paterson and/or the Daft Jamie murder only. The original list of fifty-five offered by the Crown began with the sheriff-substitute, the procurator-fiscal, and two clerks in the sheriff-clerk's office, all of whom were presumably to testify to the making of the declarations. This was relevant to the Docherty matter and even, as we may notice in the final exchanges between the defence and the Lord Justice-Clerk, it was to be a matter of controversy. But Rae may not have dared to call them, for fear the defence might raise questions about the Hares' declarations. After that there were a number of witnesses of relevance to the Paterson murder, and some for the Daft Jamie murder, with the Hares enjoying a prominent social position as numbers 10 and 11. Then followed nos. 25–36 inclusive, otherwise our old friends young John Brogan, Janet Law, Nancy Conway, William Noble, the Grays, Alston, Elizabeth Paterson, John McCulloch and John Fisher and two corroborative witnesses not called — Elizabeth (and David) Paterson's mother, and Nancy Conway's much-enduring and early-rising husband. Rae did not want too much attention on that portion of the evening when Burke was absent and the Hares at the centre of attention. He needed Nancy's evidence, but he did not require certain of its details underlined. Mother Paterson might have thrown unwanted light on her hopeful son.

But the list of police not called from among the subpoenaed witnesses is formidable, quite apart from the Captain and the Superintendent who were not even listed. And their evidence must have been entirely Docherty in relevance, and not Paterson or Jamie: the forces of law and order had played no part in the cases of the youth without wits and the lady without amateur status. Fisher alone gave evidence; Officer Findlay, Lieutenant Paterson and Sergeant MacNicol were among the many who were chosen but not among the few who were called. Again, this would seem to have been an anxiety to shift attention off police proceedings in that naturally this once again would have drawn attention to the Hares, especially should questions arise about the decision to arrest them, the reasons for a twelve-hour delay, and so forth. Had Hare admitted part in the murder, as in law he was supposed to do, the point would have not arisen, but with his insistence on his non-participation and with the unfortunate prosecution condemned either to stand over his perjury or to acknowledge it and thence be forced to prosecute him with resultant adverse effects on the informers' market, it was advisable to steer away from the guardians of the peace.

Of the next three witnesses on the original list Mary Stewart and Charles McLauchlan had given testimony on the old woman's stay in the Pleasance and the failure to call Roderick Stewart, the landlady's husband, was merely a saving of the court's time. But the next missing witness, number 43, was interesting, and, curiously, both James Gray and William Burke, severally, expressed regret that she was never heard from, and said she had much of importance to say. She was listed as Elizabeth Main although it is unlikely this was her name, and she had been maidservant in the Hares' domicile. Gray told the newsmen that two weeks after Burke's arrest she had come to him and asked him to write to the sheriff on her behalf, but no results ensured when he acted. "She said to Gray that she could tell a great many things if she liked, but only mentioned one instance, and that was of an old woman (Grannie, she called her, if he remembers right) being carried by Hare from his kitchen into the cellar, while in a state of intoxication, but she never knew what became of her afterwards. She did not mention at what time this took place. . . . She was in the witness-room during the trial, but was not called on." The absence of Burke from the story leaves the mysterious woman murdered in Burke's absence by Hare alone as the most likely candidate.

Burke in his *Courant* confession would interestingly echo Gray on the withheld evidence of the maid, although he gave her name as "M'Guier or Mair". The *Courant* were "well informed" that she was Irish (probably from Burke). Burke said "she could give information respecting the murders done in Hare's house, if she likes. She came to him at Whitsunday last, went to harvest, and returned to him when the harvest was over." (This suggests a summer corpse and hence, if the Knox tariff was in full application, it was indeed the woman murdered by Hare alone, the only possible female victim murdered at the Hares' to have obtained £8 and not £10; — another reason why the maid's evidence was not wanted by the crown.) Burke also said that the maid Elizabeth or Betty "remained until he [Hare] was confined along with his wife in the Calton Jail. She then sold twenty-one of his swine for £3 and absconded". (Hare was evidently setting up as an urban agriculturalist with his takings, a commonplace situation in those days when the cities had the filth of urban-bred livestock adding to the health hazards.) "She was gathering potatoes in a field that day Daft Jamie was murdered; she saw his clothes in the house when she came home at night." It could be argued that her evidence was primarily of relevance to the Daft Jamie murder, but she would have been in a position to document comings and goings to the Hare household during the Docherty affair, especially given the discrepancies in the Hares' narratives as to who had gone where and said what. Elizabeth might not have known the latter, but she could have thrown light on the former. But she seems to have known too much to be useful to the Crown.

The next set of witnesses were very conspicuous indeed by their absence, apart from David Paterson — Robert Knox, Thomas Wharton Jones, William Fergusson, Alexander Miller. It is true that the Docherty cadaver was the only one never examined by Knox in person, but both Knox and Wharton Jones had figured in the voyages of Burke and Hare to Surgeons' Square and Newington on All Saints' Day, Saturday, November 1, and the question of what exactly happened then became of importance as the case proceeded. Hare's version clashed with Paterson's, and Boyle was ultimately to draw extraordinary conclusions from the actions of Helen MacDougal at that point. Knox and Wharton Jones may in fact not have been called as they would have underlined Hare's perjury overmuch. But it is also clear that Rae feared the opening up of Pandora's Box if the anatomist and his assistants were brought before the court. In the absence of any corpses for the Daft Jamie and Mary Paterson murders it was absolutely vital to have the evidence of Knox and his young men, but when the defence restricted the counts to be heard to one, Rae promptly chose that which eliminated Knox from the list of unavoidable witnesses.

The decision to employ the services of a *socius criminis* really was made to avoid the searching public inquest which a prosecution of all four prisoners would have necessitated. Even Dylan Thomas's bad screenplay *The Doctor and the Devils* picked up that point: Knox may have been cordially hated by the Edinburgh intellectual establishment, old and new, but too much was at stake to allow him to be thrown to the wolves. The non-appearance of the subpoenaed Professor William Pulteney Alison in the witness-box carries its own reminder of what Rae was saving by reliance on Hare.

There was, as we saw, also evidence Rae was anxious not to have given by witnesses whose appearance before the court could not be prevented. James Gray, for instance, also told the press that Margaret Hare came into Burke's on Hallowe'en afternoon "and found the old woman Docherty sitting on the chair intoxicated, and

gave her a glass of whisky, at two or three different times, and she
refusing to take it, she poured it into her mouth and put her hand
upon her mouth, to force her to swallow it". Presumably Gray meant
that he himself had seen this; if so, here again the Crown was
deliberately suppressing evidence to keep the Hares as clean as
possible. Boyle was to squeeze inferences of Helen MacDougal's
guilt from evidence far less substantial than that. Had Gray been
permitted to tell his full story, the sheer injustice of any indictment of
Helen MacDougal as against the guilt of both Hares would have
blazed before the world. The mob demanded the blood of all the
four; few persons other than the defence counsel themselves, and the
jury, seem to have stopped to consider how little evidence against
Helen there really was. But an indictment of Margaret Hare from
the witness-box of this clarity and bite might be expected to increase
the public fury as to the escape of herself and her husband to a degree
where loss of life would be the result. Who could say what would
happen if mobs of 25,000 were to riot?

Could William Burke, William Hare and perhaps also Margaret
Hare have been convicted without the use of any *socius criminus*
whatsoever? (We rule out a trick of the kind that was turned in
England a century later, when the authorities obtained, by means
best known to themselves, a confession from one William Kennedy
implicating his colleague, Frederick Guy Browne, ensured the
maximum publicity for the document, declined to allow Kennedy to
turn King's evidence and had both men convicted and hanged.)

The odd persistence of the assertion that two jurymen wished to
find Burke not proven does seem worthy of some recognition. It
would seem that these jurymen accepted the views of Moncreiff and
Cockburn on the credibility of the Hares, and having done so found
the circumstantial evidence inconclusive. The conclusion would
seem to be that Rae really would have had very grave difficulties in
making his case stick had he dispensed with the Hares.

Yet the postulate is an unreal one. Had the Hares been among the
accused much that the Lord Advocate and his men had sealed off
would have been admissible and under discussion. It is true that there
would have been great difficulty in finding out about the other
murders, apart from the two notorious ones, Mary Paterson and Daft
Jamie. Yet on both of those there was evidence much less circumstantial than what the jury was forced to rely on in the Docherty
case. There was Janet Brown to tell her terrifying story about the
death of her friend Mary. There was the maid Elizabeth and the
evidence of the clothes left in Daft Jamie's case, to say nothing of a

string of witnesses to show that however deficient in mind he was in excellent health. There was clearly a *prima facie* case against Burke on Mary Paterson, and against the Hares on Daft Jamie. There was nothing against Helen MacDougal in either case — she simply was not present during the Jamie affair and on Mary Paterson her intervention, for whatever reason, nearly spared the victim's life — but with so many prospective victims Helen's life would be less urgently demanded by H.M. counsel. Above all, there was what might be obtained by the evidence of Knox and his boys, and there was a great deal that could be elicited from them. The little matter of Fergusson's recognition of Mary Paterson would have been hard to conceal and so, too, would the special arrangements made to conceal the identity of Daft Jamie. That such revelations would have blasted what was to be the great career of William Fergusson, to say nothing of those of Thomas Wharton Jones and Alexander Miller, may be reckoned by us now on the credit side for Rae's decision. One might even ask, what did it matter whether such concealment hanged Burke, spared the Hares and put the life of a drab like Helen MacDougal in peril? But against that it has to be said that the profession of the law, like the profession of medicine, was supposed to have its ethics, and there is no more justification for the lawyers' indifference to the fate of Helen MacDougal than there was for the doctors' insouciance about that of Mary Paterson. Yet it was the same ethics by which both were prepared for sacrifice. The Scottish enlightenment hardly found in Sir William Rae the flower of its achievement, but in its readiness to set aside normal human considerations he could place himself firmly by the side of Doctor Knox.

There remains the strange point that more was possibly chargeable against Hare than against Burke. The evidence of the maid Elizabeth deserved some study there, and the place of Hare as proprietor of the horror hotel invited some further reflection. What militated against all of these cases save that of Mary Docherty is that everything demanded a hostile examination of the Knox team in order to gainsay their insistence that nothing in the corpses was calculated to excite suspicion. So justice blinded itself, the *socii crimini* were conscripted, and the scapegoats were set up.

The Hares had captured the Government, and the Government, and the judges, were, as Emilia puts it in *Othello*, too fond of their most filthy bargain. It became dreadfully evident when a last, desperate attempt was made to bring Hare to book. The derelicts who formed the staple diet of Burke and Hare had few relatives, and fewer who would acknowledge their existence. But Daft Jamie's family, who had sent him adrift through Edinburgh with little thought, recovered dutiful sentiments as the lost waif became the property of the ballad-hawkers of the Grassmarket. Janet Wilson, mother, and Janet Wilson, sister, commenced private proceedings against William Hare and the flow of legal documents entered on its way by the end of January. The prosecution and the judges were left with one last service to perform for their servant — or master. It would go to anticipate Marx's dictum about history repeating itself, but the second time not, as formerly, in tragedy but in farce. The judgments were given in the High Court on February 2, when Burke was safely dead, before a court consisting of Lords Gillies, Alloway — and Boyle, Pitmilly, Mackenzie and Meadowbank.

Paupers' briefs were still paupers' briefs. Duncan MacNeill, fresh from Burke's defence, and Hugh Bruce, even more fresh — for he had done far less — from that of Helen MacDougal, appeared for Hare, possible conflicts of interest notwithstanding. Rae had his old team to watch the needs of their side, buttressed by that old jobman, Mr Solicitor-General Hope. Moncreiff had vanished from sight, and Cockburn with him, but to add to the gaiety of nations and specifically of the Lord Advocate, came as chief counsel for the Wilsons the third of the great Whig triumvirate, Francis Jeffrey. For support, Jeffrey had the aid of Thomas Hamilton Miller and E. Douglas Sandford. Politics would still be the name of the game.

Hare's counsel, Duncan MacNeill, stated in a bill of advocation, suspension and liberation for Hare filed on 21 January 1829 that when Hare was examined after his arrest he was then "assured by the public prosecutor, that if he made a full disclosure of all he knew relative to the several alleged murders, which formed the subject of inquiry, no criminal proceedings would be instituted against" him "in relation thereto, whatever might be the circumstances of suspicion, or apparent participation of guiltiness appearing against him" — which would mean immunity for the murders of Mary Paterson, Mary Docherty, Daft Jamie and twelve other cases (including the woman murdered by Hare alone) and accession after the fact to the murder of Peggy Haldane. But whether Hare could actually have been protected for murders not cited in the indictment of Burke is less easily said. As matters stood, his immunity proved a moot point even in Daft Jamie's case and it was only by a majority of the bench that the cards fell in his favour. A private prosecution from Mrs Haldane's respectable daughter Mrs Clark, or from Joe the Miller's relatives, would seem to have more chance of success. But, of course, their fate may have been unknown until Hare was released. Burke's official confessions were only passed by Sheriff Adam Duff to the Lord Provost for publication on 5 February 1829 on which date Hare was released and driven out of Edinburgh. Duff observed that Rae said the public had a right to see the contents of Burke's confessions "as it is now fully understood that all proceedings of a criminal nature against William Hare have terminated". The *Courant* was allowed to publish its text on the 7th, and at the moment when the public had its first chance of purchasing the printed texts Hare was crossing the English border and hence leaving the court's jurisdiction. The last time he was to be reported as having been knowingly witnessed by human eyes was the following day, Sunday, beyond Carlisle. Rae had created a gloriously Catch-22 situation in defence of his informant: promises of immunity might not hold good for cases not mentioned in the indictment but no interested members of the public were likely to have known of those cases until Hare vanished for good. The hounds could do nothing further until the scent had disappeared.

The Paterson murder, the only other case to be published by the indictment, was primarily Burke's show: it was Daft Jamie which was so flagrantly that of the Hares. Curiously enough, woman spared woman in the case. The Wilson mother and daughter almost certainly did not know what the world would only learn with the publication of Burke's confessions on February 7, that the prime mover in bringing Jamie to his doom had been Margaret Hare; and they did not connect her to the case otherwise. She had been released on the 19th of January, and although the next few weeks would see her in police protective custody on several occasions up to her voyage from Greenock on February 12, she was not again threatened with further legal retribution. The Wilsons pursued Hare alone.

Boyle and the Lords Commissioners of Justiciary considered the bill of advocation, suspension and liberation for Hare, hearing counsel for both sides on 26 January 1829 and inviting Rae to reply; he remarked that he "has not failed to observe the guarded terms in which this order is conceived, calling upon him only to give such information as he shall deem proper, and thus relieving him from the necessity of questioning the power, even of this Court, to require, in this shape, a disclosure of the grounds on which the public prosecutor has been guided in the exercise of his official discretion". It was coming right back to Boyle with the assurance that both of them knew any cover-up would be and could be justified in terms of national security, as many a rogue has sought to do before and since.

Having fleetingly flicked his tongue at his circumspect judicial protectors, Rae brought it firmly into his cheek: "Influenced, however, by those feelings of respect which the respondent has ever endeavoured to evince towards this High Court", he would let them have the following statement.

Rae laid great stress on the problem of proving that murder had in fact taken place, given that Christison and Black could not deliver an open-and-shut proof of it for him. Rae remarked bitterly that he "well knew, from long experience, how scrupulous a Scottish Jury uniformly is, in finding a verdict of guilty, where a capital punishment is to follow; and he deemed it hopeless to look for a conviction, where the fact of a murder having been committed was not put beyond the possibility of question". A Scottish jury had in fact kindly given his long experience a refresher course in 1827 when it acquitted Mary Elder or Smith on the charge of poisoning her maidservant on precisely these latter grounds (Jeffrey and Cockburn had defended). On the other hand Rae now very quickly glided over the alternative evidence available to, but unused by him, headed by that of Dr Robert Knox. Only by King's evidence, he insisted, could the missing information be obtained, indeed it was believed that there was at least one other case involved in addition to the Docherty affair and, continued the Lord Advocate unblushingly, "he felt it to be his imperative duty, not to rest satisfied without having the matter probed to the bottom". He made the point that he needed to know whether more than one gang, or more than four persons, had been involved in the murder racket. Conviction of the four in custody for the Docherty murder "appeared immaterial" in comparison with the need for information; concerning which one can only say that it was unfortunate for Helen MacDougal that she got so little benefit from this mood of academic objectivity.

Hare was promised immunity on December 1 for any crimes similar to the Docherty murder which he might disclose. "In its nature, this assurance was thus of an unqualified description, and was calculated to lead the party to believe that the *possibility* of future trial or punishment was thereby entirely excluded. The assurance was so meant to be understood."

Hare remained in jail at the instance of the Wilsons alone. Rae insisted that he was legally barred from prosecuting either of the Hares, nor would he do so, but he added a bleak dignity to his less than disinterested ruling: "He need not add that he should strongly feel such a proceeding, upon his part, as dishonourable in itself, unworthy of his office, and highly injurious to the administration of justice." Despite the importance for the Lord Advocate that the considerations of national security demanded recognition of an "informers' charter", his notions of honour certainly seem to have been much more active than those of the English public prosecutor, Sir Archibald Bodkin, a century later in *Rex v. Browne and Kennedy*.

Duncan MacNeill's information on behalf of Hare gave him his first real opportunity in this case to show the cogency of argument and succinctness of delivery which would characterise his distinguished future career and it is, in fact, a *tour-de-force* on the part of so junior a counsel. On the other hand it, too, pointed out how badly the whole case was now reeking with conflict of interest. Hare's promise of immunity must save him from any prosecution in the Docherty case in which, argued MacNeill, perhaps by his evidence alone Burke was found guilty; it had been at the instance of counsel for the defence — of whom he had been one — that the count on Daft Jamie in the indictment, for which Hare had been promised immunity, was not taken. But Hare had placed himself in a position of danger and could not be restored to his former situation. Their lordships themselves (Boyle, Mackenzie, Meadowbank) specifically ruled that Hare was immune in the Daft Jamie matter as it could again arise (should Burke be acquitted on the Docherty case, for instance). MacNeill was virtually citing Boyle, Mackenzie and Meadowbank as legal authorities and as witnesses in a plea on which they, together with Gillies, Alloway and Pitmilly, were to decide; and Boyle would preside.

MacNeill went on to stress that the public now had a compact with Hare, having through Rae forfeited rights of prosecuting him in order to get his evidence (the fact that the public in its component parts was showing every sign of desire to dissolve both the compact and Hare, was beside the point). Perhaps he reached the supreme irony when he pointed out that were Hare to admit having murdered Daft Jamie, the private prosecution still ought to fail because of the compact with the state; but in fact all Hare needed to do was to acknowledge he had placed himself "in circumstances of suspicion and danger" by accepting the bargain offered by the Crown, and not by himself.

The reply, for the Janet Wilsons Senior and Junior, was the work of E. Douglas Sandford, junior counsel under Jeffrey's leadership. The Sheriff had delivered judgment on 21 January 1829 stating the Lord Advocate's promise of immunity had not barred a private prosecution, denying Hare's petition to be set at liberty and interdicting proceedings until Hare had the opportunity to appeal before his late acquaintances and their colleagues on the Court of Judiciary. The Wilsons' case was in two parts, firstly to affirm that the right of the private party to prosecute is not controllable by the public prosecutor and is independent of him, and secondly to state that the *socius criminis* "is only protected by the indulgence of the Court, with regard to the particular crime as to which he gives evidence". The information picked up the point recorded by the Sheriff and others that the law was on decidedly experimental ground in the whole matter. Fixed procedures on *socii criminis* had never been subjected to precisely the kind of strain induced by William Hare and his fifteen murdered corpses, and private prosecutions for murder are very rare both in Scotland and in the sister kingdom. They are the more difficult in that, as their nature implies, they exist in face of the refusal of the Government to move, and, given their implication of criticism of the inadequacy of the Government, are bound of their nature to attract its hostility, active or passive. But never until now can there have been a situation where the Government was so nakedly committed to the preservation of a mass-murderer's life against private prosecution, and with half the Court of Judiciary already on record in defence of the same cause. It was no easy task which Jeffrey and his team had undertaken.

We may be very safe in assuming that Sandford's preparation of the information for the Wilsons was done under Francis Jeffrey's careful eye, and in its way one of the central arguments was as vigorous an assertion of Whig ideology as the high points of the speeches of Cockburn and Moncreiff. The idea of malefactors being protected from prosecution by Government bargains was clearly an invitation to the power of the state to express itself in tyrannical and corrupt form; it would be better to have the Lord Advocate openly remove all rights of private prosecution than to have him control its exercise in circumstances which amounted to its removal without acknowledging it. The restriction of the right of private prosecution to that of the party injured was wise, but so also was that which prevented the public prosecutor from "being able to stifle all inquiry, where private reasons might influence his conduct".

Undoubtedly Jeffrey — and, as we have earlier noted, Cockburn — were concerned about the accretion of more and more police power to the state in general and to the Lord Advocate in particular. There was poetry, then, as well as argument in the insistence that the private prosecutors could no more interfere with processes set in motion by the Lord Advocate than he could justly interfere with theirs.

Counsel for the Wilsons then went on to raise an interestingly novel point: immunity for a *socius criminis* was less than sixty years old (younger, in fact, than some of those for whose murders it was now protecting Hare). The Deacon Brodie trial of 1788 had involved some picturesque peaching. But while being called in a case relieved the witness of the penalties otherwise attendant upon the crime he had committed, he was only given indemnity for that case alone on which he testified, in the decision in *Rex v. Smith and Brodie* at least. (Burke as well as Hare departed from the Brodie precedent: William Burke's salute to his fellow-prisoner at the close of proceedings had more elegance about it than the conduct of the Deacon, who kicked his co-defendant as they left the court.)

Various other precedents were cited all to the restriction of immunity to the specific case in which evidence was given, and finally reached *Rex v. Burke and MacDougal*. The appropriate statements to Hare by Meadowbank and Boyle were cited as indicating that only on the Docherty case was Hare receiving immunity. (The statement did not say so, but it is clear that Meadowbank's generalities could have had larger application; Boyle's tying it down to the Docherty case (*"T'ould* woman") disposed of that ambiguity.) Very cleverly, the information made much of Meadowbank's opposition to Cockburn's proposed questions. Meadowbank, of course, had been trying to employ every means to tie Cockburn's hands, but one of his arguments had been to suggest that questions about crimes beyond the Docherty case would withdraw Hare from the protection of the court and were therefore unfair to him. The information insisted that that disposed of the claim of immunity. Mackenzie had also said that any words from Hare on other crimes would not necessarily protect him in the future (which, however, was not discussing anything for which immunity had been previously agreed). Boyle's stress that it was only on the Docherty case that Hare was bound to answer was taken to be further proof as to absence of immunity elsewhere. The fact that Hare had declined to answer a question on Daft Jamie was looked on as an admission he was not protected.

A series of hypotheses were then put forward, given the novelty of Hare's immunity in murder cases where no trials had taken place. If A, a *socius criminis*, appears in a list of witnesses against B, whose case is however abandoned by the Government and he himself freed without trial, is A immune from further prosecution? Had Hare been a witness against Burke on one of three separate indictments against him, was Hare immune from Government or private prosecution on

the other two? Hare's statement that he was ready to give evidence
on the Daft Jamie murder was unprovable one way or the other. The
court could not take account of deals made outside the courtroom,
and immunity could only be granted on the basis of evidence actually
given in court.

So the documents from Rae, MacNeill and Sandford duly swirled
around the illiterate heads of Hare and Janet Wilson Senior, and the
slightly more literate one of Janet Wilson Junior, and William Burke
was hanged, dissected, laid out in state and exhibited, and on
February 2 the High Court of Justiciary met for advising the papers
in the case. MacNeill did not wish to speak beyond the written
statements entered, but Jeffrey well knew the problems with half of
that Bench explicitly committed to general immunity, however
implicit in its restriction some of its earlier statements might be read
by counsel for the Wilsons now to be. He had his problems with that
Bench of whom probably only Lord Mackenzie really liked him.
Cockburn has a splendid account of Jeffrey, five years later, being
greeted by his future brothers as a Lord of Session: "Had you but seen
. . . Meadowbank taking him all in his arms with ostentatious
hypocrisy."

Jeffrey, no doubt with an eye to the vanity of the iconogenic Lord
Justice-Clerk and his fellows, argued that the court was being
reduced to a rubber-stamp if the Lord Advocate could thus presume
on its acceptance of any immunity bargains he chose to make. It was
the court which had finally to grant it; yet was it consistent in this if
such grant was entirely made on the Lord Advocate's decision? The
Lord Advocate had by custom and fashion become invested in great
part with the Royal Prerogative of pardon (a nice Whig argument,
but not going to a nice Whig Bench). A, B and C are accused of
murder, A is also accused of rape, fire-raising and housebreaking.
The Lord Advocate "in the exercise of a sound judicial discretion,
and in order to let in light upon these atrocities, guarantees to that
individual an immunity from the consequences of all the crimes in
which he has been engaged, — it is meant to be maintained that a
sufferer by fire-raising, for example, is to be precluded, years
afterwards, from obtaining redress, by reason of a compact entered
into in regard to other offences?". (The analogy was not exact, but it
was a shrewd reminder that the light which Rae had let in on the
case had been by reason of ensuring the freedom of the man who
might have been guiltier than anyone else.) Jeffrey concluded by
expressing the fear that, uncurbed by the courts, the power of the

Lord Advocate in the granting of pardon would be more absolute than that of the King.

Lord Gillies delivered the first opinion. It may be that Adam Gillies was an appropriate person to hear Jeffrey's lectures on the Rae visions of the Royal Prerogative in that he had started life as a Whig and, while having drifted into Tory sympathies in recent years, was still kindly disposed to classical Whig doctrine. Whether Jeffrey knew it or not, and it is probable that he did, the two judicial neophytes in the Burke and Hare case decidedly differed from the four who had tried Burke in the preconceptions they brought to the case. It was not, after all, going to be plane sailing for Hare — or for Rae.

Gillies began with compliments all round to the papers and pleas of counsel, and it says much for the achievement of MacNeill that he was congratulated in equal terms with the illustrious Jeffrey without mention even being made as to the difference in their status. Rae also was warmly commended for having sought to ensure that Scottish law and justice was saved from the stain of all the perpetrators of the murders escaping unscathed. Rae was held to be right in promising immunity, without prejudice to this case, as he could not have foreseen a private prosecution and as he must have intended to call Hare as a witness in each case where he promised immunity, and because he had the right to promise it. (Gillies had not considered the possibility that Rae offered immunity in fifteen or sixteen cases, most of which he could never have expected to bring to trial: Hare certainly must have considered it, and would be unlikely to testify to any case in which he was not promised immunity.) Gillies felt some embarrassment in pronouncing on the trial, which he knew only from the record and from hearsay, but it is clear he did not like all he had heard. Nevertheless he made two forcible points, regretting he was preceding his brothers who had taken part in the trial:

1. There is an *apparent* inconsistency in the opinion of the judges, as given in the report; I say apparent, being convinced that it must be only apparent, and that it may by your Lordships be explained and reconciled. I shall only add, that the explanation attempted in the Information for Hare does not to me appear to be at all satisfactory.

2. I may venture to observe, with reference to the credibility of the witnesses, that the opinions expressed to them, and the admonitions delivered to them at the time of their examination, are of more importance than the actual state of the law. These witnesses could not know how the law stood; they must have taken it as explained to them; and, therefore, upon the supposition, which I am far from stating as a true supposition, that those explanations were at

variance with the law, the credibility of the witnesses in the minds
of the jury should have been weighed to the former, and not
according to the latter. On a question being put to him, if Hare is
told that the Court can or can not protect him in answering it, the
credit due to him, so far as the situation of safety or of peril in which
he stands is a test, must be regulated by the information so given
him, whether the same be agreeable to law, or otherwise. In short,
in this respect, the impression on the mind of the witness, when
examined, as to what the law is, is of more importance than the
actual law itself.

(Two comments may be interposed here. The one is, that while
Gillies never intended it, it is a sardonic symbol of the ascendancy
which Hare had achieved over his former prosecutors that the law of
Scotland was now held for purposes of the case to be of less
significance than the mind of William Hare, if any. The other is, that
to the many phenomena in kind or number unprecedented which had
come to the fore in the case of Burke and Hare there was now being
added, long before its time, a shadow of a court of criminal appeal. It
was of small use to Burke, but it was an implicit adverse comment on
the infallibility of the Bench in the late trial as well as on the extent
to which the presiding judges were now, in addition to all else, judges
in their own cause.)

Gillies adverted to the absence of precedent in MacNeill's
information for Hare, with its demand instead that the principles of
normal protection of a *socius* be extended to the present case on an
analogous basis "and humanity justice, and policy, are said to bear
out the claim". On such principles, felt Gillies, immunity should be
given but was it possible for a court so to give it? "To require a Judge
to decide on principles of humanity, justice, and policy, is to require
him to decide on what he *thinks* humane, just, and politic; in other
words, to pave the way for the most arbitrary and despotic
procedure." (So Jeffrey's words had not, in Gillies's case, fallen on
stony ground.)

All previous authorities had assumed an examination during the
trial to be essential in any qualification of a *socius* for immunity.
Parliament stood over that and that only. A promise of pardon by the
Lord Advocate could not be held to be the equivalent of a Royal
pardon, or even its superior (in that recompense would not be ruled
out by the latter, but would be by the former). The Lord Advocate
might obtain a pardon from the Crown, but that was a different thing
from giving exemption from trial to a criminal "merely by citing
him as a witness". Finally, acknowledging the issue to be new, he
deplored the notion that the law should be stretched further merely

because it had been stretched in the past. One vote had gone against Hare.

Pitmilly took himself out of the dispute on Hare's examination as he had become ill at that point. However, he offset this agnosticism by declaring for Rae in roseate terms. If the Lord Advocate's powers overran those of private prosecutors anywhere, they did so everywhere; and Mary Docherty's relatives could not prosecute Hare because by his examination the Lord Advocate now "controls the right of the private party". It was Whig doctrine *versus* the principles on which Pitmilly had conducted the trial of Patrick Sellar, who possessed his own analogies with William Hare.

> I feel intensely for the relations of Wilson: I sympathise also with the public desire to bring a great criminal to justice. But I feel more for the security of the law; and I hold no consideration so important, as that public faith, pledged by a responsible officer, and sanctioned by the Court, in pursuance of uniform practice, should be kept inviolate, even with the greatest criminal.

Meadowbank then embarked on what was to be far the longest opinion of the proceedings. He said that he still agreed with himself on the immunity of Hare. He argued for Hare's being set at liberty on the ground that he was no longer liable to criminal prosecution for the murder of Daft Jamie, and compared Hare's position to that of "an individual incarcerated on a charge of witchcraft, which is not cognisable in our tribunals".

Meadowbank then entered on a long exercise designed to show the antiquity of the admission of *socii criminis* to give evidence in criminal proceedings in Scotland against the accused, and began with the trial of the Regent Morton in 1581, the Gowrie conspiracy, David II and statutes of 1488, 1491 and 1526, after which he explained that had the present case occurred "at the time I speak of" (a designation by now sufficiently vague) the court would have been bound to reject the application. "Whether the case can be treated in a different manner *now*, and under our present form of procedure, is next to be considered." To nobody's surprise he concluded it could not. The power of judging initially whether the private prosecution could take place had been transferred to his Majesty's Advocate. Private wrongs must give way to *raison d'état*, in fact. Having issued his *fiat* the public prosecutor could not reverse himself. He was still having difficulty in moving to the actual problem of a witness promised immunity in a case but never examined in court in connection with it, but triumphantly concluded that no precedent in history could be found for a person promised immunity from the public prosecutor being brought to trial for the matter which he had confessed. (This implied that there were no precedents for a *socius criminis* committing perjury in the course of his testimony and receiving the punishment with which Meadowbank himself had threatened Hare; but, with Burke dead, nobody was raising the delicate matter of Hare's perjury, and Burke's statements on the matter were not being made available for publication until all danger of Hare's prosecution was at an end.)

He dismissed any suggestion that a new law was being created or an old one stretched by the extension of the principle of immunity to cases not tried but for which the *socius criminis* had been promised security. Given the knowledge of the promise of immunity, and regardless of the fate of the indictment, "I held that a promise of immunity given by a party, according to Sir Ilay Campbell, 'who had authority and power to discharge the prosecution', was to be implied, by which the public prosecutor, and all others, were to be barred from afterwards putting the life of the complainer [Hare] or his wife in hazard, for anything done concerning these proceedings". (Gillies had stated that Rae could not have foreseen a private prosecution; but Meadowbank was now asserting that *he* had!)

He concluded by saying that the contrary opinion was, he suspected, "entirely founded upon a mistake as to the nature and extent of the question, which it was thought legal by the majority of the Court to put to the witness, provided that he was duly warned of his being under no obligation to answer it". (This was Meadowbank's little cock-a-doodle of triumphant reproach to the brothers who had out-voted him on the admissibility of Cockburn's questions to Hare: he no doubt suspected some collusion between Cockburn and Jeffrey on the matter subsequent to the trial, and he was no doubt right.) He ended in a paean of praise for Rae's having been actuated throughout, as anyone could see who would read the evidence in *Rex v. Burke and MacDougal*, "not only by a full sense of the duty he owed to the public, but by sound discrimination and judgment" and that his conduct there as here "has exhibited the most perfect decision, dignity, and fairness". He even managed to argue that the verdict in Helen MacDougal's case was supportive of this: "and remember that after all, that wretched woman was acquitted by the Jury".

Mackenzie came next, the son of the much-lauded Henry Mackenzie, author of *The Man of Feeling*, whom Scott had dubbed "the Addison of the North". In an interesting passage which recalls

Moncreiff's fight for the rights of Burke, Mackenzie said of Hare: "If, as is said (and in one instance, at least, it is but too difficult to refuse assent to it) *he* has forgotten that he bore the form and nature of a man; yet we must not forget it. He has still the rights of a British subject; and we are bound, by our oaths of office, to say that he shall not suffer injustice here; that he shall not be defrauded of his life by the effect of any procedure before us."

As to the question of immunity on a count in the indictment not proceeded with, Mackenzie saw Hare's presence as a witness as evidence of contract. Hare could well have pleaded that he had been promised immunity to all the charges on the indictment had he known that part of it was not to be taken. But in fact he never was told or given any impression it abridged the extent of his immunity. Had he been told that, he would have remained silent. "Not being insane, if he had believed himself in danger of being tried for murdering, and supplying the surgeons with two bodies, murdered by him for that purpose, he would never surely have given evidence that he had previously done so on one occasion, and was intimate with another murderer of that horrid sort." (Here Mackenzie, like the rest, was ignoring the fact that Hare did not testify to having murdered Mary Docherty: but his general point made excellent sense.) Any prosecution of Hare over Mary Paterson or Jamie would be most materially served by his admissions in the Docherty case. To have turned on Hare after the conviction of Burke would have been dishonourable in Rae. "I respect the motives of the respondents, one of them particularly. She is the mother of poor Wilson, and cannot be expected to weigh fairly the rights of one whom she views as the murderer of her son. But we at least must look on them more calmly, and are, I think, bound to say, that she has no right of prosecution, if the King's Advocate be barred."

The more I look to the practice of this part of our legal procedure, and to the great principles of general justice, that can never be lost sight of in considering the effect of any transaction, particularly a judicial one, the more I think that this wretched man has acquired a right to immunity in all three cases that were charged in the indictment against Burke. Remembering, as we must do, the dreadful evidence he gave, it is impossible to contemplate his escape without pain, — a pain always felt, in some degree, in every case where an accomplice in a great crime, is, however necessarily, taken as evidence for the Crown, but never, I believe, felt more strongly than in the present. I sympathise in that feeling. But I feel not less strongly that this man, however guilty, must not die by a perversion of legal procedure; a perversion which would form a precedent for the oppression of persons of far other

characters, and in far other situations, and shake the public confidence
in the steadiness and fairness of that administration of criminal justice,
on which the security of the lives of all men is dependent.

Mackenzie had offered the first judgment accorded to Hare on
liberal grounds, as opposed to the views of Pitmilly and
Meadowbank. He had also shown an important ground of difference
with Rae: he clearly did not see Hare as having immunity in the
twelve cases not listed in the indictment.

Lord Alloway delivered judgment next. David Cathcart had less
than three months to live after this date. It may be amusing to note
that his choice of legal title had arisen from his land at Alloway on
which stood the ruins of the famous kirk where Burns's Tam
O'Shanter had his unfortunate encounter with the Devil and his
associates. He paid his compliments to Rae, and curiously followed
Meadowbank, though without acknowledgement, in stating that the
verdict of not proven on Helen MacDougal justified Rae's action
with regard to Hare. (His version was more lucid than
Meadowbank's, but the irony remained. Their Lordships really
found it difficult to consider the proposition, as was their duty to do,
that Helen MacDougal might not have been guilty of anything more
than uxorial protectiveness. The verdict was seen as an indication of
how hard it was for Rae to "get" a verdict of guilty, not what it
would have been more logical to see it as — that in the midst of
murder, Helen MacDougal was innocent.) Alloway then took up the
suggestion that since the establishment of a public prosecutor, the
rights of the private prosecutor "have ceased", and he listed ways in
which the law discouraged private prosecution. But he saw the
restraints as acknowledgements of the right of private prosecution,
with restraints to prevent abuse of it.

He then argued that Meadowbank's view of the powers of the
court in times past "proceeds from a mistake". The Justice-Clerk
was then a clerk merely, "and issued all the executorial of the law".
It would have been outrageous to have the court both preparing the
evidence and selecting the culprits. "But, dreadful as the representations of many of our old trials have been, and disgraceful as they are
to the country where they took place, I do not think that the High
Criminal Court ever stood in that situation." Alloway also found
statutes encouraging private prosecution long after the Lord
Advocate had been entrusted with the work of public prosecutor on
which, therefore, "his Lordship's view is equally erroneous".

The immunity established in *Rex v. Smith and Brodie* and other cases
protected a witness "for whatever he has uttered as a witness

criminating himself", hence Hare was protected in the Docherty matter, but not in that of Daft Jamie or any other on which he did not give evidence. As to what protection had been given by the court, Alloway was doubtful if it could do so. Witness could only be given protection on evidence before the court, not to evidence not given. Alloway returned to the Cockburn questions:

> ... upon the same ground, although this protection extends to the case of Docherty, in which he had been examined, I cannot conceive how it can be extended to the other cases as to which he was told not a question could be put to him, and in consequence of which he declined to answer every question that was put to him with regard to any other murder, and particularly the murder which had taken place in his own house, in October.

If the private party discovered evidence to accuse any of the witnesses cited for the prosecution in the cases of Mary Paterson and/or Daft Jamie of being accomplice(s) in either or both of those murders, and that witness had never been cited examined with respect to Docherty, could such witness have claimed the protection of the court, or trial exemption simply because of their name being in the list of witnesses supporting the indictment against Burke? (Nobody said it, but the witness Robert Knox, not called in the Docherty matter but on the list of witnesses, was a very good example of what Alloway was hypothesising: it is an interesting thought that Knox was far less protected by the law than Hare, since Alloway cited the hypothesis as an absurdity. Knox was lucky not to be made the target of a private prosecution by the Wilsons, although it is likely they would have been less fortunate in obtaining legal services gratis. They would have been entitled to them but, with the close links between medical and legal professions, several distinguished gentlemen might have suddenly become unavailable.)

> Upon the same ground [continued Alloway], I conceive, that although Hare was examined on the trial of Burke and M'Dougal, as to the murder of Docherty, he unquestionably was never examined, nor was one question put to him, nor could it have been put to him, with regard either to Wilson or Paterson, without his being told that he was not bound to answer it; and he accordingly declined to answer all such questions.

So Hare was not protected in any case on which he was not examined. And Alloway found no authority which permitted the court to protect beyond the limits of the case on which evidence was taken. And were the court to extend protection at the expense of private prosecution, the court itself would thereby take on, or confer upon the public prosecutor, "powers which the Crown, the great fountain of mercy, does not possess". (Here was Jeffrey's point accepted once more, and here was Meadowbank's omnipotent modern state deified and denounced.) Rae ought to keep his word "even to the greatest criminal that ever existed"; and he could do it by getting a remission or a pardon from the Crown "for which he cannot in vain apply". (It did, of course, leave on Rae the odium of insisting that his gracious Majesty King George IV extend his clemency to William Hare, perhaps the least deserving criminal ever in suit of a pardon in his Majesty's Regency and reign. A Royal pardon for Hare, one feels, would in a sense have crowned the life and works of George IV and fittingly invite him to murmur his *Nunc Dimittis* the following year.)

It remained for Boyle to conclude. He was fast enough with his compliments to Rae who, in addition to the other epithets bestowed on him by the rest of the Bench was now discovered to be the author of a "manly, straightforward, and explicit statement". (One is led to feel that no public official has received such a chorus of congratulations for conduct resulting in the restoration of a mass murderer to liberty since Pontius Pilate.)

Boyle made much of the wisdom of Rae in making sure of the conviction of Burke by the promise of immunity to the Hares. Hare had sworn in his evidence to circumstances directly tending both to incriminate him and to establish a guilty connection with Burke: how they had "become acquainted" a year ago; how he had often heard Burke employ the word "*shot*" and knew what it meant; how Mary Docherty's body was sold; how he had received money via Burke for other bodies although they did not quarrel about it. Hence Hare "did surround himself with dangers from that examination". (Boyle could have put it much stronger than that — Hare's own account of his proceedings, however false, indicated habituation to accession in a going murder concern, but even now Boyle drew back from anything that looked like acknowledgement of the wholly collegial guilt with the deceased Burke on the part of the man the Government was committed to preserving.)

Boyle continued with his argument which was to the effect that the *socius criminis* was always protected save for his "being guilty of perjury or prevarication"; even when "an accomplice, though not coming up to the full expectation of the prosecutor", answered questions, he was not committed in any known instance "although instances of commitment for perjury or prevarication, may often have occurred". (But no indication of the high relevance of that exception was given, and indeed the vagueness of possible precedent with respect to it is in itself suggestive as to the legal history of the *socius criminis* as well as of the Hare case.) He stressed that the initial understanding between Rae and Hare was only the beginning of the immunity: Hare's evidence, given under that indictment, "perfected" it. But he did make one new point. While witnesses who could have testified relative to Daft Jamie's death were represented on the Lord Advocate's list, Rae had insisted that Hare alone supplied the information which led to the framing of that count in the indictment: hence it was not true to say that Hare had given no evidence relative to that murder. The public had benefited from his evidence, and the pledge of public faith must now be "preserved inviolate". (There was, of course, a distinction between evidence privately offered, and evidence rendered subject to cross-examination, but Boyle naturally did not mention that.)

Boyle then reviewed his own conduct in having charged the jury in the trial of Burke and Helen MacDougal as to the credibility of the Hares, stressed that he reconsidered it and found nothing wrong with it, denied that it had been delivered in any casual sense, and stated that if the question as to the non-credibility of the Hares because of their vulnerability for the murders of Daft Jamie and Mary Paterson had been raised before the last speeches it would have been determined then but that since "it was withheld till the addresses to the Jury, every one knows, that it could no otherwise have been disposed of than by delivering an opinion upon it to the Jury". He made a few testy remarks about alleged inconsistency of the bench in the Burke trial on a question proposed to be put to Hare, and his own charge to the jury. The debate had been whether Cockburn could ask, whether Hare had ever been concerned "in the commission of other murders". The opinions had related to that question.

> When the examination was resumed, I do not find that the question is put in the precise terms on which it had been argued; and it was only at a later period that Hare was asked, if there was a murder committed in his house in October last? But as to which the opinion of the Court was not delivered.

(But neither Rae nor Boyle nor Meadowbank objected when that question was put.)

Boyle concluded by stating that if discrepancy as to questions permitted and charge to the jury might appear to his brothers, it was to be ascribed "either to the imperfections of the report of the trial, or to the course of proceeding that was adopted at the suggestion of counsel for the prisoners". Hare, in his view, should be set at liberty, and merely to suspend proceedings while Hare obtained a Royal pardon would be against Scottish, though not English, practice. Hare ought not to be proceeded against either by Lord Advocate or by private prosecution on any matters in the indictment against Burke. (And here Boyle, like Mackenzie, was not pronouncing on the other twelve cases where Hare committed murder.) Judgment was therefore given for Hare, with an order that he be set at liberty. (It remains the case that the only two judges not affected by participation in the previous trial were unanimous in opposing the judgment for Hare; or, if one excepts Pitmilly in view of his retiral from the bench at the Burke trial, the judges not affected by involvement in previous decisions decided against Hare by a majority of two to one. It was rather an ominous comment on the earlier proceedings.)

Hare had one more legal river to cross before being set at liberty. The court's judgment was no sooner pronounced than E. Douglas Sandford, for the Wilsons, slapped a Petition on the Sheriff (who had found for them before) serving notice of their intention to prosecute Hare for £500 as assythment for having murdered Daft Jamie and asking that he be maintained in jail as he clearly intended leaving Scotland for Ireland. Hints had been dropped by several of the judges as to the possibility of such a suit was bearing fruit. Whether it was in any way a sensible proceeding is another matter. Hare had no money, nor no expectation of raising such a sum: he would have had to supply Dr Knox with fifty corpses in the winter season in order to earn it. While the Wilsons were certainly Daft Jamie's near relatives and doubtless were horrified and saddened by his murder, it is impossible to assert that they were at a pecuniary loss for it, having driven him from his home and left him to shift for himself: unless, indeed, the amiable Jamie had been accustomed to given them a little from his takings despite his hard usage at their hands. And on his family quarrel there was general public knowledge, with the assistance of the scribblers and balladmongers of the town.

It was still February 2 and Hare found himself being examined in jail. He was by now taking no chances at all. Asked whether he was concerned in Daft Jamie's death he said he would say nothing about it. Where was he born?, asked Tait; did he have a trade in Edinburgh? where would he go if released from prison now? was he afraid the mob would kill him should he be released? did he mean to go to his native country, it being understood that that was Ireland? had he any prospect of employment in Scotland? what would he do if he remained in Scotland? had he any property? To all of which he returned a great silence. Finally, he admitted his inability to write, but when the declaration was read to him and he was asked whether it had been correctly transcribed, he remained silent. Speech had saved his life on the night before Christmas; but he knew enough to see when he needed other weapons. All these questions were relevant to the likelihood of his fleeing the jurisdiction.

The Sheriff heard evidence for the Wilsons whose solicitor actually said he could prove that Hare "actually admitted that he killed Daft Jamie", but the only documents put in related to Hare's apparent intention to return to Ireland. A fellow-prisoner, William Lindsay, said that he and Hare had been prisoners in the Edinburgh tolbooth for two months, that Hare had told him he was a labourer, sold swine and herrings "and he did not say that he dealt in any thing else". Hare had said he came from Ireland and "was here two or three years before the King came", and that he had said two or three days before that he expected to be released and would at once go back to Ireland. Lindsay was literate, which may have been a reason for singling him out as a potential witness. The head turnkey in the Calton jail, John Fisher, said that Hare had told him after the Burke trial that on release he would return to his native Ireland.

Tait had one final go at Hare, and this time he would seem to have softened him up slightly. After all, the sheriff-substitute had been in on the thing from the beginning. If there were a familiar inquisitor it had been he. He had taken every deposition of which the text has come down to us, beginning with Burke and Helen MacDougal on November 3, and Hare must have come to know him well when the time came to turn King's evidence. Whether Tait advised Hare to take it coolly and await a probable collapse of the Wilsons' suit, we will never know, but it is likely that, to the very end, the ambiguity of the relationship between the King and William Hare was preserved. Tait told Hare that if he intended to remain in Scotland, any witness he wanted to bring forward to testify to that effect could be examined, and Hare replied that he had no money, and would have to go somewhere to get work, and had no home in this part of the country, and could not remain in Edinburgh. Hare did not say positively to Tait that he would go to Ireland, but that he might, and indeed did not know whether he would stay in Scotland, seek employment in Ireland or England, or what, and hence could produce no witness as to his intention to remain in Scotland. At the close he reaffirmed his illiteracy. And that statement, that he could

not write, is the very last message to the legal authorities of Scotland
from William Hare.

Tait, still on February 2, operating in his judicial capacity, granted
the appeal to maintain Hare in jail for six months to allow the action
to be brought. But it is probable that he, and/or other officials, to say
nothing of legal advisers, told the Wilsons that in view of Hare's
destitution it was a pointless exercise in vindictiveness. It was true
that the longer the Wilsons persisted in it, the longer would Hare lie
in jail, but as against that he had a roof, food, drink and security and if
released he would have none of those things. It is also clear that the
action for assythment was undertaken very hurriedly; and on
reflection the Wilsons dropped the matter. Apparently their junior
counsel, E. Douglas Sandford, may have kept an eye on proceedings,
and possibly his advice — and even that of Jeffrey — may have
decided in favour of making an end.

So on Thursday evening, February 5, 1829, the gates of Calton Jail
opened and Hare was out. The story of Hare's escape was graphically
set out in the *Dumfries Courier*, 10 February 1829, by the editor, John
MacDiarmid. John Fisher, the head turnkey, took him in a hackney
coach to Newington, where he awaited the southbound mail.
Exactly one week later the same path would be followed by an
infuriated mob carrying a lifesize effigy intending to represent Knox
which, outside his home in Newington, would be hanged and burned
to the accompaniment of ferocious damage to the doctor's windows
and garden. But it was quiet enough as the two tall men waited,
doubtless in silence. It is questioned whether Hare was particularly
gifted with imagination — he revealed far less range of it in the
imagination than did, say, Burke in his first deposition — but it is
reasonable to suppose that his mind went back to the last time he saw
Newington which was, in fact, the very last evening he had been at
liberty. Paterson had been there, and Dr Knox, and Wharton Jones,
and after them Margaret, and Helen — and William Burke. Up came
the mail coach, and Hare took his place on the outside. He had done
the state some service, and it still meant to show it knew it, for not
only must his passage have been paid and he perhaps endowed with
some funds, but Fisher, as the King's representative, took the
precaution of ensuring no danger would happen to the King's witness
within the court's jurisdiction, and took a curiously formal farewell
intended for concealment of identity, but strangely blending
clemency and irony. After all, Hare was a sneak and a murderer, a
misanthrope and a brute, yet a head turnkey can only judge on what
he sees of accused persons under his care and it may be that his last

words said something for an association that may not have been wholly disagreeable: "Good-bye Mr Black: I wish you well home". In the fullest sense of the term it was a wish Hare very much needed.

MacDiarmid's account has often been repeated, and may be briefly summarised. The coach stopped at Noblehouse for supper. Hare was cold and someone at the inn told him to warm himself at the fire. He took off his hat, and was at once recognised by someone who knew all too much about what was, perhaps, the worst crime he had committed: E. Douglas Sandford, travelling south from Edinburgh. Hare on the resumption of the journey sought a vacant seat inside the coach but Sandford, overwhelmed with disgust at the thought of proximity, ordered that he be removed. A gentleman's word had natural authority over the rights of a lower-class unknown, and back to the cold was sent Hare. But in the coach they questioned Sandford and he, wishing to justify his apparent snobbery, told what he knew. He had not acted for the state, but it was tantamount to betrayal of his general duty as a representative of the legal profession, for inevitably it set the mood in action where riot, and perhaps lynching, could ensue at the next stop. Once the mail reached Dumfries, the news spread, and a crowd assembled. Hare at this point was still proposing to go to Ireland, and four hours had to ensue before the Galloway and Portpatrick mail would leave. The crowd was estimated at 8,000 in the High Street. Hare took refuge in the King's Arms. Initially the crowd does not seem to have been hostile, and the numbers who milled into the bar-parlour to look at him even stood him drinks. But Nature took its course. Had it been Burke who had thus faced them his charm might yet have carried the day, but Hare reacted with characteristic moroseness to demands for information and said he had done his duty in Edinburgh, had said enough before and would say nothing now. The crowd began to get nastier, and as more and more arrived, he was driven into a corner becoming more and more frightened. Finally the King's men broke through, the courtyard was cleared and the police mounted guard. One report described him as being baited before the appearance of the police by a boy, and later he even determined to let himself be destroyed, it was said, taking up his bundle and walking to the door to let the mob "tak' their will o' me". A doctor — of all people — stopped him. If the story was true, both the courage and the fatalism are worthy of remark.

Finally, in the early afternoon of the Friday, with the assistance of a bogus conveyance, loaded with much fuss, the mob was temporarily deceived and Hare was got to drop out of a back window of the inn, leap into another chaise and accept a night in jail. The crowd learned of his presence and rioted outside the jail from 4.00 p.m. to 8.00 p.m. and were only dispersed by 100 special constables armed with batons, by which time the front windows in the courthouse had been smashed, and the gas-lamps extinguished. It was not until 1.00 a.m. on the Saturday morning that it seemed possible to get him out. His cloak was gone; his bundle was gone; and a sheriff's officer and militiamen saw him out of town to the Annan road. It was said that the whole population of Galloway were in arms, and that the Galloway mail had been surrounded and searched on Friday at Crocketford toll-bar, and so Hare was advised to abandon Portpatrick, for the mob might be active there too. A rumour circulated that he had been recognised at Annan and stoned to death, but it was later contradicted. A boy saw him passing Dodbeck on the Saturday at 3.00 a.m. — a fine time for small boys to be meeting William Hare. By 5.15 a.m. the driver of the mail driving northwards recognised him sitting beside two stone-breakers on the public road, within half a mile of Carlisle. The last report was that on Sunday morning he was walking on the Newcastle road two miles beyond Carlisle. And that is all.

CHAPTER

10

The Damnation of
William Burke

BURKE . . . *v.* 1829. [f. *Burke*, a criminal executed at Edinburgh in 1829.]
1. To kill secretly by suffocation or strangulation, or in order to sell the
victim's body for dissection, as Burke did. 2. *fig.* To smother, hush up
1840.
   1. As soon as the executioner proceeded to his duty, the cries of 'B.
him, B. him — give him no rope' . . . were vociferated *Times* 2 Feb.
1829. Hence BU•RKER. BU•RKISM.

—*The Shorter Oxford English Dictionary*

T HE Watergate scandal in the United States in the early 1970s
     revealed, with a wealth of documentation, how thin can be the
divide between investigation and cover-up when the government
finds its political interests confronted by its judicial investigations.
The Lord Advocate in 1828-29 was as forcibly confronted by the
conflict of interest and truth, and if personally his motives were more
altruistic than those Richard Nixon would have, his response was the
same — fear of any dissemination of information to the press, the
people and to other potential protagonists. In much of his efforts he
failed: the Burke and Hare case won universal and eternal infamy, his
own legal activities were publicly denounced and in part defeated,
mob scenes were aroused and at times on huge scales, class hostility
smouldered in Edinburgh for the next few years particularly against
the doctors. But he did dictate posterity's version of the story, partly
because, and partly in spite of his own efforts.

Rae kept his own counsel so well that Whitehall knew nothing of
what had happened until Burke and Hare had been under arrest for a
month, and then learned of it in the most casual fashion. Professor
Alexander Monro needed his subjects for dissection as fully as did Dr
Robert Knox, and was much enraged when a cargo of cadavers from
Dublin was seized by the police and customs at Greenock: it was an
understanding that Government wink at the trade. So Monro
protested to Rae, with the support of Principal George Baird of the
University, and Rae forwarded their letters to Home Secretary
Robert Peel remarking that he was privately reminding Customs of

the gentlemanly understanding and that he had been present at part of a sheriff's inquiry revealing at least twelve murders to furnish dissection subjects. So naturally restraint on the cross-channel cadaver trade was to be deplored, inviting as it did more private enterprise in the domestic market.

In the same letter, of November 27, 1828, Rae also assured Peel

> one individual, an Irishman, who has been engaged in all these acts, will be immediately brought to trial, and will to a certainty be convicted; but the charge of Murder, as against him, will be confined to *two* instances, as we are most anxious to conceal from the public the extent to which such crimes have been carried, and of which fortunately little idea is at present entertained.

Understandably, Peel saw more in this than the need for him to restrain the zeal of the customs. "Is it possible", he demanded on December 6

> that the information you have received as to the perpetuation of 12 murders in so short a space of time for such an object can be well founded? If it be well founded it exceeds any thing in horror of which I ever heard.

But where to Rae, legatee of eighteenth-century Scottish corruption, it called for squaring the customs to prevent — in a very nasty sense — the rocking of the boat, to Peel, harbinger of nineteenth-century English reform, it demanded legislative action. An Anatomy Act must be brought in to take the whole business from government *legerdemain*, grave desecration and wholesale murder alike. And that meant that the revelations of the Burke and Hare scandal had to enter the public domain, if only to alert the House of Commons to what had now emerged as the inevitable consequence of the body trade.

Either to meet Peel's demands, or to confront him with the need for suppression, the Lord Advocate sent down the precognitions or depositions of the witnesses, including, of course, the Hares. If he thought that this would reinforce the case for silence, he met with little sympathy. On New Year's Day, 1829, Peel was advocating

> the most sifting investigation into every thing deposed by Hare.
> Now that the Trial has taken place — I doubt whether uncertainty as to the extent & history of these murders — is not as great an evil as any exposure of facts can be.

But he made it very clear that what was needed was a thorough examination of the Knox medical school and beyond it to the Edinburgh medical fraternity in general.

He did not get it. And the disappearance of the depositions, especially those of the Hares, from his own archives and those of the Lord Advocate raises its questions. It is true that archivists have long noted and deplored the vanishing of such documents from official records before Scotland had obtained a satisfactory system for the preservation of official records; the Burke and Hare case might be expected to attract wanton pillagers among souvenir-hunters. Given the dissemination of pieces of Burke's skin after dissection it was hardly likely that the curious might evince more delicacy over the acquisition of public records. Yet what invites deeper suspicion is that Hare's confession after the trial seems omnipresent. The *Caledonian Mercury* seems to have had a sight of it, to judge by its issue of December 29, although it made attempts to conform with the practice of not directly citing what was disclosed with prohibition of attribution. Sir Walter Scott certainly saw it, and also discussed the case with its judges and counsel. Was this Rae's method of continuing a cover-up once press publicity had shattered his initial hopes of relative silence? If so, his freedom with the document among a charmed circle raises the question of a similar freedom with respect to a decision for its ultimate suppression. It was at least bound to raise the question of whether the confession would prove perjury on Hare's part, over which the Crown had stood. Rae would shortly see Peel when he came down for the sittings of the House and for Government discussions. Peel had with the greatest difficulty disposed of the Catholic Emancipation crisis in Ireland: he would doubtless have been obliged to listen to assurances that unwise disclosures could bring his political enemies in Scotland around the Government's ears. Rae was no Henry Dundas, but he could rely on the Tory tradition of leaving Scotland to the Lord Advocate. The issue disappears from the Peel papers, to be succeeded by discussions about giving a judgeship to Moncreiff.

But if Peel was forced to acquiesce in the aborting of investigation, he did successfully counter Rae's principles on publicity. Rae's desire to conceal the number of murders was so unsuccessful that by November 20 the *Caledonian Mercury* was "satisfied" that Burke and Hare had many active counterparts. Rae had only himself to thank for his policy of suppression of truth inviting proliferation of falsehood or unverifiable rumour. But such speculations helped Peel's hopes for an Anatomy Act, which indeed the *Mercury* demanded in the midst of its horror-mongering. Agitation had previously been allowed to die down; now Burke and Hare revived it. The *Westminster Review* for January 1829 saw the

murders as the inevitable consequence of the cadaver famine and the
suppression of straightforward body smuggling. The philosophic
radical Henry Warburton moved a bill for the provision of dissection
subjects in the Commons on March 12. Peel supported it and on May
20 during the debate on the third reading actually took the same line
as the *Mercury* had done exactly six months before. But the measure
was lost in the Lords and not until Bishop and Williams proved Peel a
true prophet by bringing burking to London was an Anatomy Act
passed, in 1832.

However much good publicity may have done the cause of an
Anatomy Bill, it did only limited service to that of truth. Rae's policy
of news control and partial blackout simply resulted in the invention
of material broadcast. The public was avid for news of Burke and
Hare, not merely for sensationalism, but also from a horrified
realisation that nobody was safe with such a murder business in
operation. Newspapers beheld their sales rise to hitherto undreamed
of figures. The result paralleled Burke's and Hare's moving into any
vacuum induced by official clampdown on the corpse trade. Bogus
confessions, bogus crimes, bogus interviews, bogus adornments
jammed the columns of the greedy journalists. January, in particular,
left a great hiatus between Burke's trial and execution; the
confessions which he made in prison to the Edinburgh *Courant* and to
the civic authorities were not to be made available until Hare was
out of the jurisdiction. The fifteen-part series Ireland was bringing
out suffered particularly from this situation. It could not afford to
lose its momentum and hence the way was open to invention. In most
instances Ireland may simply have hurled in journalistic myths
manufactured for other prints, regardless of their conflicts with one
another, but in some cases he did his own work. The first avowedly
fictional treatment of the case, *The Murderers of the Close*, has its
preface dated 28 February 1829 — but it differed from many
predecessors only in its honesty. Incidentally, it seems to have risen
to a challenge from Meadowbank's "The very announcement of such
a system is sufficient to raise ideas of horror, which it would be in
vain for words adequately to express" and certainly went to
remarkable heights in its efforts to express them, giving Mary
Docherty as last words "God abandoned! and thou, hideous carrion,
your time is at hand — the wrath of Heaven, even now, is ready to
fall on your heads — I — I — shall be the last".

Edinburgh may have sniggered over this London artefact's version
of the speech of an Irish-Scots wifie; its own fictions were,
unfortunately, much more credible. The frontier between fiction

and fact was most effectively crossed by the ballad-makers, as well also that between appeal to justice and to lynch law. Significantly, being presumably man-made, they demanded the harshest treatment for women.

> Now Hare should follow after, if right it does take place,
> For these women they should be burnt alive for such a murdering case.

By the time this was written Helen MacDougal had already been found not proven. Male chauvinism also emerges at many other points in mob and other reactions. The few women who mingled with the throng of 25,000 men to see the dissected Burke's corpse lying in state on the anatomy slab at Old College, are said to have been handled roughly and to have had their clothes torn. Even Moncreiff's speech drew a distinction between the respectable and dissolute witnesses, Janet Law and Nancy Conway falling into the latter category because of their unseasonable hours for accepting drink, while Hugh Alston, despite his very late hour of return home, was accepted by all parties as respectable. When Ireland reported on the dwellings of Burke and Hare, Alston alone remained. The West Port crowd that turned on Helen MacDougal when she so foolishly went back there after the trial may have had its word to say about Nancy Conway's evening hospitality with her neighbours, or about Janet Law's and Nancy's acceptance of those neighbours' early morning drams. Even without personal violence against the women, it must have been hard for them to find new accommodation having been driven from the old. And they indeed were innocent enough of anything save trying to lighten grinding and squalid lives by a little drink and merriment.

The ballads, lampoons, cartoons, caricatures and broadsheets ran riot and fabricated their material as it suited them. Two collections, whose lithographs are worth a glance, are "Wretch's Illustrations of Shakespeare" and "Noxiana"; the former makes somewhat laboured connections between the case and Shakespearean passages of criminological interest, e.g. Knox and Richard III (had the doctor the hardihood to prosecute the publisher of both sets, R. H. Nimmo of Hanover Street, for what was undoubted libel he would have been confronted by the unctuous assurance that the profits of the publication were going to the relatives of "the late most innocent, inoffensive, well-known, and well-liked, Daft Jamie": he could hardly have offset the effect of this by offering them £10). Bogus confessions of both Burke and Hare travelled far and wide, including the reprint of the so-called Burke statement published in the

Caledonian Mercury on 5 January 1829, rapidly incorporated in Ireland's pages and demolished in chapter six above ("the case of the broken back"). After Hare's disappearance broadsheets were on sale describing his hanging by a mob in Londonderry, and in more formal circumstances in New York. And Daft Jamie was, as stated, omnipresent whether in iconograph, in poetic fantasy, in reported haunting of his relations and in biographical effusion. The effect was enormously to heighten emotion. Initially, it was all straightforward contempt of court. Burke's guilt was being assumed in the public press before Hare had even confessed. The press, conscious of its market, had apparently not the slightest qualms of whipping up public hysteria, although it shared the prevalent social attitudes about the dangers of mob rule. The *Caledonian Mercury*, for instance, was as guilty as any in the manufacture and deployment of inflammatory fictions masquerading as news, yet on 1 December 1828 it could speak of the horrors of mob electoral power as represented by Andrew Jackson: "the mere mob of America, the most brutal and degraded on the face of the earth, are naturally attached to a man who shares their savage instincts, and occasionally exemplifies their cowardly ferocity". Christopher North's politics were high Tory, but he saw sublime virtue in the yells of the twenty or thirty thousand who saw Burke turned off. In fact, although the last century had seen in the Wilkeite, Stamp Act, Boston, Gordon and French food riots the precursors of revolution or near-revolution, and though mass popular pressure had been used on the side of radicalism by Daniel O'Connell within the last decade, the moment was arising when Tories would turn to the mob in their turn — to Orangeism in the 1830s, for example. It was a natural temptation, given the mob hysteria that traditionally attended anti-Catholicism at its most vocal.

That the Burke and Hare affair on its own would induce mass panic would have been natural enough; and when added to this there were Rae's censorship and press inventiveness the atmosphere was combustible in the extreme. Anti-Popery mobs had been really fighting chimeras, with long folk-myths about Papist massacres and Celtic slaughters. But Burke and Hare directly represented a clear threat to the life of every human being. Yet it remains the case that the leaders of the crowd, for whom historians have taught us to look, appear middle class when they can be identified at all. First of all, the writers themselves, the publishers, the artists, must be counted. The newspapers might appear more sober but were in fact even more deadly: their apparently factual accounts, often purely inventive, went to inflame the fly-by-night hawkers' material, and to lend weight and solemnity to what might otherwise appear incredible. The motives here are those of gain rather than riot, yet there does seem a thirst for blood in many of these effusions. The one person who we know personally to have started a riot is Erskine Douglas Sandford, junior counsel for the Wilsons, and he was certainly of strongly middle-to-upper class origin: his father was the first episcopalian bishop of Edinburgh since the Revolution of 1688-89. Sandford was under some strain when he put the match to the dry tinder at Dumfries: two of his father's grandchildren died just about this time, and they may have been Sandford's own infants. In politics the family was hardly typical of a Tory episcopal appointment: Sandford's brother was to be Whig M.P. for Paisley. Sandford himself otherwise survives as a legal authority on entail. Why he, a scion of church and law, should have turned to the mob, must remain a mystery: but he would not be the first figure of orthodox background to appeal to Demos at a moment of rage, grief, frustration or despair at the normal institutions. One thing is certain: he must have known perfectly well what the consequences would be when he disclosed Hare's identity to the coach. It would be interesting to know whether he added additional details for the curious at Dumfries: that particular mob took its time to reach boiling point and may have required judicious egging on from an authoritative source.

The mob actions against Robert Knox also suggest careful leadership. His being burnt in effigy on February 12 with the breaking of the windows of his house required some advance planning, and even more curious is the riot against him at Portobello, whose remoteness from the scene of action suggests at least one person there with a particular axe to grind. Relatives of the victims of Burke and Hare will hardly account for these actions: most of them known to us are women. What can be suggested is that some of this activity was kind remembrance from medical rivals who had been the victims of his vituperation, although any such activity probably took the form of inspiring their own students. Rivalry between the student followers of popular doctors was extreme, witness the Knox pupil who first sent Burke and Hare to his master instead of their proposed target Monro *tertius*. Monro himself may even have had some following, and a few sycophants might have responded to a hint from him. After all, he had had a riot outside his own theatre when he was dissecting Burke, a riot in which students anxious to gain entrance had taken the lead. Liston, Syme,

Christison, Alison, all more deservedly popular, might well have
dropped a remark before admiring students that Knox was getting
off scot-free: they could not wish anything else, for they would
suffer if he were investigated, but that would not make them love
him any better, and the age was one of ready tongues.

The situation suggests a complex pattern of class interaction, but
one in which class distinction was highly present, all the same.
Middle class knew working class in Burke's and Hare's Edinburgh:
they spoke the same language, Lallans (apart from those whose real
language was Gaelic of the Irish or of the Scottish variety). The press
and lawyers show a highly class-conscious view of the West Port,
readily and somewhat sanctimoniously attributing to its inhabitants a
lot of drunkenness and quarrelling, but the basis for such allusions
was simple enough. Drinking and fighting was the obvious way out
of the hell in which ghetto-dwellers lived during the industrial
revolution on either side of the Atlantic. To say this is not to lend
credence to the revolting and somewhat pornographic anecdotes
about Burke beating up Helen MacDougal or standing by while Hare
did, with which the newspapers filled columns deprived of harder
information by Rae. From Christopher North up there is a
widespread persistence among the journalistic brethren in seeking to
deny any truly tender sentiment between Burke and Helen. Quite
apart from this, it seems that middle-class readers were a ready
market for accounts of working-class violence between sexual
partners. Dickens, who may have owed much to Burke and Hare,
proved this last point effectively enough in *Oliver Twist* a few years
later. But the Scottish lawyers and journalists were at least realistic
in their view of the lower class, in contrast to the English legislators.
During the debate on the Anatomy Bill on March 12, 1829,
Leycester, seconding Warburton's proposal, said that paupers would
welcome being dissected after their demise in the poor-house as they
would be glad to know "that they would be able, after death, in some
measure, to repay the debt they owed to those who administered
comfort to them in the last stage of their existence". On this logic old
Donald must have been cheering enthusiastically in the next world
once he realised that the sale of his body would repay his lawful debts
to William Hare, and even the actual victims of murder at least could
rejoice in knowing they would help repay the costs of the alcohol
which so many of them had consumed in such quantity at Burke's and
Hare's expense. The Scottish commentators knew better than that.

To say this is not to argue that the journalists, who raced in and out
of the West Port to scribble down facts, half-facts, rumours,

alcoholic ramblings, vague recollections and straightforward invention from anyone they could find, had any particular respect for the workers and nomads from whom they leeched their material. The very fact that they themselves were writing in English, in contrast to the Lallans they spoke, increased the artificiality of their expressed attitudes, and apparently led them to take English condescension to be a part of English syntax. The unnatural character of writing in a different tongue from speaking enhanced the tendency to caricature. The working class might show individual personalities as three-dimensional as their material betters when both expressed themselves in the same tongue; literary formality cut away the third dimension as middle class looked at lower class. It is partly because of this that the portraits of Burke, Hare and the women have been frozen in demonic postures ever since 1829. Burke and Hare preyed on their own class, and indeed acquired some middle-class entrepreneur status by so doing, but the denial of their humanity was simply a vivid part of the denial of the humanity of those whom they devoured. It may well have been that Burke and Hare established a formidable literary convention in this respect. Dickens granted Fagin and Bill Sikes no more virtue than posterity has accorded to Burke and Hare, even if he did show more decency in the portrait of Sikes's woman. It was left for Anthony Trollope, in *The Three Clerks*, to ask what choice Sikes ever had, a question that may also be legitimate about Hare. As Sir Walter Scott pointed out in writing to Mrs Hughes on 29 January 1829, Burke's having been "rather educated above the common class" made his case "more extraordinary". There is more obvious choice in his case. But that makes him no less human.

It might be argued that one conspicuous commentator who wrote partly in Lallans, Christopher North, supplied the most demonic of all views of Burke, Hare and the women, and, in his obvious contempt for them, the most degraded vision of the victims. And it is true that the Calvinist assumptions of predestination, especially on questions of eternal damnation, invited dehumanisation in its own form. Ironically the colleague with whom North asserted himself to be speaking in *Noctes Ambrosianae*, James Hogg (who was by no means always ready to acknowledge the remarks North chose to ascribe to him), had made the great literary protest of the decade against this mentality in his *Confessions of a Justified Sinner*. On the other hand North seems to have been haunted by the thought that Burke was human and might even be saved, to judge by the violence with which he sought to expel it:

Burke, it appears, was told to give the signal with the name of his
Saviour on his lips! But the congregation, though ignorant of that
profanation, knew that the demon, on the scaffold, endured neither
remorse nor penitence; and therefore natural, and just, and proper
shouts of human vengeance assailed the savage coward, and
excommunicated him from our common lot by yells of abhorrence that
delivered his body over to the hangman, and his soul to Satan.

Scott, a witness to the execution, could at least give the lie to North
on Burke's alleged cowardice. "He died with firmness," he told Mrs
Hughes, "though overwhelmed with the hooting cursing and
execrations of an immense mob which they hardly suspended during
the prayer and psalm which in all other instances in my memory have
passed undisturbed, Governor Wall's being a solitary exception."

The Wall case alluded to an Irish-born lieutenant-governor of
Senegal whose savagery resulted in a soldier, Paterson, being flogged
so brutally on the voyage out that he died of the effects, and who
answered a deputation from his troops complaining of short pay by
having its leader, Sergeant Armstrong, given 800 lashes without a
court-martial with resultant death. He fled from trial in Britain in
1784 but returned in 1801 presumably thinking himself safe, but was
found guilty and hanged, despite earnest efforts by the Duke of
Norfolk (into whose family he had married) to have him saved by the
Privy Council. In the end it was fear of the mob which seems to have
settled Wall's fate. Sailors were at that very season being executed
for the mutinies at Spithead; it would be concluded that there was
another law for officers found guilty of cruelty to their soldiers. In
his case, and in that of Mrs Elizabeth Brownrigg, executed in 1767
for her homicidal cruelty to her female apprentices in the parish
workhouse, the mob reacted with rage even throughout the final
moments of devotions; the reasons were similar to the rage against
Burke. All three — workhouse official, military officer, doctors'
agent — represented the forces of authority and were a reminder of
the limits to which authorities in their contempt for the lower classes
might feel themselves entitled to go. In this sense the mob at Burke's
execution, which called for the blood of Knox, as well as of Burke
and Hare, was screaming against an establishment figure, like Wall,
thinking himself entitled to use his authority at the expense of the
lower classes' lives. The mob in its individual components also knew
how hideously close it came to being placed in the hands of a
Brownrigg, a Wall or a Burke; to be in a workhouse, an army or a pub
was all too likely and from there the fate of the victims of all three
moved with the speed and inevitability of a remorseless machine. It

was a class cry that assailed Burke's last moments — the protest of a people who, as they saw it, were considered not only useful for nothing but spending lives in ugly squalor and grinding labour, but worthy of casual selection for death in order to enable a doctor find cures which would benefit the better classes. Dr Robert Morris found the same mentality alive and angry during the cholera crisis of 1832, as the people rioted against the doctors, whom the Burke and Hare case had seemed to show them, thought of them only as expendable in the cause of science and research into cures for the ailments of the wealthy.

So died Burke, execrated by his fellows with justice as a murderous traitor to their class and their human right to live. Yet the Burke under observation during that last month following conviction tells another story. Much of what we know emerges from the highly suspect columns of the journalists, ready to supply copy from any who saw the convicted murderer in jail whether they could interview them or not. We may readily accept the story that his first comment on being placed in the condemned cell in the Calton Jail was "This is a bloody cold place you have brought me till!". And it seems equally reasonable that he should have been quoted as praying for Helen MacDougal, who to her bitter regret was not allowed to see him, though we may question the newspaper implication that he sought to have her "atone by a life of quietness, piety and honest industry". In any event she was to get little of it, being mobbed from Edinburgh to Stirling and thence beyond the English borders.

Boyle, in passing the statutory sentence, after a lurid statutary instruction from Meadowbank, had performed the usual task of requesting Burke to "call instantly to your aid the ministers of religion, of whatever profession you are". But Burke's response was unusual. When the prison authorities sought to know whether the usual chaplains (Presbyterian) or those of his own faith should be furnished, Burke is quoted as remarking that he never had been a bigot, and that he would like to have them all. He went on to say that in soldiering days he attended Roman Catholic Masses and also accompanied Protestant friends to the services of their churches. Contemporary newspaper reports, allegedly based on prison officials' comments, declared him to be "perfectly conversant" with the Presbyterian, Episcopalian and Methodist "peculiar tenets". The point is so unusual as to raise doubts as to its lack of authenticity, apart from some exaggeration. The reality is that as a soldier Burke was gregarious, if he resembled his future self, and sought acceptance from his comrades by readiness to accompany them to services, subsequently enjoying fairly crude comparative analysis of religious differences. The pre-famine Irish were a good deal more enquiring on this sort of thing than their more severely administered pious descendants, as Carleton's case reminds us. What gives a final support to the story is the presence of two Catholic and two Presbyterian chaplains at his execution, although it is clear that his final and most private acts of prayer and repentance took place with a Catholic priest with the usual privacy of Confession and last Communion.

But he did go to considerable lengths also to make public confession, and his doing so in the presence of a priest makes clear that what was involved for him, primarily, was some attempt to make recompense to society by disclosing all. He would, apparently, have liked to see that Helen MacDougal got money by one of his confessions but in this he was almost certainly unsuccessful. He also seems to have taken his Christian duty to forgive his enemies with the seriousness of a penitent, as well as with the reservations of a soldier. Knox he went to great length to exculpate several times, although at one point he put it a little infelicitously: "Dr Knox approved of its being so fresh, but did not ask any questions". Helen's innocence he asserted again and again. He would not even have her be thought to have accepted to status of an accessory of grave-robbery, let alone murder; he had told her the bodies were bought by him. Only against Hare, and to a lesser extent, Hare's wife, was his animus evident. Hare had informed against him, an unforgivable crime among the Irish Catholic peasantry, in the army, or within criminal circles, and of those three worlds of William Burke probably the first held it in the greatest contempt. Hare, he insisted, had drawn him into the thing, although he did not hold himself less guilty, nor question the justice of his sentence. But settling accounts with Hare does not seem from either his "official" confession, or from that to the *Courant* under official auspices, to have been his primary motive: it is much more the work of a man under spiritual direction as to the only steps left to him to make some recompense for what he had done.

His chief attendant appears to have been the Reverend William Reid, a Banffshire priest who had held office in Edinburgh, where a handful of clerics with two churches sought to minister to 14,000 Roman Catholics. Reid was then sixty-three, and his career was in fact moving into retreat, by material standards. He had been the effective administrator under the previous Vicar-Apostolic (the Roman Catholic bishoprics would not be restored for another half-century), but the new appointee was anxious to bring in his own men

and Reid would shortly be shifted back to Dumfries whence he had
come and where he would die less than fifteen years later. He won
particular fame during the cholera epidemic in Dumfries in 1832,
when he became famous for his apparent tirelessness and fearless-
ness in ministering to patients mortally ill of the contagious horror.
He died worth two pounds sterling, and a thousand people attended
his funeral, at least one-third of whom were Protestants. Given the
fact that he was Burke's spiritual adviser in his last days, his comment
when asked about his burial is interesting: "Do what you like; if my
soul be well, it is of no consequence what becomes of my body."

It was understandable that Burke would find in Reid a source of
consolation. Both as an Irish Catholic and as a wholesale murderer he
must have been an alien figure to his guards. Yet he seems to have
won some regard from them in his last days. After all, few of their
clients were particularly salubrious, and Burke seems to have been
civil and courteous as a prisoner. He retained the levity which had
characterised so much of his career. At one point he is quoted as
remarking that Knox still owed him £5 for the corpse of Mary
Docherty, and when the seizure of the body was adduced as a good
reason for non-payment Burke said that that did not gainsay his
lawful dues. His interlocutor — possibly Reid — seems to have
entered into the spirit of the thing, and ventured that Hare had the
right to half of it. Burke went on to reflect that £5 would enable him
to buy a good coat and waistcoat: "since I am to appear before the
public I should like to be respectable". It was obviously a somewhat
laboured little joke, the complaint about Knox (hardly the shadow of
a shade of what he *could* have said about Knox) being the build-up to
the black-humour punch-line. It hardly seems a proof of the
insincerity of his religious professions, as later commentators would
claim, so much as an instance of a genuinely amusing man still trying
to entertain his audience and himself in the shadow of death, and
giving an indication of the charm and manners and pleasantness of
disposition which had facilitated his murders. It also offers an ironic
reminder of the many immigrant defections from religion because of
consciousness of poverty of clothing.

On Tuesday, 27 January, about 28 hours before his actual execution, Burke was removed from Calton Hill Jail to the lock-up in
Libberton Wynd, near the Lawnmarket. The distance involved was
less than a mile, but little hope was held of saving Burke from the
mob if the journey were to take place later in the day, or on the
morning of the execution itself. (Similar consideration for his dead
body would prevent its removal to Old College for a day after its

execution, and even then there were to be ferocious struggles
between students, the public and the authorities in the struggle to be
present at Professor Alexander Monro's dissection of the brain: a
fairly uncommon expression of interest in the work of that particular
lecturer.) The scaffold was built during the Tuesday afternoon, and
an increasing crowd watched the work oblivious of what a witness
termed the "pelting of the pitiless storm". Much as children salute
the arrival of the Christmas tree as the symbolic moment in the
preparation of festival decorations, the bringing of the frame of the
gibbet was greeted with an enormous shout at 10.30 p.m. About 2
a.m. everything had been satisfactorily constructed, and the
gathering gave "three tremendous cheers" which were thoroughly
audible at the other side of Edinburgh Castle hill, on Princes Street.

Burke slept well on the night before his execution, though from
time to time his sleep had given signs of frightful tension and hideous
nightmares. To the end he offered his characteristic mingling of the
roles of penitent and entertainer. As his fetters were removed, about
5.30 a.m., he declared, "So may all my earthly chains fall!" Father
Reid saw him at 6.30 a.m., and presumably heard his final confession
and administered the Holy Eucharist. According to the principles of
his own religion, Burke, on the only evidence we will ever have, died
with every expectation of salvation. He may well have expected
some term in Purgatory for the expiation of the stains of the sins
which had themselves been absolved. But if his penitence was
genuine, William Burke, according to the Roman Catholic faith,
will be counted among the blessed in Heaven.

After his private devotions Burke heard prayers from his Catholic
spiritual advisers, in the presence of his Protestant ones. He seems to
have been momentarily overcome by the adjuration to confide in the
mercy of God, and hurried into an adjoining room. He probably felt
himself about to cry: he would not have wanted to let himself down
before his audience. The penitent might cry; but the soldier and
entertainer do not. He ran into Williams, the executioner, who
thought he was bolting. Burke gasped, "I am not ready for you just
yet." But Williams used the meeting to pinion his arms and Burke
returned with arms bound, and upper lip stiff once more. Burke told
Williams, for future reference, that his neck-kerchief was tied at the
back. Then he was offered a glass of wine. The courtesy says much
for the humanity of his gaolers, and also, perhaps, for their having
taken a liking to him. It contravened the Lord Justice-Clerk's official
sentence that, prior to execution, he "be fed upon bread and water
only". Presumably the wine had to be administered to him, but he

prefaced it by a toast "Farewell to all my friends", and talked after it
to the Protestant chaplains. The magistrates entered in their robes.
Burke then made a brief speech, thanking them for their courtesy and
kindness, and went out of his way to say a special word to Bailie
Small in that connection. He paid tribute also to Governor Rose, to
Deputy Governor Fisher, and to Mr and Mrs Christie, the
responsible officials of the lock-up.

When about to walk out the door, Burke turned to Fisher — he
who would later take leave of the departing Hare on the coach —
and said he needed a pocket handkerchief and asked for the loan of
one, adding, characteristically, that it would be returned to Fisher
after the execution. Fisher handed him a handkerchief with the
courtesy that characterised all we know of him in the case. The
handkerchief carried in its centre a likeness of Burns, together with a
quotation from "Man was Made to Mourn", a dirge written in 1784-
85 when Burns was about twenty-five. (Strangely, Burns and Burke
were both to die at the age of thirty-seven.)

> The poor, oppressed, honest man
> Had never, sure, been born,
> Had there not been some recompense
> To comfort those that mourn!

"The moment the wretched man caught the last line," asserted the
Scotsman, "he smiled and bowed to Mr Fisher, and he placed the
handkerchief under his knee on the scaffold when he knelt down for
the last time in the world." Another Scotland said its farewell to
Burke apart from that whose vituperation was screaming before
him.

The crowd was by now enormous. Estimates varied between
20,000 and 25,000 and it was universally conceded the largest ever
known in Edinburgh. The fashionable congregated at windows over-
looking the Lawnmarket, among them Sir Walter Scott, who was as
impressed by the victim's role as scapegoat as much other opinion
had been. "The mob, which was immense," recorded the novelist in
his diary, "demanded Knox and Hare, but, though greedy for more
victims, received with shouts the solitary wretch who found his way
to the gallows out of five or six who seem not less guilty than he."
The first appearance of Burke had elicited a terrific yell, and the
speed with which he mounted the scaffold impressed spectators with
the conviction that he wanted an end fast. He looked at the
screaming crowd, now adding shouts of "Hare! Hare! Bring out
Hare!" "Hang Knox!" "He's a *noxious* morsel!" Apart from the

single stare at the crowd which an eye-witness described as one of "fierce and even desperate defiance", Burke's main response was to pray as best he might amid the din. A priest and he knelt together, and one of the Protestant chaplains also said a prayer. The magistrates sought to still the tumult by making signs that the victim was at prayer, but with total lack of success. Burke rose, looked at the gallows and stood on the drop. The time was now ten minutes past eight.

Williams adjusted the rope. Burke again reminded him that the knot of his neck-kerchief was behind him. "Burke him!" shrieked the crowd. The verb, newly born, meant "smother", using the thumb under the chin and two fingers drawn in at the end of the nose, the method Burke himself had perfected. "Give him no rope!" agreed other voices. "Do the same for Hare!" "Weigh them together!" "Wash blood from the land!" The tumult was deafening, but Reid managed to make Burke hear the words "Now say your creed; and when you come to the words 'Lord Jesus Christ' give the signal, and die with His blessed name in your mouth."

It may be doubted whether any more extraordinary spectacle ever graced a martyrdom of a devout saint, executed by persecuting officials in the presence of a bloodthirsty and brutish multitude. The victim said his final prayer. The crowd howled like demons from the lowest pit. The gentlefolk behind the windows gratified their appetites to the full, at the expense of miscreant and mob alike. Only the ministers of religion existed as symbols that Burke's faith was not the occasion of his death, and they were roughly enough handled by the verbal abuse of the crowd. "Stand out of the way!" "Turn him round!" "No mercy, hangie!" and "You'll see Daft Jamie in a minute!" The white cotton night-cap was pulled over his head.

I believe in God . . .

"Choke him!"

. . . the Father Almighty . . .

"Burke him!"

. . . Creator of Heaven and Earth . . .

"Hang him!" "Hang him!" "Hang him!"

. . . and in Jesus Christ, his only Son, Our Lord . . .

THE END

A Note on Sources

Swindon: I can't believe it! What will History say?
Burgoyne: History, sir, will tell lies, as usual.
                        —George Bernard Shaw, *The Devil's Disciple*

AT first glace the trial of William Burke and Helen MacDougal, and the abortive legal proceedings against Hare, seem among the best-reported notable trials in British history before the Victorian era, and certainly the trial reports with their accompanying documents (including Burke's confessions) must form the principal source for any study of the case. Almost all accounts base themselves on the volume *Trial of William Burke and Helen M'Dougal* and the *Supplement* to it covering the Hare hearings, both of which were published for Robert Buchanan, William Hunter and John Stevenson, of Edinburgh, and Baldwin & Cradock, of London, the advertisements issued therein being dated respectively 16 January 1829 and 20 February 1829. These texts are certainly far preferable to the version in Thomas Ireland's fifteen-part publication *West Port Murders*, and are more detailed than the newspaper reports (which in any case break off during the speeches of counsel to meet press deadlines). But there are problems. The historiographical bias against Helen MacDougal is given a bad start by the publishers describing her, as well as Burke, as "criminals", although she was found not proven. The questionable practice of asking judges and counsel to "revise" the texts of their remarks was followed here as elsewhere in British official life during the last two centuries: it is this which makes *Hansard*, for instance, a source to be handled with reservation, and in so political and controversial a trial we have to allow for Rac, Moncreiff, Cockburn and Meadowbank all improving their utterances for the benefit of curious contemporaries. In Meadowbank's case it seems quite certain that his charge to the Lord Justice-Clerk before sentence was altered, to judge from Maria Edgeworth's comments in her letter to Scott and from the text as we now have it. Scott played a part in the preparation of this report for the press, and following receipt of her letter, which he took such trouble in answering, it would have been natural for him to arrange for Meadowbank's removal of the more foolish remarks to which she had taken exception. Politically and personally, he was on good terms with Meadowbank. Boyle's laziness may have prevented his taking similar steps: and the report of the opening of his speech is threadbare and clearly less than he actually said, though how much less is unknown. Mackenzie and Alloway raised decided doubts as to the accuracy of the Burke-MacDougal trial transcript used during the Hare hearings (presumably that employed was the same one, the stenographer being John Macnee), and Mackenzie was far the most impartial and alert judge in the earlier case. But it is the best we have.

William Roughead used it for his Notable British Trials series *Burke and Hare* (1921) but deleted minor details, such as the swearing of witnesses other than the Hares; and the editorial matter is equally uncritical of sources. Roughead's work in several volumes in that series was outstandingly good, in research and in analysis: e.g. his *Trial of Deacon Brodie* (1906, 1914, 1921) is one of the best in the series and both as an Edinburgh scandal much recalled during the Burke trial and as a leading case on the immunity of an informer before Hare, it has much indirect interest here. His *Twelve Scots Trials* (1913) introduces us to Rae, Jeffrey, Cockburn, Boyle (and, with very minor roles, Gillies, Pitmilly, Meadowbank, Mackenzie, Alloway, Alison and Dundas) in "The Wife o' Denside" as he has styled the trial of Mrs Mary Elder or Smith the previous year, and it was clearly a memory brooding over the Burke affair. But Roughead dealt with the latter mechanically, adding little to his earlier account when he gave a new version in *Knaves' Looking-Glass* (1935), afterwards reprinted in his *Classic Crimes* (1951, 1966). His edition of the trial (whose first publication restricted the Hare matter to a special and more expensive "limited" edition: the 1948 popular edition is comprehensive) includes a very valuable bibliography; what is somewhat disturbing about it is that it shows awareness of corrupt sources such as Ireland which the introduction does little to question. Roughead drew heavily on the C. K. Sharpe collection of MSS, pamphlets, broadsides, books, ballads, illustrations, newspapers and ephemera which formed part of the Cowan collection and is now in the hospitable custody of the Edinburgh Room of the City of Edinburgh Public Library on George IV Bridge, but his critical abilities were slumbering in his use of it.

Roughead was also influenced by accounts of the trial published in the intervening ninety years, and few of these added much save new fictions to the corpus. *The Court of Cacus* by Alexander Leighton (1861) was perhaps the worst offender here, although the student of Leighton's writings in general will find he made it clear he was a fictionist leaving little excuse to those who swallowed him. He was also subjected to admirable criticism in Henry Lonsdale's *Sketch of the Life and Writings of Robert Knox, Anatomist* (1870), although that book poses its own mysteries. It is clear that Lonsdale was put up to write the book by a decision of several of Knox's old pupils who had an interest in getting a satisfactory account in print for the sake of their reputations as well as Knox's: indeed Leighton's book may have supplied the spur. Roughead was to assume Lonsdale based his account of the case on Knox's business "books", which subsequently disappeared, but probably he had nothing more than the oral testimony and possible notes of Wharton Jones, Fergusson and Miller in addition to what had been published. There were no particular reasons for Knox to drag those "books" from 1828 on his long and sad pilgrimage from Edinburgh to Glasgow and thence London, and some extremely good reasons for them to have disappeared long before.

In fairness to Roughead he did not swallow all of the fictions in the works he diligently lists. He pays no attention to Peter Mackenzie's account of a thriving murder business being conducted by Burke and Hare across the Irish Sea (*Reminiscences of Glasgow*, 1866), or James Grant's nonsense about the execution of Hare and other myths in *Old and New Edinburgh*. He does, naturally, pay considerable attention to George MacGregor's *History of Burke and Hare and of the Resurrectionist Times* (1884), and indeed largely followed it in swallowing Ireland and Leighton wh lesale. Of the various other accounts, Camden Pelham (*The Chronicles of Crime* (1887)), Joseph Forster (*Studies in Black and Red* (1896)) and J. B. Atlay (*Famous Trials of the Century* (1899)) are distinguished by little other than a fair mixture of old myths, new myths and expressions of disapproval for murder: perhaps the palm for slovenliness in equal ratio to cant should be held back until after Roughead had published his edition, to be awarded to *Famous Trials* by the first Earl of Birkenhead.

More formal exercises in literary creativity were present from the first. Enough —perhaps too much—has been said in the text concerning Christopher North's *Noctes Ambrosianae*, XIX,originally published in *Blackwood's Magazine*, save to mention its influence on all later writers, among them Thomas De Quincey's "Murder, Considered as one of the Fine Arts", which treats freakishly of Burke and Hare in the additional matter included in its second edition. The literary fashion divided itself subsequently in vituperation and archness, apparently with North and De Quincey in mind, respectively. Neither school is wholly contemptible though few specimens of either are easily digestible. Dylan Thomas's film-script *The Doctor and the Devils* is a work-to-rule performance broken by one good epigram ("When you burn your boats, what a very nice fire it makes"), but it does illustrate how Knox's professional enemies had so much reason to prevent his prosecution. James Bridie's play *The Anatomist* throws some crude light on Knox but makes him too much of a "character" to give him real character. Robert Louis Stevenson dissected some of the medical ethics well in his short story "The Body Snatcher.", but his Burke (or Hare) though pleasingly creepy is rather too ready to kill the goose who gives out the golden eggs. Marcel Schwob's "MM. Burke et Hare, Assassins" is a very weak imitation of Wilde's "Pen, Pencil and Poison", but its attempts at facetiousness are hilariously unsuccessful. William Bolitho's "The Science of William Burke" in *Murder for Profit* is also arch, but the reader who can survive the purple of its passages will find some interesting deductions on the Edinburgh establishment, albeit with an almost Birkenhead-like indifference to facts. Much the best fictional treatment—I write it with pleasure after the above list of notable names — is Hector Bryson's *Doctors, Bodies and Snatchers* (1978) which is first-class on the Edinburgh medical world of the 1820s and of major benefit to me, although William Burke literally does not appear until the last word.

Hugh Douglas's *Burke and Hare–The True Story* (1973) is the most recent treatment. Its hearty condescension to the protagonists is no better than the officially and actually fictional predecessors from whom it draws much, but it is greatly to be commended for its work on the popular, and especially stage, image of its subjects. It does prompt the thought that the moralism and facetiousness of the historiography of Burke and Hare has proved hideously contagious, as the present writer also learned. It is also weakened, as are earlier studies, by a great divide between professional historians and amateur criminologists. But so is much formal history.

SPECIFIC TOPICS

(a) Ireland

The best book to convey the realities of the world into which William Burke was born is Thomas Flanagan's recent novel *The Year of the French*. Flanagan's earlier study, *The Irish Novelists 1800-1850*, is invaluable for an understanding of the strengths and weaknesses of contemporary writers, the most useful to us here being William Carleton and, less strongly, Maria Edgeworth. Carleton's *Traits and Stories of the Irish Peasantry* is best avoided in the recent Mercier paperback edition, being misleadingly rearranged, but studied in its correct sequence in older texts is the stuff of which social history is made. Benedict Kiely's *Poor Scholar* has useful things to say about Carleton's rural background, and Sir Shane Leslie produces important folklore evidence in his introduction to *Carleton Country*. Alistair Rowan's *North-West Ulster* in the Penguin "Buildings of Ireland" series is indispensable to any historian lucky enough to be concerned with that part of the world.

I have used old-fashioned anthologies of poetry, Gaelic and English, O Canainn's *Filidheacht na nGaedheal* and Lennox Robinson's *Golden Treasury of Irish Verse*, but the reader will have to look to a separate publication to read Brian Merriman, *The Midnight Court* (several translations). R. B. McDowell's *Ireland in the Age of Imperialism and Revolution* is rather too Dublin-centred for our purposes and while Constantia Maxwell, *The Stranger in Ireland*, has considerable insights, notably on Scott and the Halls, her *Country and Town in Ireland under the Georges* suffers from the common complaint of over-elitist perspectives. Several other travel books offer alternative accounts to the Halls'; apart from the guidance of Maxwell, the reader's first friend should be the relevant volume of *Bibliography of British History*, an excellent guide. Daniel Corkery's *The Hidden Ireland* is a stimulating, if bullying, cultural nationalist tract whose many weaknesses do not offset its value. Older books should not be neglected, Froude's *The English in Ireland* being a fine example of the provocative in its nastier forms while Lecky's multi-volume *History* is a little conventional but singularly unusual in its humanity. Finally, excellent work in integrating government and reality is to be found in Maureen Wall, *The Penal Laws*, and Gearóid Ó Tuathaigh, *Ireland before the Famine*.

(b) Burke's Military Career

Sir Henry McAnally's *The Irish Militia 1793-1816* is the basic source, though to work out the destinies of individual militias such as the Donegal, close collation of sources, text and cross-references is necessary. A little digging in Sir John Fortescue's volumes on the British Army, and Sir Charles Oman's on the Peninsular War proved mildly entertaining and marginally rewarding. I examined some military memoirs, of which Rifleman Harris proved the most interesting, and the first volume of Lady Longford's *Wellington* is informative as well as absorbing, but her son Thomas Pakenham's *The Year of Liberty* is weak on the western campaign in Ireland in 1798 and unfair to the exhausted militia. Charles Lever's *Charles O'Malley* is the classic work on Irish military life within our period. The relevant papers concerning the Donegal militia are now housed in the Public Record Office at Kew (where the student must not confuse them with those of a mid-nineteenth-century and similarly named force) and the relevant items are WO 13 2761-65 and WO 97 1096 but I suspect further records may remain in private hands, perhaps those of members of the Clements family, descendants of the Earls of Leitrim.

(c) Scotland

William Ferguson's *Scotland: 1689 to the Present* is a splendid introduction to this period: comprehensive, controversial, lucid and stimulating, as well as productive of many most helpful special lines of investigation for me. Bruce Lenman's *Economic History of Modern Scotland* opened up a fascinating background to my problem. J. Lindsay, *The Canals of Scotland*, is detailed, interesting and indispensable for this study, and unlike certain historians of such phenomena the author is highly aware of the existence of the workers involved. J. E. Handley's *The Irish in Scotland* is a pious rag-bag of invaluable materials pointing the way for later scholars; however, the same author's *The Navvy in Scotland* is a highly professional study. Several papers by T. M. Devine proved most instructive in helping me acquire a sense of the economic life of the lowlands within the period. T. C. Smout, *A History of the Scottish People 1560-1830* is a classic which illumines whatever the author touches, and occasionally infuriates by what he does not; several other papers by him proved outstanding in their integration of social and economic history. Douglas Young, *Edinburgh in the Age of Sir Walter Scott*, is a somewhat disappointing work by a great man whose main interest for me lay in social rather than cultural content. I have examined certain pamphlets and papers about the Union canal company which proved highly entertaining: the National Library of Scotland has catalogued and bound them very conveniently. Anand Chitnis, *The Scottish Enlightenment*, is painstaking if a little wooden, and opens up the topic very clearly for the neophyte, but several papers by N. T. Phillipson sparkle with excitement on the subject. On an overall basis, Rosalind Mitchison's *History of Scotland* takes the reader firmly by the scruff of the neck on the first page and keeps him on his toes to the end.

(d) Burke's and Hare's Medical Career

Apart from Lonsdale, Isobel Rae's *Knox the Anatomist* (1964) offers a later defence of the subject reflecting research but not much perspective. Knox's *Races of Men* (1850) is a vital source, and see also remarks on it in Christopher Fyfe, *Africanus Horton* (1972) and the magisterial Philip D. Curtin, *The Image of Africa* (1964). MacGregor's *Burke and Hare* is rather more useful in its collection of resurrectionist anecdotage than on the main subject although it includes interesting ballads, and James Moores Ball, *The Sack 'em-up Men* (1928), reflects remarkable scholarship and judiciousness in everything but its title. Robert Christison's *Life*, edited by his sons, has the advantage of being a personal document for some of its length, bringing a critical figure into vivid self-expression. The *Edinburgh Medical Journal*, under his influence, is a vivid illustration of the strength and weakness of Edinburgh medicine in its day, apart from Christison's own account of his experiments in its investigation which appeared in vol. XXXI (April 1829). The *Lancet*, while remote from the scene of the crimes, reflects the passions of 1828-29 accurately and venomously, no doubt with much assistance from Edinburgh sources and correspondents. Notices of the leading doctors in the *D.N.B.* are useful, if cautious. The Edinburgh *Phrenological Journal*, vol. V (1829), and the pamphlets of Thomas Stone, W. R. Greg, and George Combe disputing phrenological conclusions about Burke and Hare have a macabre use in showing some of the more idiotic lines of scientific interest at the time. Roughead gives a brief summary of the battle in his edition of the trial. I had nothing useful to add. Sir Charles Bell's *Letters* and his official biography have some value on the Sicilian relations among Edinburgh doctors. I acquired little from several official and semi-offical accounts of the achievement of Edinburgh medicine. John Flint South, *Memorials* (1884) is an acid little book of interest for its denial of a happy ending being provided by the Anatomy Act. Recent books include Hubert Cole, *Things for the Surgeon* (1964) and Norman Adams, *Dead and Buried?* (1972), which make agreeable, if somewhat inaccurate, reading: E. S. Turner, *Call the Doctor* (1958) is wide-ranging, informal — and informative. Hugh MacDiarmid and Lewis Grassic Gibbon, *Scottish Scene* (1935), includes some very instructive rude remarks on the limits of Edinburgh intellectual achievement.

The whole question is put in a major socio-economic framework in Robert Morris, *Cholera 1832* (1977), which brings class into perspective on doctors, patients and subjects. Michael Durey, *The Return of the Plague* (1979) dots some "i"s and crosses some "t"s with useful results. He stresses the Benthamism of the proponents of the Anatomy Bill, the classic exposition of which must be the *Westminster Review*'s discussion of Burke and Hare in January 1829. I have followed the debate on the Anatomy Bill in Hansard, *Parliamentary Debates* through March-June 1829. Joseph Dean, *Hatred, Ridicule or Contempt* (1954), a lively popular work on libel trials, has an instructive chapter, "Surgery in 1828", which says something on the London climate of medicine and journalism which so significantly affected the fortunes of the Bill.

(e) The Legal and Political Careers of Burke and Hare

The papers in the case have disappeared from the official archives now housed in the Scottish Record Office, although Mr Sutherland and I were but the last of many writers to seek them there including Roughead and Douglas; we saw many other precognitions in other cases of the time and got our hands gratifyingly filthy, thus correctly celebrating the rites of Clio. JC 4/E 18 and JC 8/E 32 of the Lord Advocate's papers include interesting formal documents, among them Moncreiff's acceptance of Burke's declarations, the official statements of the verdict, and of the sentence, as well as Duncan McNeill's successful plea on 26 January 1829 against the publication of Burke's confession to the *Evening Courant*, prohibited by court order until Hare's legal proceedings should be concluded. The Peel papers in the British Museum, especially the correspondence with Rae (Add. MSS 40339), have much to contribute though not, alas, Hare's confession; I had little luck with Peel's correspondence with Wellington, Sir William Gregory, George IV, general recipients and (Add. MSS 40611-14) the relevant folio volumes including newspapers preserved by the then Home Secretary. The relevant letter to Goulburn which discusses the case is printed in Parker's *Life of Peel*, and like all other students of that statesman I am indebted to Norman Gash, *Mr Secretary Peel* (1961).

The fullest account of Rae is in George W. T. Omond, *The Lord Advocates of Scotland*, vol. II, although its account of the trial is superficial; it is rather richer in its account of the lurid administration of his predecessor, Alexander Maconochie, subsequently Lord Meadowbank, throwing the political wars into relief. Omond has also left a memoir of the house of Dundas of Arniston, which reinforces the impression that the Advocate Depute in the Burke trial was more preoccupied with political jobbery and country estates, much as the literary priorities of his colleague Sir Archibald Alison are well underlined by his *My Life and Writings*, edited by his wife. Alison seems to have been a charming man. The *D.N.B.* is helpful so far as it goes: Wood is one of its odd omissions, although it notices his grandfather, and Sandford is likewise excluded although his father and brothers are not. Sandford's father's autobiographical memoir offers a personal clue to his behaviour at the time of the Hare riot. The political background to legal conflict is succinctly and brilliantly sketched in Ferguson, *Scotland*, and helpfully though conspiratorially (in all senses) in P. Berresford Ellis and Seumas Mac a' Ghobhainn, *The Scottish Insurrection of 1820* (1970): all students of Scottish history should read Hugh MacDiarmid's introduction to it.

Henry Cockburn largely dominates the historiography of the politico-legal story, although he infuriatingly has little to say about the case itself in his immortal *Memorials*. For judges and counsel his vivid if highly partisan opinions are invaluable and hilarious, both there, in his *Circuit Journeys* and in his *Life of Jeffrey*; indeed, as Ferguson suggests, Jeffrey may have been his one failure as a portrait since miniature and not life-size portraiture was his forte. Karl Miller's *Cockburn's Millenium* (1975) is a breathless switchback of a book hurling the reader from challenge to challenge, insight to insight, discovery to discovery, with the utmost contempt for the conventions of space and time: it always delighted and occasionally maddened me. Alan Bell, ed., *Lord Cockburn: A Bicentenary Commemoration* (1979) is annoying without being charming, for the most part, and the essay on Cockburn as lawyer is best avoided, but Bell's "Protector of Edinburgh", a B.B.C. talk on Cockburn, broadcast on 21 October 1979, is a splendid compilation and far more worthy of publication than the book: it adds yet further gems to his published views of his fellow-protagonists in the trial. On precedents I looked little beyond the works cited, other than for Brodie: John S. Gibson, *Deacon Brodie Father to Jekyll and Hyde* (1977) is a useful adjunct to Roughead's *Brodie*, though I disagree with Gibson's title (Knox and his rivals are better candidates, in some respects), Forbes Bramble's novel is amusing and Stevenson's play is not. George Rudé's *The Crowd in History* (1964) is of course indispensable for understanding the mob and the fears it evoked, and the greatness of R. R. Palmer's *Age of the Democratic Revolution* throws the long shadows of its period before the student of later times. As to cases inviting comparison with various aspects, I looked at the Notable British Trials volumes on Henry Fauntleroy, and Thurtell and Hunt (both heard in 1824) for contemporary English proceedings, and on Browne and Kennedy (tried 1928) and Alfred Arthur Rouse (tried 1931), for methods in the legal use of confessions a century later.

(f) Burke, Hare and Scott

The splendid edition of *The Journal of Sir Walter Scott*, ed. W. E. K. Anderson (1972), gets Patrick Robertson's name wrong in the index and is otherwise exemplary and a mine of reference. Scott's *Letters*, vol. XI, ed. H. J. C. Grierson (1936), is full of his invaluable comment, as perceptive as it is artistic. It is well supplemented by the final volume of any unabridged edition of J. G. Lockhart's *Life*. The case haunted Scott, whose last words included the repetition of "Burke Sir Walter", in allusion to a cry from a Reform Bill mob when he tried to speak at Jedburgh in 1831, the year before his death. Some of his letters about it are in the Cowan collection in the City of Edinburgh Public Library, and his correspondence with Maria Edgeworth is in the manuscript collection of the National Library of Scotland, where the original of her letter to him of 10 January 1829 is MS 3908 f. 19. Scott had some indirect remarks about the case in the preface to his dreadful tragedy *Auchindrane*, and his awareness of mobs can be readily picked up from the *Heart of Midlothian* (Roughead's edition of the Notable British Trials *Captain Porteous* I examined for that mob, not for the trial, although it was almost a century earlier). N. T. Phillipson's review of the *Journal* in the *Times Literary Supplement* was an admirable tutorial for me, and very rightly opens up the idea that Scott deserves immortality as diarist and correspondence perhaps even more than as novelist. Maxwell, *Stranger*, pays tribute to his fine sense of Ireland. Scott has a nice line or two about Rae in *Marmion*. The reader impressed by Scott's humanity on the trial will find a suitably disgusting contrast in Carlyle's letters to his brother John of 13 January and 5 March 1829, printed in the relevant volume of his correspondence so ably edited by Kenneth J. Fielding and associates. (If Lockhart and the *Journal* are followed carefully they suggest points about Scott's relations with the other protagonists — for instance Meadowbank is famous as having won Scott's public admission of the open secret that he was the author of the Waverley novels, but that did not mean close friendship although their party association and social relationship would certainly have been enough motive for Scott to take pains for such protection as could be given to Meadowbank's judicial reputation.)

(g) The Journalistic Career of Burke and Hare

The student of the press throughout the episode can no doubt draw some detailed conclusions, e.g. that the *Sun* was absurdly inaccurate up to the point of sneering at Scottish papers for saying that Burke was Irish when the *Sun* maintained he was not, or that the *Caledonian Mercury* was exceptionally fertile of invention in the pursuit of news, or that the *New Scots Magazine* was vivid in its direct reporting but credulous in its receptivity, or that the *Courant* had more enterprise in seeking hard news than most, or that the *Scotsman* was reliable and resourceful and, in Cockburn's word, "heavy". But the overall lesson to be drawn is that discussed in the text. What can be inferred to be the work of an eye-witness on more evidence than a simple but possibly mendacious statement to that effect is normally as trustworthy as such evidence is likely to be, with decided allowance for inaccuracy and exaggeration. Interviews with specific persons named, such as James Gray, have been taken by me to be reliable, especially when they include detail not likely to have been invented (in that it adds little to sensational appetite) and having a strong ring of truth (such as Gray's assurance to the press that Burke and Mary Docherty conversed chiefly in Irish), but this only applies to persons at liberty and not fugitive. Interviews with unnamed prison-warders, policemen, &c., I took with much greater reservation, but with specific emphasis on the same points in favour of provenance: allowance would also have to be made for misreading of initially accurate report (such as Burke's readiness to accept Catholic confession being construed as a repudiation of his earlier ecumenical sentiments, which clearly on the other evidence it was not). Material obviously inserted under conditions of news famine and reader voracity was much more to be suspected, and frequently proved demonstrably false. In some instances it was necessary to depend on suspect information, relying on balance of probability. The *Dumfries Courier*'s account of Hare's escape was of necessity in part derivative from other sources, but the work of the editor, John McDiarmid, shows a caution in the presentation of evidence, if not of rhetoric, which speaks well for him and his story. Folklore evidence, generally wildly inaccurate on Burke and Hare — e.g. on their careers as graverobbers which the *New Scots Magazine*, for one, picked up during the trial with reference to the Union Canal period — does support McDiarmid here, given the persistent Annan tradition about "Hare's landing", a place still shown through which he supposedly passed on his flight. Needless to say, the newspapers are valuable on the atmosphere of the times, and the flavour of life they exhibit. Even there, it must be added, there seems to have been a great tendency to depict working-class life in colours as sensational and lurid as possible, much as the visitors to the Union Canal would go to marvel at the outlandish navvies. The emphasis on the violence of the lives of the workers, especially of Burke and Helen, is suggestive here. I recently saw a play-fight in an Edinburgh pub between the landlady and a gentleman for whom she clearly had much affection; it was exotic and boisterous, and wholly without hostility, but any report of similar exchanges between Burke and Helen could well have supplied the basis for the brutality ascribed to them in the press version. Newspaper reports are digested well, and largely given ascription, in the Buchanan, Hunter & Stevenson *Trial*; Ireland largely pillages them without question and often without citation; the *New Scots Magazine* is a fair assemblage of some of the major facts and fictions. The nature of the infant press may be better appreciated if it is remembered that at this time the *Observer* was an odious purveyor of keyhole gossip with the voyeurism implied in its name, and *The Times* a hotbed of scurrilous invention, vulgar abuse and literary ruffianism of the worst kind. Having said all of which, it must be reasserted that the historian of this or any other period who neglects his newspapers is cutting himself off from his historical bloodstream — in all senses.

(h) Sex and God

The historiography of the sex controversy I have raised is laid out in the text. I owe much to Gaelic poetry for any insights it contains.

The Archives of the Roman Catholic Church in Scotland at Columba House yielded some interesting letters of the Rev. William Reid, unrelated to this case but revealing of his noble and spiritual character. The *Catholic Directory* supplied details of his career. My impression of Burke owed something to the hawker, James Maclean, said to be Irish, on whom the preface to the Buchanan *Trial* drew heavily. He was a fellow-shearer with Burke, Hare and the women at Carnwath and spoke of Burke as "peaceable" when sober and "even when intoxicated, rather jocose and quizzical".

My last primary source to be listed is the skeleton of Burke in the Anatomy Museum at Edinburgh University. It confirms his brevity of height. It is of course purely accidental that his expression remains rather jocose and quizzical, although I like to think that he would enjoy his status as the oldest Irish inhabitant of Edinburgh University.

Index

There seemed little point in indexing Burke, Helen MacDougal, the Hares or Robert Knox, the location of references to whom will be obvious on the briefest inspection. Otherwise both here and in the text I have chosen the surname mose likely to have been correct when a number of variants are offered: e.g. "Conway" rather than "Connoway", a form which clearly crept into the record by seeking to adapt orthography to Irish intonation. On the other hand I have called the last victim of Burke and Hare "Docherty" although it is clear that it was her maiden name and that she came from North-west Ulster where it is found as "Doherty"; but that spelling nowhere appears in the records and since her natural language was Irish she probably accepted the Scottish spelling and pronunciation from the first after moving into an Anglophone world.